THE MEMBER FOR SCOTLAND:
A LIFE OF DUNCAN MCLAREN

Best wishes

Willie

8/6/2011

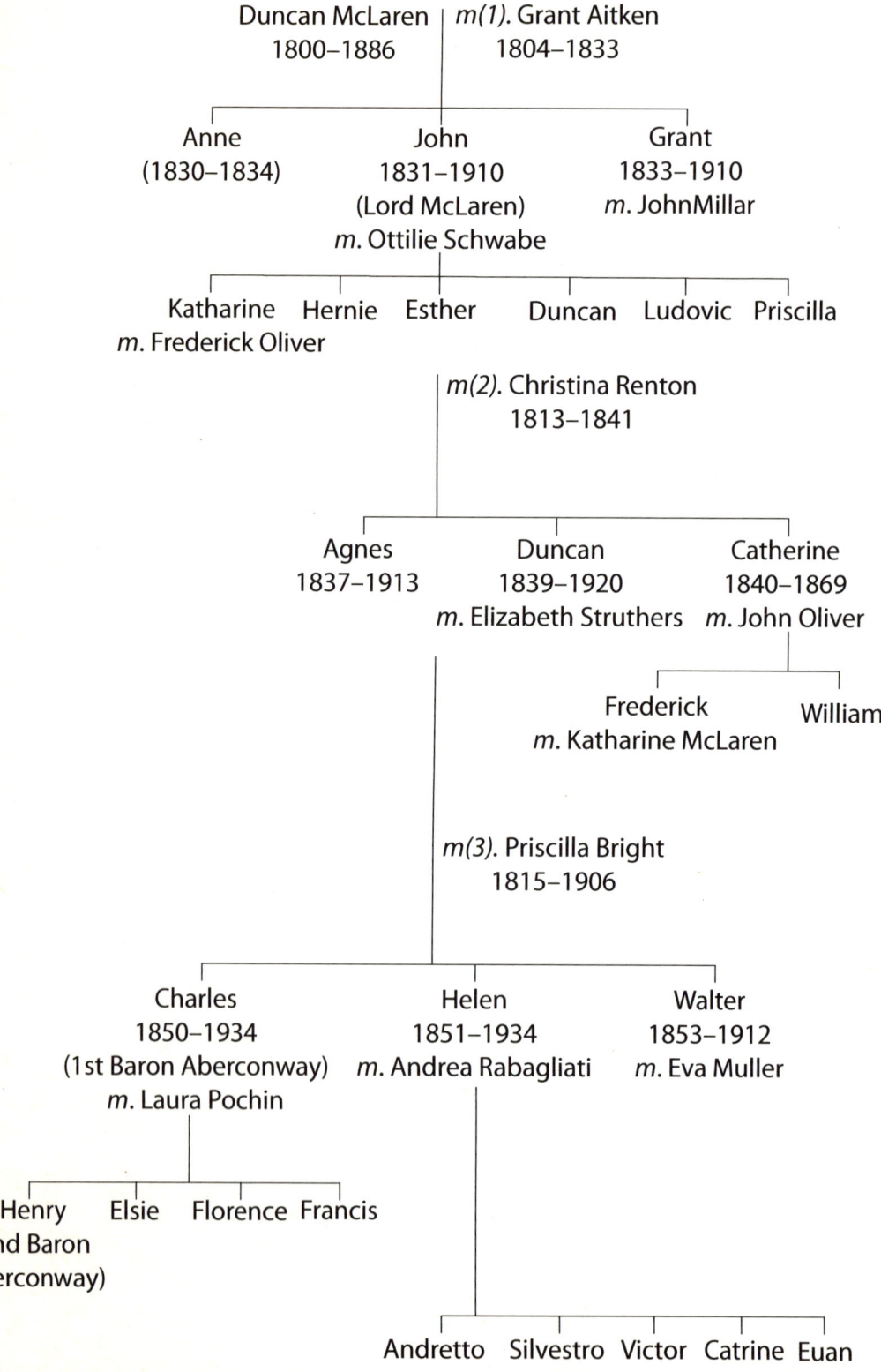

The Member for Scotland
A Life of Duncan McLaren

WILLIS PICKARD

PICTURE ACKNOWLEDGEMENTS

Acknowledgments and thanks for permission to reproduce photographs are due to: National Galleries of Scotland for John McLaren (Lord McLaren) by Sir John Lavery, George Hope by Sir George Reid, Alexander Russel by W. Brodie; National Portrait Gallery for Priscilla McLaren by Elliott & Fry, John Bright by Rupert Potter; National Library of Scotland for McLaren, Oliver and Co. trade card; Faculty of Advocates Library for James Moncreiff (Lord Moncreiff) by Sir George Reid; City of Edinburgh Council for Duncan McLaren by Sir George Reid; Royal Commission on the Ancient and Historical Monuments of Scotland for the book-jacket portrait of Duncan McLaren, Elizabeth Gray for the image of Newington House. Ann Pickard took the photographs of the McLaren monument at Dalmally and of McLaren Road, Edinburgh.

First published in Great Britain in 2011 by
John Donald, an imprint of Birlinn Ltd

West Newington House
10 Newington Road
Edinburgh
EH9 1QS

www.birlinn.co.uk

ISBN: 978 1 906566 41 8

Copyright © Willis Pickard, 2011

The right of Willis Pickard to be identified as the author of this work has been asserted by him in accordance with the Copyright, Designs and Patents Act, 1988

All rights reserved. No part of this publication may be reproduced, stored, or transmitted in any form, or by any means, electronic, mechanical or photocopying, recording or otherwise, without the express written permission of the publisher.

British Library Cataloguing-in-Publication Data
A catalogue record for this book is available on request from the British Library

Typeset by Becky Pickard, Zebedee Design & Typesetting Services
Printed and bound in Great Britain by
CPI Antony Rowe, Chippenham and Eastbourne

Contents

Acknowledgements	7
Foreword	8
1. 'For ready money': early years	9
2. Edinburgh's saviour	20
3. The 'clearest and soundest head'	38
4. The voice of Dissent	53
5. Championing cheap corn	68
6. Banker and railman	83
7. Lord Provost and failed MP	101
8. Arbiter and conciliator	120
9. A libel case won	138
10. A family at war	152
11. In Parliament at last	167
12. The busy legislator	185
13. School reform, women's rights	202
14. At odds with the unions	218
15. Father and son in and out	232
16. Campaigner to the end	249
17. Envoi	269
References	277
Bibliography	304
Index	313

For Gill and Becky

Acknowledgements

This study has led me to a range of libraries and archives. The main holdings of Duncan McLaren's family, business and political papers are in the National Library of Scotland, to whose staff I am particularly grateful. I have also been helped by the National Archives of Scotland, Edinburgh City Archives, the Edinburgh Room of Edinburgh Central Library, Edinburgh University and New College libraries, Glasgow University Library, Heriot-Watt University Archives, Manchester City Library, Nottingham University Library, West Sussex Record Office. I have to thank the Earl of Dalhousie for permission to quote from letters by Fox Maule. Wilson Bain gave me an insight into James Moncreiff, and Donald Gorrie introduced me to the advocate John Gorrie, who was a McLaren loyalist before becoming a colonial jurist. Duncan Rabagliati, a descendant of Duncan McLaren's daughter Helen, kept me right on family genealogy. My friend Michael Fry, author of a recent history of Edinburgh, takes a scornful view of McLaren; perhaps I will convert him. Ewen Cameron, of Edinburgh University's Scottish history department, read my first draft and made very helpful suggestions. He bears no responsibility for any errors that survive. Hugh Andrew was bold enough to take the book under Birlinn's wing. My editor Anna Stevenson has been punctiliously helpful, and my daughter Becky used her production skills in what I regard as a good cause. John Lawrie read the proof eagle-eyed. My wife Ann has shared her home for almost a decade with Duncan McLaren and his large family.

Foreword

Duncan McLaren was born in 1800 and for much of the century was deeply involved in the public affairs of Scotland. Yet his name has all but disappeared from public recognition. This book sets out to reassert his significance in the rapidly changing story of his times. A list of some of his spheres of activity puts him at the heart of contemporary concerns: political reform; civic government; religious controversy; public morality; free trade; the railway boom; speculative banking; national education; women's rights; Scotland's identity within the United Kingdom; the role of the press. His abilities were first recognised south of the border in the corn-laws campaign. Then he married John Bright's sister and joined the interlocked families of high-minded middle-class radicalism. He repeatedly clashed with the landlords and lawyers who perpetuated the Whig tradition of Liberalism. As councillor and MP his support lay with working men though he had no time for either Chartism or nascent labourism. He helped to build the coalition that was Gladstonian Liberalism in Scotland. Of his nine children three became Liberal MPs.

There are good stories to be told – helping rescue Edinburgh from bankruptcy, exposing the fraud of railway mania, successfully suing *The Scotsman* newspaper for libel, fighting the marriage of his daughter to his business partner. At the heart is McLaren's own personality – self-driven, unrelenting in pursuit of right as he saw it, a man who himself said he found it easier to respond to attack than to public expression of kindness. The voluminous family correspondence, much of it the Frederick Scott Oliver papers in the National Library of Scotland, shows him in his unguarded as well as his masterful moments.

1. 'For ready money': early years

The family that Duncan McLaren was born into on 12 January 1800 had just trodden a well-worn path: new Lowland industry appeared to offer a better opportunity than Highland agriculture. The previous year they had left their Argyll homeland for the village of Renton in the Vale of Leven to seek work in the flourishing world of textiles. By a quirk of the calendar the man who was to be prominent in public life for so much of the century was born on its first day, going by the 'old style' still in Scottish use.

There were 12 children in John and Catherine McLaren's family, many of whom died young, but the three youngest, Duncan and his two sisters, Janet and Euphemia, lived well beyond four score years. John and Catherine, both of farming stock, were from around Dalmally, although John had been raised on the island of Lismore. Their early married life was marred by violent tragedy. John's brother Neil, leaving Lismore for Appin, had begun to prosper as a farmer and asked John to join him in stocking a tenancy. But Neil had lent money to a friend whom he agreed to meet in expectation of repayment. Unfortunately, the friend had turned jealous, believing that his fiancée had been making eyes at Neil. When the men met, Neil was assaulted and died. In the Appin of the late eighteenth century, less than a generation after a better-remembered murder, that of Colin Campbell (the 'Red Fox'), there was no police alternative to family revenge. John, searching for his brother and finding him dead, raised a posse of 20 men who scoured the Appin countryside but to no avail. The murderer escaped to Jamaica where he was condemned to death for a different crime.

John had recently married the 17-year-old Catherine McLellan, daughter of a successful tenant farmer in Glenorchy. Not only was he now faced with the end of his prospects as a partner of his brother, but he also found that many who owed Neil money reneged on their debts and so he could not raise the capital to stock the promised farm. Like thousands of others from the West Highlands, the McLaren family decided to take the well-worn path south to where the textile industry was leading the Industrial Revolution.

Renton was a centre for bleaching and for calico printing and dyeing, in particular a Turkey red for which it became renowned. Growth was stimulated by a model village founded in 1782 by Mrs Smollett of Bonhill, a member of the family that had produced the novelist Tobias Smollett. A school opened in 1797, and significantly Renton was home to a Secession congregation and regularly to huge communion gatherings to which thousands would flock from Glasgow, Greenock and Paisley.[1] Successive generations of McLarens were to be firm adherents of churches opposed to state establishment. These churches, having been chronically fissiparous in the eighteenth century, gradually came together in the first half of the nineteenth century and formed a centre of political as well as religious influence.

For the boy Duncan the experiences of home in the Vale of Leven were early overtaken by return to Argyll. At the age of ten he went to live with his mother's nephew, Hugh McLellan, at Dalmally. He stayed for two years and it was to the country around Glenorchy and Glen Strae that he returned in nostalgic pilgrimage in later life. It is there, too, that a stone memorial honours the unprivileged lad who as a legislator came to be known as the 'Member for Scotland'.

Local tradition told of a boy devoted to his books, but his schooling ended when he was 12. He was apprenticed to his mother's brother, Nicol McIntyre, who had a shop in Dunbar. It was a long trek for a young boy across country to Inveraray, where he spent the night, and at journey's end by local carrier to East Lothian. His new employer reported to the family in Renton: 'If I had known he was so young I would have had him for four years in place of three, as he will be of very little use to me for twelve months upon account of his being so short. He cannot take down the goods nor put them up again for some time.'

The apprenticeship seems to have lasted four years. In 1816 his salary was fixed at £14 a year, including board and lodging with his employer. The following year an increase of £2 took him to work for McIntyre's brother in Haddington, the county town, where he might have bumped into a small boy by the name of Samuel Smiles, who lived in the High Street. Self-help was to be the guiding principle of both of them. Getting on in life was what led Duncan a year later to Edinburgh where a salary of £40 a year and better prospects were offered by the firm of John Lauder & Co in the High Street. It was a wholesale merchant's with contacts across Scotland as well as a retailer's. There was not only opportunity to develop business skills but also exposure to the life of the capital at a moment of imminent change.

For 20 years fear of French-style revolution and of Napoleon-led invasion had suppressed prospects of parliamentary or civic reform. The Whigs who agitated for modest changes in the 1780s had been sidelined. Tory reaction, the so-called Dundas despotism, continued to hold sway. Henry Cockburn, who had entered the Faculty of Advocates in the year of McLaren's birth, recalled the prevailing atmosphere. His was the profession that provided political leaders but 'with the people suppressed and the Whigs powerless, Government was the master of nearly every individual in Scotland, but especially in Edinburgh, which was the chief seat of its influence. The pulpit, the bench, the bar, the colleges, the parliamentary electors, the press, the magistracy, the local institutions, were so completely at the service of the party in power, that the idea of independence, besides being monstrous and absurd, was suppressed by a feeling of conscious ingratitude. Henry Dundas, an Edinburgh man, and well calculated by talent and manner to make despotism popular, was the absolute dictator of Scotland.'[2]

The coming of peace in 1815 brought no solace. Fear of sedition and civil strife persuaded Lord Liverpool's Government to tighten the laws inhibiting even mild protest. The period of high economic output needed for the war effort was followed across Scotland by a collapse of prices, wages and employment, made worse by the returning soldiers and the continuing influx of Highland labour to the industrial districts where conditions in the textile industry prompted violent outbursts that the forces of law and order depicted as revolutionary. The year 1816 closed bitterly for the poor, Cockburn recorded: 'There probably never were so many people destitute at one time in Edinburgh.'[3]

But among the prosperous classes the Enlightenment spirit of inquiry and rational debate remained alive. It took new form with the founding in 1802 of the *Edinburgh Review*, whose clever young men – including Francis Jeffrey, Sydney Smith, Francis Horner and Henry Brougham – so sparkled that its fame soon spread across Britain and the Continent. At home this new generation of Whigs, most of them making their other reputation as advocates in Parliament House, took the lead when public political meetings began again, the first in 1816 protesting against the income tax. In 1820 Duncan McLaren attended the next, more overtly political, meeting in the Pantheon at the top of Leith Walk. It had to be held indoors because one of the Government's anti-sedition Six Acts made an open-air assembly illegal. The hall was crammed. Jeffrey gave the main address and a resulting petition calling on the King to dismiss his ministers attracted about 17,000 signatures. The Tories ran a rival petition but got only 1,600 to 1,700 names. For McLaren it was not only the meeting's purpose that made it memorable. Public assemblies with their passionate (sometimes interminable) speeches and the resolutions and petitions that resulted from them were to be his kind of politics.

As he went about his business in the city, McLaren could see evidence of the post-war revival of building. After half a century the planned development of the New Town had produced about 2,000 houses by 1815. There would be around 5,000 in 1830.[4] Land beyond Charlotte Square, including Moray Place, was feued for building. Cockburn knew that progress meant change but regretted that 'everything [was] sacrificed to the multiplication of feuing feet', including the rural corncrakes that he had listened to from Queen Street. At South Bridge, work on the university building, Old College, which had lain unfinished since 1793, began again in 1817. McLaren later described conditions in the High Street as he went to work: 'The vegetables were laid down in the street and foot pavements just where the scavengers had been plying their calling immediately before; and the gutters were running near them in the most offensive way that could be supposed. This perfuming was the preliminary operation which all our fruit and vegetables then underwent before being made ready for dinner.'[5] The market was moved to a site under North Bridge six years after McLaren arrived in the city. Roads were being planned to make the city more accessible from the south and west. The Waterloo Bridge allowed development east of Princes Street, and on Calton Hill there was planned a huge classical monument to those fallen in the Napoleonic Wars. Its failure, that of ambition not met by resources, symbolised the problems confronting the city in general.

In 1819 a pamphlet was published showing the extent of the city's debt. It had risen from £52,000 in 1798 to £141,000, and still the town council authorised more expense on public works. They borrowed to build both the Royal High School beneath Calton Hill and the road from the west. They were finally crippled by their scheme for enlarging Leith Docks. The reckoning was over a decade away but it would convince even the mildest of critics that the old ways of civic government would no longer do.

McLaren stayed with Lauder until 1824, gaining in responsibility and range of experience. He was sent to London to buy goods, invaluable training for the time when he would be building his own enterprise. But he claimed in later life that he was restless, even contemplating a job in South America as representative of a trading house for £200, far more than even regular pay rises were giving him in the High Street. His opportunity came with Lauder's retirement in 1824 and an offer from a contact in Glasgow to set him up in business on his own account. McLaren recorded the story in the course of a public lecture in 1868:

> I became acquainted with Mr White of White, Urquhart & Co, Glasgow, an excellent man in all respects, who took a fancy in a certain sense to me, and thought, from what he had seen and heard of my talents and industry and my desire to promote the interests of my employers, that I would be certain to succeed if I began business on my own account. He knew that I had no money of my own excepting a trifling amount from savings on my salary, after assisting near relatives who were poorer than myself; and to my surprise, he one day told me that he had formed such an opinion of me, that, if I desired to begin business, he would lend me whatever money I required at a low rate on interest and without any security.[6]

McLaren asked for six months to think over the offer. As he told his friend George Combe, the phrenologist, many years later[7] he had only about £25 saved at the time and he was worried about how he would repay the money if his business did not take off. He came to a decision: 'I said I had carefully considered the matter, and thought that £800 would be the requisite sum. My friend thought this was rather a small sum, but said when I had occasion to go to the markets (London and Manchester), as was customary in spring and autumn, he would give such additional temporary loans as I might require. He gave me a draft for £800, for which I gave him my promissory note, and I took a shop in what was then an excellent central situation, and succeeded beyond my most sanguine expectations.' The extra temporary loans for the markets were given and in a few years repaid by McLaren along with the principal loan and interest on it.

The shop was certainly in a 'central situation', at 329 High Street, immediately across from St Giles' Cathedral and only two doors away from Lauder's. McLaren rapidly expanded his premises, as we shall see. The building has formed part of the City Chambers since the 1890s but it served its mercantile purpose throughout McLaren's long career and that of his son. With £800 he was well set up. Retailing businesses could be started at the time for £100.[8] The High Street, bustling with people, was a main shopping centre while the New Town, certainly the western part of it, was still predominantly residential. The city directory for 1834–5 listed among the premises in the High Street spirit dealers, silversmiths, fleshers, saddlers and tailors. There were 70 drapers in the city who helped to support 180 milliners and dressmakers. Some of the drapers' businesses were substantial. The first Lord Provost under whom Councillor McLaren was to serve, Sir James Spittal, had set up as a mercer on South Bridge in 1807 (in premises that in the twentieth century were J&R Allan).[9] His political mentor, Adam Black, had a bookseller's round the corner from the High Street on North Bridge. Within a few hundred yards of where McLaren worked were the centres of civic life in the council chambers, of the law in Parliament Square, of churches of several denominations and of the twice-weekly *Scotsman*, which had been founded to promote the cause of reform and to which he would at first contribute and from which he would take decades of abuse.

How prepared was the 24-year-old McLaren for business success and a place in Edinburgh's public life? He was largely self-taught. Starting as an apprentice in Dunbar, he recalled in his 1868 lecture: 'I could do what in England they call the three Rs pretty well; and that was about the bulk of it.' But he had plenty of leisure time and read voraciously. A friend gave him two volumes of Gregory's *Encyclopaedia*: 'I was not daunted, but began at the beginning and read them through, excepting the articles on mathematics and algebra, and matters of that kind, in which I was not sufficiently instructed.' He gained a smattering of knowledge in everything – gunnery, fortifications, shipbuilding, 'cannon-foundling'. When *The Scotsman* was founded in 1817 a friend subscribed and gave McLaren his copy: 'The foundation of all the political knowledge I ever had was derived from that paper, which was most ably conducted at that time.' In Edinburgh the opportunities widened even for a young man who had to be in the shop from eight o'clock in the morning until well into the evening (shop hours were to be one of McLaren's later campaigns). He joined a subscription library. A university student of mathematics taught him Euclid in the evenings. He attended public lectures, and 'before the dreadful Burke and Hare murders I attended a full course of lectures on anatomy by Dr Knox, who figured so conspicuously in that affair.' Edinburgh at the time was aware of the need for what we would call further or adult education aimed at improving tradesmens' skills. The first mechanics' institute in Britain, the brainchild of Leonard Horner, later one of the founders of the University of London, opened in Niddry Street off the High Street in 1821. Its name encapsulated its purpose: 'The School of Arts of Edinburgh for the Education of Mechanics in such branches of Physical Science as are of Practical Application in their Several Trades'. It would later add 'the Watt Institution' to its title and in the year before

McLaren's death would join forces with George Heriot's Trust to form Heriot-Watt College, now the university of the same name. Grateful for the self-betterment opportunities he had been given, McLaren was a lifelong campaigner for both 'the Watt' and Heriot's Trust.

Set up in his own shop, McLaren was admitted as a burgess of the city on 1 June 1825. The relationship between the old craft guilds and the town council was complex and contentious and as city treasurer a decade later McLaren would seek to clarify and simplify it, but tradesmen and merchants were supposed to buy their ticket of admission, an expense that must have been a deterrent to new enterprises and essentially just a local tax. Not surprisingly, the number seeking entry went down, from 64 in 1830 to 17 in 1837, the year of his proposed reform. The average cost of a ticket was then £7 14s 3d.[10] He was admitted as a member of the Merchant Company on 7 March 1826 and kept his membership for almost 60 years. The company of businessmen, established in 1681, was by the 1820s keenly in favour of reform, political as well as commercial, and it gave McLaren an opportunity to hear the arguments and to join in. Ironically, its members wielded great influence in the unreformed town council and so had to bear some responsibility for the growing problems which would soon undermine the city's financial independence. McLaren's drapery business flourished from its earliest days, the result of hard work, eight years' learning from others and a knowledge of how to buy goods advantageously in the markets of the south. Just as textiles led the Industrial Revolution through the mass production of the great northern mills, so wholesale and retail textiles were the first to adopt modern ways. Michael Winstanley, historian of shopkeeping, explained the opportunities in drapery: 'Recruits required just enough working capital to purchase stock or convince suppliers to advance credit on goods, not difficult in an industry prone to crises of overproduction' until 1850.[11] McLaren embraced the new sales technique of fixing a price and sticking to it. He later claimed to have led the way in Edinburgh in abolishing 'prigging', or bartering, which was common in Scotland, though other retailers abandoned the practice around the same time. McLaren's newspaper advertisements for bolts of material and made-up garments included the tag line 'For ready money'. Often his advertisements would cite that new purchases had been made in England. On one occasion goods on offer included 'An immense variety of new merinos, new patterns in printed cottons and muslins, cotton shirtings, stripes and checks, linens, sheetings, muslins, shawls, furniture prints, stripes and dimities, blankets, bedticks, counterpanes, drapers, black silks, bombardines, crapes, janes, long lawns, French cambrics, fancy handkerchiefs, stockings etc. The same price is invariably charged to all classes, and no abatement made, consequently the most inexperienced are served on the same terms as the best judges.'[12]

Five years after setting up in business the 29-year-old McLaren married. His bride was Grant Aitken, aged 24, whom he had known since his time in Haddington; he had probably delayed marriage until he felt secure in his business. She was the youngest daughter of William Aitken, who had been a merchant in Dunbar until he retired to the county town. Her sister was married to McLaren's former master, Nicol McIntyre, with whom McLaren seems to have continued to do substantial business until the latter's retirement in 1831. A letter to her fiancé survives from two months before the wedding.[13] Writing from Dunbar, she reminds 'my dear Duncan' that she writes once a week on Mondays because McIntyre generally has a parcel for him that day. She misses him and hopes he has got into his fine new house. She also gently ribs him and makes it clear she will continue to do so in future. She appears a spirited girl who ends her letter with three lines of doggerel:

> The motto for your carriage must be
> 'Who would have thought it
> Cheap cotton goods got it.'

They were married in Dunbar on 7 July 1829 and settled in the fine house at 118 Princes Street, at the corner of Castle Street, later moving to 2 Ramsay Gardens. Grant was to survive less than four more years, during which time three children were born – Anne in April 1830, John almost exactly a year later and another Grant on 5 March 1833. By 27 April that year, Nicol McIntyre was writing to McLaren lamenting that 'your poor wife continues still so distressed' but gratified that the infant was doing so well.[14]

Grant had in fact died three days before, and McLaren expressed his bitterness as well as anguish in a letter in which he said that although his wife had been ill for seven weeks after her confinement woman friends of his correspondent had not visited her despite being told of her condition.[15] He went on to say ironically that 'the contemplation of death must have been peculiarly painful to their feelings; and of course the reality would be still more so.' Therefore he had not asked them to the funeral but if they wanted 'to see the lifeless corpse of one who had such a warm heart to them, and indeed to all her friends', they should come without a formal invitation.

'For ready money': early years

The nineteenth-century obsession with the physical aspects of death is evident in another letter written the same day: 'There is less of the disagreeable and more of 'the loveliness in death' than is usually met with.' He had anticipated more decay. Three-year-old Anne was very distressed:

> I took her to see her she loved so ardently, and whose loss to her is so irreparable, the moment the vital spark had fled, and told her her Mama was dead. She immediately went into the most violent fit of crying I ever heard, in old or young, kissed the lifeless features over and over again, and at every interval, when she could find utterance in words, she repeated 'Mama is not dead, Mama is not dead.' After she was taken to another room she continued inconsolable, repeating the same words, and weeping most bitterly, for half an hour. It would have melted the hardest heart to have witnessed such acute distress in one so young. She appeared perfectly to understand that death was a great calamity, and also that it really had taken place. She was evidently giving vent to her wishes, rather than to her beliefs for after she became composed she observed me distressed and said in a consoling tone 'Pappa I'll be good to you when Mama is dead.' John was taken to the room at the same time and kissed the body without appearing to understand the loss he has sustained, for he did not even weep.[16]

The baby Grant was not baptised until ten months after her mother's death. The year 1834 also brought the family fresh tragedy: Anne died of what was described as croup, not five years old. Her loss was especially hard on McLaren. Whereas his wife had been increasingly ill after the birth, his eldest child died almost without warning, the hardest blow her father ever had to endure, he said in later life.

He had the support of his family. Indeed, the domestic hardships that McLaren experienced until his third marriage would have made a public career and frequent absences from home impossible if he had not had support from his mother and two unmarried sisters who moved through from the west and ultimately settled in the seaside suburb of Portobello. If he took solace from religion he had a solid framework there, too. He had been brought up in a household that attended a Secession church, Presbyterian in belief and organisation but divorced from the Church of Scotland and one among several fractious factions. In 1820 two of these churches outwith the Established Church came together to form the United Secession Church. It is not necessary to trace the century-long story of breakaways from the

Established Church and breakaways from breakaways. By the early nineteenth century there was a new spirit of cooperation and reunion.[17]

Arriving in Edinburgh, McLaren joined the United Secession congregation in Bristo Street.[18] In this expanding part of south Edinburgh (now a university quarter) a new building had been opened at a cost of £3,000 in 1804. It was the meeting place for the 1820 union and it held the pulpit of the Peddies, father and son. James Peddie had been minister since 1783 and continued preaching until 1843. His son William was called in 1828 to assist him. At both inductions there was dissent and some members 'disjoined' themselves, but that was common at the time. James Peddie was a leading theologian, recipient of an honorary degree from St Andrews University and a founder of the missionary movement in Scotland. He was regarded as a practical preacher who saw liberal political causes as part of his mission, and that must have impressed young adherents like McLaren. Today if James Peddie is remembered at all it is for his sermon after the fire in 1824 which destroyed a stretch of the High Street killing 10 people, making 400–500 homeless and causing damage estimated at the huge sum of £200,000. The Rev. Dr Peddie took as his text Numbers chapter 10, verse six: 'Let your brethren ... bewail the burning which the Lord hath kindled.'[19]

The newly reunited Secessionists, or Dissenters as they were often called, were on the march. They numbered about a quarter of a million and were strongest in central Scotland, especially Glasgow and Edinburgh where they flourished among the commercial middle classes and skilled artisans. With allies among Congregationalists and Baptists they formed what became known as the Voluntary movement, recently described as 'the first truly national agitation in Scotland'.[20] Perhaps a third of all churchgoers in the 1830s attended Dissenting churches, yet the agitation they stirred up is barely remembered compared to the attention given to the divisions in the Church of Scotland that led to the Disruption of 1843 and the founding of the Free Church. The Voluntaries, specifically those who made a further union – that of 1847 which produced the United Presbyterian Church – ensured that there were not two but three competing Presbyterian allegiances for most of Queen Victoria's reign. The political as well as the religious history of Scotland cannot be understood without that context; nor can Duncan McLaren's career.

In May 1829 the Rev. Andrew Marshall, minister of the United Secession church in Kirkintilloch, published a sermon he had preached in Glasgow. He argued that religion was at its purest when it was 'voluntary'. Established churches were corrupted by their association with the State, which unfairly endowed only one church and taxed members of other churches to support the established one. By the early 1830s Voluntary church associations were springing up in large towns and cities.[21] The Edinburgh one was founded at a meeting in September 1832 chaired by James Peddie. Its fundamental principle was that 'compulsory support of religious institutions is inconsistent with the nature of religion, the spirit of the Gospel, the express appointment of Jesus Christ, and the civil rights of man'.[22] Duncan McLaren was soon to be a powerful lay voice of his denomination's resentment. He found allies and a platform in the town council which he joined in 1833.

2. Edinburgh's saviour

It was only the day before the first elections to the reformed town council in November 1833 that Duncan McLaren consented to stand in the Second Ward. Friends encouraged him to become involved in public affairs as a way of assuaging his grief at his wife's death six months earlier.[1] He had shared in the febrile excitement in the city from 1830 to 1832 as the prospect of parliamentary reform came closer, for a time stalled and was finally achieved in July 1832. The celebrations and the lauding of Whig leaders in Scotland as well as at Westminster were out of proportion to the extent of reform north of the border. True, the electorate went up from only 4,500 to almost 65,000 as the vote was given to owners of property worth £10 a year as well as, usually, to tenants occupying such properties in the burghs (though not so straightforwardly in the counties). But there was to be little change to the nature of representation at Westminster. Edinburgh won a second seat, but there were only seven other extensions, all in the burghs: Glasgow, with two members, and Aberdeen, Dundee, Greenock, Paisley, Perth and Leith, with one each, had their own MP for the first time. Many small, easily manipulated burghs retained their separate representation and the counties were hardly affected, a sure sign that Whig gentry had as much interest as the defeated Tories in maintaining a tight grip. New men might have a vote but they were still expected to choose an MP only from among their betters. It has been calculated that between the Reform Acts of 1832 and 1867 barely 1 in 10 Scottish MPs had been engaged in commerce and trading and only 1 in 30 came from manufacturing.[2] In the 1832 elections Edinburgh comfortably returned two leading Whigs. Francis Jeffrey as Lord Advocate had brought in the Reform Bill. James Abercromby, who lived at Colinton outside the city on an estate now occupied by Merchiston Castle School, was later to become the successful candidate in a fiercely contested election for Speaker of the Commons. Edinburgh Radicals tried to challenge the two Whigs but failed to find enough support before polling day, though they did field a candidate at the by-election two years later when Jeffrey became a judge.

In Edinburgh, as in the other burgh seats, the Tories, no longer the masters of the self-serving, introverted system, were now on the sidelines. Their unyielding opposition to reform had sealed their fate. They returned only one Scottish burgh MP at any election until 1841 and few thereafter. Such minority successes as the party had were in the counties, where they recovered steadily from 10 seats in 1832 to 22 in Sir Robert Peel's victory of 1841. The effect of this decline was to remove a serious threat to the Whigs in the towns and cities. Another challenge, however, filled the vacuum. Radical opinion soon tired of the timid approach to further reforms by the Whig Governments of Earl Grey and, more markedly, Lord Melbourne. Radicals, many of them religious Dissenters north and south of the border, demanded speedier action on a broad political and social front. The Whig establishment, always wary that the dire predictions of French-style revolution that had accompanied the Reform Act might be coming true, rebuffed Radical demands, which they mistakenly associated with the Chartist agitation that was beginning to attract large numbers of, mainly, the unfranchised. Where there was no serious challenge mounted by Tories, the stage was set for a battle for liberal supremacy among those who had been on the same cheering side in 1832. It might have made life more comfortable for the Whig leaders if there had been a serious but familiar Tory challenge. In the county seat of Midlothian, where there was a series of tight Whig–Tory contests in the 1830s, Radicals as well as Whigs had to confront the common enemy. Duncan McLaren and 11 other supporters from the city played their part by creating 'faggot', i.e. fictitious, votes. In a coordinated registration campaign their names were added to the Midlothian voters' roll by the device of jointly buying a property in Ratho owned by the Whig grandee Sir James Gibson-Craig. His son William had been the unsuccessful candidate in the 1835 election. Outmanoeuvring the Tories in the contest to create voters he went on to win the seat in 1837.[3] In Edinburgh itself the Tory parliamentary threat remained modest; this was also the case also in the council chamber which McLaren entered in 1833.

The Burgh Reform Act had just come into force and so in Edinburgh as elsewhere in the country there was a General Election for the council. The old system by which councils chose their own members had long been indefensible but had to wait for parliamentary reform and a new Government before it could be tackled. Cockburn famously described the council chamber as 'a low-roofed room, very dark, and very dirty, with some small dens off it for clerks'. There was no public scrutiny of what went on: 'Within this Pandemonium sat the town-council, omnipotent, corrupt, impenetrable. Nothing was beyond its grasp; no variety of opinion disturbed its unanimity, for the pleasure of Dundas was the sole rule for every one of them. Reporters, the fruit of free discussion, did not exist; and though they had existed, would not have dared to disclose the proceedings. Silent, powerful, submissive, mysterious, and irresponsible, they might have been sitting in Venice.'[4] Although the three Scottish Acts sweeping away such excesses were passed after truncated debate and retained many anomalies and too many tiny burghs, at least the problem was addressed two years before municipal reform legislation south of the border. The second Lord Melville (to Cockburn the Doge of Venice) had retained a Dundas-family grip on Scottish politics until reform but even he had been moved to complain of the state of Edinburgh and 'the public inconvenience, to say nothing of the personal and constant plague arising from an inefficient and unsafe magistracy'.[5] He was right. The Burgh Reform Act became law on 28 August. The following day an Act was passed appointing trustees for the creditors of the city. The nation's capital was bankrupt.

A clean sweep in the council was inevitable in the elections just over two months later. Not a single member of the old regime survived. There were six vacancies in each ward and McLaren, whose electors voted at the recently opened Waterloo Rooms to the east of Princes Street, came fifth out of 10 candidates, with 179 votes, the top candidate winning 257. As an indication of the kind of men putting themselves forward, those in the Second Ward were listed[6] as a druggist, two merchants, three booksellers, two tailor/clothiers, a silversmith and a printer. Across the city only 2 in 5 of the electorate of about 3,500 bothered to vote – much the same as in local elections today. *The Scotsman* analysed the results and found 24 or 25 Whigs, 7 or 8 Radicals and no Tories. Candidates had not stood under party labels and the paper[7] noted that all had been returned as independents and hoped there would be no sectarian dissension, for example between Whig and Radical. An anonymous diarist wrote: 'The outcry against the annuity tax has brought forward more radicals or ultra-liberals than were at one time expected particularly in the old town, still they form the decided minority.'[8] Henry Cockburn, who as Solicitor-General had helped to draw up the reform legislation, wrote about the results across Scotland: 'The people have in general chosen better councillors than were produced by self-election; and it is curious that they have often chosen persons higher in station and in wealth than their predecessors. The great comfort is that all classes are represented, and a legitimate vent given to all opinions.'[9]

Duncan McLaren, like others among the incoming councillors, was pledged to right a particular wrong. It was to take him almost 40 years as councillor, Lord Provost and member of Parliament, but the grievance felt by the city's inhabitants gave him not just a popular cause but continuing political support. At 7 p.m. on 14 August 1833 a procession of 8,000 led by members of an Inhabitants committee and trades delegates formed up at the Calton Jail to mark the release of William Tait, a Radical publisher, and to accompany him to his home across the city and then to a rally at the Mound. The horses dragging the martyr's carriage were released and replaced by manpower, which *The Scotsman* thought degrading to people who expressed their feelings by such action.[10] The newspaper nonetheless supported Tait's cause: he had been jailed for refusing to pay the city's annuity tax. He was not the first protester to face legal redress, nor the last.

A month previously the Court of Session had decided that non-payment of the tax could be punished by a jail term as well as by distraint of goods. This inflamed passions about a levy that was peculiar to only two towns in Scotland, Edinburgh and Montrose. In a form still by and large existing in the nineteenth century the tax went back to 1661 and provided for the upkeep of ministers of the Established Church. It amounted to 6 per cent of the annual rental value of properties, but there was an exemption that particularly riled the inhabitants of Edinburgh: no member of the College of Justice had to pay, and that included most lawyers, who were among the most prosperous of the citizens. In 1809 a further twist was added. Parliament acceded to a request by the unreformed town council to make the tax applicable in recently extended areas of the city but added a 'submerged' (that is undebated) clause which imposed a permanent level of assessment without imposing a maximum level of stipend. Thus any increase in tax collected simply augmented the ministers' stipends, which by the 1830s could be a healthy £650 a year in the 18 churches supported by the town council. McLaren, like fellow councillors, was elected on a 'scrap the tax' ticket. They objected to the modest change that had just been unsuccessfully proposed in a Bill by the Lord Advocate and city MP, Francis Jeffrey. It would have made lawyers contribute their share and would have fixed the sum to be raised and permanently awarded to the clergy at an average of the previous five years' total. The other source of council funds for the churches came through the rent paid for a seat in the pews. However, the £7,200 thereby raised was one of the sources of revenue in a city now officially bankrupt. The city's creditors, as we shall see, did not want such a steady source of revenue upset. Therefore, as *The Scotsman*, a reasoned opponent of the annuity tax, argued, the tax regime proposed by Jeffrey was unavoidable.

The merchants and tradesmen of the city and Dissenters' meeting disagreed and sought abolition. The new council elected in November 1833 would become a platform for the campaign. Although many members of the Church of Scotland agreed that the annuity tax was no way to pay for the churches they attended, the Dissenters had a more fundamental ground for objection and they were numerically strong among business and trading interests. They saw no reason for paying a tax for the upkeep of ministers of the Established Church from which they or their forebears had removed themselves. After all, they already paid for their own ministers, who enjoyed no such civic subvention. Thomas Russell was an ironmonger and a town councillor living in the High Street. In 1836 he was sent to Calton Jail for refusing to pay £7 5s 6d in annuity tax. He passed his five weeks there issuing a flurry of letters explaining his position as a Dissenter. He told the clergy of the Established Church that hurting Dissenters was not the right approach if 'your object is to induce them to desert the unscriptural views they entertain and act upon'. Non-payment was founded on Christian principle which from the Old Testament down to the Reformation and modern authors found it right to refuse to obey a human law when it was opposed to divine institutes. He also answered those worried Dissenters who felt compelled to pay up because it was the law of the land. The tax was for religious purposes and not for support of the Government, and since it was levied in breach of the Commandments, Dissenters and others should not comply.[11]

In 1834 and 1835 the town council sponsored Bills to abolish the annuity tax. The Lord Advocate, who was in charge of Scottish business at Westminster, at first did nothing and then said he would bring in a Bill of his own. In 1836 pressure on the parliamentary timetable was the excuse, but two prominent MPs, Henry Labouchere and Sir James Graham, suggested they might frame a Bill. However, nothing came of that either. Four years passed and an 'Annuity and Poor's Money' Bill was introduced to Parliament, but because it would have raised the stipends of the ministers, 10,000 people petitioned against it, while for their part the city's lawyers also opposed it on the grounds that they would lose their immunity. There was to be a flare-up of violent resistance to the tax in 1848. As a councillor and leading Dissenter McLaren made himself an authority on its history, its spurious basis in law and the principled reasons for opposing it. His pamphleteering brought him to the attention not just of his own side but of spokesmen for the Established Church, including its Evangelical champion Thomas Chalmers. Yet even a later admirer of McLaren, writing while the abolition of the tax was still within living memory, could only say of McLaren's published account that it 'fairly bristles with facts, dates and figures, which quite repel the ordinary reader, although it may possess some interest for persons of a legal and antiquarian turn of mind'.[12]

The early years of the reformed town council were dominated by the city's bankruptcy. New, untried councillors faced an immediate challenge in dealing with creditors who inhibited policy and spending decisions in order to protect their own interests. Hitting back, councillors pointed the finger at the irresponsibility and extravagance of their predecessors going back many years. McLaren, with colleagues who were at first his mentors and then his followers, argued that they not only had a mandate from the voters, but that that their ideas and leadership represented the future. Government-appointed Commissioners on Municipal Corporations had examined the state of Edinburgh. Their report paved the way for the declaration of bankruptcy but ensured that time would not be wasted in dragging guilty councillors or their officials through the courts:

> We have not found sufficient evidence to entitle us to report that the disastrous state of the city's affairs has been caused by actual embezzlement or fraudulent malversation ... The closeness and irresponsibility of the Corporation could not alone account for the continuance of such a system [of wastefulness and letting expenditure continually outweigh revenue]; the studied concealment of the affairs of the community for a long period, and the partial and confused statement of them which was afterwards periodically made, probably kept the respectable members of the Corporation in ignorance of their financial embarrassment, and it is that ignorance and reckless confidence in the future improvement of their finances which can alone save the city managers from a charge of fraud both as regards the community and their creditors.

This was a damning indictment whose consequences left the 130,000 citizens with a local government that was not its own master.

The largest creditor was central Government. It had become involved as long ago as 1805 when the Treasury gave a loan of £25,000 for the improvement of Leith as a port and took as security the rates and property associated with the harbour and docks. New docks were opened, but the debt to private creditors and the Government grew. In 1825 the council was bailed out by a Government agreement to take over the whole dock debt, now £240,000, and have rights to parts of the dock for the navy. All port revenues went to the Government as security. Leithers, who resented Edinburgh's role, saw their economic lifeline slip further from their grasp. Meanwhile trade continued to find other Forth harbours cheaper to use – and safer. In four years 40 people drowned at Leith through lack of chains and lamps. The reform legislation made Leith a parliamentary burgh, but its council had in effect no revenue or common good fund. It is little wonder that a subplot to the tale of Edinburgh's long-drawn-out bankruptcy was the fractious relationship with its burgh port.[13]

The trustees for the creditors appointed in August 1833 included Sir William Rae, until recently Tory Lord Advocate, the Whig leader Sir James Gibson-Craig, the departing Lord Provost Sir John Learmonth and the most influential Lothian magnate the Duke of Buccleuch. They were faced with a debt of some £400,000 which had risen at over £15,000 a year for the six years to 1832–3. Yet the city's annual revenue was only about £25,000, of which £7,000 came from seat rents in the city churches.[14] The trustees, one of whose roles was to safeguard the interests of small creditors and protect them from ruinous litigation, were vested with assets that might be realised to tackle the debt. Much controversy turned on what revenue the city needed to keep functioning. Although the trustees remained constructive and business-like during the four years searching for a permanent settlement, spokesmen (including councillors) for some importunate creditors were determined to put a spoke in the wheel.

In the council the main burden of running a bankrupt machine and finding a solution fell at first on Adam Black, chosen as treasurer in November 1833. The 49-year-old Dissenting radical bookseller, who had bought the copyright to the *Encyclopaedia Britannica* in 1827 on the collapse of publishers Constable, had shown his political standing in proposing Jeffrey and Abercromby as MPs. William Tait, the recent annuity-tax martyr, was his brother-in-law. Black strove for a settlement that would be acceptable to the creditors and would 'save the inhabitants of Edinburgh, if possible, from an additional, heavy, and interminable assessment'. In 1835 he wrote a pamphlet[15] setting out his proposals and frankly acknowledging the strain felt by the council. He said that councillors had been deterred from taking office because of the restrictions placed on them by the trustees and the repeated threats of legal and financial action against them. But there would be no point in councillors resigning because that would result in 'a general state of anarchy'. He also warned the city and those councillors who were increasingly frustrated by the stranglehold imposed by the creditors on use of revenues raised that 'we are in the situation of unfortunate bankrupts, who must submit to the hardship of their situation. We cannot get rid of it.' Yet get rid of it they had to. Edinburgh's good name was being besmirched, and its financial situation was a deterrent to inward investment. Notoriously, salaries of professors in the university – a civic-funded institution – had not been paid.

One of the problems standing in the way of a solution was defining the council's actual and potential revenues. If figures could be agreed, the amount available to settle the creditors' claims and the time required might be negotiated. When Henry Labouchere, as vice-president of the Board of Trade, was asked in 1836 to report to the Chancellor of the Exchequer on the impasse in Edinburgh and Leith, he put the total revenues of the city as low as £22,000 including the £7,000 from seat rents in the churches. In 1834–5 the Court of Session allowed civic spending of £8,030 but of that £1,400 was in dispute between the council and the creditors. Labouchere reckoned the expenditure to keep the city going was not less than £11,000, but the actual spending was only £7,000. He estimated that sale of council-owned properties, one of the proposals put forward to meet the creditors' claims, would bring only 9s 3d in the pound. There were other problems. An ale duty of 2d a pint was due to run out in 1837. The revenue shortfall could be met by a local assessment, as had just been provided for in the Act establishing reformed corporations in England, but it was not the practice in Scotland. Edinburgh had a range of tolls and taxes on goods brought into the city, including basic foodstuffs, and there were levies on imports through Leith. The latter were a serious obstacle to trade. A new port was being promoted for Granton by the Duke of Buccleuch, in the teeth of Edinburgh's opposition. Meanwhile, in Adam Black's view no new tax was possible: 'The city is already overburdened by so many heavy impositions, that an addition to our assessments in the present languishing state of the town would be disastrous.'

A parliamentary select committee in 1835 came up with no proposal worth putting to the creditors. The next year Henry Labouchere tried to cut through the tangle. His report is a mine of statistics producing proposals of sound sense that would two years later contribute to a solution. He estimated free revenue from the operations at Leith at £14,000 of which £6,000 should go to the ministers, the university and the schools. Creditors should agree to 3 per cent annuities on three-quarters of the debt owed them. The proposals appealed to neither side. A public meeting of creditors debated the report at the Waterloo Rooms and a majority of the 279 or their representatives turned it down. At the next town council meeting the Lord Provost described the decision as 'dreadful' and proposed raising the amount payable to creditors by a half per cent. A deputation would go to London to negotiate. There another parliamentary committee recommended 3.25 per cent annuities and £7,000 for civic institutions. In subsequent negotiations between the creditors and the council, the latter suggested raising the benefit to 4 per cent and putting £2,000 a year into a sinking fund. This would mean annual spending by the city of £14,000 until the debt was extinguished. By taking power to levy an assessment on householders this solution would be underwritten. The trustees agreed, the creditors did not. As a result several influential trustees resigned. The next suggestion was to give up the disputed attempts to make a total of the town's revenues, and instead to work out which city properties could be used to service the debt and which had to be retained for municipal needs. Herein was to lie the key to an eventual agreement.

By this time responsibility for representing the town's interests had been handed on. In 1834 McLaren had been re-elected to the council as one of the original intake who had to face a new poll in order to establish a cycle of triennial elections. His success was accompanied by the kind of controversy that would attach itself to his later electoral forays. Across the city the issue of the day was bizarre: how many churches should the council support – 18 (as wanted by the Established interest) or 13 (as proposed by Dissenters and others keen to cut spending)? At a pre-election meeting in the Tron Church John Anderson, a defeated candidate of the previous year, announced that McLaren was not fit to be a councillor because he was a Dissenter. Alone among newspapers the *Courant* reported this outburst but did not include the protests voiced against Anderson, including by McLaren himself. On 1 November *The Scotsman* wrote a ward-by-ward summary of the campaign and said of McLaren: 'He has done his duty admirably; and a man of sounder judgment, or firmer integrity, the town does not contain.' The paper rallied its readers to vote for the 13-church option. It also drew attention to an advertisement in its columns from McLaren, who attacked the one-sided *Courant* report and added that he had told the Tron meeting that he did not want to serve for a long period on the council and would stand only if the burden of committee work was shared more equally among councillors and the length of the weekly council meetings was curtailed. In the previous year he had been a member of 22 special and ordinary committees 'including nearly all the most laborious, which made it necessary for me to take part in the discussions at the council table more frequently than was agreeable to my own feelings, in defending and explaining measures in public which I had assisted in perfecting in committee.' He had told the Tron meeting that he would not canvass but with this publicity he did not need to. Beneath the professions of reluctance there was perhaps a sign of artful public relations. His reward after topping the poll was to be appointed one of four bailies, which involved sitting as a magistrate – more work, not less.

He was also closely involved in settlement of the city debt and supported his friend Adam Black's proposals. He thought the creditors grasping, and his own calculations suggested that even the council's offer in the wake of Labouchere would prove too generous to fund.[16] McLaren was by now a prominent member of the treasurer's committee, which dismissed the creditors' attitude: 'By grasping at too much, they will lose the benefit within their reach, reduce many of the poorest creditors to destitution, embroil themselves in expensive and protracted lawsuits, raise insuperable obstacles to the deliverance of the town from its embarrassments, and prevent the improvements of the Port of Leith.'[17] But rhetoric from either side would solve nothing. McLaren would soon have to wrestle with the facts and figures because when Black retired from the council in November 1836 McLaren had already proved that he had an accountant's mind, political acumen and willingness to exert himself to negotiate a way forward, which would mean going to London and dealing with Government ministers. He became city treasurer and made his reputation.

An immediate problem was a demand from the Treasury for overdue payment of interest on its loan. All payments had been suspended during negotiations with the creditors. The Lord Provost told the Treasury in February 1837 that money from Leith harbour and docks would now be used to make regular payments. McLaren brought to the council a proposal that lists of non-payers of the annuity tax should be given to church ministers and that the council would, if requested, help to enforce collection 'either by rouping [publicly selling] the goods or taking steps for imprisoning the persons of defaulters.'[18] He opposed the tax but had to try to make the books balance. At the same time he came up with a bizarre solution to the tax itself. Citing provisions in English and Irish Bills before Parliament to fund local government, he suggested that the annuity tax would no longer be needed if revenues from the bishopric of Orkney and the deanery of Edinburgh were made available. These and other ecclesiastical funds had belonged to the city for the support of its clergy until taken by the Crown on the restoration of episcopacy in 1661 and they had not been given back after re-establishment of Presbyterianism in 1689. Six councillors objected to taking a lead from Ireland where many towns were under the influence of Popish priests and where Protestantism would be impeded if not overthrown. McLaren's scheme got nowhere.[19] Meanwhile, attempts to make progress with the city's creditors also yielded nothing. Councillors sympathetic to the creditors objected to a majority decision not to renew the ale duty of 2d a pint. The resulting shortfall in revenue would, they claimed, affect professors whose salaries depended on it, as well as charitable institutions. The council's action was 'vindictive' and the only beneficiaries of scrapping the tax would be brewers, who would pocket £2,000.

In May the creditors again tried to protect their interests by seeking an interdict against the council, which wanted to make money available to Leith harbour. Better accommodation was needed for steamships which were preferring Granton to Leith. The absence of nine vessels meant a reduction in dues of over £3,000. The next month McLaren had to report to the council that negotiations with the trustees had broken down. The Solicitor-General, Andrew Rutherfurd, had offered to act as an intermediary and had held many meetings involving McLaren, the Lord Provost and magistrates. The proposal was to split the use of revenues, some to be allotted to the creditors, others kept for the city's use. Again the money coming from the port was an issue. Rutherfurd persuaded a reluctant council that it should hand over harbour and dock revenues to the trustees, but whether they could surrender powers of management that had been vested in the council by Act of Parliament could only be decided by the Court of Session. McLaren told the council[20] that the trustees insisted on total surrender. Yet he counselled against attaching blame: the trustees had acted conscientiously and were relying on counsel's opinion that the council could abandon rights of management at Leith given by Parliament, an opinion he described as 'extraordinary'. On the failed negotiations he concluded: 'The asperities which it was occasionally difficult to withstand, did the very reverse of promoting conciliation or of serving any good purpose.'

At the end of September McLaren announced he would resign as treasurer and councillor but did not carry out his threat, which was just as well as the Lord Provost, Sir James Spittal, also said he would not continue in office, and any chance of reviving negotiations would have been set back had the two departed at the same time. The Lord Provost told the council that in this his second term he had hoped for a settlement but 'every proposal made by the city to the creditors has, one after another, been rejected ... and the prospect of bringing matters to a settlement is still indefinitely distant'. His health had 'yielded under the burdens and anxieties of public duty'. McLaren used a series of letters to municipal electors to remind them how the city had got into its mess. His investigations had shown that in allowing debts to run up, the pre-1833 councils had not only been imprudent but had breached rules governing their conduct. Parliament had expressly prohibited them from letting the debts increase. For three-quarters of the debt neither the city funds nor the property of burgesses could be made liable, and the creditors should be limited to claiming repayment from councillors who had contracted the debt. McLaren's sustained campaign was meant to put pressure on creditors, their mouthpieces in the council and those voters who might have forgotten that the blame lay with a corrupt Tory regime. He must have known that the chances of getting redress from past councillors were minimal but he mounted a clever public relations campaign to accompany the series of detailed and laborious calculations which he produced in the search for a settlement. At a banquet in honour of the retiring Lord Provost the proposer of a toast to 'Duncan McLaren and the finances of Edinburgh' said he had been reading a report by the treasurer 'which probably few accountants in Edinburgh would have drawn up under a few hundred guineas'.[21] The last council meeting before the November election heard that further efforts to strike a compromise had failed. Councillors did, however, pass a motion reinforcing their recent strategy, which was to offer a 3 per cent annuity on the amount of the debt, secured against most of the revenues of the city except the common good fund, petty customs, duties on goods brought to the city and burgesses' fee tickets. In time this would form the basis for agreement.

McLaren again topped the poll in his ward and was reappointed treasurer, with James Forrest of Colinton becoming Lord Provost. At the first meeting of the new council further conciliatory efforts by Rutherfurd and Sir William Rae, spokesman for the remaining trustees, were made public. Rae had told the Solicitor-General that a considerable number of the most influential creditors had approved the compounding of all debts for a 3 per cent annuity. McLaren was asked to convey the council's approval to Rutherfurd, who replied: 'The creditors will gain immediately more than any reasonable man would promise himself, even from a successful contest; and the city will be raised from the unbecoming – I had almost said degrading – situation, to which the extravagance and mismanagement of former councils had reduced it.' He commended the efforts of Spittal and McLaren. The details of the settlement, including maintaining the level of dues at Leith unless the creditors agreed to their reduction but allotting £1,000 to harbour or docks improvement, were put to the council. Twenty-three councillors agreed but six wanted a week's delay before the creditors were informed. The next step would be to seek parliamentary approval through a Bill drawn up by Rae and Rutherfurd. Following this momentous debate the council moved to next business – a report that the stove at St Mary's Church was not working. Rutherfurd wrote to London to Fox Maule, undersecretary at the Home Office in charge of Scottish business, on November 20: 'I have been oppressed beyond all bearing for these five days past, particularly in bringing to a conclusion, which I hope is now done, the settlement of the city debts.'[22]

The group of councillors unhappy with the proposals made further trouble at a meeting on 28 November. Led by Robert Deuchar, they were depicted as the voice of creditors. They failed in arguing for a delay while accountants calculated the exact total revenue the city would have at its disposal. Deuchar entered a formal protest at the majority's decision, claiming that the creditors might take possession of city property. McLaren said that Deuchar wanted to become 'sole trustee and accountant'. The series of council meetings in November and December at which the proposed settlement was debated were marred by a bitter row between McLaren and his opponents, especially Deuchar, who, McLaren said, had been elected as a Radical and was acting as a Tory spokesman for the creditors.

McLaren sent an open letter addressed to his fellow councillors but intended as an appeal to the bar of public opinion.[23] He explained that at the council meeting on 12 December he had attempted to answer the letter of protest sent by Deuchar after the previous week's meeting. He was assailed for three hours, he said, by a cabal of five councillors as he tried to read his reply to Deuchar, whose letter of protest he had received only the previous evening. He had immediately begun to draft a reply but after finishing the first part was interrupted by a visit from a fellow councillor who stayed two hours. He finished the second part at midnight. The third part was completed between 10 and 11 the next morning before an important meeting of the committee of Heriot's Hospital. He had only resumed work on the fourth part when he had to go to the council meeting at 12.30. 'The remainder, forming a considerable portion of the whole, was written at the council table, while the public business was in progress, in which you all know I had to take a considerable share.'

The *Weekly Journal* then gave[24] what McLaren described as a biased report of what followed – attacks so virulent that McLaren felt absolved from the ordinary rules of courtesy to opponents. The newspaper did not report McLaren's interventions, and he complained to the manager of the paper, John Harthill, about the reporter, who remained in employment only 'because he is your son'. Deuchar and his supporters objected to McLaren tabling his answers. The Lord Provost in the chair said he could not intervene 'in the personal abuse which existed between Mr McLaren and Mr Deuchar' but threatened to suspend the meeting. *The Scotsman* ignored details of the ructions pleading lack of space and a desire not to perpetuate bad feeling but it approved the accuracy of McLaren's reply to the *Weekly Journal*. It also stated that Deuchar, despite claiming to be a Radical, generally sided with ultra-Tories and having come into the council to get rid of the annuity tax was now standing up for the claims of the church. But 'if there is one man in the council, in whom more than any other, the friends of religious liberty and the opponents of the annuity tax have entire confidence, that man is Treasurer McLaren'.[25] McLaren had to answer the criticism that the terms for a possible settlement ignored his earlier claim that responsibility lay with those who had contracted the debt. He replied that he had not changed his view and, applying pressure, he warned that redress remained 'the ultimate resource in the event of the trustees refusing any reasonable compromise'.

In Edinburgh the efforts of McLaren and Rutherfurd had gone as far as they could. The scene moved to London where the details of a Bill had to be thrashed out and passed through both Houses of Parliament. It proved time-consuming and burdensome. On 24 April 1838 McLaren received a commission from the town council to go to London with full powers to act on its behalf. He travelled alone and in his negotiations with ministers, MPs and lobbyists for the various interests, he had the support of no officials apart from the council's London agent. He was of course familiar with the imperial capital, though so far his experience had been with its business houses where he bought his firm's goods. He now had to mingle in Whitehall and Westminster. In particular he dealt with members of a select committee chaired by Henry Labouchere, author of the report two years earlier which had mapped out a possible solution. McLaren had a high regard for him, as he did for another member of the committee, Sir James Graham, who had been in Earl Grey's Cabinet and was similarly to serve Sir Robert Peel and Lord Aberdeen. An indication of the obstacles he faced was the presence of John Murray, as Lord Advocate the Government leader in Scotland, but also MP for Leith, which resented the way its interests had been sacrificed to Edinburgh's and which sought the best deal for the port. In a letter home to his second wife he recalled one meeting which included Murray: 'I debated the different points at great length, and gained nearly every one of the least importance that I thought worth pressing; *but you must not say this until the Bill is passed.* The committee always paid great attention to what I said, and seemed disposed to make allowances for my deficiencies.'

He had to face down opposition from several quarters. The Duke of Buccleuch was concerned about the effect on his properties at Granton, including the new harbour, if the boundaries of Leith stretched as far west as they appeared, from the Bill, to do. An hour and a half's interview with Scotland's leading Tory settled ducal fears. McLaren and Buccleuch remained on good terms for nearly five decades. No doubt it had helped that in 1836 McLaren stood out against councillors who had opposed Buccleuch's enterprise: it was absurd, he said, that 'because we could not improve our own harbour, we should oppose another Bill for building a harbour and docks in the neighbourhood'.[26] More prolonged was the opposition of the Church. It demanded preference in securing city funds to build its new churches, a thorny subject as is explained in the next chapter. McLaren told the town council and Sir William Rae, the trustees' spokesman at Westminster, that such interference with the principles of the settlement was mortally damaging. The Bill was about to go to the House of Lords, which could be expected to back any demand by an Established Church. Withdraw your proposal or take responsibility for wrecking the whole settlement, McLaren told the presbytery of Edinburgh. Graham, a keen churchman, was inclined to support funding of new places of worship but after summoning McLaren for interview agreed not to press the matter.

Another example of McLaren's persuasiveness is found in correspondence with the second Viscount Melville, whose family's long stranglehold on Scottish politics had delayed the reforms that might have forestalled Edinburgh's plight. McLaren wanted to change clauses in the original Bill governing repayments so that investment at Leith would be promoted and the Government's loan better secured. He sent drafts of two new clauses to Melville, who though out of office since 1830 remained an influential fixer. The new provisions might postpone repayment of all debts from 25 to at worst 27 years but £25,000 would be freed up. 'This £25,000', he wrote, 'would all be expended on the improvements of the harbour-docks, and would, most undoubtedly, be so applied as to prevent, to some extent, the trade from going from Leith to Granton, or, in other words, would prevent the revenues from falling off at least to a certain extent, and consequently would, as I said before, make the Government loan more secure than it could possibly be without this outlay.' In this cautious sentence he was trying to reduce the annual repayment from £12,750 to £11,750 without risk of invoking the provision in the legislation that the Government could through default take possession of the harbour and docks. An extra £1,000 a year would be available for improvements.[27]

The Act 'to regulate and secure the debt due by the City of Edinburgh to the public; to confirm an agreement between the said city and its creditors; and to effect a settlement of the affairs of the said city and the town of Leith' was commended to the town council by McLaren in a long statement on 31 July 1838. The Act, running to 83 clauses, provided creditors with 3 per cent annuities on a total debt of £400,000. At a public meeting later in the year the many small beneficiaries, often ignored among the pleadings of the major creditors, were remembered: 'A considerable portion of this sum was held by ladies and women with small means, whose all was invested in what was considered at the time a safe deposit. Very many of their cases were extremely hard. Let them only think of these poor women – their breadwinners gone, and their necessities compelling them to sell to the cool, calculating holders of money, who purchased, or were ready to purchase, the debts below their value – a settlement was to these poor creatures saving them from starvation or the poorhouse.'[28] Some £100 annuity holders lost out by selling at only £80, but those who held on were adequately rewarded in the long run. McLaren's aim, stated in a letter to municipal electors first published in *The Scotsman* on 15 August, was to prove that the settlement fulfilled his pledge the previous year that the outcome would not be less favourable than the proposals rejected by the creditors in 1836 and subsequently agreed by most councillors as having been too generous to the creditors and probably unaffordable by the city.

The final agreement absolved the city from paying interest on debts to the Government of almost a quarter of a million pounds, though the claim was not formally abandoned. The creditors' interests were secured by making over to new trustees the city's properties, but the common good fund was excluded, in return for paying £1,000 a year, as were customs and other dues, including a penny rate which would have brought in about £1,350 but which McLaren, having done his sums and with rising revenues from elsewhere, was able to tell the council in November would not have to be exacted. The ale duty which had expired would not have to be reinstated. The value of the creditors' security he calculated at about £12,000 a year. The city would have free income of almost £4,300.

Although that figure seems very little even at the money values of the time, just as the finances of the harbour and docks had been central to the city's problems (not to mention those of Leithers), so the settlement hung on the value of the port revenues. Annually £7,680 would be used from that source – £3,180 going to the creditors, who then discharged all their claims on Leith revenues, £2,000 for ministers' stipends and £2,500 for the university and schools. The professors' salaries could now be paid, and the 'college debt' amounting to £13,000 would be discharged. The burgh of Leith was a main beneficiary of the settlement. The Government would postpone security on loans for improvements at the port up to £15,000. The Docks Commission established by Parliament in 1826 and much resented in Leith for the power it gave Edinburgh councillors over the revenues was swept away and replaced by a new commission of 11 representing the Government and the councils of Edinburgh and Leith (but with no councillor members) to manage the harbour and docks and superintend the improvements. Trade was given a boost by abolition of the ancient merk per ton levy on imports. The burgh was completely separated from Edinburgh and its council furnished with a common good fund and customs revenues. McLaren later commented: 'Our Leith friends insist that they have got the best, the creditors contend that the best lot has fallen to them, while the city think they have not got the worst.'[29]

In a report by the treasurer's committee and unanimously approved by the council on 2 November McLaren was upbeat.[30] Having set out figures for revenue and expenditure and made provision for payment of the annuities, he concluded: 'It thus appears that when the new [1833] council came into office, there was an annual deficiency of revenues to the extent of £9856 2s 4d, which has been converted into a surplus of £2688 2s 6d.' And citizens no longer had to pay £2,400 because the ale duty had been abolished.

The treasurer's achievements as accountant and negotiator were widely praised. A public meeting on 3 October chaired by the Lord Provost heard many tributes, among them one from Sir James Gibson-Craig who said that it would be impossible to find anyone who had acted 'with more respect to himself and more utility to the community'. The Whig patriarch would not be so fulsome to McLaren in later years. A subscription list was started and on 6 February 1839 a presentation was made at the Merchants Hall of a silver plate worth over £500. Rutherfurd, the Solicitor-General, was the principal speaker. As a representative of the Government he knew how much the final negotiations had depended on McLaren: 'I knew well that at the last hours, when other parties were in London, and all hopes of passing an Act of Parliament were nearly gone from some hitch or other, they were anxious to have his services; and so fully impressed were parties on the other side with the conviction that without his hand the work would not be accomplished, that they made a point, and I was applied to use my influence to persuade him in the first instance to go to London, and then to remain there till he saw the measure safe and secure.' McLaren's last service as treasurer before resigning the post in November 1838 had been to reform the way the city's accounts were set out. Perhaps if the clarity that he brought to columns of figures had been evident before 1833 Edinburgh would not have blindly slid into debt and suffered five years' embarrassment.

3. The 'clearest and soundest head'

On 7 January 1835 *The Scotsman* carried an advertisement publicising the names of 30 members of the Central Board of the Committee of Scottish Dissenters who had been chosen at a founding meeting a month earlier in Rose Street Chapel, a regular venue for promoting the Dissenters' causes. The convener of the board was Duncan McLaren, and the list included council allies like Adam Black and Thomas Russell, as well as McLaren's later adversary Robert Deuchar. James Peddie, a lawyer and son of the James Peddie who was McLaren's minister at Bristo Street, was another driving force. It was a busy time: on 21 November 1834 McLaren had spoken at a meeting of 15,000 in the Grassmarket protesting at the fall of the Whig Government and the return of the Tories under Sir Robert Peel. The meeting, full of Whig luminaries, pledged support for continuing with the principles of reform. The Rose Street meeting gave a similar pledge and set out to publicise its resolution across Scotland where dozens of local associations had sprung up in the last two years to rally Dissenting (or Voluntary) opinion. The Edinburgh association had met in 1833 – 50 strong in Rose Street Chapel with McLaren in the chair – to consider a campaign to separate Church and State.[1] The Church of Scotland was beginning to flex its muscles and was demanding investment in new churches. Leadership of the General Assembly passed into the hands of Evangelical churchmen in 1834. The Rev. Thomas Chalmers, their inspiring leader, launched his campaign to bring the Gospel to the thousands who were beyond its reach, and that meant seeking money for new buildings. Dissenting churchgoers were affronted by the prospect of the public purse contributing, and they realised that a revitalised Established Church would pose a challenge. Although statistics are not wholly dependable, it appears that about a third of churchgoers were members of Dissenting congregations, rising to half in Edinburgh.[2] They were alarmed by Chalmers's aim of a 'sufficiently thick-set establishment' which they thought meant setting up a parish church in opposition to Dissenting churches no matter how sparse the local population.[3] The contemporary historian of the Secession Church wrote of the collapse of relations between churchmen and Dissenters: 'Religious societies where churchmen and Dissenters had long co-operated harmoniously together, were broken up ... and in many instances, the ties of friendship were broken asunder.'[4]

The Committee of Scottish Dissenters had pressing political as well as ecclesiastical business. The accession of a Tory ministry made an election likely. So the Central Board interviewed Edinburgh's two Whig MPs, James Abercromby and Sir John Campbell, 'at considerable length' and 'without entering upon the great question of separation of Church and State, brought under their notice the views entertained by Dissenters on various points.'[5] The result was to promise 'undivided support' especially since the likely Tory candidates were 'opposed to Dissenters on almost every point'. A month later at the town council McLaren returned to the issue of city church funding, giving notice of a motion to inquire whether any reduction was possible. Councillors who had been elected because they favoured the support of 13 rather than 18 churches tried to get Parliament to reduce the number. Chalmers had already been wrestling with the opposition mounted to his plan for a new church in the Cowgate, a particularly deprived area. He blamed the stroke he suffered in January 1834 on the obstacles that Dissenters were putting in the way of his godly Commonwealth, though he had doughty opponents in his own church too.

The battleground was the number of seats needed in churches. Both sides lobbied hard in Westminster as well as through pamphlets. James Peddie denied that one publication by the Central Board of the Committee of Scottish Dissenters was necessarily the work of McLaren and himself simply because it bore their names as office bearers. McLaren, however, was never happier than when publishing statistics to prove or disprove a case and he raised the wrath of Patrick Clason, minister of Buccleuch Parish Church, who riposted with a series of letters addressed to 'Bailie' McLaren, whose Central Board 'was hatched in some dark corner on the 17th December last'.[6] McLaren had only become chairman because he was a bailie, Clason alleged. He accepted that McLaren was 'very able at figures', but because there were errors and distortions and because of the 'utter inefficiency' of Voluntaryism Clason had ignored the position of Dissenters in the tables of church statistics which he had drawn up for the Church of Scotland deputation that had gone to the Prime Minister. The Dissenters were allying themselves with Roman Catholics in an effort to pull down religious establishments, he charged, and he hoped that McLaren would now see that 'there really is a very serious deficiency in the means of religious instruction, particularly in the manufacturing districts of Scotland'. McLaren, however, told the town council on 15 March 1836 that there was 'a mania' for erecting churches 'similar to that for promoting railways'. The Edinburgh debates had their effect elsewhere. From Coupar Angus a James Miller wrote to Fox Maule, MP for Perthshire from 1835, using the evidence of over-provision of church places in the capital to counter the demands by Church of Scotland ministers (mainly Tories) in Perthshire.[7]

At Westminster MPs plagued by religious pressure groups sought ways of establishing the facts, and on 1 July 1835 Lord John Russell as Home Secretary set up a Royal Commission on the opportunities for worship, figures on attendance and the funding available to the Established Church. Neither side was happy at the composition of the commission. Dissenters, with only one representative among the members, thought it was predisposed in favour of endowments to the church. Chalmers thought it contained too many churchmen opposed to his plans for church extension. He was also furious when the commission, working at a snail's pace but finally arriving in Edinburgh in January 1836, took evidence from the Central Board of Dissenters. He gave his testimony on 13 and 20 February. McLaren rose to the challenge, saying that although he had been sitting in on the commission meetings he had not been going to give his own evidence until he heard Chalmers's: [8] 'For several days I have been obliged to sit up a considerable part of the night, in order to get it completed in time', he told the commissioners on 17 and 19 March. His aim in getting together facts and figures over three weeks was to counter claims that 'there is a want of pastoral superintendence and church accommodation in the city'. In amassing his own evidence 'I did not occupy the whole of my time, nor the fourth part of it in making them [his statements] up. I could not afford to do so without neglecting my other duties'. But he claimed deep acquaintance with the subject and boasted: 'I dare say if the commission had employed an accountant to make them up, with all the facts to collect, in place of taking three weeks, the statements would not have got out of his hands for three months to come'.

McLaren's 33-page pamphlet includes 23 tables of statistics about Edinburgh's population, the income from seat rents and ministers' stipends. The aim was to show that the Established Church in the city had been 'a complete failure'. In 13 churches only 6,385 seats had been let out of a possible 14,000. The position was much better in the churches recently built in the more prosperous suburban areas but the key point was that Chalmers's case did not stand up. Far from there being too few places of worship in the Old Town (where Chalmers wanted another in the Cowgate), only 1,070 people rented seats in the Established churches there. In other words, there was plenty of space but the churches were not attracting adherents. McLaren had been in the High Church (of St Giles) across the High Street from his shop several times in the previous two years and there were many pews unlet or, if let, unoccupied. The average number of families for each Old Town minister was 354 – 'he could visit them all in 35 days, at the rate of 10 families each day'. McLaren played his local card: 'I know the ancient royalty intimately, as I know the operations which have been going on. I have taken down buildings myself, and converted them into places of business, which are occupied by a population of at least 100.'

The Royal Commission, which expressed irritation at the late date on which McLaren had come forward with his evidence when it wanted to set off to hear about the position in Glasgow, began a series of reports in February 1837. It found 40,000–50,000 inhabitants of Edinburgh capable of attending a church but not doing so, mainly among the lower working classes. The Government was not pleased that Chalmers, a Tory, chaired the committee promoting church extensions. It would have preferred leadership from Whig-inclined moderate ministers and Parliament House lawyers in the pews. Playing for time, ministers hoped that the enthusiasm for extensions would wane. The Dissenters, however, remained an irritation. When the Royal Commission reported, McLaren was contacted by Henry Renton, who was not only making a reputation as a minister in Kelso but had just become McLaren's brother-in-law. The Government, Renton said, should be told of the Dissenters' concerns about the report, and McLaren was the man to get the Central Board to act.[9] In November the Solicitor-General Andrew Rutherfurd wrote a long and pained letter to Fox Maule as a junior minister.[10] The Committee of Dissenters had been to see him 'and certainly expressed for their party great hostility to any grant for further endowment'. Dissenters would not support the Tories but there would be 'a very lukewarm and partial support, if not abandonment of the Whigs'. Rutherfurd expressed his own support for endowment to Fox Maule but he had not let on to the delegation: 'I heard them with exemplary patience for an hour, and received thanks for it; but if they had overheard the 'man within the breast' that Adam Smith speaks of, they would have felt how little merited their acknowledgments were.' In December the Central Board sent 362 petitions containing 148,000 signatures attacking endowments, and in March 1838 there was a mass protest rally in Edinburgh.[11] The Government announced its refusal to sanction endowment grants for new churches anywhere in urban Scotland, and it would apply only unclaimed teinds (tithes) in the possession of the crown to build where there was a need in the Highlands. The Dissenters were mollified but still sent a delegation to London to complain about this State use of the teinds. The Church of Scotland, with rather more ground for complaint at the lack of State support for an Established Church, also tried lobbying. Lord Melbourne, easily wearied by religiosity, told the delegation: 'You may not be better for our plan, but – hang it – you surely cannot be worse.'[12] Rutherfurd, who had many dealings with McLaren around this time on the Edinburgh settlement as well as Dissenters' claims, recognised the qualities of the man. In June 1838 he asked Fox Maule to receive McLaren as 'an able and excellent man, and a thorough good Whig'.[13]

When it became clear that the Government would not support general endowment of churches, particularly not in urban areas where Dissenting congregations were strong, the Central Board ceased its propaganda war and stopped sending out orators from Edinburgh to stir up protests. Within the Church of Scotland there was resentment among landowners about the threat that teinds they had hung on to might be used to build churches in rural parishes needing accommodation. And the succession of court cases about who had the right to install ministers in parishes began to call into question the integrity of the national Church. The Government, Whig until 1841 and then Peel's, wrestled with the challenges to ecclesiastical authority. The Dissenters nursed their grievances, but public attention was diverted elsewhere. The Disruption of 1843 and the founding of the Free Church are inescapable landmarks in Scotland's story. As for Dissenters, their campaign was and remains all but forgotten. Yet it has been described as 'the first truly national agitation in Scotland', using methods that would be adopted by both Chartists and the Anti-Corn Law League, which was to find some of its strongest supporters among Dissenters.[14]

As a national spokesman for the Dissenters McLaren argued with Government ministers. As member of an Edinburgh Dissenting congregation and until late in 1838 treasurer of the city, he pursued his campaign, almost a vendetta, against the claims of the Church of Scotland ministers. The annuity tax was still there to attack since it gave the ministers comfortable stipends. However, there was also the question of the rents charged for seats in the pews. These were a source of revenue for the council and were factored into the calculations surrounding the City Agreement Act. Litigation was underway about the level of rents charged. The church ministers accused the council of milking a source of income. McLaren set out to rebut their claims and in 1840 published a series of seven letters, originally contributed to *The Scotsman*, with a title page proclaiming 'One fact is worth a ship-load of arguments'.[15] The city creditors have a right to income from the seat rents, McLaren stated, and any threat to the revenue stream is bound to affect creditors' interests. Uncertainty over the litigation had reduced the value of the £100 bonds issued in 1838. They had gone down as far as £70, but McLaren believed that settlement of the seat rents issue would see them go up again to £85. McLaren's aim was to disprove the ministers' accusation that the town council had raised the rents and thus deterred the poor from attending church. That was 'a perfect chimera', he said, armed with his usual array of figures.

By 1839, two years before a General Election, disillusionment with the Whig Government was spreading. It had lost the reforming impulse. It was offending its natural supporters – in the case of Scottish Dissenters on matters which now appear tangential but could feed underlying resentments. The composition of the Bible Board was a case in point. The role of the board was to license printing of Bibles but the Government restricted it to members of the Church of Scotland, and McLaren wrote to Fox Maule[16] on the damage caused to the Liberal party by this kind of discrimination: 'There is *not one* burgh or county constituency in Scotland in which the Church could return a Liberal candidate to Parliament without the votes of Dissenters and having the occasion to meet Dissenting ministers I am satisfied from what I hear from them that many Dissenters will not in future vote for ministerial candidates ... They have for years been complaining that they were not eligible even to the humble office of parish schoolmaster, and that they were excluded from professorships in the university and the removal of their disabilities was what they were always looking for from a Liberal Government, but in place [*sic*] getting any existing grievance removed they cannot avoid feeling that another has been wantonly imposed on them which must exist for at least 20 years.' McLaren hastened to assure Maule that he would not desert the Liberal cause or advise others to do so 'for my principle has been 'better half a loaf than no bread' but I am telling you honestly the feelings which I *know* to exist with many liberal minded men – their interest in the excelence [*sic*] of the present Government is by no means strong and is diminishing'. The back of the letter has in Maule's writing several comments – 'read and master', 'learn and inwardly digest', 'a queer fish'.

The pretext for McLaren's letter was the composition of the Bible

Board and his attempt to involve the Rev. John Lee in its doings. Lee was prominent in the Church of Scotland, a Whig Evangelical who had fought several bitter battles for supremacy with Chalmers. He had a long friendship with McLaren, who in 1837 praised his resistance to pressure from Chalmers's party but regretted that 'you did not brush away the falsehoods and sophistries of your calumniators sooner'.[17] In 1839 McLaren tried to persuade him to become secretary of the Bible Board for which he was eminently suited as he had earlier led a successful campaign to overturn the right of the royal printers to print the Bible in Scotland, but Lee would not resign his ministry at St Giles. He shared his dilemma with McLaren in a series of letters in which McLaren showed sensitivity and diplomacy.[18] One problem was that Lee had recently resigned as principal at St Andrews University. To dither publicly over the secretaryship of the board might affect his reputation, but McLaren thought that Lee would have given standing to the Bible publishing project. McLaren pragmatically did not press Lee further but he was not a man to give up on a principle. Although the Central Board ran down its campaigning after 1839, Dissenters' grievances continued. McLaren summed them up at a public meeting in Edinburgh on 14 July 1841 called to devise measures for 'protecting the civil rights of Dissenters from the unjust encroachment of the High Church party and their abettors in Parliament'.[19] There was a political point to his argument that these civil rights were being undermined: McLaren argued that one of the city's MPs should be chosen to exert himself on behalf of Dissenters who formed 'a large portion of the Liberal constituency'. The electoral implications of that will be examined in the next chapter. McLaren listed the grievances that were being ignored. There was the composition of the Bible Board. Under a recent Prisons Act no Dissenters were eligible to become prison chaplains. In 40 schools set up to fill gaps in provision across the Highlands, teachers were paid from public funds (not by local heritors) and they had to subscribe the Church's confession of faith. Finally, the first Inspector of Schools had been appointed in 1840 with the proviso that he should 'possess the confidence of the Church of Scotland'.[20]

To McLaren's rise to prominence in representing organised Dissent there was an intimate side. On 22 March 1836 he married Christina Renton, the 23-year-old youngest daughter of a prominent Dissenting family in Edinburgh. Her parents, William and Agnes, at their home in Buccleuch Place hosted frequent social gatherings that appealed to the young widower McLaren and included leading Liberal families of all hues. His family correspondence from later years often refers to visits to this sanctuary where William and Agnes were increasingly venerated.[21] William, like McLaren, was a successful draper and for more than 40 years treasurer of Broughton Place Secession Church. The Rev. John Lee, a frequent visitor, called him the 'very milk of human kindness'. His wife Agnes bore him 12 children but still found time to be involved in many good causes, from the Voluntary controversy to anti-slavery, temperance reform and the society devoted to world peace. Their second son, Henry, minister in Kelso since 1829, remained a close friend of the McLaren family till his death in 1877.[22] His letter to Duncan on 14 April 1837, referred to above, contained a reference to his sister Christina, 11 months after her marriage. He is happy to hear she is now well 'although we deeply regret that the account of the improvement is still qualified by the notice that her old complaints have not altogether disappeared'. Her health was perhaps not helped by pregnancy: her first child, Agnes, was born on 4 July. Duncan junior came in February 1839 and Catherine in May 1840. In Agnes's babyhood, Duncan spent much time in London sorting out Edinburgh's finances. He was conscious of his absence, sending many letters to Christina. On 4 July 1838 he reminded her that if he had not 'come up' to London the city's affairs would have been in a worse state than they were, and the agent who acted in London for the interests of Leith would have had everything his own way.[23] He was staying with a Miss Goudie in Cecil Street off the Strand.[24] He had arrived there on 28 June, the eve of Queen Victoria's Coronation, having suffered delays on the journey south. It was a period when old and new forms of transport were called on: he had had to travel by Oxford, Windsor and Maidenhead, using the Great Western Railway and sundry coaches which had been held up for lack of post horses. He was met by a message from Sir John Campbell, one of the Edinburgh MPs, to say that a Coronation ticket had been got for him by Campbell's wife, Lady Stratheden, who qualified for an invitation as a peeress in her own right. He would not have taken a ticket any other way since they were selling for up to £25. The problem was that attendance demanded court dress, and that meant blue coat, white vest, white buttons and white neck-cloth. He went to see a friend in the hope of borrowing vest and coat, but the man was as gravely attired as McLaren himself in black. So he bought a pair of ready-made white trousers, neck-cloth and gloves: 'And what do you think', he wrote to Christina, 'I took the black buttons off my black coat and got fancy yellow ones to put on which made it a very qua [sic] blue for me! You would not know me in my smart new dress.'

Following Lady Stratheden's advice, he got to Westminster Abbey at half-past five the following morning and remained until four in the afternoon.

> I had a delightful view of the Queen and all the company as they arrived for several hours before her. They passed in review before me, and it was a splendid sight, – the whole nobility of the land passing before one leisurely from six to ten o'clock. I only wished you had been with me to make my enjoyment greater. There was nothing struck me so much in seeing the peeresses walk along before me in procession as the fact that, with very few exceptions, they were all very stout women. I really never saw so many stout ladies, or women of any rank or class. I remarked, too, that when any one of about 15 stone weight appeared who was well made, the whisper among the gentlemen near me was, 'She is a very fine woman.' All those of a more slender form were allowed to pass without notice. It was very beautiful to see them in their crimson velvet robes, with trains three or four yards long, sailing along the ground like peacocks. The Queen is rather little as compared with those whom I have been describing. I saw her for at least ten minutes, as there was a stoppage in the procession, or at least a very slow movement, when she was near me; and I saw the Duchess of Kent for a much longer time.

The day gave him a chance to meet valuable contacts – Sir William Rae, Henry Labouchere, the Speaker of the Commons (James Abercromby) and Fox Maule ('a very nice man'). They were all involved with the Bill to sort out Edinburgh's debt, and McLaren added: 'I think our matters are getting on well.'

His retirement from the council soon after the council's affairs were sorted out was as much because of his wife's health as from the needs of the shop. His son John would later recall life at Ramsay Gardens, just down from the Castle and close to both the shop and the council chamber.[25] His father 'was in the habit of dining at four o'clock, and after dinner he went back to business, for at that time a great deal of shopping was done in the evening'. In summer they would take a little house with a walled garden in South Queensferry, and his father would travel in to Edinburgh in the morning, returning in the afternoon. This happy existence was to be short lived. There were alarms about the children's health. In April 1840 their father noted that all of them had been poorly with a sort of 'fever of cold or influenza. The baby [Duncan] has had an inflammation of the lungs and is very dangerously ill. We had very little hope of him this morning but he seems if anything easier this evening.'[26] Around this time John began to be ill with the chest problems that dogged him well into adulthood. McLaren noted the symptoms early. In the summer of 1841 John and his sister Grant were on holiday in Arrochar while the younger children stayed with their grandmother in Portobello. John had written about 'a slight cough' and McLaren replied: 'You must take care of this for 'a slight cough' was the beginning of Mamma's trouble, and a great many people die of very painfull [sic] and lingering diseases which have their commencement in 'a slight cough' ... Don't go with wet feet after you come into the house, but always put on dry stockings and shoes.' It cannot have helped the boy's peace of mind that the letter also reported on his stepmother having 'a good deal of reaching [retching] and pain.'[27] McLaren and Christina travelled a good deal in the hope of restoring her health, but she died on 1 November 1841. Later that month the widower, now with five children from 10 years to 18 months, had a letter from his sister Janet offering the services of herself and their sister Euphemia without reward 'to lighten in some degree your domestic afflictions and to take care of your children and household property'.[28] The offer was made partly because of McLaren's kindness to their mother and others in the family. Henry Renton remembered his sister as 'most fair and beautiful, most artless, affectionate and disinterested, in moral and religious principles inflexible, and in her long and severe illness most patient and resigned'.[29]

At the time McLaren withdrew from the town council there was much goodwill towards him. Aside from a handful of fellow councillors, there was no lasting rancour among men who had been on the other side of an argument with him. They recognised his abilities, commended his unceasing hard work and, while realising he did not suffer fools gladly, saw evidence of the practical philanthropy valued in an age when the State did not assume the burden of caring for its citizens. To the middle classes he was the skilled negotiator who restored the city's financial reputation. To the poor of the old town he was the man who used charitable funds to set up free schools. By 1854 he was responsible for having founded 10 non-sectarian schools educating 2,800 children. From first joining the town council he took an interest in education, being appointed a representative on three trusts that operated 'hospitals', that is, residential schools for needy children. He remained interested in the George Watson's and James Gillespie's trusts throughout his life, but it was to the Heriot's Trust that he devoted his energies and creativity. The trust had prospered in the two centuries since it was founded with £25,000 (over £2 million in today's value) left by George (Jinglin' Geordie) Heriot, jeweller and banker to James VI and I. The hospital school had opened, just outside the city wall, in 1659. By 1833 the trust that supported about 180 boys was awash with money. Much of the land being built on as Edinburgh expanded was owned by the trust, which enjoyed the revenues as feudal superior and the largest landowner in the city.[30] McLaren in 1835 brought to the town council what the historian of George Heriot's School has described as 'the most dramatic and far-reaching proposal' for the future of the hospital.[31] He pointed to the annual surplus of £3,000 – in contrast with the fate of the city's finances. He proposed establishing a school in each of the 13 parishes at a cost of £800 a year, which would offer better value than the £8,000 spent on 180 boys in the hospital. It would be 'amply sufficient to educate gratuitously all the poor children in Edinburgh, besides fulfilling, in the most ample manner, the liberal intentions of the pious founder respecting burgess' children, and thus the revenues of the hospital would become an estimable blessing to the community'.[32] On 12 October 1835 the hospital governors approved the plan, and the following year a Bill promoted by MP Sir John Campbell allowed the trust to extend its powers. The trades guilds, however, were opposed to the project because they saw it as a threat to their preferential rights as burgesses to have their children admitted to the hospital. McLaren became chairman of the 11 governors responsible for the out-schools, as they came to be known. They insisted on free education, a controversial principle since other schools, especially those being opened as 'sessional schools' by individual churches, charged small fees. Several times McLaren successfully fought the argument that a penny a week would secure more regular attendance and help to build a fund for books. The first school enrolled 318 pupils from 700 applicants and opened at Heriot Bridge – between the hospital and Grassmarket – on 15 October 1838. By the following year there were four schools for children of five and over and two infant schools. In 1842–3 the first national Inspector of Schools, John Gibson, reported favourably on 'by far the most valuable educational machinery in the country'. Teachers were paid above the norm, which ensured competition for posts and high standards.

The children of burgesses and free men in poor circumstances had priority for admission, followed by children of the poor who had resided in the city for at least a year. McLaren tackled the problem of burgess rights. Many people from outside the city had paid the burgess fee to get their sons into the hospital, depriving some residents of the opportunity. The level of fee was a deterrent to tradesmen and small businessmen, and so McLaren persuaded a majority of councillors to reduce the fee on the argument that more people would apply to become burgesses and so income would be maintained or increased.[33] The number of burgess entrants had fallen from 64 in 1830 to 17 in 1837, but a report to the treasurer's committee argued the arithmetical case in characteristic McLaren style: 'The average sum formerly payable to the city for each entry, after deduction of all expenses, being £7 14s 3d and the sum proposed to be charged by the city in future being £3 2s 6d, it follows that if the number of entries on an average of the next four years shall increase from the present rate of $15\frac{1}{2}$ annually to 38, the revenue derived by the city from the entry of burgesses will be the same as it has been during the last four years.'[34] The city's creditors disagreed, fearing a loss of income, but McLaren persisted and won his case in 1838. His projections proved over-optimistic and the town council was told in 1845 that the revenue had not recovered and that most entrants were seeking not the status that went with being a burgess but only a place at Hospital.

The future of the hospitals and education of the poor were matters that were to exercise McLaren as Lord Provost, MP and into retirement. His six years as a councillor saw the start of controversies that marked later years of public prominence. Two of them – the influence of Parliament House lawyers and the relations between town and gown – came to the fore as early as 1835. In that year the council considered the report of Burgh Commissioners on municipal corporations in Scotland. It suggested, among other things, that councillors were not equipped to judge the merits of candidates for chairs in the university. Needless to say, that went down badly not only because of the slur on members' capability but because the council was deeply proud of the fact that the city had founded the university two and a half centuries earlier and maintained close scrutiny over its Government – even when unable to pay professors' salaries on time. The commission stated: 'The class of persons of which the town council is chiefly composed, is not of sufficient intelligence either to estimate for themselves the merits of candidates, or to weigh the representations put forward by others.' It drew no distinction between the old, unreformed council and the new one. McLaren told the council meeting on 21 October 1835 that all the commissioners were members of the bar, 'some of them in small practice, most of them little known beyond the walls of Parliament House, while some of them are chiefly distinguished for an extreme anxiety to serve their country as advocates-depute and as sheriffs'. He had 'often heard of the superciliousness of the Tory aristocracy: but this contemptuous language was used by Whig commissioners'. Their report and an additional one on the financial affairs of the city 'was one of the most erroneous, in regard to details, which had ever been laid before Parliament'. Any committee of the town council, 'whom they appeared so much to despise, would have been ashamed to append their names to such a tissue of ignorance and misrepresentation'. The figures on the city's revenues were wrong, he said, especially the statement that Leith docks brought in no money for the city when in fact they were making £7,000 a year. He devised an ingenious way of comparing the relative prosperity of the commissioners and the disdained councillors. The rental value of the eight commissioners' houses was an average £64, having deducted a quarter for their chambers which were 'in fact, their *shops*, in which they conduct their business'. Nineteen councillors were shopkeepers, whose average rental for their businesses was £83, over and above the value of their houses. Other councillors had offices, workshops or manufactories rated at £120.[35]

With deft figuring and a keen turn of phrase McLaren was welcome when he turned his hand to journalism. In the 1830s he wrote mainly for *The Scotsman*, at this time a bi-weekly paper selling about 2,300 copies an issue at 7d each, the high cost restricting its circulation to the middle classes being the result of Government stamp duty.[36] The paper had been founded in 1817 to promote the cause of reform and its views on many issues accorded with those of the young councillor. In particular under the editorship of Charles Maclaren, one of the paper's originators, it sympathised with the claims of religious Dissenters and wanted to ensure that the momentum for political and social reform should not be lost. McLaren's articles, which appeared as editorials voicing the views of the paper, were like those of all writers, anonymous, but it does not take much analysis to spot pieces where the amassing of facts and figures to support an argument suggests his pen. An indication of his range was given by Charles Maclaren in a letter in April 1838 to the editor of the *Morning Chronicle* in London introducing McLaren:

> The articles [on church affairs] in *The Scotsman*, have, with few exceptions, been written by my friend the Treasurer [McLaren]. The long one you copied ten days ago was his. The shorter one, copied in the *Chronicle* on Saturday 21st, was his also. Previous and elaborate articles on Funds and the Scottish School Bill were his too, with most of those on the pretended *religious destitution* of Edinburgh and Glasgow, on our Annuity or Stipend Tax here, and similar subjects. There is no man living who has so complete a hold of the *facts* on these matters, and he is unequally unrivalled in the minute accuracy with which he treats whatever topic he

touches. If, therefore, he should see occasion to attack or reply to any article in the *Times*, he will send it to you, and you may rely on its correctness with the most entire confidence. All his articles in *The Scotsman* go in as editorials, but on this point you will, of course, do as you think best. I may add that my friend is a man of sterling principle, and has one of the clearest and soundest heads I ever met with.[37]

McLaren and Maclaren exchanged ideas on matters of the moment, including the appointment of university professors in which the paper took a keen interest. In 1836 they discussed the vacant chair of logic. One of the candidates was George Combe, phrenologist and best-selling author on the principles of government, and a friend of McLaren's. Editor and councillor agreed that he was not the man for the chair, especially since his rival was the much better qualified Sir William Hamilton. McLaren wrote[38] that he had no intention of voting for Combe, against whom many councillors had a 'strong prejudice'. For his 'own amusement' he had drawn up a list of the thirty-three councillors and found only two likely to opt for Combe. Hamilton was chosen but soon ran foul of the council over the fees he claimed. Treasurer McLaren mollified the professor's feelings but could not reduce his demands. *The Scotsman* editor sought to retain McLaren as a valued writer. 'Your article in yesterday's paper is excellent ... Will Mrs McLaren and you favour us with your company to tea and supper next Wednesday evening at seven?'[39] McLaren took no payment for individual contributions but in October 1836 received from the paper a complete set of the *Edinburgh Review* from its founding 34 years earlier . In 1838 he was given a token £50 for his work over the previous year. To fears that the writer's freedom might be compromised, Charles Maclaren explained on behalf of William Ritchie, the paper's proprietor: 'Our rule is to pay all who contribute to the paper at the rate of £1 per column ... No reason exists why you should not accept a very moderate remuneration for the labour which puts money in our pockets. Had your articles been connected with some event or business which was to lose its interest in a few months, we would have presented you with a piece of plate or something similar, but it is our wish and hope that they may be continued for years, and we are therefore anxious to place them on a business footing.'[40]

As a businessman McLaren was concerned about Edinburgh's prosperity and like other councillors looked to the day when the burden of bankruptcy would be lifted. As early as 1835 a committee led by Councillor Thomas Grainger, who would one day contest the Lord

Provostship with McLaren, set out the terms for turning Edinburgh into a manufacturing centre. All four bailies, including McLaren, were on the committee which identified five necessary strengths possessed by the city. These were: abundance of cheap, high-grade fuel (from the Midlothian coalfield); good water ready to be tapped (from the Pentland hills); cost-effective male and female labour in the area; an accessible port and good internal communications (the Union Canal linking Edinburgh to central Scotland had just been opened); and a ready supply of building materials (from neighbouring quarries). In 1839 McLaren added another requirement to these essentials. On behalf of a Committee of Farmers and Traders he drafted a series of recommendations to the council under which restrictions on the movement of goods would be eased.[41] The existing customs charges were complex. Farmers bringing produce to the city were faced with paying $1/2$d on every quarter of wheat, pease and beans. For butter the charge of 3d was by hundredweight. Apples and pears were levied $3/4$d per bushel. And for 'each burden carried by a woman $1 1/2$d'. The farmers and traders pointed out that such charges were on essential commodities, including those in leather and hide, whereas some dearer products were excluded. The plan was to replace all customs with a fixed commutation charge on each cartload. An extra tax could be levied if the city found that its customs revenue went down as a result. McLaren expected farmers and traders to save £3,500 a year but in setting out the proposals, he hastened to assure fellow councillors that he would not be bound by its provisions if the figures did not add up. In 1840, after he had left the council, the farmers and traders asked him to go to London to oversee the passing of the Edinburgh Customs Bill. He worked closely with William Gibson-Craig, MP for Midlothian, and in the Upper House with Lord Melville. The battle for free trade was soon to be joined on a grander scale, but McLaren kept up the fight for unencumbered local trading.

4. The voice of Dissent

As Duncan McLaren rose to local prominence, it is a mistake to look at the Edinburgh of the time in isolation, tempting though that is because of the peculiarity of its annuity tax and its crippling bankruptcy. The sharpness of religious divisions in the city that were to dominate the politics of the 1840s and culminated in the ousting as MP of a national figure, Thomas Babington Macaulay, makes Edinburgh appear a community turned in on itself and betraying the rational tolerance of its Enlightenment heritage. Protagonists like McLaren and his allies are readily demonised. But in their ambitions and convictions they were not a race apart; they came from a background shared by other local leaders north and south of the border. They had aims in common, too.

In the three other cities, Glasgow, Aberdeen and Dundee, the reformed councils were dominated by businessmen with the time and money to make their mark. In the balance between commitment to political causes and local bigwiggery they varied. Mainly Whig or Radical, they included in Glasgow an important element of revitalised Tories by the end of the 1830s. In civic life across Scotland as a whole were many men of McLaren's stamp. A good example[1] is to be found in Paisley where Peter Brough, three years older than McLaren and from humble beginnings in Perthshire, served his apprenticeship as a draper in Edinburgh but then, failing to find a permanent post, was appointed by a Glasgow firm to its branch shop in Paisley, which he bought in 1816. Like McLaren he found his stock in the wholesale houses of London and eventually acquired three shops in Paisley and others in Alloa, Crieff and Kinross. He, too, made a point of abandoning customer-bargaining or 'prigging'. He joined the unreformed town council in 1830 but retired in 1833. He was a moderate Whig uneasy with the pace of reform. Shares in banking and railways were the foundation of his later fortune, which as a lifelong bachelor led him

53

into the philanthropy from which Paisley was to benefit after his death in 1883. Offered the opportunity to become the town's Liberal MP, he lacked McLaren's political drive.

Sustained commitment to radical causes brought McLaren into contact with fellow spirits south of the border. In fighting the annuity tax the Dissenters of Edinburgh were not alone. They had natural allies among Nonconformists of various hues in England – Unitarians, Wesleyan Methodists, Congregationalists – whose target was the church rate, levied to support the 'national' Church of England. The Whig ministries of the 1830s dallied and dithered with its abolition or commutation. Refusing to pay church rates sent men like William Baines of Leicester to prison and led to the founding of a paper, the *Nonconformist*, which gave a national voice to local resentments. In Northern and Midlands cities, where opposition was strong, the indifference of London ministerial Whigs, even ostensible allies like Lord John Russell, turned the campaign towards outright disestablishment.[2] The rhetoric against a State Church was exactly that of Scottish Dissenters. In 1837 McLaren presided at a 1,500-strong meeting in Dr Peddie's chapel to highlight the iniquity of church rates wherever they applied.[3] It is little wonder that his journalism when copied into the powerful press of towns like Leeds and Manchester found an understanding readership.

At the point when McLaren was preparing to leave the council and devote his time to business and family, Liberal politics were entering a difficult phase. The optimism of the early 1830s had faded. 'Finality Jack', a nickname given to Lord John Russell, the embodiment of traditional Whiggery, indicated the refusal of ministers to continue with a reform programme, much less to listen to Radical MPs. The General Election of 1837 saw the number of Radicals elected reduced to only about 50. Social and political unrest did not help their cause. The cotton spinners' strike in Glasgow in 1837 brought arrests, trials and deportations. The rise of Chartism, which was strong in Scotland, dismayed middle-class Radical leaders whose meetings in Edinburgh they disrupted and whose stridency (and lower position on the social ladder) turned people off reform altogether. The embattled Whig leaders in Edinburgh as well as London represented safety and stability. So in 1839 when Macaulay, his political reputation already made in India and his literary one developed through contributions to the *Edinburgh Review*, was persuaded by Adam Black to offer himself as a successor to Abercromby (now Lord Dunfermline) who had retired from the House of Commons, it was a coup for the Whigs. The Radicals were disconcerted and divided. Sir James Gibson-Craig told of a private meeting they had had: 'I understand they were very reasonable. They have asked for a meeting with some of our friends [i.e. Whig leaders]. They propose a meeting to address the Queen and that measures be taken to prevent such disgraceful proceedings, as the Chartists, or rather the sweepings of our streets, adopted on the last occasion. The Chartists have no weight whatsoever – and in an election, are not worth speaking of.'[4]

All was not quite plain sailing. Gibson-Craig reported on a meeting of the Liberal Aggregate Committee, which represented activists throughout the city. It agreed to a requisition to Macaulay but 12 members had dissented, arguing that a general meeting of electors should be called and a wider choice of candidate discussed. McLaren moved that motion but 'became ashamed of it and wanted to have it negatived without a division but Tait the bookseller and his Radical friends would not allow him'.[5] James Ivory, the new Solicitor-General, told Lord Advocate Rutherfurd that Macaulay should get to Edinburgh as quickly as possible since that would show that his supporters were in the majority and that despite the mention of several names, McLaren and his allies had no alternative candidate to propose. A rumour was going about that Voluntaries in Glasgow were willing to pay McLaren £500 a year to be their MP, and so the Whig leaders were on the alert. On 24 May Ivory again wrote: 'McLaren is most unreasonable. However, he says we shall have no danger this bout. But that hereafter on a general election, his friends and he are determined to propose two candidates, such as they are satisfied, with reference to their local connexion – knowledge of the city affairs – and business habits ought to represent Edinburgh and would rescue it from being a mere Treasury burgh ... He is a man, not much to be operated on from without – and may endanger the cause, in a Tory contest.'[6]

Arriving in Edinburgh Macaulay won over a public meeting and was elected unopposed. Gibson-Craig celebrated prematurely: 'The extinction of the Rads and Charts [sic] and the whole proceedings must tell well hereafter.'[7] In the end McLaren 'after another blow out today at the Merchants Hall ward meeting'[8] joined the Whigs on Macaulay's platform but would not have been happy with the tone of a letter from the new MP to Black. He wanted to be an independent member and was disinclined to seek ministerial office. He would have half the year in which he could 'be at leisure for other pursuits to which I am more inclined and for which I am perhaps better fitted', citing the *History of England* which he was about to start writing.[9] Four months later he made Edinburgh a 'Treasury burgh' by joining the Government as Secretary at War; the other city MP, Sir John Campbell, was also a

55

minister. Macaulay told Melbourne that there was strong support for the Government in the city even among Radicals.[10] The Whig Cockburn took a dim view of McLaren who 'has behaved like a fool about Macaulay ... I fear he has been spoiled by praise, and that he is not to be an exception to the rule that, even in the humblest walk, the pipe clay of low training will break out, – especially in the form of conceit.' But he had a warning for the future: 'The modest Duncan McLaren says, with a resigned indignation, 'this bolus will be swallowed but don't try it again'. He will be your next candidate.'[11]

Resentment at McLaren's influence outwith the council, where his services had been widely acclaimed, was clearly growing among the landed and lawyerly Whigs accustomed to calling the electoral shots. It is hard, however, to estimate the extent or depth of his power. Party organisation was in its infancy, confined in many constituencies to ensuring that supporters were registered to vote and opponents excluded wherever possible. Throughout the run-up to Macaulay's election the correspondence of Whig leaders is full of rumours of rival candidates who might be being persuaded to stand as a Liberal, Whig or Radical. It was in the ability to control nominations that electoral power rested in the burghs and counties. Political activity at grassroots level was deemed necessary to turn away unwelcome candidates, though its effectiveness varied from constituency to constituency depending on the safeness of seats and the commitment of local leaders. Midlothian, a seat with contending Tory and Whig magnates and a record of changing electoral fortunes in the 1830s, was well organised.[12] In Edinburgh the threat of a Tory revival was regularly used to keep Whigs and Liberals in line, but in practice civic leaders, senior lawyers and Whig magnates exercising influence from their estates in Midlothian assumed that they would decide who represented the city at Westminster. In 1839 McLaren and his supporters threatened to challenge the established order, although the threat did not materialise. Cockburn sitting at Bonaly in the foothills of the Pentlands was not the only Whig lawyer to see the threat only postponed.

At this period of his career McLaren did not lead a Radical faction; its mouthpiece was James Aytoun, an election candidate challenger as far back as 1832.[13] McLaren did agree with the need for further political reform through the ballot and a wider franchise, but the arguments he raised in meetings with ministers were directed at religious discontents, from the Bible Board to prison chaplains. That is because he was spokesman for the Central Board of Dissenters and by extension for the wider Dissenting community in Edinburgh. The influence he could exert, threatening the withdrawal of Dissenter support at a future election, was far greater than that of Aytoun or Tait, the Radical bookseller and editor. *The Scotsman* supported the claims of a Presbyterian community complaining of discrimination, but not of a political minority whose manifesto was close to Chartism. Within Edinburgh Liberalism alliances waxed and waned, as McLaren found out on the council. Altogether more substantial was the potential of an organised religious community whose leading adherents were largely from the business middle class. Given leadership they had the money and men to look for electoral representation either directly or by putting pressure on MPs and candidates. McLaren had the family tie with the Rentons, respected Dissenters. He was adept at using ward meetings to press a case. In the absence of permanent political organisation the committees that backed councillors in their wards were a power base since ward representatives sat on an Edinburgh-wide Liberal Aggregate Committee. Following settlement of the city's affairs McLaren's reputation was high, extending to the Dissenters' stronghold in Glasgow. The shop in the High Street whose premises he had extended gave him the income and apparent leisure to remain to the fore in public life.

James Ivory, a Whig insider, summed up the man during the Macaulay by-election.[14] He would require 'great management – and I doubt whether even that will do. He has long had the crochet that moves him ... The Voluntaries have of late entertained views, which they are most anxious to have a mouthpiece for the expression of in Parliament. And McLaren is so thorough an enthusiast – if not a bigot, – in his Voluntary notions, – that I should not at all wonder to find him willing to do the work of his friends.' But he would not encourage the Radicals. 'It is not at all in that direction he is inclined to bolt. Moreover not one of his friends at present goes along with himself. His namesake of the *Scotsman* is decidedly against him. But for hereafter I have the greatest apprehension. There is some reasonableness in the principle, as a mere abstraction, that Edin'r should not be left in the hands of strangers and ministerialists whether in or out of office.' Many would support an inferior candidate even if he stood in the way of strengthening a popular Government. There was still a possibility, Ivory feared, that McLaren might intervene in the by-election directly. If he stood it would be reckless of the consequences: 'He has such a following, – as though assuredly not able to carry his own ends, – could yet weaken the liberal side, – as to cause the most eminent hazard of letting in a Tory.'

By January 1840 peace appeared to reign in the Liberal camp. Ivory reported to Rutherfurd that the Aggregate Committee was in safe hands with Sir James Gibson-Craig elected chairman and Sir James Spittal, the former Lord Provost, as his deputy. 'Duncan Maclaren [sic] behaved with great temperance and forbearance in this matter, and I believe we are now able to stand the brush even of a general election.'[15] Yet before the end of the year another of the Lord Advocate's correspondents, Fox Maule, was describing McLaren as a 'vile brute' and suggesting castration to 'make him sing smaller'.[16] What changed the atmosphere?

The answer lies in growing sectarian intolerance. McLaren was no longer the de facto leader of a group of councillors, but those of his Dissenter persuasion still on the council – reckoned at 8 out of the 33 in 1840 – looked to him. Their nominal leader and elder statesman was Adam Black, who came forward as a candidate for Lord Provost in November 1840. McLaren as a controversialist and member of the Central Council of Dissenters was regarded as the mouthpiece and manipulator of political Dissent in the city. His role was not the immediate issue in the bitter contest between Black and the incumbent Lord Provost, Sir James Forrest, seeking a second term, but when the rivalry degenerated into claims and counter-claims about whether a Dissenter (Black) should occupy the civic chair, the hand of a kingmaker (McLaren) was assumed to be at work. In the opposite camp were influential Non-Intrusionists – the Evangelical party taking up an increasingly aggressive position within the Church of Scotland and against the power of the State. Both Black and Forrest were Liberals with a radical history, but Forrest was ready to ally himself with the Tory minority on the council to retain the Provostship.

Just before the municipal elections *The Scotsman* published a long open letter from McLaren to voters.[17] In it he denounced the pretensions of the Non-Intrusionist faction, alleging that 'although the practical application of the "Church in danger" cry is to be limited, *on the present occasion*, to the attempt to exclude Mr Black from the civic chair, if they have confidence in their own principles, and are successful in their present object, they must, as a matter of course, on future occasions, attempt to exclude all Dissenters from the office of councillors and magistrates. And they must likewise exclude all those members of the Established Church connected with the *Moderate* party, who oppose their Non-Intrusion principles.' McLaren was trying to widen the rift to make it appear that the equivalent of a Test Act was being brought to bear against all Dissenters seeking public office, and at the same time to seek support from the Moderates in the Church of Scotland whose fears grew as Thomas Chalmers and his allies took the Church ever nearer the brink over who had the right to appoint parish ministers.

One of the Non-Intrusionists' arguments against Black was that Dissenter councillors were prejudiced against the Established Church when the council as patron of the city churches appointed ministers. McLaren in his letter 'carefully analysed' all 220 votes since 1833 on such matters. Categorising appointments as favouring either the popular wing of the Church or traditional Moderates, he found that whereas the votes given by councillors who were Church members were 55 per cent in favour of the popular party, the figure was 62 per cent among Dissenting councillors; therefore Dissenters were more liberal than churchmen. McLaren was trying to undermine the Non-Intrusionists' case that only their predominance in the Established Church could carry liberal causes, such as the end of appointment of clergy by patronage. He ended by promising that Dissenters in self-defence would extinguish the Whig Non-Intrusionists as a party 'by throwing all their friends out of Parliament at the first general election'. The threat carried by organised Dissent was to be used by McLaren many times in the future, first against Non-Intrusionists and then against a wider array of Whigs.

The council election day saw business suspended in many parts of the city as crowds perused the lists issued every hour on the state of the poll. For *The Scotsman* there was no doubt of the reason for the excitement – the alliance between Non-Intrusionists and Tories to exclude a Dissenter from the Lord Provost's chair. In the most keenly contested First Ward where the paper labelled candidates as either 'Liberal' or 'High Church', McLaren took charge of publicly stating objections to 'High Church' voters when he could think of a reason for seeking their exclusion from the poll. In McLaren's old Second Ward, a row brewed because one of the Liberal candidates, William Johnston, was elected having given a pledge to support Black as Lord Provost. He later reneged and helped Forrest secure a majority of three through a combination of Tories and Liberals, or, put another way, of Tories and Churchmen. A war of pamphlets between Johnston and McLaren about ill faith followed.[18]. *The Scotsman* pointed out that Non-Intrusion claims that Forrest's victory was one for their cause did not add up: 12 of his 17 backers were opposed to the Non-Intrusionists. Black's biographer ascribes his defeat to a combination of 'the first of those heterogeneous and mutually hostile elements which afterwards became a distinguishing feature of Edinburgh politics at election times.'[19]

For the Whig leaders the fear was of a permanent split and damaging defections. Sir James Gibson-Craig had appealed to Fox Maule as an influential Non-Intrusionist to dissuade Forrest from challenging

Black. Maule refused to intervene despite Sir James's concerns that upsetting the Dissenters would leave the Whigs at a general election 'to be overwhelmed by the Tories'.[20] Instead, Fox Maule launched into an attack on the Dissenters in general and McLaren in particular. The Dissenters 'have been insufferably dictatorial, and refusing all proffers of compromise, have ventured on a contest with the church in which they have found their weakness. Had they been content to share Empire, they might have had Black as the Provost, but they were resolved to rule with an iron rod, and they must abide the result.' As for McLaren, let him beware, 'or I will give the world a specimen of the *honesty* of a Dissenting councillor, should I have occasion to cross the Dissenters in their headlong acts of insanity'. Thus spoke a Minister who had been repeatedly faced with the litany of Dissenters' complaints. Gibson-Craig was sympathetic, in December sending Maule a copy of a letter he had written to Black condemning the Central Board of Dissenters for attacking Maule, whose Government position meant that he could not answer back.[21]

The Whigs faced a delicate situation immediately after Forrest's victory. Black's friends, led by McLaren, arranged an 'entertainment' with fruits and wine to thank the defeated candidate for his history of public service. Dunfermline was asked to take the chair, failing whom Gibson-Craig. The two elder statesmen agreed that, in Gibson-Craig's words, the entertainment must 'not make breach among the Liberals wider but to smooth things over ... Dunfermline will not mention Forrest's name'.[22] In the event the evening, attended by 700 with 200–300 unable to obtain tickets at six shillings, went off without embarrassment, although *The Scotsman* regretted the absence of some Whig lawyers, whose 'timorous and fastidious spirit' augured ill for the future of the Liberal party.[23] There were twenty-six toasts, one proposed by McLaren, each accompanied by a musical air.

The next flashpoint concerned the city's parliamentary representation. A general election was looming. There was no threat to Macaulay despite the fact that he was a minister in a Government that had run out of steam. But who would occupy the second seat? Even as a small minority in urban Scotland the Tories had new hopes and it was clear that Non-Intrusionists were looking to a Peel-led Government to resolve the dispute between the Church of Scotland and the State. Liberals of all shades feared that division within their ranks would allow Tory gains, but unity was easier to preach than to accomplish, especially in Edinburgh. The Dissenters were unhappy with 'the Attorney', Sir John Campbell, long-serving Attorney-General, as their MP. He was not enthusiastically supported by the city's Whig leaders either, and there was little surprise when, after months of manoeuvring, he announced in June 1841 that he was standing down. It is clear from Whig letter-writers that they did not think McLaren would seek nomination himself. He led a committee of 150 Dissenters and it was their intentions that concerned Sir James Gibson-Craig and his allies. On 20 May Sir James had written to his son William, MP for Midlothian,[24] that McLaren was calling a meeting of his committee to discuss a successor to Campbell. Sir James had already called a meeting of 'our' committee of 32 chairmen of wards, of whom 23 came. It was agreed that five representatives from Sir James's committee and five from the Dissenters' would try to reach agreement on a candidate. 'But for Maclaren [sic] I can not doubt everything would go right, but I am afraid he will not yield – and that he will try to get his meeting to declare that they are determined not to have the Attorney [Campbell], and that they will name some one, whom they will support.' That 'would be forcing a disunion by attempting to dictate to us – and forcing all the mischief of a contested election long before there was any occasion to sever.'

Meanwhile McLaren wanted a speedy decision by the Dissenters. He told John Hill Burton, the historian, that he did not approve of delay and the 'do nothing' policy of 'our friend' Adam Black.[25] The committee of 150 considered the relative merits of Joseph Hume and Sir Culling Eardley Smith, a religious enthusiast. As chairman he had not expressed an open view but although he had a preference for Smith he thought Hume would prove more acceptable to the constituency in general, churchmen as well as Dissenters. Hume, at the time MP for Kilkenny in Ireland, sought 'to forward the cause of the people, as opposed to the cause of the aristocracy, which both of the great parties have kept so much in the news'. Sir James Gibson-Craig told his son that the Dissenters' committee was divided, with Black remaining faithful to Campbell and opposed to Hume. 'I hope we shall be able to shew that Duncan is not as all powerful as he supposes,' wrote Sir James.[26] William had hoped that Fox Maule might be persuaded to stand, which would be a blow to McLaren.[27] But that idea failed and by the beginning of June McLaren was pressing for an early decision. Sir James told William, whose Midlothian seat was marginal, that he was the only possible choice. If the Dissenters were allowed to name a candidate, both seats would fall to the Tories, who were bestirring themselves, with Lord Provost Sir James Forrest a possible nominee.[28] On 9 June Sir James Gibson-Craig wrote to Maule having told McLaren of the attempt to persuade William to stand. McLaren, Sir James complained, 'would object to an angel from heaven, if not brought forward by himself'.[29] It immediately became clear, however, that the Dissenters, including McLaren, recognised that William, together with Macaulay, could not only win but probably do so without a contest.[30] McLaren had a last attempt at promoting the possibility of William Ewart, a Radical MP who had persuaded Parliament to abolish hanging for cattle theft, but that failed. Gibson-Craig reported that Black was very upset at McLaren's attitude and that there was 'a complete schism' among the Dissenters. Black had allegedly told Gibson-Craig that he had joined the Dissenters' committee to support their rights, not to forward the ultra-Radicals, and he would no longer have anything to do with them.[31] Gibson-Craig in the same letter summed up the Whigs' feelings about McLaren: 'Duncan will prove his own weakness. His whole object is mischief, in which, to a certain extent, he will succeed at the expense of his own character for consistency and plain dealing.'

At the election on 1 July William Gibson-Craig and Macaulay had no opposition though Chartists demonstrated noisily at the hustings and demanded a wider choice of candidates. The Tories recognised that there was no chance of unseating either representative of the Liberals, united as they appeared on the hustings. The episode showed that the Dissenters, despite their numbers, were not able to pull the Liberals in their direction, partly because of internal disagreement (between McLaren and Black) and partly because they had no candidate to offer. They were outwitted by the traditional leaders of the party, who looked to their own number to find a credible representative. The state of party organisation, or rather the lack of it, at the time allowed Whig dominance to continue. The decision by MPs whether to seek re-election could be left, as it was by Sir John Campbell, until almost the last minute. There was no formal mechanism for the organised Liberals of whatever hue to call for nominations and to vote on them. The Aggregate Committee was intended to represent Liberal activists across the city but although it contained members of different backgrounds (and religious groupings) it did not have the powers of constituency associations later in the century, much less in the modern era. Sir James Gibson-Craig's committee ended up negotiating with the Dissenters' committee only because the latter was numerous and led by a man unafraid to question, though not yet defy, the local Whig oligarchy. McLaren was, however, a divisive figure, and not all Dissenters would follow him all the way. Nor did McLaren have the connections to find and persuade a credible challenger like Joseph Hume to come forward in the Dissenting and radical interest. Black had shown in

1832 and with Macaulay in 1839 that he had that stature. It is little wonder that relations between him and McLaren would move from strain to hostility. And McLaren was about to make common cause with Radicals from south of the border.

Immediately after the election there was a large meeting of Dissenters at South College Street Church.[32] McLaren proposed a resolution that laid down a challenge: in future one of the city MPs should be required to have knowledge of Dissenting principles 'and tried attachment to their cause' since Dissenters represented a large proportion of the Liberal constituency. 'In this coming forward as a distinct party,' he went on, 'I expect that we shall be greatly blamed ... for dividing the Liberal party.' Their grievances, however, had been ignored, and he singled out Maule for blame among ministers. 'It has been notorious that for the last year or two the government of Scotland has been carried out, not so much for the advantage of the people as a whole, not even for the advantage of the Established Church as a whole, but to please a section of a sect', by which he made clear he meant 'the High Church Non-Intrusion party'. The resolution was carried by a large majority, and the Rev. James McGilchrist then expressed the hope that McLaren would represent Edinburgh after the next election. The idea had come up before the election just concluded, and, with the same reluctance to discuss his own position that he had expressed then, McLaren told the meeting that he would not have taken part in it had he known he would be proposed as a candidate, which he could not become for reasons of family and business. The chairman, McLaren's ally Councillor John Gray, said he hoped that McLaren would consider the proposal seriously.

The Tories took office at Westminster, but their hoped-for revival in Edinburgh proved illusory. After the council election in autumn 1841 Sir James Gibson-Craig wrote: 'We have totally demolished the Tories ... Every one of their candidates defeated – seven Tories are replaced by seven Whigs ... Four non-intrusion Whigs in the fifth ward in place of four Tories.' Two years later, after the Disruption, the reckoning was 24 Dissenters on the council and 9 churchmen.[33] Despite the best efforts of Peel's ministers, such as Lord Aberdeen and Sir James Graham, it was clear well before the final schism in May 1843 that the Tory Government was no more inclined than its Whig predecessor to allow the Church of Scotland to challenge the institutions of state. So the alliance of Tories and Non-Intrusionists was short-lived. Freed from the threat of Tory advances in the burghs, the Liberal party was able to turn in on itself and resume its sectarian and personal squabbles. In Edinburgh McLaren's influence continued to be detected and mocked. A 'new song' was published about Duncan 'MacLaren' in 1842.[34] Here are four of its nine verses:

> Town Councils of old kept up Self-election,
> And the old Thirty-three incurred direful reflection -
> But now the Electors their votes may be sparin'
> For I'll choose all myself, says great Duncan MacLaren.
> I have set myself up as the City's Dictator -
> I'll propose whom I please, like the great Liberator;
> And you, noodles and dupes, by your votes be declarin',
> You are glad to be the tools of great Duncan MacLaren.
> Your Judgments and Wishes I greatly respect them,
> Therefore *I* choose the Members, *and then you* elect them;
> Be they Tories or Whigs, you needa be carin',
> But do as you're bidden by Duncan MacLaren.
> In tapes, threads, and cottons, I used for to deal in,
> But trade's turned slack and business is failin',
> So now, being tired of dealin' sma ware in,
> I mak' Provosts and Bailies, says Duncan MacLaren.

McLaren's attention turned to the performance of the city's MPs, Macaulay in particular, with whom he conducted an increasingly tetchy correspondence. It began on issues of religious dissent, widened into the defining controversy of the age – the abolition of the corn laws – and ended when the MP lost his seat and expressed relief at being free of the city and its awkward squad. It would be a classic tale of misapprehensions and misconceptions and a demonstration of mismatched talents if only it were complete, but unfortunately we have only Macaulay's side. The MP did not keep most letters he received and none of McLaren's survive, though it is possible to gauge their tenor by Macaulay's comments and by our knowledge of how McLaren conducted a case – with unrelenting facts and figures used as hammer blows, Pelion heaped on Ossa. Macaulay's olympian urbanity, expressive of the archetype Whig historian, was never likely to convince plain-speaking Edinburgh Liberals of the merchant class, especially at a moment when the future of their Presbyterianism was being determined by a Parliament incapable of understanding the passions that were tearing it apart.

Macaulay was at first constrained by being a minister in Melbourne's Government but in opposition from 1841 he did not use that freedom and his own eloquence to charm the voters. He tried to stay away from them as much as possible and when confronting them in correspondence he appeared increasingly patronising or dismissive. That was despite conscientious attention to Scottish affairs in the Commons and cooperation with William Gibson-Craig in forwarding Edinburgh's interests in matters such as its water supply. McLaren was his most persistent and troublesome opponent, and potentially the most dangerous. It is entertaining to read Macaulay's correspondence with McLaren alongside his letters of the same period to Macvey Napier, editor of the *Edinburgh Review*, with whom he exchanged views on the literary scene. He enthusiastically sought to review a work on Addison, and he explained his distaste for public meetings in Edinburgh. As he told Napier, if he were in town on a Sunday 'to whatever Church I go, I shall give offence to somebody'.[35]

McLaren embarked on the correspondence just before Macaulay faced re-election in January 1840 because he had become a minister. The issue was mistreatment of Dissenters and the pretensions of the Non-Intrusionists.[36] Macaulay hastened to reassure McLaren, and indeed he made religious freedom a major part of his speech at the Assembly Rooms where none of his 1,500 audience challenged his defence of the Government, and he was re-elected without a contest.[37] But the bulk of the letter is in response to a slight that McLaren claimed to have detected. Macaulay sought to assure McLaren that it was Dissenters in general and not McLaren as their spokesman who the MP thought overstated their grievances: 'I should be a mere flatterer if I did not say that I think their present temper a little punctilious and resentful, and that I am afraid of their being hurried by angry feelings into courses which will not raise their credit or give them satisfaction in the retrospect ... I by no means arrogate to myself any superiority over so many good and able men, except the superiority which necessarily arises from the circumstance that in the present unhappy disputes I am impartial, and they cannot be so.'

One of the Dissenters' campaigns, as we shall see, was for a national system of education in both Scotland and England. Macaulay[38] recommended caution to McLaren, who had threatened withdrawal of Dissenter goodwill: 'There is much hostility to national education in both the Established Churches. To maintain such a system against the opposition of both these Churches would be impossible. Is it not wise then and right in the Government to humour these Churches in matters not essential, even at the expense of the Dissenters? The consequence may be that a few unreasonable, irritable, or greedy Dissenters may desert us. I do not believe this of the body. It would give me the deepest pain to believe it. I am ready for my own part to quit office and Parliament later on. I am sick of both. But I should be sorry that the blow came from the Scottish Dissenters.'

Later in the year Macaulay told McLaren that he had to remain on the sidelines when Black was defeated for the Provostship by Forrest but privately he deplored the treatment of Black and gave his assurance that Black's supporters (including, privately, himself) would not suffer. But in a series of letters in December 1840 and January 1841 Macaulay spelled out his disapproval of the Dissenters' campaigns and tactics. He was frank to McLaren because 'I have seldom found among men employed in the highest functions, and accustomed to the management of great affairs, a mind more statesmanlike than yours'.[39] But should 'some trifling matters of punctilio' such as the printing of the Bible or appointment of school inspectors be allowed to dictate Dissenters' views on whether to support the Whig Government or allow the Tories to come in?

This made necessary another letter a week later[40] in response to a paper on Dissenters' claims and assuring McLaren that he knows 'wounded pride and vindictive feeling are not the motives by which you are actuated'. He defended himself and the Government against charges that Dissenters were being ignored. He had spoken to Lord John Russell about contracts for printing the Bible. The exclusion of Dissenters as teachers in prison was unfortunate but not enough to oppose a much needed prisons bill. 'There are bad clauses, very bad clauses in the Reform Bill, in the bill for abolishing slavery, in all the best bills of my time. The question is one of comparison. Does the measure on the whole do more good or harm?' On national education and the need to heed English bishops and the Established Church in Scotland, Macaulay got into his polemic stride:

> You are not only Dissenters – you are also citizens. As citizens, you must feel that there may be evils even greater than the giving to the Kirk a feather in her cap, which I acknowledge to be something more than her due. That millions of children should grow up with as little moral or intellectual training as the Hottentot, – that while we are squabbling about Intrusion or Non-Intrusion, multitudes of youth should, in every great city of the realm, be ripening for the brothel and the treadmill, – this is, I do think, as serious a public calamity as can well be imagined – a much more serious one than is set forth in your paper. The etiquette between Scotch sects is not the only thing that a Government has to look to.

As for 'tests, pledges, or whatever else you may call them, my mind has long been made up and has often been publicly declared. My opinions, except where secrets of State are concerned, may be known to anybody for the asking. But I will never, while I live, give any promise as to any particular vote.' If honest attachment to the principles of religious liberty were not security enough for Dissenters, 'I have no other to give them.' McLaren sent Macaulay another paper on aggression by the Established Church and the demands of Non-Intrusionists. In reply[41] Macaulay supported the notion of an Established Church but agreed that the State should allow a veto on the appointment of a parish minister where that would be for the good of the Church. Parliament's refusal to accept that view was leading towards disruption, but for Macaulay the demands of Non-Intrusionists went damagingly beyond that. 'They deny the right of the State to do anything with respect to the Church, except to give it money and to imprison Dissenters who refuse to pay rates.' In a striking phrase he dismisses their claims: 'The civil magistrate in their system is nothing more than a bum-bailiff to the priest.'

5. Championing cheap corn

On 10 February 1842 Duncan McLaren led a march of 600 men, their arms linked, along the Strand and bound for the Palace of Westminster. They had come from the Crown and Anchor, meeting place of an Anti-Corn Law League conference. It was timed to coincide with an annual ritual in the House of Commons, the vote on repeal of the corn laws, called for by Charles Villiers MP. The vote was always doomed to failure although support for it became a badge of acceptability in Radical circles. On this occasion the conference had two reasons for paying attention to events at Westminster. For the first time Villiers was making a plea for total repeal, and Sir Robert Peel as recently installed Prime Minister was due to state his intentions on altering the sliding scale of duty on imported corn. The conference was being chaired by McLaren, giving him, in the words of two recent historians of the Anti-Corn Law League, 'a brief moment of fame'.[1] He was having his work cut out. There was division between those who wanted total abolition and those who would be content with a fixed duty. A split was feared, but McLaren and other leaders were able to avert that. On the second of six days the camaraderie of a march must have come as relief, but when the marchers arrived at Westminster they were met by a police barrier: 'Out truncheons, close the gates,' was the command. The middle-class League may not have looked like disruptive working-men Chartists, but the authorities were taking no chances. Some delegates made off up Parliament Street to intercept Peel's coach as it made its way to the House. The Prime Minister at first thought he was being hailed by supporters but the shouts made it clear he was not, and he was reported to have slunk into a corner of the carriage. About a hundred League delegates were eventually admitted to the Commons where Peel's proposals fell far short of their hopes. Later, at Brown's coffee house, they unanimously passed a resolution which McLaren signed as chairman. The Government's measure 'so far from holding out the slightest prospect of any relief of the distress of the country, is an insult to a patient and suffering people'. It was 'an indication that the landed aristocracy of this country are destitute of all sympathy for the poor, and are resolved, if permitted by an outraged people, to persist in a course of selfish policy which will involve the destruction of every interest in the country'.

This is not the place to tell the story of the long campaign to end the corn laws, nor even of the contribution of Scotland to the campaign.[2] McLaren was involved from the 1830s until victory was secured – and the Tory Government rendered asunder – in 1846. His role was significant but as a lieutenant not a general. When others took the lead and called for help, he responded efficiently. When the campaign languished, as it did at several points, he had other calls on his time and energies. Contrast that with John Bright's singlemindedness. Shortly after being elected to Parliament for Durham in 1843 he wrote to McLaren, with implied rebuke to the Scot's Dissenting activities: 'To talk of overturning the Church is treason to my constituents. As I was elected to do the League's work I intend to steer tolerably clear of other matters at present.'[3] The Anti-Corn Law League was born in Manchester and its members campaigned throughout the country. McLaren's prominence in its Scottish activities brought him for the first time recognition in Radical circles across Britain. He was regarded not just as a successful civic leader and polemical writer but a trusted ally and counsellor of the men who, by inspiring the League, changed Victorian society and politics. His first meeting was with Richard Cobden, the Sussex-born calico printer deeply involved in Manchester agitation. They were introduced by a radical Glasgow minister of the Secession Church in 1840 and soon were corresponding not just about the recently established Anti-Corn Law League but about parliamentary reform, household suffrage and the gamut of radical causes. McLaren, like other Scottish campaigners for free trade, welcomed the founding in Manchester of a League which could bring together the work of anti-corn law associations in many British towns and cities. McLaren as a businessman was familiar with Manchester as home to the textile industry, just as he was with London where the League recognised that the battle for change had to be fought. In 1834 he had been involved with an Edinburgh association for speedy abolition of the corn laws as contrary 'to the principles of free trade'. The Lord Provost, James Spittal, had been a member, as had working-class leaders of an earlier mechanics' movement. The Chamber of Commerce, of which McLaren was a member, was early in the campaign, too. A petition with 18,000 signatures was got up,[4] but neither in Edinburgh, nor in Glasgow,

Dundee or other centres where associations sprang up was there sustained activity, much less cohesion of effort. Good harvests from 1836–8 made corn readily available at a low price, relieving evidence of poverty. By 1839 the economic climate had darkened. William Weir, a Glasgow journalist, had been involved in earlier efforts across Scotland and at his instigation the Manchester League sent Abraham Poulton and J.H. Shearman on a tour, principally to raise funds from businessmen. They had little financial success and much Chartist interference at their meetings. Yet there was progress. Glasgow showed the way by affiliating to the League in April 1839. A meeting in Edinburgh almost three months earlier, presided over by Lord Provost James Forrest, had heard a barrage of statistics from McLaren, which *The Scotsman* said 'excited intense interest'.[5] Scotland had one advantage: League speakers could hold meetings in Dissenting chapels from which in English towns they were barred. True, there was trouble at Dr Peddie's chapel when Shearman was interrupted by Chartists, and McLaren had to appeal for order lest the church be no longer made available.[6] It was as a lay leader of Dissenters that McLaren would at first prove invaluable. The Central Board, though by now in decline, had campaigned across the country. It had the techniques and the contacts. From 1840 access to the new penny post made distribution of propaganda easier. McLaren had learned a lesson that the council of the League would apply on a scale never before seen in Britain. A campaign – be it for ending religious discrimination or the corn laws – needed to have two focuses, the campaign in the country and the pressuring of Government and politicians. Cobden would call upon McLaren's 'cooler judgment' to help determine the way ahead in and out of Parliament when the League was divided and all sorts of 'violent remedies' were being suggested. MPs in applying parliamentary pressure had to take account of what was being done for the free-trade cause 'out of doors'.[7]

With his record on the Central Board it was not surprising that McLaren was called upon to lead a major initiative outwith Parliament by convening the committee that organised a conference of ministers in Edinburgh for January 1842.[8] The result was an 'Address to the People of Scotland', which was reprinted several times. The event was part demonstration, part opinion poll. McLaren did not take part in the 700-strong meeting itself because of a family bereavement, but he had done the groundwork and afterwards he convened the group that issued the 'Address'. Tickets for the event, he told invitees, were available 'at my warehouse'. Ministers of various denominations had been invited to take part and to declare their attitude and that of their congregations to repeal of the corn laws. The main argument in the organising committee had been about inviting ministers of the Established Church. In the end it was unanimously agreed not to because they were unlikely to attend. 'As a body they had a deep pecuniary interest in maintaining corn at the highest possible price, because their stipends were, with comparatively few exceptions, payable to the price of certain fixed quantities of corn.' Roman Catholics were contacted. None came to the meeting but of 55 replies, most favoured immediate repeal. Ninety circulars went to the Scottish Episcopal Church. There were 21 replies, none in favour of the proposed meeting. The overwhelming majority of responses were from Dissenters – comprising members of the Secession, Relief, Independent and Baptist churches and some smaller sects. Of 494 ministers returning answers, none was in favour of the existing corn laws, and 431 wanted total repeal. It is little wonder that the replies and the conference itself were dominated by Dissenters. The initiative came from a group of Edinburgh ministers who had attended an anti-corn law conference in Manchester. The meeting was a triumph. Aside from ministers, there were 500 family tickets and 150 for friends. In all between 1,400 and 1,600 people milled around the Relief Church in South College Street. *The Scotsman* gave full-page reports of the speeches and opined that thousands of churchmen 'disgusted with the selfishness, corruption and tyrannical spirit of the Established clergy, now exclaim – "thank God we have a large body of Dissenters"'.[9] Several MPs attended. Cobden did not but sent a letter to McLaren regretting his absence and suggesting that 'some practical agriculturalists who are corn-law repealers' should attend the meeting.'[10]

Involvement of country people in the urban-dominated League became a concern of McLaren's too. He relied on advice from his brother-in-law, the Rev. Henry Renton, in Kelso. A local hero was found in George Hope, tenant farmer at Fenton Barns in East Lothian. He submitted one of the three essays that won a national League competition and were published. Cobden sent McLaren a copy, and Cobden and Bright later visited Hope's farm: here was a man in whose economic interest the corn laws were supposed to exist and yet he was an ardent free-trader.[11] Amid calls at the Dissenters' conference for total repeal, a resolution summed up the tenor of the poll of ministers' views and the mood of the meeting: 'The tendency of an immense majority of these answers is to show that the middling and working classes in Scotland, not even excepting the agricultural districts, are nearly unanimous in regarding the corn and provision laws as unjust in principle, vexatious and oppressive in their operation, and the main cause of all the distresses of the country.'

McLaren first met John Bright, the Rochdale mill-owner, at the Crown and Anchor conference early in 1842. He soon cemented his new friendship by a visit to Bright's home when attending a conference of the British Association for the Advancement of Science in Manchester. Looking after her recently widowed brother's daughter was Priscilla, who was later to tell of the impression McLaren immediately made. Priscilla's housekeeping skills were much in demand because Bright was away a great deal as he embarked with his friend Cobden and other League leaders on the nationwide tours that made them famous. Back home in Edinburgh McLaren's organising skills and contacts, as well as the accommodation he offered at Ramsay Gardens, were called upon when their itineraries included Scotland. Cobden's correspondence deals in detail with arrangements for a swing though central Scotland in January 1843.[12] Could he have a day off between the Glasgow and Edinburgh meetings, he asks McLaren, for 'the flesh is weak'. A week later he accepts that the meetings have to be on consecutive days. As the time for the tour drew near, he was writing again. A muddle about the dates meant he could not fit in a proposed visit to Dalkeith in Midlothian. And he did not want a separate event or 'scene' for his 'personal glorification and I am a very bad actor'. Perhaps Bright, 'who is a stronger man than myself and a better speaker', could visit Dalkeith between the meetings in Edinburgh and Leith.

Cobden wanted McLaren to galvanise the League north of the border. McLaren held back, pointing to apathy in Edinburgh and Glasgow and to opposition in country areas. Among supporters of the League, many would be content with a lowering of the duty rather than total abolition. 'I do believe', he complained to Cobden, 'that if twenty people I could name were to resolve no longer to move in the matter there would be a great deal of apathy both in this city and in Scotland generally. Individually, I have for the last ten years done much to promote the liberal cause for its own sake and thus have made many sacrifices the least of which were of a pecuniary kind although indirectly these were not small. You will thus see that you have not much to expect from me in the way of greater exertions to "go ahead" or to get others to do so.'[13] The way to animate McLaren was to pose a practical challenge. He became the League's principal fund-raiser in Scotland. Cobden was ambitious, telling McLaren in November 1842 that his target was for £100,000 across Britain although the League council had agreed to find only £20,000. He asked McLaren to raise money in Scotland, probably in small sums.[14] In January 1843 McLaren placed an advertisement in *The Scotsman* listing all subscribers in Edinburgh so far to a national fund whose target he gave as £50,000.

His own contribution was £30; the running total was £1,078.[15] Glasgow raised rather more, but Cobden was critical of Scotland's efforts. He thought that Edinburgh's leaders like McLaren and John Wigham, a Quaker shawl manufacturer, were abler than their Glasgow counterparts, though their task was harder in a city where manufacturing – the core of Glasgow support for the campaign – was of less importance. On one occasion McLaren got his business clerks to write to every Edinburgh elector, on another he circularised every name in the *Edinburgh Directory*.[16] Bright was more enthusiastic about the results than Cobden. 'Your subscriptions are of appalling length,' he observed, meaning that he had difficulty finding space for them in the League's journal. Late in 1843 he suggested targeting members of the new Free Church, not least because they had had help from south of the border in establishing themselves. Rochdale had given the Free Church £400. But McLaren reported back that Free Churchmen were understandably preoccupied by their own affairs and not much could be expected of them. The great rallies, however, raised significant sums. In January 1844 at the City Hall, Glasgow, a meeting addressed by Cobden, Fox Maule and the local Radical MP James Oswald brought in £400. The following day at the New Music Hall in Edinburgh the audience included 34 clergymen and deputations from several burghs. Cobden and McLaren spoke. The collection amounted to £1,362.[17] A feature of League fund-raising was massive bazaars in Manchester and London. True, there were few products of local manufacture that Edinburgh could send for sale. A ladies' committee led by Mrs Wigham and Mrs Agnes Renton, McLaren's mother-in-law, instead oversaw the production of fancy goods which were sent free to Covent Garden by two steam navigation companies. Among the ladies attending from Rochdale was Priscilla Bright.

It is clear from correspondence that McLaren was more than the eyes and ears of the League north of the border, or even just its chief money-raiser. In 1842 he was exchanging letters with Cobden about once a month. They discussed Cobden's ideas on taxation and the policies that bound Radicals together in and out of Parliament – among them household suffrage and triennial parliaments. But by 1842–3 there was evidence that despite the round of campaign meetings, progress was slow. The economic climate was better, any hopes vested in the Tory Government were soon dashed and the Whigs did not use their period in Opposition to devise fresh policies. If Villiers's annual motions were a guide to MPs' opinions, support for repeal was confined to an unspectacular minority. The problem, too, was that mild reformers could talk of a fixed duty and of repeal over an undefined number of years, thereby giving a nod in the direction of freer trade while not offending too much those constituents who favoured faster progress or those who feared that an open market in corn would damage agriculture and/or depress wages. Among Radicals parliamentary reform was being talked about more than the anti-corn law cause. So the League launched a new campaign which in Scotland should start in Glasgow, McLaren advised, because the fragility of economic recovery would persuade businessmen that further freeing of trade was necessary. His standing with Dissenters was important because their congregations were full of businesspeople. Encouraging their ministers to appear in every greater numbers at League meetings 'helped to contribute both an evangelical zeal and a moralistic cover to the self-interested motivation of the commercial and manufacturing interests'.[18] McLaren also had the political contacts that most League supporters in Scotland lacked. He and Sir James Graham, Peel's Home Secretary, respected each other. In reply to a letter of McLaren's which Graham described as denouncing the corn laws in 'no measured terms' but written in 'a friendly spirit', the minister declared: 'I am the last man to undervalue or disregard the deliberate judgment of the middle classes; and when it has been formed on sound reasoning and is distinctly pronounced, it will never fail to overpower all opposition. But you must not mistake the views of public meetings in cities for the voice of the community; and I suspect that Free Trade in foreign corn has stronger and more numerous opponents than you may be prepared to admit.'[19]

It was a point that from the Whig side Macaulay understood as well. His relations with McLaren and supporters from 1841 to 1846 were increasingly strained. Macaulay thought he made plain enough his opposition to the corn laws by his votes and his speeches but it was an opposition tempered by caution about the depth and breadth of support for repeal and therefore about the extent and pace of reform. In his constituency this prudence was misunderstood or misrepresented as bad faith. Wider disenchantment with his performance as a city representative and his attitude to critics was ventilated in attacks on his refusal to follow the Radical line on repeal. The fact that his Whig supporters in the city, including his fellow MP, William Gibson-Craig, were also suspicious of anti-corn law agitation and of McLaren in particular meant that disagreement about repeal became a breach between parties within the Liberal camp. Gibson-Craig was a tactful man who understood local sensitivities. Macaulay distrusted zealots be they religious or political, and as a Whig student of history he not only followed Burke in believing that he was his constituents' representative and not their delegate but was unafraid to tell them so.

On the eve of the 1841 election Macaulay predicted that the leaders of the Opposition might well carry through corn-law reform if they became the Government as he expected. He told McLaren that a fixed duty of 8 to 10 shillings was possible, though that would not answer McLaren's hopes.[20] In February the following year McLaren was one of a delegation that called on the MP at his London home in the Albany bearing a petition with 27,000 signatures from the Edinburgh Anti-Corn Law Association calling for immediate repeal. They asked Macaulay to present it to the Commons provided he would vote for Villiers's motion. McLaren reported that Macaulay declined because he favoured a fixed duty. The following year another petition, this time with 30,000 signatures, was presented by Fox Maule because neither of Edinburgh's MPs would support it. By 1844, when relations between Macaulay and many of his constituents had worsened, Macaulay's voting record was dissected by McLaren. Macaulay said he had supported Villiers. McLaren argued that in 1843 his support had only been for a motion that the House go into committee to consider the corn-law issue in detail. The sophistry is unimportant. The fact is that Macaulay did not support immediate and total repeal as demanded by some of his Liberal voters. He thought it neither practicable nor desirable and in December 1842 he rejected a request by McLaren that he associate himself with the League and attend a public meeting arranged by McLaren.[21] In further letters the pair debated tax policy. McLaren argued that free trade ought to forbid any duty on an import unless an equivalent duty was imposed on the same article produced at home. Macaulay rejected the notion that a government needing to raise money should reject any tax that interfered with freedom of trade. It might be right to tax imported timber but to impose a tax on home-grown timber would 'need an army of spies' in every wood and park. In January 1843 he told Adam Black that he would not side with the League and would sacrifice his seat because opinion in Edinburgh had hardened over the previous year.[22]

At a meeting of the Edinburgh Anti-Corn Law Association in March 1843 a letter by Macaulay to Wigham was read out in which he claimed never to have promised to vote for total and immediate repeal or even for total repeal at all. The meeting registered its disapproval of the stance taken by both Edinburgh MPs. Macaulay wrote to McLaren that he was convinced by the commercial case for repeal but not the fiscal one. He accused McLaren and his friends of 'dissolving the alliance which at the last general election seemed to be firmly established between all who are honestly desirous to give a large extension to the freedom of trade.'23 He also took issue with McLaren over the support in Edinburgh and Glasgow for repeal. Great cities, he pointed out, were not alone. 'You must admit, I think, that almost the whole strength of the party which is for perfectly free trade in corn lies in towns of 10,000 inhabitants and upwards. The inhabitants of the small market-towns are generally, as far as I have observed, more prejudiced in favour of agricultural protection than even the neighbouring farmers. Now, what proportion of the people of the United Kingdom lives in towns of 10,000 inhabitants and upwards? In England, I think, not quite a third. In Scotland, certainly not a third. In Ireland, not a tenth.' Strength of feeling in Edinburgh was decisive only if 'the object you suppose me to have in view is the keeping of my seat in Edinburgh'. McLaren would surely not think him so selfish: 'God knows, I would gladly resign [my seat] today if by doing so I could make a quarter loaf a farthing cheaper.' Then Macaulay's irritation burst forth: 'I know that yours is the stirring party and the noisy party; but I know that it is the weaker party – weaker in numbers, in wealth, in constitutional power, in physical power.' The weaker party ought to be willing to compromise.[24] After the rebuke from the Edinburgh Anti-Corn Law Association Macaulay returned to the attack. McLaren was wrong to suggest that 'the time has happily gone by when the enlightened public opinion of the middle classes can be turned aside by the chiefs of parties'. For Macaulay, as a Whig, governments could not be made without men of weight: 'Try to make a list of a Cabinet of Total and Immediate Repealers. I will engage that you will yourself burst out laughing at it.'[25] To William Gibson-Craig he wrote that McLaren was guilty of 'dirty proceeding'.[26] Seven months later he told William's father: 'The demands of the liberals, heated as they are by religious fanaticism, are such that I will not comply with.' He prophesied that he and William would lose their seats – to a Tory and an ultra-Radical.[27]

Throughout 1843 McLaren was involved in the politics as well as the organisation of the corn law campaign. To Cobden he criticised the weakness of Villiers's annual motion for repeal. Cobden replied that it had been as strong as possible and that Villiers, having been told of McLaren's criticism, was very cross. 'Really I think he is rather entitled to our support as a martyr than to our censure.'[28] Cobden had a task for McLaren: organise the small burghs of Scotland into an 'electoral union' or 'moral Hanse Town confederacy' to put down the confederacy of monopolists. Larger burghs, which were pro-repeal, should take smaller ones under their wing.[29] In December Cobden asked McLaren to keep a watch on the selection of a parliamentary candidate for Glasgow lest they nominate 'any half-and-half man'. McLaren had suggested that it would be good propaganda to have a Tory free-trader returned somewhere but Cobden replied that such a 'rara avis' might turn out to be less than a true man.[30]

Meanwhile McLaren's activities in Edinburgh were concerning the Whigs. William Gibson-Craig received a letter from a supporter saying it was time to wrongfoot McLaren and reconstitute a defunct election committee because 'the only known existing body at this moment is Duncan McLaren', whose speeches ought to be attacked since they were 'a matter of mere abuse and offensive words'.[31] By the end of 1843 the stage was being set for a decisive confrontation. McLaren invited both city MPs to a meeting of the Edinburgh Anti-Corn Law Association to be addressed by Bright and Cobden. Macaulay's refusal was abrupt, and he later regretted its tone. When it was read out by McLaren it was greeted with 'general hisses'.[32] McLaren used preparations for the annual meeting of the Edinburgh ACLA to challenge both Macaulay and Gibson-Craig. A resolution was produced asking for the city's representatives to have views in accord with 'those of the great body of Liberal electors' and of the League, and to call a meeting of Liberals to ascertain their opinions. For *The Scotsman* this pressure on the MPs was too much.[33] The resolution would cause dissension in Liberal ranks and would be 'a threat suspended over the heads of our present members'. They might have made a few mistakes but had served the city diligently. The paper hoped they would vote for repeal but it was wrong 'to erect any single question into an exclusive qualification for the office of representative'. *The Scotsman* was breaking with McLaren whom it had backed for a decade. At a Chamber of Commerce meeting on the same topic he lost the support of Adam Black, now Lord Provost, and of the rising Liberal star in Parliament House, James Moncreiff.

The controversy drew 600 League subscribers to the Edinburgh ACLA meeting in the Waterloo Rooms in January 1844. McLaren professed to identify a 'clique' who, not only in Edinburgh but also in the Commons, were saying that he was prominent in the League because he wanted to oppose the sitting MPs. This was an 'unalloyed falsehood'. Repeating an earlier mantra, he said that nothing would induce him to stand, 'neither the arrangements of his business nor the arrangements of his family'. But if a free-trade candidate did come forward he would beat Macaulay two to one (loud cheers). An advocate, Edward Maitland, said that McLaren was diverting attention from the association's business. He was loudly hissed and had to sit down. In the days after the meeting *The Scotsman* reflected on its disorderliness and said McLaren should not have talked of a clique. The ACLA and the Liberal party were being damaged, and if there was too much emphasis on total, immediate repeal 'a great number of Whig noblemen and gentlemen' would withdraw from the anti-corn law cause. 'No one knows better, or respects more, the high character and extraordinary talents of Mr Duncan McLaren than we do. There are few men who see so far, and on whose judgment we would generally rely with so much confidence, but we have a firm conviction in this case he has committed a grave error; and we feel a decided opposition to it to be so much more necessary, because his well-earned influence in the city renders any wrong measure which he supports doubly dangerous.' That was recognition at least of the support McLaren enjoyed in the ranks of those who would hiss at Whigs.

Macaulay made his views clear in a letter to John Wigham.[34] Repeating that he had always voted for Villiers's motions, he said he wanted union, not division, among those favouring repeal. He would continue to act according to his beliefs and if he offended any constituents, he was sorry. 'They must do their pleasure – my mind is made up, and I am ready to abide the consequences.' If Edinburgh wanted to be represented by a 'sycophant', they wouldn't find it hard to find such a man. The letter and one from Gibson-Craig reiterating support for repeal were read to the ACLA amid general disapprobation.[35] McLaren pounced on Macaulay's voting record and, unwisely, broadened his attack. What were Macaulay's views on the growing debate about the state of Ireland and endowment of its Roman Catholic clergy? And 'what is the next great question? I say it is the extension of the suffrage question.' (Applause.) To James Moncreiff this was too much: in a body seeking to advance repeal, McLaren's speech was 'suicidal'. Instead of attacking Macaulay they should welcome his conversion to the League's cause and acquisition to their ranks.

Macaulay was angry that his voting record had been subjected to what he regarded as distortion, that his broad support for repeal had been dismissed, that his independence of judgment had been challenged, that the Edinburgh ACLA had been used as a platform to attack him across a broad political front and that McLaren and supporters were apparently seeking to take over Liberal leadership in the city and thereby remove him. But he hastened to mend relations with the ACLA in a brief accommodating letter committing himself to repeal. On 1 June a leader in *The Scotsman* announced that the difference of opinion in the city Liberal party 'is terminated'. For McLaren, however, the breach with both the newspaper and Macaulay was to be permanent. In August he told George Combe[36] that the MP should not be sticking by Lord John Russell who, as a party leader, refused to move on issues like the corn laws beyond his position before 1841. As for *The*

Scotsman, he complained that its criticism had become personal, not just political. It 'had said more about my moral character than any tory paper had ever ventured to assert'. In a further letter three days later McLaren spelled out his views on candidates. He told Combe, a Liberal activist, that if in a constituency a more liberal candidate would have a greater number of friends than a sitting MP of less liberal views and have a better chance of winning, it would be 'both just and politic' to bring him forward. On the other hand parties should try by argument to promote opinions 'without giving battle on their own account, as a separate section of a party, while there are good reasons for holding that they form the majority of the party with which they have been acting in harmony, or have power in some other way to return their men according to the reasonable probabilities of the case'. Not the clearest of McLaren's formulations but one that he said 'would sanction the starting of League candidates for Edinr., for all sections and parties here have admitted (including the most zealous friends of the sitting members) that the supporters of League principles form a large majority of the Liberal constituency of the city'.

In September 1844 Macaulay risked a trip to his constituency. Reporting from Oman's Hotel to William Gibson-Craig on a cordial reception he claimed that 'even those whom I regarded as the tools of Duncan Maclaren [sic], Howison for example, and Gray the Quaker, have assured me of their approbation and support'. But there was a small section of the party trying to draw a distinction between him and Gibson-Craig. 'Just scorn and disregard' which both MPs felt against McLaren should 'not lead us to do anything which may look like disrespect to any knot of well-meaning liberal electors'. He was sorry to have responded so tartly to McLaren's invitation the previous December out of 'contempt for his dirty artifices'. Having advised Gibson-Craig also to show civility to honest and friendly Leaguers as Howison and Wigham appeared to be, he added a personal note: 'I stole yesterday to Riccarton, saw your house and pleasure grounds in high beauty, and made my acquaintance with the children who were in high beauty too'. Their grandfather Sir James was in excellent health.[37]

John McLaren, reminiscing after his father's death, depicted the argument about corn-law repeal as one between landowning Whigs who refused to go farther than their leader, Lord John Russell, in arguing only for a fixed duty and out-and-out repealers, of whom McLaren had been among the first in Edinburgh, ahead of most of his former allies on the council.[38] That judgment is based on hindsight. There was a range of opinion in Liberal ranks about the pace and extent of reform, and until December 1845 Russell gave little leadership at all. The Edinburgh Whigs certainly lacked McLaren's single-minded commitment and were wary about the activities of the Anti-Corn Law League. But it was not disagreement about the repeal campaign, or even about the position adopted by Macaulay and Gibson-Craig, that brought the fracture in Edinburgh politics. The break did occur at that time, as John McLaren noted. But it was his father who split the party. His speech at the city's Anti-Corn Law Association meeting in April 1844 turned the Whigs and some of his former allies against him and his noisy supporters. Disagreement about the technicalities of free trade was one thing, and criticism of MPs' voting records was nothing new. What was intolerable was the hijacking of the ACLA by the Radicals when McLaren issued his challenge on Ireland and suffrage reform. For Adam Black as Lord Provost it was too much. Henceforth he would side not with his Dissenter protégé McLaren but with the Whig leadership and Macaulay. James Moncreiff as a Parliament House man was also alarmed. He and leading members of the Free Church had other concerns than riding radical hobby-horses: they had churches to found and finance and their corner to fight. There was no love lost between the new Church and the Dissenters, as we shall see. Finally, *The Scotsman* turned against McLaren and radicalism. McLaren had stopped writing for the paper by 1842. As he told Cobden,[39] his articles had become 'somewhat out of joint' with other contributions and, although anonymous, were attributable through 'internal evidence'.

Charles Maclaren, an editor with an inquiring mind, retained admiration for McLaren's skills, and the admiration was mutual. Over the next decade Combe was to try to bridge the gap between the two, both of whom he regarded as friends, but McLaren said[40] that although he bore no grudge against 'our friend the editor', the attacks over Macaulay and the corn laws had continued without abatement and so he had no alternative but to put an end to cooperation 'even if I approved of the policy of the paper which I do not'. A political disagreement need not have turned into open hostility. But Maclaren was soon to be joined in the editorial office by Alexander Russel, previously editor of local newspapers and a vigorous writer, whose influence on the leader columns was evident long before he succeeded to Maclaren's chair. He and Duncan McLaren clashed early and often.[41] A later editor, Charles Cooper, suggested a reason for their initial hostility.[42] While still a local editor Russel had been asked by McLaren to write some papers for the Anti-Corn Law League attacking *The Scotsman*'s attitude. Russel knew that McLaren and Maclaren had been allies and he refused. 'It may be that here was the groundwork of the subsequent strong antagonism between the two men.'

When Macaulay was contemplating his autumn visit to Edinburgh he must have been delighted that McLaren was out of town, accompanying his son John on a trip round the west coast and the Highlands and preparing to leave with him in October for a winter in Madeira. The 13-year-old boy had a weak chest and was unable to go to school or leave the house in winter. Thus confined he had developed a precocious interest in his father's public life and writings. In Madeira Duncan immersed himself in geology, vulcanology and economics. John tried to interest him in the flowers that bloomed all winter. It was Andrew Combe, the doctor brother of McLaren's friend George the phrenologist, who suggested that John join the many British visitors who nurtured their health on the island. Leaving the rest of the children in the care of the aunts, father and son set off from Liverpool on a stormy voyage lasting 14 days. Bright regretted that he could not be in Liverpool to see off his friend but offered to meet in Manchester. He wished the pair a prosperous voyage: 'I would have been far more glad, had the voyage been unnecessary.'[43] Duncan wrote a 32-page pamphlet about the trip he made with 'a young friend'.[44]

Madeira might be made 'the garden of the world', McLaren declared, and its industrious, if backward, inhabitants were in many ways superior to those of their Portuguese motherland. The land laws might teach Britain and Ireland how to treat tenants. If a tenant wanted to leave the land, he must be fully contemplated for improvements he had made. There were about 250 British visitors, including invalids, although McLaren said that the island with its steepness and lack of carriages was better suited to those able to take vigorous exercise. He and John rode most of the day, covering 1,500 miles in five and a half months. The boy much benefited from his stay, though he noted that his father, while popular with those he met, did not enter much into the gaiety of 'English' society. One person McLaren did meet was John Oliver, who later became his business partner and son-in-law. Father and son travelled back to Europe by way of Tenerife in the Canary Islands, where their fitness was put to the test by a 30-mile, 2-day climb with mules to a volcanic peak. 'I shall not be charged with exaggeration to say that my pulse beat quicker, and that I felt my cheek flushed with surprise and satisfaction, when I found myself at length standing on the spot which, from the earliest hour that I can recollect I had never ceased most ardently to desire that I might reach.' The return home was by Gibraltar and then through Spain, north Italy and Germany. Duncan was not to visit continental Europe again until he was in his seventies. John spent the rest of summer 1845 at home and then went abroad again for two and a half years, this time to Jamaica. His sister

Grant wrote to him at Christmas about the younger children: 'Agnes, Duncan and Catherine each got a shilling from Papa and they are all going to give half of it to the Colection [sic] on Sunday. I think it is very generous of them but I forgot to say that Catherine is not.'[45] Dedication to his son's welfare won McLaren wide admiration and to celebrate his return and perhaps put aside the political tensions of the months preceding his departure, there was a dinner in his honour chaired by Adam Black as Lord Provost.

By the autumn of 1845 Government ministers realised that the famine in Ireland was reaching such proportions that the corn laws must be suspended, and that it would be impossible to reintroduce them. The failure of the potato crop was doing the League's work for it. With the tide of moderate opinion now in its favour, the League campaigners stepped up their fund-raising efforts. In December a Manchester meeting raised £60,000. More modestly McLaren summoned a few friends to his home on New Year's Day to discuss subscriptions and to ask Cobden to come to Scotland.[46] Edinburgh had just been the focus for a shift of opinion on the Whig side that was to affect significantly the political outcome. While in the city Lord John Russell as party leader had published a letter declaring that it was no longer feasible to contend for a fixed duty on corn. Events moved quickly. Peel resigned on 6 December. Russell failed to form a Cabinet. Peel, reinstated, introduced proposals for repeal on 27 January. The Whigs and League leaders were now largely in agreement but still had to face Peel's proposal that abolition would take three years of reducing duties. McLaren assessed Edinburgh opinion and informed Cobden that although the feeling was for immediate repeal, there were two views about tactics.[47] He himself would not side with protectionist Tories to throw out Peel's Bill although the outcome would be either an election or an immediate Whig Government. He understood, however, that most Whigs at Parliament House were for that course. *The Scotsman*, he added, wanted Peel's measure passed although he had not seen the editor on the matter or had any contact with him for some time. On a second reading vote that split the Tory party down the middle Peel carried his measure, and although there was concern in the League lest Whig landowning peers destroy it in the Lords, its passage into law on 25 June was greeted with celebrations across the country. On the national stage McLaren had been only a bit player but in Scotland his reputation had grown. His support had been longstanding, he had mobilised opinion and brought in cash, he had encouraged the now famous Bright and Cobden to visit Scotland on several triumphal occasions and in his own city he had created a team who would go with him on new campaigns.

6. Banker and railman

Promising cheaper corn and thus bread was politically popular. McLaren latched on to another staple issue that won him support across the classes – obtaining a reliable water supply in Edinburgh. By the 1840s the link between rotting waste, sewage and disease was beginning to engage medical and social reformers.[1] Worst affected were the poorest areas, but all classes suffered from a lack of piped water, notably residents of the upper storeys of new tenements. The first of several crises that spurred McLaren's intervention occurred in the drought of autumn 1842. Supply was reduced to as little as once every four days. Even in ordinary conditions it was reckoned that the population of Edinburgh and Leith, totalling 167,000, was getting only 13.41 gallons per head per day. The Edinburgh Water Company, which had taken over the duty of supply from the town council in 1819, was meant to solve the problem by tapping new sources and building a reservoir in the Pentland hills. In 1826 a new Act increased the company's powers, and in 1835 its financial problems were debated in Parliament. The matter came up again in 1843 with a Bill allowing the company to tap new sources and increase its income from householders' rates.[2]

McLaren had no time for the water company and he undertook to represent the complaints of his fellow citizens while in London on other business. The town council also sent representatives to keep the water company in check while MPs debated the Bill. From March to May a parliamentary committee took evidence, and McLaren and the council representatives spent up to 15 hours a day in attendance and in briefing counsel and preparing answers to the company's pleas. McLaren was happy with the commitment to constituents of Andrew Rutherfurd, the MP for Leith. But he took issue with Macaulay and Gibson-Craig, accusing them of 'frigid neutrality'. If only the two MPs had come out against the water company's Bill as the city wanted, other members of the committee would probably have thrown it out but 'when the city members were so lukewarm in the cause, there could be no very general or intense feeling on the subject among their constituents'. Gibson-Craig replied that in a committee considering a private Bill like this no MP should express an opinion before hearing the evidence. McLaren had left London and responded from the Royal Hotel in Manchester on 13 April: he understood the principle well but 'in this case the promoters had violated every pledge which they had previously given to the inhabitants, and they were in the course of being compelled by the inhabitants to perform their duty under the powers of the existing Acts'.[3] It was such pressure that led Macaulay the following week in a letter to Gibson-Craig to refer to McLaren's 'dirty proceeding' and to hope that the good sense of their friends would make public comment unnecessary.[4] His optimism was misplaced. By publishing the details of the proceedings in London[5] McLaren wrongfooted the two MPs and gained kudos for himself. He claimed to have secured a guarantee of new spring water within five years and a reduction of the rates, saving the community £4,000 a year. His exertions did not convince Lord Cockburn. Writing to Gibson-Craig from his Pentlands estate at Bonaly, the judge admitted that the city was paying a lot for a small quantity of bad water, but 'that modest man Duncan Maclaren [sic] thinks he secures his return next election, by telling the people that they may all drink liquid crystal, till they have dropsies, for nothing, if they will only believe him to be infallible'.[6]

McLaren's attention-winning public commitments were combined with a branching out in business life. On return from Madeira in July 1845 he embarked on a new venture. *The Scotsman* of 16 August carried an advertisement announcing the Scottish Exchange Investment Company which, under an interim committee, was offering £500,000 in £10 shares 'for the purposes of affording accommodation to the holders of Railway and other Stocks, by advancing money on the security of such stocks'. A second advertisement said that all stock had been taken up and the capital would be increased to £1 million. By 24 September another notice recorded that John Maitland who had been appointed as manager had resigned and McLaren was taking over. The editorial columns proclaimed that 'Mr McLaren's knowledge of business, his high character for integrity, his foresight, prudence and sagacity, eminently qualify him to be the head of a great monied establishment'.[7] Better that than upsetting the Whigs, it seems. The company was soon renamed the Exchange Bank of Scotland and found offices in St Andrew's Square, at the heart of New Town business. It had a tie-in with the London and Westminster Bank and was overseen by a committee comprising advocates and merchants. The new enterprise soon joined forces with the Edinburgh and Leith Investment Co. to create extra shares. In October McLaren's drapery business was renamed McLaren, Renton & Co. on the same principles of 'personally selecting all their goods in the best Markets, in large quantities and under every advantage'. A member of the Renton family now shared responsibility.[8] Until at least 1850 McLaren would spend much time at the bank. Political and personal correspondence was often on the bank's headed paper. He told Cobden on New Year's Day 1846 that he had time for a meeting at his home about Anti-Corn Law League subscriptions because he did not have to be at the bank.

McLaren had long been interested in railways. He may have been enthused by Charles Maclaren whose articles in *The Scotsman* showed a grasp of the technology and potential of steam trains before the tentative developments in the 1830s turned into boom and mania. Scotland lagged behind England in opening lines but that did not prevent Scots with money to invest from doing so in English companies, especially when with the completion of lines, the companies began to pay good dividends.[9] Peter Brough, the Paisley draper, was like McLaren accustomed to buying textiles south of the border and realised the potential of rail travel, buying large holdings in the York and North Midland railway. McLaren became a shareholder in the associated York, Newcastle and Berwick Company, with consequences when it ran into trouble in 1849. He was also for a time auditor of the Edinburgh and Glasgow Company, whose line connecting the cities opened in 1842. The majority of its shareholders were Lancastrian though its directors were mostly Scots. McLaren's study of accounting had been in order to run a draper's business, but his guidance of Edinburgh's financial affairs must have convinced the rail company of his care and astuteness. As the network across Britain developed, he became an enthusiast for timetables, a walking Bradshaw as his letters to family members show, always keen to plan their journeys for them. Every issue of *The Scotsman* in the mid-1840s carried advertisements from companies seeking finance. Parliament became concerned about the number of private Bills seeking authorisation for rail schemes. George Hudson of York, with his ambitions to see the lines from London to Edinburgh completed largely by his companies, was being popularly crowned the 'railway king'. The problem was a lack of capital to feed the frenzy. The banks had been reined in by Peel in 1844 and were reluctant to lend money on the security of railway shares. The gap was briefly filled by exchange banks, nine of which were set up in Scotland, starting in Glasgow in 1844. The Exchange Bank of Scotland was incorporated by Act of Parliament in 1846.[10] Such official recognition aroused resentment since the Government had refused incorporation of joint-stock banks with large capital and many proprietors; so why give a blessing to what were indubitably speculative concerns? And why should a man as financially cautious as McLaren become heavily involved?

The answer is that the sums appeared to add up. Depositors were to be paid more than by joint-stock banks but with railway stock, on which investments were secured, paying up to 8 per cent, there was a profit margin of a least 2 per cent. The railway companies were happy to welcome a cash injection and investors were happy to find a banking mechanism which brought them into a lucrative market. Writing to George Combe from the Exchange Bank in December 1845, McLaren struck an optimistic note.[11] The initial £4,500 cost of uniting the Scottish Exchange Investment Company and the Edinburgh and Leith Investment Company had been met. All securities were good and apparently prospering. There was a provision in place by which if a stock fell by 10 per cent or more, anyone who had been advanced money on its strength had to pay two-thirds of such a fall or the stock would be sold. Security was therefore good even in time of depreciation.

Two years later boom was turning to bust, and the situation further deteriorated as investors learned the extent of malpractice in some companies, most notably those controlled by Hudson. *Tait's Edinburgh Magazine*, which chronicled the difficulties in detail, described 1849 as the 'most disastrous year for the holders of railway property' in the life of the industry.[12] The exchange banks, for which railways were only the most prominent of speculative investments, were in collapse by 1850. McLaren had to wind up affairs in the Edinburgh bank, which caused him much anxiety.[13] He never again became involved in the financial world, which as he admitted many years later might have brought him great prosperity. Property – building Edinburgh in stone and mortar – was to prove a less worrisome investment. But meanwhile he was still a railway man.

For those like McLaren who were by the standards of the time frequent travellers to London, the benefits of new stretches of track and bridges were obvious. However, the North British line from Edinburgh to Berwick was opened only in 1846, and that from Tweedmouth in Northumberland to Newcastle in 1847. In 1849 only 5,792 passengers were booked through from Edinburgh to London by the North British Railway, compared with 11,584 by steamer from Leith or Granton.[14] There was a ferry across the Tweed until the Queen opened the Berwick bridge in August 1850. George Hudson, who was born in the same year as McLaren and had run a draper's business in York before inheriting enough money to embark on railways, sought to dominate the creation of lines in the North and Midlands of England, but in 1849 his fraudulent methods of business were revealed in one of his companies after another. On 20 February shareholders in the York, Newcastle and Berwick Company questioned his share-dealing. Three months later an extraordinary meeting of the company in York heard the results of a preliminary inquiry and appointed a committee of shareholders to report on the company's affairs. Representatives from five large cities where important shareholders lived were nominated to the committee – including, from Edinburgh, McLaren as manager of the Exchange Bank. Hudson resigned as chairman. Similar investigations went on at his other companies. The Railway King had been deposed but he avoided the courts because he was an MP. In August the committee of inquiry revealed that Hudson's dubious transactions and false accounting dated back to 1844, but there was still enough profit to pay a 3.5 per cent dividend. The existing directors resigned and a new board including McLaren was appointed. He remained for six years having given up his connection with the Edinburgh and Glasgow company. John Benjamin Smith, the Unitarian Manchester mill-owner and MP for Stirling who had been active in the Anti-Corn Law League, shared information with McLaren about the rail industry in which both had investments. They agreed that the controversial issue of Sunday trains was best left to individual conscience. A seven-day service should be available, and it was up to travellers to decide whether to avail themselves of it on the Sabbath. As an MP Smith was able to keep a close eye on the City of London and gave McLaren updates on the state of the market. When the Hudson scandal began to unfold, Smith wrote to McLaren: 'I think you have never had much confidence in his lines ... The temptation of gain has been too strong for weak morals.'[15] He was worried that McLaren in helping to clear up the mess was taking too much upon himself: 'I scarcely see how you can get out of the mire.'[16]

But the industry with its opportunities as well as perils continued to interest McLaren, and he was tempted to go into railway management himself. He found a congenial associate in Harry Thompson, a Yorkshire landowner and keen Liberal who became chairman of the York and North Midland Railway, which had been one of Hudson's companies. In 1850 Thompson, who wanted a manager for the business, wrote: 'Would you, after your Exchange Company's affairs are wound up, accept any place connected with the management of a railway company, with an adequate salary?' McLaren was tempted and conditionally said yes. But he had second thoughts and withdrew, telling Thompson that it was the only time 'in the course of my public life in which I have halted between two opinions'. Thompson promised him more time to consider, and there was a second offer from the Lancashire and Yorkshire Railway Company based in Manchester. John Bright advised against the Lancashire and Yorkshire because of its management structure but approved Thompson's offer.[17] McLaren decided against both, reluctant though he was to disappoint Thompson, who was to become first chairman of the North Eastern Railway, created by an amalgamation of three companies in 1854, and who kept up a relentless vendetta against Hudson.

McLaren's attention was never away from politics for long. He forged an alliance that inflicted defeat on the Edinburgh Whigs but failed to survive long enough to create a permanent Liberal party. It was too contrived, born as it was in the febrile conditions of the Disruption in the Church of Scotland and the coincidental upsurge of evangelical and anti-Catholic sentiment across Britain. If this had seen the birth of a new Liberalism in Scotland, it would have had the most dubious parentage. The Whig tradition had been of tolerance and the removal of religious barriers. In the mid-1840s, and not just in Edinburgh where the atmosphere was most heated, the new Liberals sought to ground their electoral support in sectarianism and prejudice. It was not a glorious episode, and even contemporaries were dismayed. McLaren wanted to engage with secular issues such as the franchise and national education but for at least a decade that proved premature. The clash of personalities, not least his own, reinforced prejudices and made long-term unity impossible.

At the outset the bond that held sectarian campaigners together was Maynooth; the target was Macaulay. It is hard for us to understand why the increase in a modest Government grant to the Roman Catholic seminary at Maynooth outside Dublin should have aroused such passions in England and Scotland. The famine would have been a better reason for intervention in Irish affairs, but to orthodox laissez-faire opinion starvation among peasants did not need state intervention beyond removing the duty on imported corn. On this side of the Irish Sea latent anti-Catholicism was stirred by the influx of Irish families in search of work, and south of the border by ritualism that seemed to be dragging some Anglican churchmen too close to Rome. In reaction to Peel's support for Maynooth there was formed the Central Anti-Maynooth Committee under Sir Culling Eardley Smith, an earnestly evangelical member of the Church of England. It is reckoned that 1 in 20 of the entire population of Great Britain and Ireland registered their opposition to increasing the college grant by signing 10,000 petitions to Parliament. After Peel's Government fell in 1846 – not directly because of corn-law repeal but on another Irish measure, this time coercive – the incoming Whig Prime Minister, Lord John Russell, appointed both Macaulay and William Gibson-Craig to Government posts, which in these days prompted by-elections. Gibson-Craig was not opposed, though like Macaulay he had backed Peel over Maynooth. Macaulay found himself in the eye of a storm as Free Churchmen and Dissenters were joined by some members of the Established Church in expressing their resentment at the Maynooth affront to Protestantism.

For such a narrowly based challenge to a Whig moderate the ideal candidate may have seemed to be Sir Culling Eardley Smith, who had become the prime mover in an Evangelical Alliance that brought together evangelicals across the Protestant denominations. Elsewhere in Scotland by-election challenges to the Whigs were being mounted by Free Church/Dissenter combinations. In Edinburgh McLaren's followers joined forces with a Free Church group led by Sir James Forrest. Their election committee, according to Cockburn, 'contained Establishment Churchmen and wild Voluntaries, intense Tories and declamatory Radicals, who agreed on nothing except in holding their peculiar religion as the scriptural, and therefore the only safe, criterion of fitness for public duty'.[18] The choice of Smith as a candidate from outside was prudent but it showed the narrowness of the attack on Macaulay, who won comfortably and was glad to have got off with spending only £400. Some Free Churchmen did not want to undermine the new Whig Government and possibly endanger free trade. McLaren, steering clear of public confrontation, realised that the challenge had been misdirected but could be successfully remounted in the forthcoming General Election with a better candidate.[19] Maynooth was too narrow an issue. It evoked a spurt of anti-Catholicism but that was undesirable: Dissenters like McLaren felt that Roman Catholics shared their sense of religious exclusion and that there was almost a bond. The Maynooth grant should be opposed but on the ground that all State support of religious establishments was wrong. So the Dissenters, who had resuscitated their former Central Board as a new Scottish Board of Dissenters in July 1845, highlighted their parallel objection to Government aid for the work of Irish Protestants. On the other hand the Free Church was not opposed to an Established Church, only to the practices of the Church of Scotland, and its rhetoric was markedly more anti-Catholic. So on sectarian grounds amity could not be guaranteed among campaigners against incumbent Whigs. Nor might an alliance withstand personal disagreements. McLaren looked to the success of another recent alliance, the Anti-Corn Law League. It had brought together men of varied backgrounds and vocations. A challenge to Whig domination of Liberalism had likewise to be broad based and well focused.

The vulnerability of Macaulay was recognised as the 1847 election approached. When Peel got his Corn Bill through the Commons, Macaulay made a point of shaking Cobden by the hand and congratulating him on the success of his campaign.[20] But the gesture counted for nothing among those in Edinburgh who recalled his treatment of the Anti-Corn Law League. Discontent with his voting record and with his offhandedness in dealing with constituents, especially the prickly ones, had built up. On his rare visits to Edinburgh, according to the judge Lord Neaves, he wore a 'septennial, supercilious smile', which was a snide reference to the statutory length of Parliaments and Macaulay's appearance for elections only.[21] It is untrue, as his biographer Trevelyan asserted, that the worst to be thrown against him in the election campaign of July 1847 was that he was too much the literary man and not enough the politician and 'that one who knew so much about Ancient Rome could not possibly be the man for Modern Athens'.[22] The most that the new Free Church/Dissenter alliance could hope for was to defeat one Whig, and of the two incumbents Sir William Gibson-Craig was much the more secure, coming from a family wearing the battle honours of earlier reform and with an understanding of Edinburgh social and religious affiliations. But targeting Macaulay meant identifying a candidate acceptable to both sides of the alliance and that posed problems. From the days of Non-Intrusion, there had been rivalry between Dissenters and those who were to leave the Church of Scotland in 1843, exacerbated by personal animosities. The Free Church, building congregations and churches, could be seen as a challenge to Dissenters who had prospered amid the troubles of the pre-Disruption Church. Sir Culling Eardley Smith was denied another attempt because he opposed Sunday trains, and many voters did not. McLaren, despite being leader of his side of the alliance, was too divisive to be a parliamentary champion and anyway he continued to deny ambition for Westminster. The choice as candidate fell on Charles Cowan, a Free Churchman but pre-eminently a businessman, member of a paper-making family in Midlothian. Cowan was not a politician by nature, and Adam Black, loyal to Macaulay, attacked his lack of experience. But he had a cause to promote – the excessive excise on paper. Spirit dealers looked to him to oppose the excise on whisky. The pro-Cowan alliance embraced drinkers as well as the teetotallers prominent among his religious backers. According to Cowan's own reminiscences Macaulay was damaged by mocking the opposition to the Maynooth grant as 'the bray of Exeter Hall', the headquarters of London evangelicism. During the election campaign one of Cowan's supporters, William McCrie, reminded a public meeting that 'the same animal which could bray could also kick'.[23]

Two days before the election Andrew Rutherfurd, Lord Advocate, wrote to Fox Maule: 'We are down in the mouth about Macaulay. He is personally unpopular in the last degree ... Shall we carry him through? He made such a powerful speech and what requires to be added is tact. [Gibson-]Craig is safe.'[24] Four candidates came to the poll – Macaulay, Gibson-Craig, Cowan and Peter Blackburn, a Tory. Electors could make two choices or plump for one only. McLaren, voting at a shop in Victoria Street, plumped for Cowan. Macaulay spent the day at the Liberal committee room in the Merchants' Hall in Hunter Square, sitting on a sofa reading, or appearing to read. About an hour before the poll closed at 4 p.m., one of his workers came in apprehensive of the result. Then Black, who was Lord Provost, arrived distraught: 'I am ashamed, Mr Macaulay. I am ashamed of my fellow citizens.' Macaulay replied placidly: 'Chances of war, Mr Black, chances of war.' Gibson-Craig arrived having learned that he and Cowan were elected. In tears he said: 'Would to God, Mr Macaulay, that I was rejected and you returned.' Later, addressing supporters in the hall, the defeated Minister said: 'My connection with Edinburgh is terminated – terminated for ever.'[25] During the day he had written to his niece Hannah: 'I am not vexed, but as cheerful as ever I was in my life. I have been completely beaten. The poll has not closed; but there is no chance that I shall retrieve lost ground. Radicals, Tories, Dissenters, Voluntaries, Free Churchmen, spirit dealers who are angry because I will not pledge myself to repeal all taxes on whisky, and great numbers of persons who are jealous of my chief supporters here, and think that the patronage of Edinburgh has been too exclusively distributed among a clique, have united to bear me down. I will make no hasty resolutions; but everything seems to indicate that I ought to take this opportunity of retiring from public life.'[26] At Christmas 1848 he wrote to Rutherfurd: 'I have really great reason to feel obliged to Mr Cowan, Duncan McLaren, Sir James Forrest, and other gentlemen whose names I have very ungratefully forgotten. If I had still been member for Edinburgh and Paymaster of the Forces, I should not have been able to bring out these volumes before 1850.' He had just published the first two volumes in his *History of England*. Cowan, showing his political naivety, was disqualified because he had been a Government contractor, and a by-election was called in which he was returned unopposed. Macaulay was asked to consider fighting it but replied: 'Under no circumstances will I ever again be a candidate for Edinburgh.'

The 1847 poll was immediately put under psephological scrutiny. Cowan had received 2,063 votes to 1,854 for Gibson-Craig, 1,477 for Macaulay and 980 for Blackburn. The new MP's supporters were described, significantly, by religious affiliation: 567 Free Churchmen, 492 United Presbyterians (following the union of the Secession and Relief churches), 160 members of the Established Church, 71 Congregationalists, 65 Baptists, 35 Episcopalians, 20 Seceders, 9 Wesleyans, 8 Quakers, 6 Roman Catholics, 6 Unitarians and 621 whose religion was unknown.[27] The question was whether this coalition could do more than remove an unpopular MP. The terms 'independent Liberal' and 'advanced Liberal' began to be attached to candidates and their supporters around this time[28], but party labels were everywhere still loose. There was no formal structure to the groups that convened when a candidature had to be considered. Forrest took the public lead in bringing forward Cowan; McLaren stayed in the background. When McLaren referred to a Whig 'clique' everyone knew whom that was intended to include, just as his own leading supporters were designated as such. Many were councillors or former councillors who several times in the 1840s sought to bring McLaren back into the council chamber.

In the language of modern political reporters Macaulay was one of the high profile casualties of the election. Lord John Russell told the Queen his defeat was 'disgraceful'. *The Times* was among southern newspapers that thought Edinburgh had disgraced herself: Macaulay's only mistake was that he had not exhibited the qualifications of a parish beadle or a district surveyor. For the Prime Minister the overall results were confusing. A Commons rendered unstable by the division of Conservatives into Protectionists and Peelites had been made even more unpredictable. The Radicals gained in numbers. How estranged from the Whigs would they prove to be when ministers sought approval for specific measures? Russell might have had Edinburgh in mind when he explained to Victoria that 'the absence of any party contest, or of any great question has led to results of a very unfortunate character – the indulgence of caprice, ingratitude and injustice'.[29] Elsewhere in Scotland the anti-Maynooth alliance saw two Whig candidates replaced in Glasgow, and in Aberdeen a Free Churchman replaced a member of the Established Church. In urban areas where many electors belonged to the Free or Dissenting churches, Whigs found themselves swept aside, or barely clinging on.[30]

In Edinburgh a curious comment was made at a public meeting four months before the election by an ardent Dissenter, the Rev. Lindsay Alexander. He was not afraid of Macaulay or Gibson-Craig, or even of the talents and tactics of Parliament House. 'Forgive me if I say that I am more afraid of the petticoats. I am afraid of the ladies who come into shops and say, "Mr So-and-so, do you vote for Mr Macaulay and Mr Gibson-Craig?" "Not quite sure, madam. I am rather thinking of voting for the Dissenting candidates." "Oh, very well, you will be so good as to send in your account."' Alexander was addressing a meeting called to oppose the Government's proposals for education.[31] The issue of national education was coming to the fore in both England and Scotland. Before the 1847 election the Russell Government decided to reform the grants paid to schools and to offer teachers better conditions. But with so many schools owing their existence to the churches, the question of State support for religion reared its head on both sides of the border. In Scotland the Free Church was hard-pressed to finance the schools it was founding, or had inherited at the Disruption.[32] Deciding whether or not to accept grants was divisive, though pragmatism won out. The Dissenters, who had far fewer schools to support than either the Established or Free churches, could make the debate one of principle. They disliked the Churches' grip on education, including the employment of teachers, supervision of the curriculum and standards in individual schools, and the content of religious instruction. They realised, as many did in all denominations, that school provision, especially in the fast growing industrial towns and in the more remote country areas, was inadequate and they doubted whether the Churches could meet the challenge even if that were desirable. So when a campaign for national education was launched they took a leading part. McLaren was knowledgeable as a promoter of schools using Heriot money, and he followed his own children's education closely in the middle-class schools of the city. His friend George Combe, after early success in publicising the merits of phrenology, moved into a commitment to the education of all, regardless of the shape of their heads. Combe gave a wide-ranging series of adult education lectures, and one such delivered in the winter of 1834–5 to a mixed audience was attended by the young Councillor McLaren, who had some cause to blush.[33] He wrote to the lecturer that 'if I had been walking home with any unnamed lady I could not have ventured to ask her opinion on some parts of the lecture, but I am very far from wishing to obtrude my feelings on others, and I know you must necessarily be a much better judge of the proper boundaries in such cases than I am'. Combe took the view that 'no important truth, if clothed in pure language, is indelicate'. McLaren hastened to say that he had no issue with the content, except for Combe's assertion that it was sinful of ladies to marry under the age of 23. Combe scribbled at the bottom of McLaren's letter that 'if there *are* important truths which, when expressed in pure language, are indelicate, then the Creator is indelicate'.

By 1844 the pair were together in facilitating the visit to Scottish schools of a leading American educationist, Horace Mann of Boston. McLaren accompanied Mann on visits to Edinburgh schools, including some Heriot foundations, and he was pleased by the American's praise for the able and energetic teaching. But he pointed out to Combe that if Mann had gone to some country schools where the teachers were ill-qualified, the verdict would have been different.[34] McLaren also gave Combe his own experience of being taught the Scriptures at school: 'My teaching was all mere *words*. No attempt was made by my teachers to make me understand the meaning of the words, and I thought nothing about the meaning.'[35] But in Edinburgh's hospital schools he had seen the great pains taken to make children understand the meaning of the Catechism and scriptural passages. He agreed, however, with Mann that more needed to be done to turn meaning into moral conduct. 'It is manifest that a clever boy may know the history of all the Scripture characters and be able to recount all the miracles and leading incidents in the New Testament and yet be a great rogue.' McLaren's contribution to the education debate was applauded by John Benjamin Smith, the Manchester-based MP for Stirling, who asked him to formulate a plan for Scottish education which would improve the 'moral and physical condition' of the people. Smith thought that Dissenters were too negative in criticising Government inaction: 'A plan emanating from Scotland would be well received in England and would go far to neutralize [sic] the sectarian jealousies amongst us since there would be no doubt of your being opposed to a "godless scheme of education" ... You have great influence, cannot you collect a few good men of all parties together to talk over this important matter.'[36]

The meeting where the Rev. Alexander worried about the politics of petticoats was called to protest at the Government's Bill on education grants, which was directed mainly at English schools but which Scottish Dissenters read as a boost for Established Churches in both countries. The chairman of the meeting, which lasted five hours, pointed out that the purpose was not to debate the role of the State in education but to take issue with the Bill itself. McLaren's role was to give a vote of thanks to Edward Baines, who had come up from England at his own expense to proclaim his belief that education was a matter for parents and not the State. Baines, whose Dissenter family owned the influential *Leeds Mercury* and who had made a study of the potential for voluntary expansion of education, became a close associate of McLaren, on this occasion receiving reassurance that a press attack on his presence at the meeting was only to have been expected: 'I can assure him that the Dissenters look with disgust on the course which *The Scotsman* follows on this question.' But on the need for national provision of education McLaren differed from Baines and the majority of Dissenters. In April 1850, when the National Education Association of Scotland was launched, McLaren joined its Edinburgh committee. The first president was Sir David Brewster, principal of the United College of St Andrews University, and the vice-presidents and directors included 38 clergymen, 7 professors, 6 teachers, 4 Lord Provosts and a number of doctors and advocates.[37] Its aims had wide support but debate about religious instruction in schools meant that implementation of these aims was to be long postponed. The first Bill presented by Lord Melgund, MP for Greenock, came just a month after the launch of the NEA. It was defeated on second reading by six votes, though it had a majority of three among Scottish members.

The Dissenters could now speak with greater cohesion on education as on other matters. The coming together in 1847 of the United Secession and Relief Churches meant that the two largest Churches with histories dating back to eighteenth-century dissensions now formed a strong third force among Presbyterian denominations. The negotiations that led to the United Presbyterian Church started in 1835, and there was common cause during the Voluntary controversy. A scheme of union was agreed in 1840, but the Secession Church found itself in a doctrinal tangle about atonement and it was not until May 1847 that the two synods agreed the final terms.[38] Four hundred clergymen then joined in procession to Tanfield Hall, consciously following where another procession had gone four years earlier to launch the Free Church. There was not enough space for the 3,000 adherents who wanted to partake of the 'fruit soiree'. Cockburn was sardonic about the union: 'Their alliance seems to have been distinguished by as much grandeur and etiquette as if it had been a marriage between the houses of Austria and Bourbon.'[39] The United Presbyterians distinguished themselves from their Free Church brethren by insisting in their new constitution that theirs was a Church free of association with the State. They did not seek to mimic the Established Church but with over 500 congregations, 400,000 in the pews and an astutely run building programme they became part of the framework of Victorian towns and cities. Their culture was urban, like the bulk of their membership, and they exhibited the values of thrift and self-help which they practised in their trades and businesses. As the historians of the Victorian church noted, 'the sites of United Presbyterian churches were frequently selected with an acumen which any property developer might envy'.[40] There was a self-confidence about the UPs with whom the middle-aged McLaren mixed that was different from the inward-looking sects among whom he had grown up and cut his political teeth. The well-to-do laity held much power in these churches of a 'polite' character, and it was claimed that ministers were chosen more for their oratory or social connection than for religious zeal.

At different times McLaren was associated with several congregations as new churches were erected in the suburbs. Family and church connections went together. For example, Agnes Renton, sister of McLaren's wife Christina, married the Rev. John Robson, a leading UP minister in Glasgow. McLaren's family as they grew up took many a rail journey to Glasgow to spend time in the Robson household. Shared churchgoing and family friendships went with a shared outlook on politics. The United Presbyterians were more understanding of other faiths than many other Presbyterians, especially in the Free Church. Their reliance on the Westminster Confession and the Larger and Shorter Catechisms was accompanied by a statement repudiating intolerance. Members of other churches were welcome at Communion. In the selection of elders women as well as men had a vote (although only for male candidates, of course). The mission field was important. Sunday services were often enlivened by the accounts of missionaries home from Calabar or, later, China. The anti-slavery tradition among Dissenters turned into a mission to relieve the plight, material as well as spiritual, of millions overseas. Jamaica was an early commitment, and by 1852 the island had 18 UP churches with pastors, catechists and teachers. An academy at Montego Bay had a teacher of the classics and another of theology, who happened to be an Alex Renton.[41] To the island in search of the health that continued to elude him after returning from Madeira went 14-year-old John McLaren at the end of 1845. He remained for two and a half years, during which his health improved with regular exercise.

Shortly before he returned home he had a letter[42] from his father, which told him:

> I expect to be married in June or July to Miss Bright whom you saw in her brother's house at Rochdale. I have got her consent and

have to see her father in two days but the post will not wait these two days and hence I must write to you in this state. Like all members of the Society of Friends (Quakers) he will be much opposed to the marriage of his daughter with anyone not of that body and I believe will also be afraid of the responsibility of her having to attend to the welfare of a family not her own; but I do not suppose he will have any *personal* objection to myself on the ordinary grounds on which such objections are usually rested. She was at Ben Rhydding [a Yorkshire hydropathic establishment] when the children were there and has seen them all but Grant and knows them well. She has seen you also and always takes a great interest in your welfare. She is 33 years of age and, as you know, I am 48. I need not say anything about her as you will probably be here soon. She is of a *very* kind, gentle disposition and I am sure her teaching *by example* will be of inestimable value to the younger children. She will I think love you all and be as kind to you all as any person possibly could be. I believe there *never was* a lady who could have *precisely* the same feeling for children not her own as if they had been her own; but from what I hear of her I believe she will come near to that standard as any one could be expected to come ... She makes a great sacrifice of independence and position by taking charge of my family and I hope that you and all the others will show by your respect for her that you feel this to be the case and that you will appreciate the kindness you may experience. In worldly matters, too, I dare say, she will make a sacrifice, for her father will be so averse to the marriage for the reasons mentioned, that she expects he will resent it.

Writing to his adolescent son about Priscilla cannot have been easy for a Victorian father, and John's reaction is not recorded but he and his second stepmother developed a sound relationship. John admired her unremitting dedication to his father's well-being, and Priscilla knew the efforts John made to support her husband's political work, sometimes to his own detriment. The pre-marriage problems that Duncan foresaw with Priscilla's father were well anticipated. Jacob Bright, the self-made mill-owner, was indeed a patriarchal figure with nine children and at this late stage in life he was causing his family embarrassment by embarking on a third marriage, with his housekeeper.[43] Priscilla and her three sisters had made an impression on Thomas Carlyle when he visited their home. He dubbed them the 'Brightesses' who had minds of their own.[44] McLaren as a suitor for Priscilla was undesirable as a non-Quaker, but Jacob might have admired his campaign against the annuity tax; he himself had had many warrants against him for refusing to pay church rates. The age gap between Priscilla and Duncan should not have been a problem: Jacob's second wife was 14 years his junior. Priscilla's brother John, however, disapproved of the marriage because of the age difference and the fact that McLaren had so many children already. By befriending him and relying on his political counsel, John had brought the pair together. It is little wonder that Priscilla, at home looking after her widowed brother's daughter, looked forward to first meeting the man whose appearance as chairman of the 1842 London anti-corn law conference John had described – of large head, clear open brow, gentle Scottish voice.[45] She found him looking older than she expected but realised he was suffering from the recent loss of his wife Christina. Their friendship took six years to result in marriage. Priscilla did not lack other suitors, but her freedom was constricted by the responsibility of looking after John's daughter Helen. Then in June 1847 John remarried, his choice Elizabeth Leatham, the daughter of a well-to-do Yorkshire Quaker family. Priscilla told him he was too old, at 35, for a romantic attachment. But now over 30 herself, she lost her role as Helen's guardian and John's housekeeper. It is little wonder that, attracted as she clearly was, she overcame the opposition of her father and brother and accepted McLaren. The religious question could not be overcome. On 6 July 1848 they were married in the Rochdale registrar's office, which would have been the choice of neither, and set off on a honeymoon tour of northern England and Wales. The following spring Priscilla was summoned to attend a monthly meeting of the Quakers but refused on health grounds. She wrote expressing her sorrow at disunion from the Society whose principles were dear to her through education and conviction.[46] This attitude gave the meeting 'lively satisfaction' but she was disowned nonetheless. Her brother John was furious, writing in his diary: 'Today my dear sister Priscilla was disowned on the grounds of her marriage contrary to the rules or practices of the Society. I protested against this course as unjust to her and injurious to the Society. But our Monthly Meeting seems to be unable to perceive any distinction in cases; flagrant immorality and the marriage of a member with a religious person not a member are visited with the same condemnation. The Society may well not extend. It is withering to almost nothing. Its glorious principles are made unsightly to the world. Its aspect is made repulsive ... Can the Society reform itself, or will it slowly sink?'[47]

Early in their marriage McLaren made an effort to understand Quakerism.[48] He read the lives of Quaker heroes like Elizabeth Fry and studied their doctrines and practices. Writing to Priscilla in April 1849 he was almost jocular: 'I am satisfied you do not fully understand them [the bases of Quakerism]; and that my opinions on all the essential points of religion are nearer the opinions of Friends than yours are.' They shared McLaren's belief in the 'apartness' of the Sabbath even if they did not use the term 'Sabbath'. On the evidence of the book on Elizabeth Fry they gave the Scriptures an importance Priscilla did not. The practice of silent worship he found difficult – 'only advanced Christians can profit by it' – and he concluded: 'The great body of Christians require teaching from day to day, to be "built upon" in newspaper language. I am more a Friend than my beloved Priscilla is, she not being well "built up" yet.'

When they were apart, which even in their early days was frequently as Priscilla sought health cures or visited her family while Duncan made trips to London on business or public affairs, they corresponded regularly. Duncan wrote about family affairs, especially his wife's health, but also about politics, frequently citing her brother John's activities. Two days after the letter on Quakerism his theme was a speech by John, the best that year. The newspapers were saying that Bright's influence was becoming greater than Cobden's. This letter from Edinburgh would arrive by the same train as he was taking to meet her, and McLaren signed off affectionately, even ardently – the letter would 'get to your *hands* about the time I get into your *arms*'.[49] Throughout her life Priscilla referred in public to 'McLaren' rather than by his first name. Formality of the age apart, she confessed to a friend soon after their marriage that she did not like the name Duncan: 'In the presence of others I adhere to "McLaren" or "my dear" as best suited to his serious judge-like demeanour.'[50] She suffered from ill health early in the marriage, and her husband, no doubt mindful of the fate of his two previous wives, was solicitous and even interfering. Their first child, Charles, was born in May 1850. Two others, Helen and Walter, arrived in 1851 and 1853. For the first half of 1849, however, she was poorly and went to the Hydro at Ben Rhydding near Ilkley, which had been recommended to McLaren by John Benjamin Smith two years previously. In May she was back in Edinburgh and feeling better, with less pain. William Renton called and kept asking 'innocently' what ailed her.[51] Bearing in mind the reticence of the time and social class, one wonders if Renton's innocent query was to a pregnant woman. If so, there must have been a miscarriage. Certainly, Priscilla was to suffer one in 1856. Writing to her at the Hydro McLaren expressed his concerns, not least about her taking long walks and rides on a donkey. He had no confidence in water cures (though he himself was frequently to visit Ben Rhydding where, as Smith said, 'you generally meet with some agreeable people').[52] Nor did McLaren trust Dr Macleod, the medical director at the Hydro. Still, he was 'quite willing that you should think for yourself and judge for yourself'. He would think no less of her or be less kind if she returned an invalid. But he added: 'If you had not married me perhaps you might not have had this illness.' He thought she might be having doubts and fears, but he assured her that if they had not become married he would have continued to want to be so.[53]

In November 1849 McLaren again took issue with Priscilla's medical treatment.[54] 'The fact is that I cannot write on the subject without feeling a tendency to lose my temper. It is a sore subject with me, for I think you have not been properly treated, but feeling a tendency to go too far will say no more.' He turned to the question of the stepchildren, reassuring her of their affection. 'I am not at all surprised at their loving you so warmly. You know I *always* told you it would be so ... I never saw one of their letters to you. They all have the liberty to write when they like and what they like and they get no tutoring or inspection; and my belief is that they don't copy the letters they send you but give them just as written off hand.' Duncan, he reported, was down in his class to about 10 but Catherine was still up. 'I find Agnes had most dux medals of any girl in the class. She had 11 and the next highest was 7. I agree cordially in all you say about high places in the classes. I don't care about it at all. I said to Duncan a few days ago in the presence of the others that I didn't desire him to be very clever if he were only very good. And that is my heartfelt desire respecting them all.' This tolerance did not extend to handwriting. He complained several times about the illegibility of John's hand. But for anyone having to read McLaren's own letters, that is a case of the pot calling the kettle black. Priscilla took her role as stepmother seriously, corresponding with the children regularly when she or they were away from home. Early in 1849 she tried to sort out Agnes's problem of fitting in music practice with her other studies. 'Papa would like you all three to play nicely,' she wrote, 'and it is worth making the effort a little longer to please him.'[55] If that concern still strikes a chord with parents, two other worries can probably be disregarded today. She warned Agnes and Catherine not to read novels because 'both Papa and I disapprove.'[56] Grant's problem, however, could not be addressed by admonition alone. The 15 year old, in a long letter to Priscilla, expressed Calvinist fears for her soul because she was not one of the elect. Priscilla told her husband that it was difficult to reassure the girl because Quaker beliefs and his Presbyterianism did not accord on the matter.[57]

7. Lord Provost and failed MP

'The electors of the second Municipal Ward, in consequence of my known hostility to the Annuity-tax, having in June last, without my knowledge or consent, unanimously elected me a member of the Town Council, while I was in attendance on the Select Committee of the House of Commons for the purpose of giving evidence respecting the injustice of that tax, and the necessity of its immediate repeal, I have taken the liberty of dedicating this reprint of my Evidence, that they may have an opportunity of judging the manner in which the trust committed to me was discharged.' That clunking sentence signals McLaren's return to elected politics in 1851.

After a lull during the excitements of the Disruption and the founding of the Free Church, resentment against the annuity tax and the way it was imposed grew again in the late 1840s. There were numerous poindings of non-payers and some imprisonments, notably that of Bailie J.H. Stott, a McLaren follower. The decline in the number of churchgoers belonging to the Established Church added to the anomaly of supporting the clergy of one denomination alone. Concern in Parliament in 1849 led Lord John Russell to dispatch John Shaw-Lefevre, a Board of Trade official, to investigate on the ground. He met the council and the Anti-Annuity Tax League, which had been set up to coordinate resistance. His report proposed a new way of paying the Established Church ministers through a parliamentary annuity, but with their numbers and salaries reduced. Shaw-Lefevre, who was also retained at this period to look into Scottish fisheries and the management of Scottish art, remained concerned at the continuing action against non-payers of the annuity tax which he feared was a cause 'of dissention [sic], if not of serious disturbance'; he came up with a revised system of payment through a municipal tax from which the city's lawyers would not be excluded. The House of Commons created a select committee, to which 23 witnesses (including the Provost of

Montrose, the only other town with an annuity tax) gave evidence. McLaren was a witness but without the standing of a councillor. It became clear, however, that his erudite researches in the history of the tax and his forensic skills were crucial if MPs were to act as well as to listen. It was clear, too, that the city's MPs, though well intentioned, did not have much clout. Charles Cowan in particular was a lightweight.

So the reason for the rare unanimity of a council initiative to re-embrace McLaren is obvious: he commanded attention. Opponents of the annuity tax went far beyond his Voluntary supporters. The need of a credible spokesman in pushing for parliamentary intervention outweighed personal feelings. But what would his role be? His supporters declared that he must become Lord Provost after the autumn elections. The contest in the wards turned on whether candidates would support or oppose him. He claimed to Combe that he was reluctant to stand having 'become such a recluse in my domestic habits' but Priscilla's 'patriotism' had helped him decide, for 'she hopes that I may be able to assist the cause of liberal principles more in a public than in a private situation' although her private situation would suffer, and indeed she was ill when he wrote the letter from London.[2]

The select committee's hearings showed him in a good light. He argued that a reduction in the number of ministers receiving payment would satisfy him and the citizens. That could be achieved by removing the clause in the 1809 Act which had allowed magistrates to levy for 18 ministers instead of the earlier 6.[3] He would even settle for 9 and not trouble Parliament again. The spirit of compromise was too much for one member of the select committee, John Benjamin Smith, MP for Stirling and McLaren's ally and correspondent. Surely even a reduced level of public funding for the Established Church was an affront to Voluntary principles, he suggested. McLaren stood his ground. The money could be found from the Crown's acquisition of the ancient bishops' teinds, £200,000 of which supported Scottish parishes, although none in Edinburgh. The money would not be a tax on the people. Sir William Gibson-Craig, whose support for ending the annuity tax McLaren commended, gave him the opportunity for a passage of rhetoric that resonated with the wider Edinburgh public. What about the exemption of lawyers from payment, Gibson-Craig asked. McLaren replied:

> In Edinburgh the aristocracy are the lawyers. They occupy the highest-rented houses, and they are exempted; they are the parties who chiefly remain in the Established Church. The poor, and what we call the shopocracy, have almost all left the Church. The effect

therefore is, that the annuity tax is levied in Edinburgh on the poor for the support of an establishment for the rich. The poor man living in a £20 house, and paying £20 a year for the rent of his shop (take the case of a grocer, or a shoemaker, or a spirit dealer), has to pay annuity tax on his house and his shop; and in fact on everything that he has, in order that the rich gentlemen may receive the benefit of religious instruction from the Established Church at his expense.

It is little wonder that McLaren easily topped the poll in the Second Ward with its preponderance of small businessmen whose plight he had depicted. His pledge that as Lord Provost he would make abolition of the annuity tax his priority brought in councillors pledged to him. Whether there was still a recognised alliance between Voluntary supporters and the Free Church is debatable but many Free Churchmen realised that McLaren was best qualified to lead the council. His nomination was opposed by Tories who wanted Thomas Grainger, distinguished as a railway engineer but untested as a politician. James Aytoun, that rare bird a Radical advocate, said he could no more vote for Grainger as Provost than he would ask McLaren to make a railroad from Edinburgh to Queensferry.[4] McLaren defeated Grainger by 20 votes to 10, and the defeated candidate, resigning from the council, was dead within a year from injuries in a rail accident at Stockton. McLaren said it was natural for Free Churchmen to have supported him since they were no more for a Church Establishment than the Voluntaries (which was a distortion of Free Church thought). Grainger, he added, had had the support of the Established Church to a large extent, plus the Parliament House/Whig interest. But 'we are met here for secular business, and if the annuity tax were settled, I hope never to hear the words Churchman, Free Churchman, or Dissenter, mentioned at this board'.[5] *The Scotsman* grudgingly recognised the Lord Provost's abilities: 'To get a good Provost in Mr McLaren, there is a call upon us to return a bad council', full of Voluntaries, Free Church bigots and Tories, all the paper's enemies.[6]

The select committee had suggested a municipal tax to replace the annuity tax and pay for 15 ministers at a fixed £600 stipend. A Bill was brought forward with town council support to set such a tax at 3.5 per cent, well below the level of annuity tax and chargeable on lawyers. In March 1852 McLaren went to London to lobby for it. His report to councillors was pessimistic. The Bill had had its second reading and Gibson-Craig was trying to take it further, but the new Tory Government led by Lord Derby was against it. Not that the Tories alone dragged their feet: a Bill in the previous session had been turned away by the Whig Home Secretary because it was not supported by everyone in Edinburgh. Another parliamentary issue engaged the Lord Provost's interest. Growing agitation for voting reform led to a Scottish Bill tabled by the Lord Advocate in February 1852, although it too fell prey to the departure from office of Lord John Russell, a proponent of moderate change. In Edinburgh the council, Chamber of Commerce and Merchant Company met to arrange a public meeting to promote reform. McLaren favoured a wider franchise, perhaps encompassing £5 ratepayers but with the ballot a necessity. Unless there was the secrecy of a ballot, he would prefer the £10 franchise to a £5 one.

A General Election was now imminent. Gibson-Craig sent a letter to Andrew Rutherfurd on 10 April: 'It is *quite clear* that keeping my retirement secret was a most politic course, and our best means of defeating Duncan MacLaren's [sic] intrigues.' Since his father's death in 1850 Sir William, as he had become, bore responsibility for the estate and family at Riccarton. He had served as a junior minister but was not an ambitious or career politician. He was keen to ensure a safe succession, and McLaren was a threat, not necessarily as a candidate but as leader of the Radical and Voluntary Liberal grouping. Sir William Johnston, influential on the Free Church side, had thought of putting himself forward, Gibson-Craig claimed, but had decided not to because of adverse reaction to his proposal for a fixed duty on corn, an impossible stance for a free-trade electorate. Gibson-Craig told Rutherfurd that Charles Cowan would be thrown over. So two amenable candidates were needed. Lord Provost McLaren chaired a public meeting in April to thank Gibson-Craig for his services as MP. Behind the scenes debate about the city's future representation was underway. Since McLaren eventually contested the seat and lost and since the previous alliance between Free Churchmen and Voluntaries was sundered, he bore most of the animus for what was an unpleasant episode. But the evidence does not place the blame at McLaren's door. Until it became clear that agreement among Whigs and representatives of the Free Church and Voluntary factions was impossible, McLaren tried to find common ground. Immediately after Gibson-Craig announced his retirement McLaren called a meeting of electors. Both sections of the Liberal party wanted a period of deliberation, not precipitate nominations. It is convenient to refer to the Whig committee by the name given to it at the time – the Aggregate Committee. Those who split off (Free Churchmen and Voluntaries) at the time of Sir Culling Eardley Smith and Cowan in 1846–7 formed the Independent committee, and McLaren claimed that its Free Church leaders had sought him as a future candidate. The hope now was for an agreed Liberal candidate, and seven representatives of each committee were nominated to discuss names. Since the retiring MP was a Whig, there was a presumption that his successor would be from that side of the party. In strongly Liberal urban constituencies with two members, a Whig and a Radical were commonplace at this period. Various names were mentioned, but at a joint meeting of the two committees on 4 May, with the Lord Provost in the chair, people were reluctant to speak, rather to McLaren's embarrassment since he knew that some members of the Independent committee wanted him to declare his hand. A week later there seemed to be agreement that Edward Bouverie should be approached. He fitted the bill as a regular Whig – he was Episcopalian, second son of the Earl of Radnor, a Harrovian, Cambridge lawyer, landowner and former junior minister. But he was MP for Kilmarnock and why should he move?

The Independent committee was unhappy with Bouverie because he was unsound on Maynooth, i.e. he would not fight against the grant. Combe, who as convener of the sub-committee representing the two sides of the party was striving to broker an agreement, tried another noble-born compromise candidate, Lord Melgund, heir to the earldom of Minto and as MP for Greenock twice promoter of a Bill for national education. He was sound on Maynooth, but that was not proving enough to protect his seat from a Free Church/Voluntary challenge, and he wanted to move.[8] He said he would not stand against McLaren, and McLaren made clear he would not stand against Melgund. From Lord Dunfermline's seat at Colinton Castle, his son Ralph wrote on 11 June to put Melgund in the picture: 'The great object of hatred to Gibson Craig, Lord Panmure and Rutherford [sic], and all that faction is the Provost, and I believe that there are very few lengths to which they would not go to thwart and oppose him. Party feelings, and personal jealousies run so high just now, they have rendered all union impossible and the consequences have been that the Provost, who I sincerely believe was not desirous of coming forward as a candidate, has been driven to enter the field irrespective of all other parties.' Abercromby concluded that whatever McLaren's faults, he had 'acted frankly and honestly'.[9] Melgund drew back and put his name forward for a Glasgow seat but withdrew before the poll. By now Macaulay, the defeated statesman of 1847, was being wooed by the Whigs, some of whom still hoped to bring in Melgund as well and win both seats.

Meanwhile the Independent committee was splitting irrevocably. In so far as blame can be attached to McLaren, it was his general reputation with Free Churchmen that caused a problem, and not his actions at the time. Some members of the Independent committee had wanted his name substituted for Bouverie's. McLaren made it clear he would not stand if Bouverie was in the field since the MP held the same opinions as he did on free trade and parliamentary reform. To Combe he disclaimed any ambition, and to John Benjamin Smith he wrote: 'I really cannot afford it [life as an MP]. No consideration would induce me to live in London apart from my family; and according to my calculation I could not get a furnished house in London suitable for us and pay the additional expense of being here and of moving the family and servants up and down under £500 extra for the six months, over and above whatever expenses would be in Edinburgh.'[10] In focusing on McLaren's politics, it is easy to overlook his responsibilities for a large and expanding family.

Meanwhile the Free Church Liberals were seizing the initiative. Their spokesman, Sir William Johnston, McLaren's predecessor as Lord Provost and an engraver who founded the map-makers W. and A.K. Johnston, let it be known that he could not support any candidate in favour of the ballot and triennial parliaments. That was a hit at McLaren (as well as Bouverie). It exposed the instability of the alliance between the Free Churchmen and Voluntaries. Whereas most Voluntaries favoured parliamentary reform as well as disengagement between religion and the State, the Free Church was not politically Radical. In the Independent committee its representatives looked for a candidate hostile to the Maynooth grant. That was acceptable cover for an animus towards Roman Catholicism not shared by most Voluntaries, who were against Government support for Maynooth and other religious institutions of whatever denomination. Being anti-Maynooth had succoured the alliance that got the Free Churchman Cowan elected in 1847. It was not enough to paper over the cracks in 1852. Lord John Russell's Government had acted against what it regarded as 'papal aggression' through the creation of Roman Catholic episcopal sees in England. Encouraging the spasm of anti-Catholicism throughout Britain was not Liberal, but it appealed to the Free Church in Scotland. McLaren was more tolerant. In 1850 he had refused to take part in a meeting of the Edinburgh Anti-State Church Association, the successor to the Scottish Council of Dissenters, because in reality it was called to condemn 'Popery, and almost nothing but Popery'. Now in the election campaign, as *The Scotsman* pointed out, the attempt in the Independent committee to find a candidate acceptable to both sectarian groups was absurd since the position of Voluntaries was not that of the Free Church which continued to believe in a religious Establishment. With Whiggish distaste the paper pronounced, 'A candidate's qualifications are made to consist, not in holding this or that set of political opinions, but in "sitting under" the Rev Mr This or the Rev Dr That.'[11]

McLaren was asked at an Independent committee meeting what his position would be if Bouverie declined nomination – as he was shortly to do. 'Sufficient for the day is the evil thereof' was the enigmatic reply, one he liked to use when asked a tricky hypothetical question. For the Free Church section there was no more delay. At the beginning of June they named a candidate of their own, Alexander Campbell of Monzie, who was a strange choice in that he was a former Tory MP for Argyll, but he held the required religious opinions. So when the Independent committee next met, it heard a letter from Johnston saying that his 'section' could no longer remain members. A significant majority of those remaining wanted to requisition McLaren. At this point the Whigs still had no nominee. The Free Churchmen believed both seats could be theirs – with Cowan and Campbell.

On 12 June 1852 *The Scotsman* carried an advertisement in the form of a letter from McLaren accepting nomination and saying that the Independent committee's views reflected those of ward meetings. He hoped for 'a large majority of the whole Liberal electors'. There was also a news report that the Aggregate Committee had nominated Macaulay. That was a coup led by Adam Black who had been so upset by the defeat of 1847. Black told a crowded public meeting that Edinburgh should make up for its mistake by restoring to 'the British Senate one of its brightest ornaments'. He added: 'If Mr Macaulay has a fault, it is that he is too straightforward; too open; that he uses no ambiguities to disarm opposition. By many his early, his eloquent, his constant, his consistent advocacy of civil liberty is forgotten, while a few unconsidered words are harped upon.'[12] 'Unconsidered words' on the Maynooth grant may have contributed to his defeat in 1847. The question is whether the issue still swayed many votes. That it would come up in the campaign was inevitable. To his sister Macaulay wrote that Edinburgh was Maynooth-mad. If elected he would remain unpledged although everyone knew that he was in favour of the Maynooth endowment.[13] He insisted on remaining away from the campaign, relying on his Whig supporters to canvass for him. To be elected without appearing would be 'a high and peculiar honour', he told Black, who was concerned two weeks before the poll that Cowan and McLaren were campaigning actively and making play with Macaulay's polite refusal to answer the Scottish Reformation Society's request for a pledge to oppose Maynooth.

The Whigs had wrongfooted both sides of the severed Independent committee. Macaulay was bound to be elected. For Whig voters he was a more than adequate replacement for Gibson-Craig. For waverers the memory of the embarrassment caused to the city's reputation in 1847 meant that one of their two votes was likely to go to Macaulay. The Free Church lobby no longer had any hope of returning two MPs, although they hoped that by having Campbell in the field as well as Cowan they could prevent Free Churchmen from giving a vote to McLaren. On 16 June McLaren published a letter to electors that touched on all the usual Radical causes. He also stated opposition to the Maynooth grant but only because all such grants to religious bodies should be opposed. Notwithstanding this Radical and Voluntary platform McLaren believed that he and Macaulay could seek votes in tandem. The hope was illusory. The heart of Macaulay support – the legal profession, which formed a significant chunk of the electorate – was ill disposed to McLaren. Inevitably the contest for the second seat became one between Cowan and McLaren. Campbell was an outsider in all senses of the term. So was the final candidate, Thomas Bruce, representing the Tories, whose second vote, however, might be important.

McLaren has been blamed for splitting the Independent Liberal alliance, but that is true only if he and his Voluntary supporters were expected by the Free Churchmen to be passive partners. He wrote to Melgund on 19 June that 'The intolerance of the Free Church leaders and their hostility to me is very great. They know that I have a will of my own and will not be an instrument in their hands for any purpose whatever.'[14] Animosity between him and Sir William Johnston went back a long way. They had published recriminatory pamphlets about each other's conduct in the 1840 election for Lord Provost. They now had new accusations to exchange. In his adoption speech McLaren had suggested that Johnston was backing the candidature of the former Lord Advocate James Moncreiff in Leith although Moncreiff was in favour of the Maynooth grant. On the Edinburgh side of Pilrig Street, the boundary between the two constituencies, Johnston and other leaders of the breakaway committee were against Maynooth. Johnston in a paid-for letter on the front page of *The Scotsman* of 16 July vehemently rebutted the charge. The spat would probably have been forgotten after the election if Johnston had not included a description of McLaren that was to lead to a court action four years later and to colour his reputation ever since. McLaren's speech had been 'a miserably shuffling address' containing 'false and slanderous statements' and 'gross untruths'. Johnston had been told that McLaren was a dangerous person but had not expected practical demonstration of that. 'I hope my fellow-citizens may learn something from this little incident, and take care that they, too, do not take into their bosom the cold little snake that may turn round and bite them as soon as it gets warm enough.' Hard words even by the standards of abuse in electioneering at the time, but rendered more offensive in that they were uttered by a former Lord Provost against his successor. McLaren's opponents seized on the 'snake'. At one of Campbell's meetings there were three cheers for him and three groans proposed for the snake. Among the cheaply printed squibs that mocked or praised candidates in execrable verse was one with a song to the tune 'The Mistletoe Bough' which defended Johnston and had as its chorus, 'Oh, the cold little snake, Oh, the cold little snake'. Posters went up questioning the character of 'snake the draper'. He was accused of betraying Macaulay in 1847 and Cowan now. He had allegedly made money out of the Exchange Bank and had destroyed the oyster beds of the Forth estuary (a town council issue going back to the 1830s). He was even accused of bankrupting the city.[15] McLaren's supporters struck a confident note:

> Maclaren [sic] we'll gi' ye a
> blaw, blaw, blaw!
> Your [sic] the best o' the five after a'
> You're as sure o' your seat,
> As there's wit in your pate,
> And that the week comin' will
> shaw, shaw, shaw!

The fact that McLaren's first hope was of allying his fortunes to those of Macaulay and not Cowan shows the depth of the split in non-Whig Liberal ranks. Later in the campaign he asked his supporters to 'plump', that is to use only one of their votes. His calculations showed that the destination of second votes would determine the outcome. With Macaulay a likely winner, 'the strain of the contest will lie between the Lord Provost and Mr Cowan', as the *Caledonian Mercury* put it.[16] McLaren did not want anti-Whig Liberals to give a vote each to the leading Free Church candidate and to a Voluntary, since that would hand the second seat to Cowan, but he also did not want to alienate Cowan's supporters who might give him their second vote. *The Scotsman* was committed to Macaulay but recognised that McLaren was an abler candidate than Cowan – and less of an intolerant sectarian. McLaren did not short-change his supporters when it came to policy statements: his first campaign speech lasted two hours. He repeated throughout the campaign that he was not 'a political Voluntary', but only a religious one. Therefore those who had broken with the Independent committee because they could not support a Voluntary were misguided. The problem was that some Free Churchmen who might have accepted the distinction were put off by McLaren's political Radicalism. Some electors also no doubt questioned why he was so anxious to move on from the Provostship having just won it. He made reference to his work on the annuity tax but he might have emphasised that the fate of the tax rested with Parliament and as an MP he would be a more convincing advocate of its abolition than the distant Macaulay or the ineffectual Cowan. He wrote to Combe that with these two representatives city business in general would be neglected: 'Neither of them can do it for want of knowledge and Cowan for want of talent.'[17] John McLaren also had a poor opinion of Cowan. He told his father he would rather have Macaulay than 'such an entirely respectable and commonplace individual as Mr Cowan'.[18]

Polling took place on 13 July. There were 4,700 on the electoral register. According to one estimate at the time, 1,500 were 'old Whigs', 1,200 Free Church, 1,200 Dissenters and 800 Conservatives.[19] At Edinburgh Academy the pupils assembled behind the railings and roundly hissed a passing cab placarded 'The Lord Provost's Committee'.[20] The well-to-do New Town with its boys at the Academy was not McLaren's strong area. It was Tory territory, and although Bruce had no hope of winning, his supporters helped to determine the outcome. McLaren accused them of uniting to give their second vote to Cowan to keep him out. He also alleged that some Tories were told not to vote until late in the day when the state of the poll could be assessed. They were then instructed to go and plump for Cowan, safe in the knowledge that Macaulay (their natural second choice after Bruce) was home and dry. Public voting not only meant that everyone's choice was on show but that excitement was whipped up – and tactics were deployed during the day to affect the result. When the poll closed at 4 p.m., the figures were: Macaulay 1,872, Cowan 1,754, McLaren 1,559, Bruce 1,066, Campbell 626. McLaren's aim in defeat was to show that among Liberals he had a majority; Cowan had depended on Tories. As for Macaulay's votes, many were second choices by McLaren's men: 'A few of his friends, no doubt, gave votes to us; but we gave them in hundreds, and we got them in tens.' The alliance that McLaren had tried to create worked only in that his Liberals were willing to vote Whig as well, and not the other way round. Addressing his committee in South Bridge, the defeated candidate said: 'One influential party – I mean the Parliament-House Whig party, gave us their undivided opposition, except in two or three cases. Then we have had the hostility of the Free Church, including all their influential men. Many gentlemen connected with that Church, who were not subject to their influence, did me the honour of giving me their vote, but, speaking on the gross, the great bulk of the Free Church party did all they could against me, and with an envenomed bitterness which has not been exampled in any contest which has taken place in the city of Edinburgh.'[21]

Priscilla told her sister that McLaren was unfazed by defeat – and she was delighted at not having to go to London. People were surprised when he arrived with 'a happy face the day afterwards at Holyrood Palace, to see the election of Scottish peers'.[22] Two weeks later McLaren's committee published in full the poll-books, which caused offence to individuals (since their votes were there for all to see) and which, according to *The Scotsman*, was unprecedented in Scotland. The paper saw no value in the action, but it has allowed historians to make detailed analysis of who voted for each candidate and from which social groups they drew their support.[23] McLaren was defeated because he was not strong enough in any of the pairings of candidates. Like the Tory Bruce he did well among the minority of voters who plumped for a single candidate. But his hope that Macaulay's supporters would give him their second vote largely failed. True, Macaulay/McLaren was narrowly the most popular of any combination but it was not enough to bridge the 195-vote gap between Cowan and McLaren. Cowan did rely on Tory voters, as McLaren alleged, and so the latter's claim to be the choice of most Liberals has validity. Little can be divined of religious preference. McLaren must have won his own Voluntary constituency, but his level of success with a chunk of Macaulay's supporters was founded on non-sectarian grounds. The two Free Church candidates, Cowan and Campbell, did help each other, but Campbell received so few 'first' votes that Cowan's success cannot have depended on Campbell's adherents playing the Free Church card. A main conclusion from the 1852 result in Edinburgh is that although sectarian loyalties were meat and drink to contemporary political commentators, they did not determine the outcome of the election. The falling out between Free Churchmen and Voluntaries meant that they no longer worked in combination against the city's Whigs, whose re-established authority was not seriously challenged for more than another decade. But when men cast their individual votes, denominationalism was not their priority.

So what was? It was their occupation. Not their class as understood by Marxists since political loyalty based on consciousness of class was not yet a meaningful concept. Edinburgh, a city of professional men and small businesses, was not likely to be in the forefront of that development. The electorate intentionally excluded those who in the view of the age were without a stake in society. The three largest occupational groups defined in the pollbook were 'distribution and processing', 'craft' and the 'legal profession'. The political loyalty of occupation groups explains the election outcome in a way that religion does not. The three main occupation groups cast almost half of the votes. There were only five votes by policemen and two by railwaymen. Those calling themselves 'merchants', and the grocers and shoemakers polled strongly for McLaren, but Macaulay and Cowan also appealed to them. McLaren's glaring weakness was among lawyers who because of the narrow scope of the franchise had a numerical influence far beyond that in any modern constituency. Macaulay, Cowan and Bruce all scored well; McLaren had hardly any votes. The Lord Provost's long campaign against lawyers' exemption from the annuity tax and his colourful attacks on the Parliament House Whigs cost him election to Parliament. Six months before the election Priscilla McLaren had written to her stepson John that they had had an invitation to dinner from the Lord Advocate and commented, 'The Whigs must like his independence'. She was wrong.[24]

McLaren had said he would resign as Lord Provost if elected to Parliament. He now embarked on the remaining two and a half years as first citizen with undiminished energy. The annuity legislation remained a prime concern and his prediction was fulfilled that Macaulay and Cowan were unable to exercise enough pressure on either the Tory Government that continued after the election or the Peelite/Whig administration under Lord Aberdeen that took over in December 1852. The Lord Provost led a delegation that was cordially received by Aberdeen, a Scots peer with a long history of seeking to resolve the disputes of his native land. McLaren said that there was no need to convince ministers because they were convinced already of the iniquities of the tax. He wanted them to act. The Lord Advocate, James Moncreiff, took charge of a Bill along the lines of that in the previous Whig Government, and McLaren spoke in its favour at a public meeting in the Queen Street Hall in July 1853. Ministers, however, listened to opposition not only from representatives of the Established Church but also from some clergymen hostile to the vestige of state support for religion provided for in this Bill as in its predecessors. They allowed it to be talked out in the Commons. *The Scotsman* attacked McLaren for not working hard enough to convince MPs, but he responded in the council that backbench lobbying had not been the deputation's job. He unburdened himself to Combe on the pressures of promoting the city's interests: 'I am great slave, and feel like a person hurrying forward on a rapid journey with only time sufficient to glance at passing objects.'[25]

The office of Lord Provost was dignified, its holder always addressed as 'your Lordship'. But its three-year term was much more burdensome and time-consuming than being an MP in a Parliament that sat for just over half the year. McLaren chaired the weekly meetings of the council and the Lord Provost's committee to which much detailed business was referred. He chaired the Police Commission, which oversaw sanitary and public health matters, and he chaired Heriot's Hospital and an endless procession of public meetings and dinners. His name led subscription lists for good causes and he was the recipient of notices from the Home Secretary when a prisoner in Edinburgh appealed against execution. He told Priscilla: 'Today's post brought me, from Lord Palmerston, a respite for the man now under sentence of death. It was addressed to me *inside* but to the keeper of the prison *outside* of the letter so that he got it first and communicated its contents to the poor man before I got the letter from him. The sentence of death is always addressed to me – that is the Lord Provost and Magistrates are required by the terms of the sentence to causing it with effect and hence the respite becomes the warrant for *not* executing the sentence.'[26] In 1854 the town council unanimously passed a motion against executions in public. McLaren said the last one had cost £75.[27]

Sir James Marwick was a council official during McLaren's Provostship and later became town clerk. He objected to McLaren claiming authority to rewrite the council minutes, and they later clashed over who should print a reference work about a parliamentary Bill in which Edinburgh had an interest. McLaren, by now ex-Lord Provost, wanted the job to go to a printer whose family were political supporters. Marwick set off to McLaren's home to tell him that such interference in an administrative decision was intolerable. McLaren 'was a good deal disconcerted and asked if I had not employed another printer. "That," I said, "you must allow me to tell you is a matter with which you have nothing to do. I am responsible to the town council and the community for having the work properly done, and I cannot allow you or any other citizen to interfere."' Marwick's memoir adds that he had later evidence that McLaren did not think the less of him for asserting himself.[28] Not that city officials were allowed to ride roughshod. The police surgeon paid the price for insubordination over an issue dear to the Lord Provost's heart: drainage in the city. The Police Commission, which McLaren chaired, had powers over drains that were extended by a Police Bill brought to Parliament and enthusiastically supported by McLaren and the council. A delegation was sent to ensure that MPs backed the measure. It included McLaren and the police surgeon Glover, who not only stayed on in London for ten days after his work was done but behind the scenes was lobbying against the Bill on behalf of some landowners concerned about drains across their land. Glover was dismissed.[29] The police itself encountered the Lord Provost's wrath just before his term of office ended. The superintendent of the force, Thomas Linton, responded to a request by the sheriff to send some of his men to help quell a riot in Kelso over a toll-bar on a bridge. McLaren and the council challenged the right of a sheriff to call out the police, who were responsible to the magistrates.[30] Here was another case of lawyers disregarding local government. Episcopal authority did not count for much either. In 1854 a stretch of city wall beside the railway at Leith Wynd fell down, and because it adjoined a school run by the Episcopal Church Bishop Terrot asked the council to fund the repair. As recounted over 30 years later in Mackie's biography, McLaren refused to pay heed to a clergyman claiming superior rank. The incident was not highlighted at the time by a press ready to pounce McLaren's failings, and it seems harsh to regard it as a case of Presbyterian intolerance.[31]

No one can have been surprised that McLaren was an interventionist Lord Provost. His achievements were significant in the city's development. He reduced the number of toll-bars as an inhibition on trade and a discouragement to the feuing of land beyond the bars.[32] His plans to lay out the Meadows as a public park matured only after he left office, and it was his successor Sir James Melville whose name was given to the road through the middle. But McLaren's readiness to involve national figures in his campaigns paid off when he took a Cabinet Minister, Sir James Molesworth, the Chief Commissioner of Works, to see how much a connecting road was needed between the new Queen's Drive and Portobello by way of Duddingston. Molesworth agreed, their joint efforts succeeded and the Minister received the freedom of the city in 1854. McLaren's ultimate aim was for 'one of the finest drives in the kingdom' from the west end of Princes Street via the Meadows and Queen's Drive to Portobello. But the Crimean War became a deterrent to public investment and imperilled another of McLaren's plans – for an Industrial Museum. Following the success of the 1851 exhibition at the Crystal Palace there was a call for permanent showpieces across the country to encourage inventors and promote industrial design. McLaren led several deputations to London, which eventually secured a promise of nearly £8,000 from the new Chancellor of the Exchequer, William Gladstone, only for the grant to be struck from the estimates because of the war. Just before McLaren demitted office, the pressure he had put on Gladstone and the Prime Minister, Lord Aberdeen, paid off. A new building was planned which would incorporate the natural history museum of the university. The keeper of the museum, Robert Jameson, who was professor of natural history, disagreed with McLaren about the development but had to accept another of the Lord Provost's policies, that museums and gardens should be accessible as possible to ordinary citizens. The natural history museum would allow the working classes in on Thursdays, Jameson reluctantly informed McLaren.[33] Opening up West Princes Street Gardens took much longer. The proprietors, who were the shopkeepers, were reluctant to abandon privileged access, claiming a lack of legal power to make the change. Who would pay for the maintenance of good order? Surely no respectable female would frequent the gardens. McLaren was one of those who paid 2 or 3 guineas as a key-holder. More than 20 years were to pass before open access was secured, but as Lord Provost McLaren scored one victory thanks to representations from the Scottish Association for the Suppression of Drunkenness. The gardens would be opened on Christmas Day and New Year's Day 'with a view to keeping parties out of the dram shop'.[34]

Priscilla recorded that on New Year's Day Professor Jameson had to accede to free entry to his museum, which was visited by batches of 200:

> We drove to all the rational places of amusement – enjoyed seeing the troops of people pouring into them. Papa had managed to put a stop to the boys at Heriot's Hospital drinking the health of the founder on that day in *toddy*, and had an apple and an orange given to each boy instead, with which they seemed much pleased, but some of the governors were sadly annoyed at the improvement. We stood in the midst of the boys as they were assembled in the quadrangle to receive their bun – the head person among them whose name I forget, introduced the Provost to them, whereupon they gave several rounds of cheering and Papa gave them a nice little appropriate address ... I was much pleased as I like Papa's straightforwardness and good principles to be appreciated by the people.[35]

McLaren had to confront a conservation issue that still strikes a chord 150 years later. Proposals to facilitate economic development clashed with the protection of historic heritage in a row over Trinity College Church which began before McLaren became Lord Provost and continued long after he demitted office – in fact up to the present day. The fifteenth-century church, founded in memory of James II and associated with a hospital charity, was described in one of McLaren's pamphlets on the subject as 'the finest specimen of Gothic architecture in Edinburgh'[36], but it sat where the North British Railway was building Waverley Station. Environmental protection was becoming an issue: Lord Cockburn led a famous campaign to prevent building on the south side of Princes Street. In 1844 the town council unanimously agreed to dispose of the church to the railway company, which would provide another church somewhere else. Debate then broke out about whether the former building should be rebuilt stone by historic stone. In 1848 the railway agreed to pay the council a sum of money which the council could spend on a church, possibly on Calton Hill. Two years later the ever helpful Lefevre suggested postponing any rebuild and using the money to help with ministers' stipends, thus easing a solution to the annuity tax. But the parliamentary select committee that considered Lefevre's report wanted the town council to set aside £10,000 of the railway money for a church, though not specifically a copy of the demolished building. Bills came forward in Parliament but no progress was made and McLaren was under pressure from the conservationists to rebuild Trinity on an unspecified site; there were many suggestions, from Princes Street Gardens to the site of the Bank of Scotland headquarters on the Mound and a woodyard belong to a Mr Ireland. McLaren favoured a site in the High Street but, that having failed, could not secure a council majority for the woodyard. His principle was that any new church should be in a place suitable for the poor and not in the New Town where there were churches in plenty. Belying his reputation as a friend of hard-nosed Manchester utilitarianism, he wrote that the 'Goths and Vandals' who had encouraged, or at least allowed, the railway company to destroy Trinity Church were the town council and the presbyteries. 'There was no necessity for removing it; the ground was not required for the line of the railway or for the station, but merely for coal-depots, or something of that kind.' As Lord Provost he was accused of being a vandal by antiquarians and polite society, including Adam Black, for leaving the church unreconstructed, but among the people who did not write letters to newspapers, his arguments found favour. Only in the 1870s was a partial solution reached: parts of the old church were rebuilt in Chalmers Close off the High Street as Trinity Apse, and in the late twentieth century became a centre for brass-rubbing. McLaren was vindicated by a House of Lords judgment in 1864 that £10,000 should go to the fund for Trinity Hospital pensions rather than be spent on yet another city church.

Edinburgh society was divided again by McLaren's campaign against public drunkenness. He himself was neither a drinker nor a confirmed teetotaller like his mother. He imported Madeira wine after his time on the island. When he married a Quaker he married an abstainer but not a crusading one. As hostess to receptions when her husband was first citizen, she made alcohol available. In the letter about the withdrawing of New Year's toddy from Heriot's boys she described her role as provider of dinners for councillors: 'The first party among whom were the adverse ones, was apparently the most lively – they took the most wine, and were in my opinion the most gentlemanly set – not that I mean that wine drinking is a proof of gentlemanly nature. The second set were quiet but there was a cordial friendly feeling.' The Tory councillors, it seems, were the best party animals. According to Mackie McLaren did not drink at all for 12 years, including during his time as Lord Provost.[37] It was the effects of drinking on public order and family life that concerned him at this time, not the sin of letting alcohol pass one's lips. Drinking had been part of social and business life in Scotland from time immemorial, but by the early nineteenth century the problems it caused were changing the climate. A reduction in whisky duty in 1824 was followed by an increase in consumption and in the number of public houses; there were 733 of them in Edinburgh in 1833.[38]

McLaren's name is associated with the attempt to solve a social problem by increased regulation, first in Edinburgh and later across Scotland. But in Glasgow there were already regulations in force to keep pubs closed on Sundays, and the first restrictions in Edinburgh were put in place three years before he became Lord Provost. Licensees staying open after 11 p.m. were liable to a £5 penalty and loss of licence.[39] His initiative in 1852, as he explained 16 years later to the House of Commons, was to call a meeting of magistrates in Edinburgh and Midlothian to discuss intervention and then to pass regulations at a special licensing session. Where publicans were charged with offences contravening their licence, the fact that they stayed open on a Sunday was to be regarded as aggravating their offence. 'The change that took place was almost instantaneous ... I made it my business to walk through the lowest parts of the city on Sunday evenings, and I can say, as the result of personal experience so gained, that the effect was really startling.'[40] The support he gained went far beyond his own Voluntaries. Abstinence was most strongly backed by the Free Church. Temperance advocates like William Collins, the Glasgow publisher, had struggled to make progress for 20 years. McLaren struck a chord, and the pamphlets he published linked his name to a successful initiative.[41] In 1853 a Scottish-born MP, Forbes Mackenzie, introduced a Bill that allowed restriction of licences across Scotland along the lines of

McLaren's Sunday initiative in Edinburgh and the earlier one on 11 p.m. closing. Taken up by Lord Kinnaird in the Upper House, the law came into operation in 1854. A year later McLaren reflected on a year's experience of the Act, linked to his own work. Many publicans had lost their licence because they allowed Sunday drunkenness. 'In walking along the streets, as I have done during the last year, one can hardly believe that the quiet orderly groups whom we see are in any way connected with the crowds of disorderly persons who were formerly to be seen, quarrelling, fighting, swearing, using obscene language, and on too many occasions – under the influence of intoxicating liquor – behaving more like savages than Christians.'[42]

Not everyone was convinced by regulation and the accompanying rhetoric. The drinks trade was understandably hostile and many middle-class citizens of moderate opinions were sceptical. *The Scotsman* took issue with McLaren's claim that drunkenness had increased in the four years before he took action. The number of pubs had gone down from 854 to 511 in the same period, the paper said, and so the link between the number of pubs and drunkenness was questionable.[43] McLaren and the 'suppressors' had not curbed whisky drinking, only its public appearance. The Lord Provost also ran into a row over whether he was selling his city short. The *Edinburgh Evening Courant* said he had worked out that Edinburgh was more drunken than Glasgow, but that was a misreading of the statistics. 'We may be permitted to hope that when his inexorable virtue next aspires to the heroic height of volunteering judgment against his own city, he will take pains, in the first place, to see that the judgment is a righteous one.'[44] McLaren, as always, bridled at a slight on his arithmetic. The truth is that the figures for Edinburgh and Glasgow measured different things – in one case disorderliness through drink, and in the other just drunkenness.

As Lord Provost, McLaren played host to one figure of international repute – and missed the opportunity to meet another whose reputation was still growing. Harriet Beecher Stowe, author of *Uncle Tom's Cabin* and campaigner against American slavery, visited Edinburgh in May 1853 as part of a wider tour. McLaren's radicalism, like that of many Dissenters, had been fostered in the years when slavery was being outlawed in the British empire. Its continuance in a country whose democratic constitution they in other respects admired was an affront, and so Stowe's visit afforded the opportunity to laud her and affirm their own principles. At the Music Hall people of all political and religious affiliations gathered for a banquet. The 100th Psalm was sung, and McLaren in his speech took pride in the abolition of slavery from British colonies and called on Americans to, as they would say, 'go the whole hog' as well.[45] In 1853 the city also prepared to pay tribute to a rising political star. William Gladstone's free-trade Budget was warmly welcomed by the town council and its merchant members. They sent the Chancellor of the Exchequer a letter and followed it up with a decision to make him a freeman while he was travelling in Scotland. He was told in a letter sent to the Duke of Sutherland's seat at Dunrobin but by then he had gone south to the Duke of Buccleuch's at Drumlanrig in Dumfriesshire. The Chancellor expressed his thanks and wished his engagements could have allowed a visit to Edinburgh, but his letters to McLaren betray some bemusement at the arrangements. The Chancellor, who got his burgess ticket by post, was still a Tory, or at least a Peelite seeking to further the fiscal policies of his dead mentor. McLaren and the Liberal-dominated council expressed admiration for principle and policy and set aside party label.

The verdict on McLaren's Provostship as it ended in November 1854 was favourable.[46] The Tory *Edinburgh Evening Courant* stated that 'the throwing back of the toll-bars which impeded the traffic of the city, and the improvement of a drainage previously prejudicial to its health, were both measures inviting a host of petty and wearisome contests, quite sufficient to dismay any man not actuated by public spirit of a high order'. Extending public parks and opening buildings were other advances that would 'reflect honour upon Mr McLaren's name, long after the differences of mere opinion are forgotten.'[47]

8. *Arbiter and conciliator*

The good merchant councillors of Edinburgh may have been disconcerted when they received testimonials in Latin from professors in Germany supporting the candidacy of John Stuart Blackie for the university chair of Greek in 1852. But appointments to most professorships in the 'tounis college' fell to the 33 councillors and they took the task seriously. Controversy was regularly whipped up in the city as rival testimonials flooded from the printers. As Lord Provost, McLaren saw one controversial figure depart and another arrive. He sent a letter to John Wilson, better known as Christopher North, the poet, novelist and contributor to *Blackwood's Magazine*, when Wilson retired after holding the chair of moral philosophy and political economy for 32 years.[1] Wilson had been absent for several months through ill health and McLaren, in wishing him a happy retirement, noted the councillors' sensibility 'of the lustre which your name has shed on the university'. In truth, Wilson was an eloquent lecturer who mightily impressed young students but he was not a distinguished philosopher and he held his chair too long. Yet for those who think of Edinburgh descending at this time from Enlightenment to strait-laced religiosity, a description of Wilson by his friend William Maginn suggests that devil-may-care individuality was still appreciated: 'a sixteen-stoner who has tried it without the gloves with the game chicken, and got none the worse, a cocker, a racer, a sixbottler, a twenty-four tumblerer, and out and outer, a true, upright, knocking-down, poetical, prosaic, moral, professorial, hard-drinking, fierce-eating, good-looking, honourable, straightforward Tory ... A Gipsy, a magazine, a wit, a six-foot club man, an unflinching ultra in the worst of times! In what is he not great?'[2]

The second controversial figure was John Stuart Blackie, another extraordinary man. Was he right for the chair of Greek? He was professor of Latin in Marischal College, Aberdeen, and he had strong views about the poor grasp of the classics, especially Greek, among boys coming up to university. He wanted a benchmark test to avoid the professor having to deal with entrants who barely knew the Greek alphabet, and he was an admirer of the rigour of German Hellenists. But he defended the traditional Scottish curriculum rooted in philosophy and was increasingly an outspoken nationalist. The academic issues were debated in pamphlets by his supporters and those of the 18 other candidates for the chair. The councillors no doubt grappled with recondite arguments but they could be swayed by other considerations. Blackie sported eccentric garb complete with tartan plaid. There were doubts about his religious orthodoxy. When he sent out his first testimonials he forgot to pay for the postage. He called on the councillors individually and his exuberance was disconcerting, although he attributed his success to impressing their wives. His supporters instructed him not to come back to Edinburgh during the campaign.

In the wake of the Disruption professorial appointments had become embroiled in Church politics. By longstanding legislation designed to keep out Episcopalians candidates had to profess allegiance to the Church of Scotland, but that was now impossible for Free Churchmen, one of whom having been appointed to an Edinburgh chair had to wait several years for induction. As Lord Provost McLaren called a meeting at the request of the committee of inhabitants to object to the way in which the test was being applied in the post-Disruption squabbling between the Established and Free churches.[3] Only in 1853 did the Lord Advocate bring in a Bill substituting an innocuous statement that any professor could accept. The introduction of sectarian divisions into academic appointments was deplored but undoubtedly guided the preferences of councillors. As the historian of Edinburgh University puts it, 'electors to chairs often preferred a less qualified candidate of their own denomination to a better qualified candidate of another denomination.'[4] A leader like McLaren would be looked to for guidance by less confident councillors. He was experienced in contentious professorial elections; in 1836 he had helped the distinguished Sir William Hamilton secure the chair of logic. But when the field of candidates for the Greek chair in 1852 narrowed, McLaren's role became an issue. A first ballot removed candidates who did not receive a minimum vote, including the rectors of the Royal High School and Edinburgh Academy. There remained two contenders besides Blackie. The Rev. Charles MacDouall of Belfast had been rejected for the chair of Hebrew two years earlier having fallen foul of the Church of Scotland presbytery. He was now the favoured candidate of the Free Church. Dr William 'Dictionary' Smith from London was author of classical dictionaries and a Dissenter. McLaren was believed to favour him, which annoyed Blackie and his backers, who thought they had secured the Lord Provost's support. On the second ballot Smith was eliminated and there was a tie between Blackie and MacDouall. McLaren had the casting vote, which he gave to Blackie. It was a wise choice. Blackie's Greek scholarship was not always approved by the classicists of Oxford, and his claims that the Scottish pronunciation of Greek was more authentic than the English brought him ridicule. But for decades he was an instantly recognisable Edinburgh character who contributed richly to political debate, as a nationalist Tory, just as he did to arguments about the curriculum and governance of the universities. McLaren wrote to him in Aberdeen after the election result and followed with a letter saying that Blackie should make a formal response to the council without mentioning the casting vote.[5] They became friends. Blackie sent him the four volumes he had written to make Homer accessible to non-Hellenists. In 1866, at the height of the agitation for voting reform, McLaren wrote to Blackie that 'although we don't sail in the same boat as respects politics', he held the professor in high regard for moral courage and honesty of purpose. Blackie was opposed to reform and said so straightforwardly. McLaren added that his own son Charles would be joining Blackie's Greek class.[6]

Only months after Blackie's election the choice of a successor to John Wilson for the chair of moral philosophy turned out less successfully. McLaren supported the winning candidate, P.C. MacDougall, but MacDougall was an undistinguished nominee of the Free Church and was opposed by James Ferrier, well known as a writer on philosophy and successful holder of a chair at St Andrews. One of Ferrier's supporters was Sir William Hamilton, who fulminated: 'The Edinburgh academical patronage has reached the lowest level of subsidiation; religious parties now co-operate with secular corruption in seducing the incompetent elector to violate his duties.' Hamilton led an attempt to exclude the victor from the chair by invoking the religious test and so made a bad situation worse. Although the battle between MacDougall and Ferrier descended into one of sectarian allegiance, obscuring the gulf in academic merit between the candidates, McLaren from the council chair avoided being drawn on the reasons why fellow councillors might be irrelevantly influenced in the choice they were about to make. He said he had read all the testimonials for the candidates and made his own inquiries. When the vacancy had been first announced, he had suggested that councillors should not make open pledges and he had 'made it a point not to mix himself up with any of the candidates; and he therefore neither knew how any member of the council intended to vote, nor did any member of the council know how he intended to vote, until within the last few days'[8] He added that MacDougall appeared the best qualified even although his testimonials were very inflated in their encomiums. Ferrier's proposer also referred to the writers of testimonials and invoked Hamilton, the essayist Thomas de Quincey, the novelist Bulwer Lytton and several other household names. On merit it should have been no contest. But MacDougall won by 20 to 13; Ferrier was left in St Andrews embittered. McLaren's support for MacDougall, whom it was said the Free Church wanted to remove from the payroll of its college and put on the university's, shows that a month before the 1852 General Election the Free Church/Voluntary coalition still worked at council level although it was fracturing in parliamentary politics.

After decades of debates and inquiries the Scottish universities were reformed in 1858. In each was established a court to oversee finance and administration, with a general council of graduates to give a public voice. In time the structure of courses and degrees was modernised. Although the development of the universities was keenly debated then and since,[9] the 1858 Act, sponsored by the Tory Lord Advocate John Inglis, was controversial in only two aspects – a proposal to amalgamate Aberdeen's two colleges (King's and Marischal) in a single institution and the removal of the power of Edinburgh town council to appoint professors. McLaren, out of the council but with long experience of civic patronage, was outraged, especially since Inglis's first preference had been to retain the council's role. It was pressure from MPs that prompted a change of mind and the creation of a new body, the curators of patronage, with only a minority of councillors, to make appointments. McLaren was in favour of university reform but not of removing the rights of elected councillors. He lobbied the former Prime Minister, Lord Aberdeen, who expressed sympathy, but the will of the Commons prevailed.[10] Years later McLaren compared his experience of council patronage and that of the curators. He did not dispute that the curators were doing a good job; he served as one on behalf of the council. But he defended democratic participation. It was true that no single councillor was equipped to choose among professorial candidates, but 'a jury of 33 impannelled to try the cause' listened to the arguments and made sensible judgments. He singled out Blackie as evidence of a wise appointment in the face of doubts about the candidate's Presbyterian orthodoxy. He recalled that in the 1830s he had supported the choice of a Church of England clergyman as professor of mathematics (despite the statutory Presbyterian requirement) because he was the best-qualified candidate.[11]

Debating the rival merits of aspirant professors was as much a middle-class Scottish pastime as savouring the choice of bishops in Trollope's England. The condition of the nation's schools was of more deep-seated concern. The Church of Scotland, for so long the promoter and funder of education in the parishes, was faced with an intractable problem. Its education committee reported in 1850 that its funds were completely exhausted, and yet the Church was to block all attempts to create a national network of schools. The Free Church wanted State-led reform partly to scupper the Established Church and partly out of recognition that its own attempt to create a school system to match the existing one was financially crippling. The United Presbyterians shied away from creating a third faith-based network of schools and were opposed to state funding of religious instruction in schools – a difficult case to maintain when conventional opinion dictated that education instilled morality, which in turned flowed from religious understanding and practice. After the failure of Lord Melgund's Bills in 1850–1 the pressure intensified for legislation by the Government rather than through a private member. Parliament was due to review schoolmasters' salaries in 1853 – an exercise undertaken only every 25 years. The National Education Association led the agitation. George Combe, who devoted more of his latter years to educational reform than to phrenology, urged McLaren to take a lead as the capital's first citizen. In early 1852, just before the Whig Government lost office, he wrote to McLaren to say that the Lord Advocate was working on an education Bill, but if he did not bring it forward, Melgund would try again.[12] Would McLaren call a public meeting to put pressure on the Government? If not, Combe would take the lead. He was a religious sceptic unsympathetic to the claims of religious education. McLaren knew the need for a national school system and one where religious instruction had a place for those who wanted it. He wrote to Melgund in June 1852 that the schools should be managed by the people just as burgh affairs were managed by the people. 'I do not want the Bible and catechism to be made compulsory but the contrary. If the people wish them to be used, which I think would be the case, then I would desire a fraction of the quarterly school fee to be specifically charged for the religious instruction just as a fee is charged for Greek and Latin.'[13] There would be no hardship for parents who did not want religious instruction.

When James Moncreiff as Lord Advocate published the first of his education Bills in 1854, McLaren led the town council's approbation of its aims and principles.[14] He took issue with a Central Board which Moncreiff proposed to oversee the extended national framework of schools supported by State funds: it would have too many university professors and not enough representatives of the burghs responsible for so many of the schools, including new ones that were to be created. McLaren also pointed out that Edinburgh did not need more schools because there were enough already, thanks to the Heriot schools. The clause in the Bill providing for religious instruction was the most controversial. McLaren was criticised by *The Scotsman* for being too close to the 'secular' position – that is, like Combe, disputing the place of religious instruction in schools at all. He also faced opposition from some Voluntaryists because he accepted that increased State funding of teachers meant funding their teaching of religious instruction, which amounted to State support of religion and fundamentally objectionable to Voluntaryism. McLaren argued that Voluntaryists who were happy to send their children to Church of Scotland or Free Church schools should have the right, along with other parents, to opt for religious instruction taught by the master but paid apart from his state-supported salary.

In the event, although religious pressure killed not just the 1854 Bill but the Lord Advocate's subsequent attempts in 1855 and 1856, it was the Church of Scotland, protecting its own interests especially in the rural areas where many of the landowning heritors were its members, that persuaded first the Commons and then the Lords to block reform. Moncreiff was a leading Free Churchman and was accused of acting under pressure from his denomination whose 500 hard-pressed schools were, in the phrase of the *Daily News*, ready to 'roll over' in gratitude for the proposed new national levy for education. McLaren was concerned about parish schools in rural areas where one landowner was the dominating or even the sole heritor. A large and increasing number of these landowners were Episcopalians, he told the council. 'I have no objection to Episcopalians or the Episcopalian religion, but I have great objection to what is known as Puseyism, which I consider is next door to Roman Catholicism, and I should greatly dislike

if these heritors were to do what conscientiously they ought to do – namely, to appoint a man of sound religious opinion according to their views – in other words to appoint a Puseyite schoolmaster and an Episcopalian minister to form the committee. In that way the whole management of the school would be in his hands.'[15] The debates on Moncreiff's Bills showed that despite the widely accepted need for greater Government involvement in education, the curriculum to be taught was hardly addressed, except for religion. More schools and more teachers would have been provided but the problem of persuading parents in poorer communities to send their children and pay fees was sidestepped. There was much rhetoric about the age-old virtues of Scottish schooling and some concern about the influence of English and even Irish educational changes on Scotland, but the case for addressing the country's social needs was drowned out by the clamour of competing sectarians.

These sectarians were of course home-grown. The interest in education in the 1850s has been described in terms of national identity.[16] That is justified in only a limited sense. The distinctiveness of Scottish education had survived the Union of 1707 largely because education could not be separated from religion. Any reforms of the kind so badly needed by the 1850s had to be considered separately from changes advanced south of the border because of different histories and structure. As an issue national education would be affected by patriotic feeling only if there was a prospect of English solutions being promoted for Scottish problems, or if the will of Scottish reformers was thwarted by English votes. The former risk was not yet evident. It was discernible only from the 1860s and 1870s when English educational reform gathered pace. The second concern, of Scottish solutions being blocked, has more force. Scottish MPs voted for the succession of Bills in the 1850s, only to find themselves outnumbered by English and Irish members, or outmanoeuvred by parliamentary business managers unwilling to give time for Scottish legislation. However, non-Scots who were hostile or just lukewarm were not in the main activated by anti-Scottishness. The messages they picked up in the debates and from the lobbying that went on in Westminster and Whitehall were of a nation divided: the opponents of change were led by the Established Church. So did even the reasonableness of the Free Churchman Moncreiff deserve support, much less the clamour of radicals?

Far from embodying revived national sentiment, the reform of education was not central to the campaign launched at this time to address Scottish grievances. The National Association for the Vindication of Scottish Rights was inaugurated in 1853 at meetings in Edinburgh and Glasgow which attracted thousands of supporters. The range of opinion was impressively wide – from the Earl of Eglinton, who became its president, to McLaren and dozens of other council leaders across the country, and embracing well-known figures like the high Tory sheriff and author Sir Archibald Alison and the geologist turned Free Church editor Hugh Miller. The Scottish rights deserving vindication were similarly comprehensive – from restoration of a

Secretary of State and a more equitable share of Government spending in Scotland to a claim that the revenues of the Bishopric of Orkney had been purloined to fund the lighting of London streets.[17] At the launch meeting in Edinburgh on 11 November McLaren was entrusted with moving the first resolution which called for a Scottish Secretary of State to take responsibility for the growing weight of parliamentary business. Two years previously he had explained his concerns about the neglect of Scotland to the publisher of (the Tory) *Blackwood's Magazine*: 'One day at the Exchange Bank we talked of getting "justice for Scotland" as regards public grants, which although paid by us equally with England were seldom distributed here.' He had prepared a paper on the subject and he wanted 'one of your clever writers' to search miscellaneous estimates for grants to local purposes and their distribution in England, Ireland and the colonies.[18]

In helping to launch the National Association for the Vindication of Scottish Rights, McLaren was as usual concerned with practicality, not sentiment.[19] He pointed to the strain on successive Lords Advocate, who led Scottish business in the Commons (as Moncreiff was preparing to do on education) and were also responsible for criminal prosecutions, appeals to the House of Lords and (in whatever time remained) their own private practice. McLaren also noted that in Governments since Canning's in 1828 the Lord Advocate was 'merely an assistant to the Home Secretary'. McLaren had been on a deputation about a Scottish Bill to a previous Home Secretary who had not had time to 'get crammed' by his officials and could only ask 'What is the Bill about?' despite the fact that his name appeared among its proposers. McLaren took up a cause he was to promote for years to come – under-representation of Scotland at Westminster. Ireland returned 105 MPs; on a population basis Scotland should have 73, not 53. 'Put us in the position in which Ireland is, and then let us have a fair race together' for parliamentary time and Government investment, in which Scotland trailed both Ireland and England.

The National Association was launched with enthusiasm and tracts. The first of several rounds of petitions was sent to the queen. But official Britain was uninterested and in the case of London papers like *The Times*, dismissive. The Whigs in particular regarded the association's complaints as a slight. At Parliament House Lord Cockburn said of the sponsors of the association that the names were respectable, 'but it was all trash'. He sympathised with complaints about the loss of Scottish influence, but the wide assimilation with English practices was irresistible.[20] Only one Scottish MP, Charles Cowan, joined the association. A prominent Free Church minister, Sir Henry Moncreiff, the Lord Advocate's elder brother, wrote a letter to McLaren in the form of a pamphlet explaining why he declined to sign up.[21] Pouring scorn on the divisions among members, he pointed out that McLaren was an advocate of world peace, while Sir Archibald Alison gloried in the thunder of military victories. In July 1854 Palmerston as Home Secretary said there was no intention of creating a Secretaryship of State. By this time public attention was diverted to the war in the Crimea. The National Association continued to air grievances that appeared insignificant alongside the military campaigns and loss of lives. In 1856 the queen was again petitioned. The association intervened in a by-election in Edinburgh and told electors not to pledge their votes until a deputation met both candidates. By now McLaren had lost interest. He left the council of the association when he ceased being Lord Provost. Its principal practical aims he would pursue in other ways. But to mere gestures of sentimental nationalism he was no friend. He turned down an invitation by a clergyman in Stirling to join the committee for a monument to Sir William Wallace.[22] Unlike the Anti-Corn Law League, whose success the National Association for the Vindication of Scottish Rights sought to repeat, there was no strategy and no core of activists like Cobden, Bright and McLaren who were prepared for a long haul. The association withered away. Since it did not seek a Scottish Parliament and sought remedy for all grievances within the Union, it is hard to see it as a trailblazer for twentieth-century nationalism.

Nor did it rank alongside the eruptions of national feeling that threatened to destabilise Europe and made heroes in Britain of the exiled Hungarian Kossuth and the Italian Mazzini. Among radicals there was hope that autocracies would be swept away but concern also that Europe was slipping towards war that would involve Britain. The Peace Society, founded in the aftermath of the Napoleonic Wars, seemed to offer a way of avoiding conflict, and it grew in influence in the 1840s with congresses in various European capitals. Both Cobden and Bright sensed that British politics were becoming bellicose. The two radical leaders in Parliament diverged in their interests after the excitements of corn-law repeal. Cobden involved himself in international affairs, believing that freeing up trade across the nations would reduce the risk of war. Bright came to believe that a radical agenda would not make progress in Britain unless there was further parliamentary reform. The two colleagues largely went their own ways until both detected a drift towards war, first in response to fears of a French invasion under the new Napoleon and then directed at thwarting Russian threats to the Turkish empire. Cobden became an enthusiastic supporter of the peace movement.[23] Bright, as a Quaker, was committed to peace as a matter of principle although he doubted whether international congresses of the well-meaning would be more than talking shops. There was a Peace Congress in Manchester in January 1853. Bright, though MP for the city, was reluctant to attend but was persuaded by Cobden. Amid mounting anti-French hysteria, the delegates tried to revive the spirit of corn-law campaigns across the country, with a fund of £10,000 to train lecturers and distribute anti-war leaflets.

McLaren, who listened to the peace message from his Quaker wife and brother-in-law, was among those impressed. With Priscilla he visited Bright in Rochdale in August and outlined his plans for another peace conference in Edinburgh in October to maintain the momentum. Bright was at first reluctant to participate, but Cobden encouraged McLaren and wrote him a long letter, praising his initiative, especially given the character of the Scots: 'Nowhere has the movement fewer partisans than Scotland – and the reason is obvious – first because your heads are more combative than even the English, which is almost a phrenological miracle, and secondly the system of our military rule in India has been widely profitable to the middle and upper classes in Scotland, who have had more than their numerical proportion of its patronage.'[24] The peace movement, he went on, was unfashionable because of the power of military establishments and the fact that its supporters were branded as all unrealistic Quakers, which was not the case. Whereas some people opposed all wars, even those in self-defence, he argued from an economic and financial position that wars and the establishments associated with militarism were cripplingly costly. He hoped that McLaren would induce as many influential people as possible to meet on the platform in Edinburgh. From Blackpool John Benjamin Smith added his support: 'It requires a little moral courage to face the rampant war spirit which seems to exist all over the country.'[25] He and Cobden would come to a preliminary meeting just before the conference started. As it happened, the two got on the wrong train and reached Edinburgh late and unfed. 'On our arrival we were marched off to the committee room to hear the resolutions read and to listen till 10 o'clock to the hairsplitting of the members some of whom were very sharp theologians.'[26]

The conference was an opportunity to rally opinion against the threat of war with Russia.[27] Two hundred thousand leaflets were distributed in Scottish towns. On 12 October, the first day of the conference, which had had to be switched from the Queen Street Hall to the larger Music Hall, it was clear that McLaren had rallied large numbers of Dissenter ministers and dozens of prominent laymen. The presence of Bright and Cobden was undoubtedly a draw. McLaren gave the opening address and emphasised the breadth of the coalition that had formed at Manchester. He said there were 'two sections', one of which argued that 'war is every form and for every purpose is unlawful, as being opposed to the precepts of Christianity and the whole spirit of the New Testament'. The other section merely deprecated 'the war spirit wherever it may be found'. Referring to press criticism before the conference, he went on: 'We have been misrepresented as being all non-resistant – that we are for disarming this nation, and leaving it prey to any unprincipled nation that chooses to invade us.' Whatever opinions individuals might have, that was not the policy of the organisers. That statement helped clear the air and allow Cobden to concentrate on ridiculing the war crisis: 'Nobody intends to invade you, nobody wants to invade you.' Russia, he went on, was not responsible for the weakened state of the Turkish empire. 'Nations don't perish from without: they always perish by suicide from within.' Over several days the conference called for arms reduction and the arbitration of disputes, non-intervention in the affairs of other nations and the reform of colonial government to avoid conflicts. This modern-sounding agenda was complemented by calls for an international mercantile law, cheaper international postage and common weights, measures and coinage.

A diversion was caused by the incongruous presence of Sir Charles Napier, the Scottish naval hero soon to lead a Baltic expedition against Russia. According to the Peace Society magazine, the *Herald of Peace*, he had come 'to redeem a somewhat foolish boast made at the London Tavern'. Bright's biographer, John McGilchrist, who was sitting in the Music Hall behind McLaren, recalled that Napier, a bulky man with a war-wound limp, pushed his way to a seat of honour on McLaren's left.[28] No one recognised him until Cobden made reference to the admiral, who had declared he would 'beard the Peace Society in its den'. Napier insisted on making a speech and was heard tolerantly when he claimed: 'I am as fond of peace as any one can be, although I am not one of those who will support non-resisting opinions.' Press comment on the conference was largely hostile, asking whether the aim was peace at any price and alleging that the debates would give support to aggressive elements in Russia. Bright recognised the public relations problem and said that people were asking 'whether we have a screw loose, which, I believe, is the favourite term'. *The Times* was particularly scathing but nevertheless gave a generous account[29] of the soiree in the Music Hall that ended the conference: '400 to 500 ladies and gentlemen intermingled in the greatest good humour, chatting over the cause of peace and interchanging civilities with each other while the organ boomed forth appropriate music. Messrs Cobden and Bright were the lions of the evening. Wherever they moved they encountered groups of admirers; there was no end to the compliments and congratulations which they received, and the shaking of hands which they had to endure for fully two hours must have been attended with no small physical suffering.'

Bright assured Cobden, who was a less accomplished platform orator than his friend, that he had never spoken so successfully at a public meeting: 'It was a great intellectual gathering.' *The Times*'s hostility, he judged, had been no more than the Anti-Corn Law League endured in 1842. Cobden summed up the conference to his son Fred as 'very profitable'. McLaren was 'a very remarkable man to lead others', and he had had the great advantage of being Lord Provost. 'His house was full of visitors and every day he has 20 or 30 to dine – there was a strong muster of good men from all parts, and the seed sown in Edinburgh will bring forth good fruits in Scotland.'[30] Unfortunately for the peace campaigners, Turkey declared war on Russia on the second day of the conference. A leading Quaker at the conference, Joseph Sturge, made a fruitless personal pilgrimage to plead with the Tsar in St Petersburg. By the next year Britain and France were embroiled in the Crimea and bellicose Napier was blamed for a fruitless expedition to the Baltic.

The McLarens' flurry of entertaining during the peace meeting was possible because they had recently moved into a larger home. Their West End flat in Rutland Street, home since their marriage, was too small for their growing family, visitors (since there was only one spare bedroom) and the demands of civic hospitality. Newington House, to which they flitted in 1852, was in Priscilla's description 'very ugly outside but most commodious within'.[31] It was set in two acres of land on the south side of the expanding city. McLaren was instrumental in ensuring that a new drainage system was installed for the new suburb where desirable villas were being erected. Built at the turn of the century by Benjamin Bell, who made his fortune as a surgeon, Newington House was described as a mansion with stable and garden house. The policies were well wooded, and in the early years of their occupancy the family spent time reorganising the layout. An opening in the wood was filled in and another made at the top of the garden, which made the walk in front of the house warmer and more pleasant.[32] For the rest of his life and for Priscilla in her 20-year widowhood Newington House was home and a base for entertaining the extended family and a wide political circle. The Post Office needed no more precise identification than its name and that of the city. Before the family moved in Agnes McLaren wrote to her brother John in Madeira that Papa and Mamma were very busy choosing wallpaper and marble.[33] McLaren's delight was the garden, where he often worked alongside his outdoors staff. Eager to get started as soon as they moved in, he bought plants at a sale from the late Professor Deuchar's garden. They were stored in East Princes Gardens until they could be transplanted – one of the perks of being Lord Provost, it seems.

On a day in 1857 when McLaren suffered a setback in one of his political campaigns he took refuge in the garden and finished cutting down and pruning trees.[34] The same year he told his daughter Catherine that there were no more trees or shrubs to be dealt with and the garden was finished. But Catherine commented to Priscilla: 'I daresay it will not remain *finished* very long.'[35] In her letters to the family Priscilla would fuss that their father insisted on working outside while still suffering from flu or a cold. But he kept up his interest in plants, breaking off business during a visit to London in 1858 in order to view the horticultural displays at Crystal Palace.[36] The younger children kept pets in the garden. The fate of hens and rabbits recurs in their letters.

Before the decorators had finished the alterations to the house, McLaren entertained more than 350 of his helpers in the unsuccessful parliamentary election campaign. 'Our house is a very tall queer one,' Priscilla told her sister. 'The kitchens are on a level with the garden and the sitting rooms are so high as not to admit of any entrance into the garden except by the front door.'[37] So a wooden staircase was made to allow access to the lit lawn where a band played. For a party in March 1858 McLaren brought in hyacinths and camellias. 'I had no idea we could have such a show on the landings and stairs – the effect was beautiful indeed,' Priscilla said.[38] The catering on this occasion may not have matched the decoration. The guests were offered potatoes and lemonade and a few dishes of orange and coconut. The party was not wholly dry because Priscilla revealed that despite being a teetotaller herself she had drunk bitter beer, which she preferred to wine. She described her stepdaughters' party outfits. Catherine, in white, was 'the most truly lady-like looking girl of the evening'. Agnes wore a simple coloured muslin, 'very genteel'. But Grant 'somehow was shockingly dressed'. Ladies sang and played music, but there was no dancing. John and Agnes had wanted quadrilles. 'Nothing weighs me down so much as to have to go against the wishes of the elder ones – however Papa put in his potent voice – and although not objecting to dancing himself – knowing mine, he would not allow any yielding on my part and the young folk gave up with great apparent cheerfulness, but I always think on such occasions they must feel annoyed inwardly that their father married a Friend.'

A whimsical series of articles published in 1859 as *The Castes of Edinburgh*[39] depicts the life of the prosperous 'shopocracy' as one of the divisions in society: 'Just look along the suburbs of our city and see these mansions. Get over the threshold if you can – for the "cave canem" of exclusiveness is here also – and view the shining mahogany, the Turkey carpets, the six-feet chevals and the piers, the costly pictures, the elegantly bound books, and all the rest – most of them belong to the aristocratic shopkeepers.' The writer, John Heiton, says that the shopkeeper is 'above all, a very progressive personage, almost always a Liberal of some kind, for he feels that his nature requires an outlet on the other side of that where he is pressed by the necessity of an oppressive fealty or obedience to haughty customers. The Ballot is his god, and through his influence it will sooner or later be carried, for he must strive for liberty against the bondage of an obligation to those on whom he lives.' McLaren's business was thriving in the 1850s. Divesting himself of the concerns of the Exchange Bank and English railways, he had time to devote to its expansion. The Lord Provostship was very time-consuming, but when McLaren was in Edinburgh everything in his business and public life took place within a few hundred yards. He could move between shop and council chamber without wasting any time, and from his days as a young councillor he was adept at working on official papers while minding the business. He had a new business partner. John Oliver, whom he had met in Madeira in 1845 and had told that a business opportunity back home in Scotland would be difficult to find, had nonetheless joined the firm in 1846 and by 1852 replaced Renton as a partner. The shop, now describing itself as McLaren, Oliver & Co., featured regularly in the advertising columns of city newspapers, those politically hostile to the senior partner as well as the sympathetic. A carpet saleroom was added to the premises in 1852. At Christmas 1853 there appeared an advertisement for a new room to display evening dress, 'fitted up with gas for the convenience of those who may wish to see the effect of the different fabrics and colours for evening use.'[40] In 1856 there were 94 employees: 54 dealt with the sale and delivery of goods, with 40 working as milliners, upholsterers and so on. McLaren recorded that from the 11 o'clock post one morning he opened 45 letters containing orders, invoices and receipts.[41]

Profits grew steadily rather than spectacularly. John Oliver recorded in 1861 that they had increased from £1,400 in 1847 to nearly £7,000. The business was run with prudence, money being carefully set aside for planned expansion. Figures for 1854–5 suggest that McLaren took £4,000 from the shop and Oliver £1,500, with £500 each for Duncan junior, who had joined the firm, and John Towers, who was an increasingly key employee. McLaren had a business gauge: stock should be turned over 2½ times a year, and therefore stock worth £2,504 should have brought in £4,174 in sales at cost price in the first eight months of 1855. The actual sum, however, was £4,044 and so there had been a shortfall.[42] Oliver's health was at this time a problem – and it was to become more so again. He had to spend over a year in Madeira and, apologising for his long absence, paid tribute to McLaren's success in maintaining sales while he had been away.[43] It is clear from a letter he sent to Priscilla about life in Madeira – and the state of his own flatulence – that, 18 years younger than McLaren, he was a subservient as well as junior partner:[44] 'I frequently imagine us all seated around the dining table and I, or some other unfortunate makes a remark which is quietly and good humouredly taken to pieces by Mr McLaren, then to be followed by a genial smile at the unfortunate's expense. I know I owe my recovery so far as it has taken place very much to the kind, inlivening [sic], cheerful society I enjoyed at Newington House.'

In the wake of his successful Lord Provostship McLaren attained social status beyond the ranks of fellow merchants and co-religionists. He continued to champion the cause of reform in politics and public administration but did so more through participation in mainstream bodies such as the Chamber of Commerce than as a spokesman for militant Dissent. He had sought a compromise parliamentary solution to the annuity-tax question. He backed Lord Advocate Moncreiff's education Bills and discountenanced many Voluntaryists by accepting the need for State support of denominational schools, which was the Free Church position. But at the same time McLaren remained the de facto leader of the Independent Liberals, who had split in 1852 and allowed the Whigs to take advantage. Macaulay had been the beneficiary then but it became clear early in the next Parliament that ill health was limiting his activity. Despite his distaste for the narrow wranglings of Scots sectarians, he tried his best to respond to constituents' wishes and especially those of the town council. He spoke in favour of the abolition of university tests. He met McLaren and other members of the deputation at the House of Commons pressing the annuity-tax Bill. His last speech on 19 July 1853 was on the subject and 'without any preparation as to language, but with perfect fluency, and with considerable effect ... I have done the handsome thing by my constituents'.[45] In supporting the Bill he was backing moderates like McLaren as Lord Provost against the protests of extreme Voluntaries, including John Benjamin Smith, now MP for Stockport, for whom any continuing support of Established clergy was anathema. Macaulay's final words to Parliament were a warning about the dangers facing an Established Church north or south of the border. McLaren could only have admired Macaulay's peroration:

> The unpopularity of an Established Church is a very different thing from the unpopularity of the preventive service, of the army, of the police. The police, the army, and the coastguard may be unpopular from the nature of the work which they have to do; but of the Church it may be said that it is worse than useless if it is unpopular; for it exists only to inspire affection and respect, and if it inspires feelings of a character opposite to respect and affection, it had better not exist at all. Most earnestly, therefore, I implore the House not to support an institution, which is useless unless it is beloved, by means which it can only cause it to be hated.

It was not until January 1856 that Macaulay resigned his seat. Adam Black, Macaulay's leading supporter since 1847, was the choice of Sir William Gibson-Craig and the Whigs to fight the by-election. That seems to have been arranged before Macaulay's resignation became public. Black's committee of support was immediately in place, his canvassers started knocking on doors and the poll was arranged for barely a fortnight after the resignation. The Independent Liberals were caught on the hop and they complained of a fix. McLaren made it clear that he would not be a candidate,[46] 'especially after having so recently devoted three years of my time to its [the city's] interests'. But he was determined not to cede the seat to the 72-year-old Black who having been his guide and friend was now in thrall to the Parliament House interest. McLaren told Combe, whose Aggregate Committee was as usual trying to find common ground between Liberals, that among the newspapers only *The Scotsman* supported Black, at the prospect of whose return 'there is an intense feeling of dissatisfaction in the city'. The Independent Committee in apparent desperation talked of Lord John Russell, Lord Melgund and even McLaren's antagonist Sir William Johnston as possible candidates. None took up the challenge and time was very short. Meanwhile Macaulay was 'mortified' that there was opposition at all to Black: 'I shall not be free from anxiety till our friend is fairly returned.'[47]

The choice of challenger fell upon Bailie Francis Brown Douglas, an intensely devout Free Churchman who had been a member of the town council since 1850 (and was to become Lord Provost in 1859). He was an advocate but with a substantial private income he no longer practised, devoting his time to evangelical causes such as working-class housing and temperance.[48] For McLaren, who mentored his campaign, there were three problems. Was Brown Douglas actually a Liberal? His election address proclaimed support for the seemingly endless war in the Crimea and loyalty to Lord Palmerston, Prime Minister since the fall of Aberdeen's Government the previous autumn. Like Pam he was in effect a Liberal-Conservative and his candidacy was endorsed by the city's Conservative Committee, to *The Scotsman*'s scorn. The second problem was the incongruity of a leading lay Dissenter backing a Free Churchman and intolerant anti-papist against Black, a former leader of the Dissenters' campaigns for religious inclusion. As was pointedly noted, McLaren in 1852 had described Brown Douglas as a 'calumniator'. The third difficulty was that in terms of experience and standing in the city Black was much better equipped to be an MP than Brown Douglas. McLaren, however, questioned whether a man of 72 could adequately fulfil the needs of Edinburgh and Scotland. He cited the dispensation given to any MP over 60 of not having to serve on Commons committees and thus not take a full part in the House. Events were to show that both Black and McLaren, an MP until he was 81, had parliamentary energy in plenty.

The anti-Black coalition around Brown Douglas was described as comprising 'Tories and Radicals, Churchmen, Free Churchmen, and Voluntaries, silly Teetotallers and bigoted No-Popery men'.[49] To Black's supporters, the 'real' candidate opposing them was McLaren, who certainly made longer and more detailed speeches than the nominee. McLaren took up Brown Douglas's support for the Forbes Mackenzie Act of 1853 and claimed that Black wanted to relax its conditions in the interest of spirit dealers. Black riled him when he accused his former friend of abandoning the Voluntaryist attacks on 'political Protestantism and Orange Associations', which the two of them had once conducted.[50] There was a robust rally of Brown Douglas's supporters at the Queen Street Hall which provoked *The Scotsman* into a bitter attack on McLaren, describing his speech as a 'feculent mess'. As an election diatribe McLaren's was no worse than Black's at the nomination hustings a few days later, and other newspapers reported it without regarding it as exceptional, but Russel, the *Scotsman* editor, decided it was the last straw and mounted a sustained assault on McLaren. The paper virtually played the role of Black's agent, requesting that electors intending to vote for him should come forward early on polling day to get up a head of support. Victory by 2,429 votes to 1,786 brought exultation and a further attack on McLaren as 'designer and worker of the conspiracy which was yesterday shivered'.[51] Two days later, claiming that so great had been the interest in the paper's reporting of the by-election that recent issues had sold out, it reprinted all its reports and editorials in a special supplement. The consequences were to land the editor and proprietor in court.

9. *A libel case won*

At the end of July 1856 the libel case brought by Duncan McLaren against the proprietor and editor of *The Scotsman* excited attention far beyond middle-class Edinburgh where the animus between the former Lord Provost and the acerbic Alexander Russel, editor of the voice of the Whig establishment, was already well known. McLaren claimed that he had to have recourse to law because of a campaign of vituperation by the paper during and after the by-election that pitted Francis Brown Douglas against *The Scotsman*'s favourite, Adam Black. He had been held up 'to public hatred, contempt, and ridicule.'[1] In the edition of the paper which reprinted its coverage of the whole election campaign, his name had appeared 57 times.[2] For several weeks the paper's election coverage extended beyond news reports and hostile leaders to publication of squibs mocking McLaren and spoof advertisements for his business – a sale by Messrs Wylie, Spiteful & Co. 'including a large lot of damaged remnants of a former popularity'. Ham-fisted, student-like humour perhaps, but how much was it deemed to damage a reputation that stood higher than ever before in the city following a successful Lord Provostship? McLaren pointed out that Messrs McLaren, Oliver & Co. had been one of the paper's best customers, spending £130 on advertisements in the last two years.

The hand of Russel himself can be seen in much of the vituperation. The editor attended the meeting of Brown Douglas's supporters: 'Every class of creature known to the political world was there represented – Mammalia, Aves, Pisces and Reptilia.' Among the 'viperidae' 'what could be a more delightful object of Christian contemplation than Sir William Johnston and Mr Duncan McLaren lovingly intertwined in the folds of their affection, no longer with anything "cold" between them?' This was a reference to the infamous letter by Johnston in 1852 denouncing McLaren's cold, snake-like behaviour. At the libel trial the defenders claimed that it was a common joke in the city to refer to 'snake the draper'. But Russel had a point to make: Sir William Johnston and McLaren were now allies, backers of Brown Douglas, having been enemies for 16 years. In court McLaren admitted he and Johnston were still not on speaking terms. Russel wanted to show a lack of principle and consistency among Brown Douglas's variegated supporters. He had also sustained a campaign over many years against McLaren and the Independent Liberals. Charles Cooper, who worked closely with Russel before succeeding him as editor, recalled that Russel was 'a good hater; I suspect Mr McLaren ran him close in that respect'.[3] But McLaren had none of Russel's slashing wit. As an experienced journalist Russel was careful to distinguish the private man from the public figure and it was on that distinction that the paper relied when matters went to court. 'There is no man of whom ... we have had to say harder things than of Mr Duncan McLaren – at this moment, not insidiously, but to his teeth, we charge him with deserting principles, and traducing his friends, and deceiving enemies, and acting only for his own purposes, and especially his own malignities; but we speak on no other data than his own public speakings, writings, and actings. As to his having private or meaner personal motives ... we are most willing to add ... that Mr McLaren is far removed from sordid motives, and the private qualities contrast very favourably with his public.'

So why did a dispute prosecuted in the heat of an election campaign end five months later in court? Partly by mistake. McLaren began by seeking the redress of recantation and apology. Unfortunately he did not make his intentions clear enough, or at least *The Scotsman* said it was unaware of the depth of his concern until a writ was executed on 20 March, and there was ample time between then and the hearing at the end of July for a resolution to be achieved. McLaren relied on his friend George Combe to mend bridges, and Combe in turn relied on Charles Maclaren, also a friend of McLaren's and former editor. Maclaren was still with the paper, from which he received a retirement annuity. But when Combe told Maclaren about Duncan McLaren's upset, it was unclear whether the intention was for Maclaren to pass that concern to Russel and John Ritchie, the paper's proprietor. Certainly, McLaren assured Combe from the outset that he was ready for the first time in his life to go to court to clear his name, but Maclaren thought that the articles were not libellous and merely 'ebullitions of election violence' (Combe's phrase) not to be taken too seriously.[4] McLaren insisted that only if the paper learned the error of its ways would it restore its good name and stand once more for liberty of opinion. While Combe continued to counsel caution, McLaren insisted he was acting 'from judgement and not from impulse'. If Russel offered reparation only in response to the writ and not from a change of heart he would pass the matter off as a joke at a dinner party and write another attack the following day.[5] By 1 May McLaren was willing to accept a printed apology and £100 plus expenses rather than the £1,000 claimed in the action. But later in the month he ended the correspondence with Combe, thanking him for his efforts and, while accepting that they differed on the seriousness of the case, pointed out that as the injured party he was more sensitive than could be expected of his friend. McLaren's family cut off social contact with Charles Maclaren, who by now was worried that if the paper was ruined by the court action he would lose his annuity.[6] McLaren himself, while putting Russel beyond the pale because of his 'personal rancour', reflected on the good relations he believed he had with the co-defender, Ritchie. 'I once was the instrument in the hands of Providence to save his life when a stage coach, on top of which we were both sitting, was in the act of turning over an embankment (he being at the falling side). I caught him firmly round the waist with one arm as he was being pitched over and held on by the iron bar with the other, and then he got down with only a few bruises from some trees with which he had come in contact. I suppose he did not think of this when he authorised the libellous matter against me to be collected and republished in one number.'[7]

The case in the Second Division of the Court of Session occupied the last two days of July and was presided over by the Lord Justice Clerk, Lord Hope. If the public were still unaware of its significance, they would have been alerted by the names of the two principal advocates appearing. *The Scotsman* was represented by the Lord Advocate himself, James Moncreiff. At that time the Lord Advocate could maintain a private civil practice alongside official duties. McLaren was represented by George Young, Dean of the Faculty of Advocates. The jury of 12 had to consider a substantial booklet of extended reports from and comments by *The Scotsman*, plus extracts from coverage of the by-election in other newspapers. It was clear from the outset that the complaints cited from *The Scotsman*'s coverage were expected to speak for themselves. The jury would have to decide whether they constituted libel or were merely robust journalism. The testimony of witnesses was of little significance. Even McLaren was subjected to little more than perfunctory examination and cross-examination. Since the newspaper's ridicule had been prompted by McLaren's support for a candidate whom he had described as a 'calumniator' only four years earlier, the circumstances of that disagreement were explored. The jury in effect had to consider whether it was honourable, or at least understandable, for the enemies of one election to become allies in the next. Asked about his recent relations with Brown Douglas, McLaren said there was no animosity and when they had both been in London on the town's business they had stayed at the same hotel.

Moncreiff's closing speech, lasting two and a half hours, drew a distinction between treatment of public and private life. The paper had expressed approbation for McLaren as a private citizen but 'for any man who engages in politics to have recourse to a jury ... is contemptible'. McLaren was complaining 'like a schoolboy'. The paper took issue not with McLaren himself but with his role in leading the unseemly coalition formed to oppose Adam Black. Moncreiff accepted that the squibs and mock advertisements were vulgar and stupid but not libellous. In its comments the paper could be sharp and, to some people, offensive. He himself had not been happy when it accused him of debauching Parliament House by making offers of sheriffships but he had not thought of raising a libel action. In the end – and this was Moncreiff's final flourish – he had to safeguard the freedom of the press no matter the discomfort that might bring. Finding for McLaren would undermine that freedom. George Young in his address painted a picture of a man and a family constantly exposed to repetition of falsehoods and ridicule over the ten days of the election. Despite attempts by McLaren to extract an apology for this behaviour the paper had not responded, and the campaign of vilification continued. The judge told the jury to look at the offending articles in full and to decide whether McLaren was too thin-skinned for the robustness of an election or whether the articles had been 'calumnious and injurious'. If they found for McLaren it would not be a threat to freedom of the press, which did not extend to publishing calumny. The jury retired at 3.30 p.m. and took only half an hour to find in McLaren's favour and award him £400 damages, less than half of what he sought but four times what he had been willing to settle for privately.

The Scotsman took the verdict badly. Its leader talked of 'the first political trial in Scotland since 1795'. Freedom of speech and reporting had been assailed. McLaren had not sought an apology as he claimed. Besides, everyone knew more about his conduct than had been brought out in the case. In a sentence dangerously close to contempt of court, the paper suggested that the 12 men on the jury had been more ignorant of the matter as a whole than 'the first 12 you may meet on Edinburgh streets'. The London papers had taken an interest in the case, and *The Scotsman* was anxious to encourage *The Times* in its view that the verdict cast Scotland in a poor light. North of the border the press was divided; the divergent opinions were widely reported and the number on each side totted up. The *Dundee Advertiser* in supporting *The Scotsman* suggested that the jury should 'draw up an index of naughty and objectionable words'. Probably a majority of papers, however, saw no threat to their freedom of expression.[8] John McLaren, who was embarking on his own career as an advocate, wanted to write a letter to *The Times* because the English did not understand Scottish libel law, but his father said no. If the letter appeared under John McLaren's name, *The Scotsman* would immediately reprint it, along with a fresh attack, on the assumption that the letter was really by McLaren senior. Duncan told John that other papers were 'clearing up' the real meaning of the verdict and all would be reprinted in the *Herald*, a sympathetic organ with a large circulation. But he was concerned that 'there is still an immense mass of people who never see any of the papers which are friendly to me. They are the Conservatives, Free Church and old Whigs. The more independent party are the *News*, *Scottish Press*, *Express*, *Herald* and other such papers in the different towns.'[9] McLaren continued to worry about the support he was getting. He told Cobden: 'The newspapers are nearly all against me, especially the Whig ones. Their despotism has got a blow and their self-importance has been brought down.'[10] Perhaps in that sense – of a contest between old Whiggery and new Liberalism – *The Scotsman* was right: it had been a political trial.

There was a strange sequel to the story. On 8 January 1857 the governors of Heriot's Hospital heard that McLaren had gifted his £400 damages to the outdoor schools so that two boys and two girls in each school would receive a reward for good conduct, including a pocket Bible and a sum of money. At first the governors were happy but two months later they had second thoughts. The dean of guild, a town council representative on the governors, said that acceptance of the money would perpetuate the feud between McLaren and *The Scotsman*. James Marwick, later the town clerk, wondered what the governors would think if the newspaper offered to buy psalm books to go with McLaren's Bibles. Russel immediately jumped at that media opportunity and offered £150 to buy the psalm books. The money would come from the residue of an appeal made to the public to pay the paper's bill for the damages and expenses, totalling £1,200. The Heriot's governors realised that things were getting out of hand and turned down both offers. Russel said: 'I have got back my £150, which I would have been awfully sorry if the governors had kept. I have had my fun, and shown up the affair – making all the parties look ridiculous.'[11]

The court case offers an insight into the practice of journalism at the time as well as its high (and low) politics. Two days after the verdict *The Scotsman* commented on the previous day's edition containing the closing speeches. There had been a large number of typographical errors but that was because of a 'great mass of matter' taken down and printed in a very few hours. 'One portion of the report alone – the Lord Advocate's speech, which occupied two hours and a half in its delivery, and filled *eleven* of our columns, had, as it happened, been all written by our reporter – Mr J. I. Smith of our own office – between six in the evening and three in the morning, being the greatest feat in reporting in our experience.'[12] The paper was under stress. A year previously it had moved from twice-weekly publication to daily. That was in response to the abolition of newspaper stamp duty. Like other established papers *The Scotsman* had not been happy at the legislative change because although it offered the opportunity of a lower cover price, it opened the way for other titles to come into the market place and muscle in on advertising revenues.[13] Ritchie, the 78-year-old proprietor, opposed a daily edition but eventually gave in. In 1856 the financial verdict on the change was still open. The paper, like others, had sold well during the Crimean War. With peace came a slackening of interest in news. We know now that by stealing a march on its competitors, most of whom remained twice- or thrice-weekly publications, and by pioneering use of the telegraph to gather news and the railways to distribute each day's edition, *The Scotsman* was destined to become pre-eminent, but at the time of the court case there was stiff competition – including from a paper that reflected the views of McLaren and his followers. The *Scottish Press* had been founded in 1847 when the United Presbyterian Church also came into being. McLaren always disclaimed credit for its arrival or involvement in its running. But he was among the subscribers who raised the launch money and he knew it would be a rival to the paper for which he had previously written. Before the launch he wrote a letter to Ritchie at *The Scotsman*. After the court case the paper dug out this letter and printed it[14] to show that McLaren had bitten the hand that fed him, and in taking *The Scotsman* to court he was acting for a rival organ. In fact the letter shows what was in McLaren's mind in 1847 and not nine years later. The tone was friendly, simply giving notice that Dissenters in Edinburgh and Glasgow, disillusioned with *The Scotsman*'s recent policies, were starting their own paper which would be 'free from more political partisanship to any Whig Government or other measures'. It was not intended to be in opposition to *The Scotsman*, but McLaren recognised that it would become a competitor, especially for advertising. He himself had not written more than three newspaper articles in three years, although he had often been asked. Now 'occasionally I may devote an hour or two in the evenings to help forward any good cause by my pen; but it will be purely as a volunteer, and not as having any kind of connection with the management of the paper or the pecuniary concerns.'

The *Scottish Press*, while not under his control, was generally loyal to his causes and those of United Presbyterians, though it challenged his support for national education. Newspapers of the time were intensely partisan and each church sought a voice as well as each political party. *The Scotsman* spoke for ecclesiastical moderation and the old Whigs. The *Courant* was Conservative and sympathetic to the Church of Scotland. The *Witness* was founded in 1840 by the Non-Intrusionists of the Church and became the mouthpiece of the Free Church, although its editor, Hugh Miller, then famed as much for his pungent editorials as for his geological insights, often tangled with the Church's egotistical leadership. Circulations were small. *The Scotsman* was selling about 3,500 when it went daily, rising to 10,000 by 1859-60. The *Scottish Press* registered 1,734 copies for each edition in 1854, the *Courant* slightly more and the *Witness* 2,700. Newspaper titles came and went but there was always a wide choice and therefore commercial rivalry as well as editorial backbiting.[15]

McLaren told Combe in 1858 that he had no commercial or editorial interest in any newspaper although he took all the Edinburgh papers except two.[16] At another time he said he did not read *The Scotsman* at home, though we can be sure that he saw it in the shop. Throughout his life he was a press addict, on holiday found waiting impatiently at the Oban pier for the arrival of the boat with the newspapers. Press cuttings would be sent with letters to and from his family. The Glasgow papers and the provincial English titles, then more important politically compared with the London papers than nowadays, he also kept abreast of. The *Leeds Mercury* belonging to the Radical Baines family was regarded as particularly significant, and McLaren contributed to its letters columns. No doubt it was among his reading matter when at the Ben Rhydding Hydro. Described as the most important paper outside London, its successive owners Edward Baines senior and junior owed their standing as MPs to their newspaper's hold on the Yorkshire middle class.[17] Edward junior had been MP for Leeds for six years when McLaren joined him on the Radical benches in 1865. McLaren never enjoyed the power that newspaper ownership gave the Baines, and he did not aspire to it because he saw that papers were more likely to lose money than make it for their owners. Richard Cobden was another believer in the power of the press[18] and in 1856 was instrumental in founding the *Morning Star* in London to give the peace party a voice. Later he sought to set up an advertising sheet to take a chunk of revenue from *The Times* and consulted McLaren several times about the economics of such a project. McLaren was sceptical, especially after consulting a longstanding contact at the *North British Advertiser*.[19] It was personal influence with newspapers rather than their ownership that McLaren found valuable. In 1857 he wrote to his son John from Llandudno congratulating him on his handling of a court case. The full report that had appeared in the *Express* (a short-lived Edinburgh paper) would do John's reputation good, he added. 'I believe they would do the best they could in that way on my account.'[20] Not surprising considering the extent of McLaren's contributions to the *Express*. In one letter the editor sent him a proof of an article on Black's attendance at committees and thanked him for his letters on a Lunacy Bill before Parliament. The paper had space for only one or two though there was material for a dozen long articles, squeezed out by 'that dreadful trial' – of Madeleine Smith for poisoning her lover.[21]

Three months after the libel case Priscilla wrote that her husband 'is over head and ears in the business of trying to procure good men to go into the new council, but they seem very unwilling to stir, tho' the enemy is very active.'[22] Edinburgh's boundaries had just been extended and wards redrawn. The powers of the police commissioners over civic amenities were being absorbed within the town council. It was important to continue to have a secure phalanx of allies, as duly came about. But supporting Brown Douglas's campaign had done McLaren no good with some Voluntaries, who detected in the artificial coalition too much emphasis on anti-Catholicism.[23] At a General Election the Independent Liberals would have to find a more credible candidate than Brown Douglas or sit on the sidelines. Lord Palmerston was defeated in Parliament early in 1857 when Conservatives and Radicals came together to condemn his provocation of the Chinese. He called an election confident that defending British interests would reinforce his reputation with the electorate. Throughout the country candidates had to take the field quickly. Cobden, who decided that Huddersfield would offer a safer seat than the West Riding he had been representing, urged McLaren to stand: 'For Heavens sake come into the House for one of your Scottish boroughs, or try an English one that you may endeavour to set up something better in the House than the present forlorn state of the representation of Scotland.'[24] He repeated the appeal days later: come in 'if for only a session or two.'[25] But McLaren was adamant that he would not stand – for Edinburgh or anywhere else. The Independent Liberal Committee knew that Black was unassailable. Cowan they regarded as inadequate and there was no longer any sense of an alliance between Voluntaries and Cowan's Free Church. Priscilla told her stepdaughters that 'he [Cowan] has fairly sold himself to the Whigs'[26], which was true in that the Whig leaders were content to see him returned alongside Black. McLaren toyed with tempting Alexander Murray Dunlop to abandon his Greenock seat for Edinburgh. Dunlop had for many years been the Free Church's legal adviser, and it is a sign of changing times that his church allegiance was regarded as unimportant compared with a reputation for good sense, hard work and radical views. But Dunlop stuck by Greenock, his home town, and was rewarded with an uncontested election. Cobden wrote to McLaren that Dunlop was a good man with high moral qualities 'but it is *you* we want in the House'.

Another possible candidate, McLaren believed, was Lord John Russell. The former Prime Minister had become a forlorn figure, out of Government and overshadowed by his arch-rival Palmerston. He was thought likely to lose his London seat. He embodied Whiggery but was a persistent advocate of parliamentary reform. As McLaren told his fellow Independent Liberals, 'he is head of the reforming party in Parliament in opposition to the no-reform policy of Lord Palmerston'.[27] London went to the polls before Edinburgh, which would thus be in a position to rescue him if he were defeated. To general surprise Lord John proved to have no need of a bolt-hole, and it was too late for McLaren's party to find another champion The situation, Priscilla wrote in the same letter to her stepdaughters, was 'heart embittering – I feel so much for Papa'. The election went well for Palmerston and the Whigs, who increased their majority. For the Radicals the setback was severe. The peace party lost ground to Pam's aggressive populism. Cobden was rejected by Huddersfield. Bright, too ill to campaign, lost Manchester.

The prospect of parliamentary reform, central to Radical hopes, was dashed. Palmerston did not want it and was under no pressure to accede to it. In Scotland McLaren saw an opportunity, however, to maintain interest through focusing on the freehold movement, which sought to extend north of the border the voting rights of those who in England had been enfranchised as freeholders in 1832. A series of meetings had started at the Queen Street Hall on Christmas Day (of all days) 1856. Priscilla wrote to John, who was in Glasgow on his first court cases, that she was looking forward to a 'rousing' reform meeting, though Papa 'discourages the idea of ladies attending it'. She was going anyway.[28] McLaren's ally in this campaign was James Begg, a Free Church minister dedicated to improving the conditions of working people, especially their housing. McLaren sought to prove that freehold was as ancient a right north of the border as in England but it had disappeared by 1832 and therefore did not feature in the Reform Act, with the result that the number of householders in the counties eligible to vote was lower than in England where 40-shilling freehold was the main voting qualification. Another anomaly affected Scottish county electorates because parliamentary burghs had been created by removing burghs from their surrounding counties and artificially lumping them together. The result was very small county electorates readily influenced by local landowners. 'Burghs had been made parliamentary burghs in order to leave the counties to the aristocracy,' McLaren told the Queen Street meeting.[29] He drew up a Bill extending the franchise. Begg praised it but it did not meet with the approval of either the Convention of Royal Burghs or the Lord Advocate. A parliamentary supporter, Samuel Laing, MP for Wick Burghs, wrote just before the March General Election to ask McLaren for 'a large public meeting in Edinburgh comprizing delegates from the principal towns and districts so as to give it a national character, and held before the elections.'[30] That proved impossible, but the following month Priscilla noted that McLaren was looking forward to a meeting that he and Begg would address in Ayr. The next week there was one in Hawick 'where no doubt they will meet with a warm reception.'[31]

Following the campaign to vindicate Scottish rights, the freehold movement was a brave attempt to secure equal treatment with England. But there was no appetite in the Cabinet for legislation, and Lord Advocate Moncreiff would not have got the go-ahead for a Scottish Bill even if he had been less lukewarm than he was. However, the man who could energise a much wider reform campaign was about to come back into Parliament. In the summer of 1857 John Bright was continuing recuperation from long illness through his new hobby of fishing in the Highlands. While staying at Castle Menzies in Perthshire he received a telegraph message from McLaren in Edinburgh: Joseph Sturge, the peace campaigner, who lived in Birmingham, was trying to contact Bright urgently. One of the Birmingham MPs, George Muntz, had died. Bright must succeed him. Sturge travelled from the Midlands, Bright from the Highlands. They met at Newington House. 'We have been literally inundated with telegraphic messages wanting my brother to go to Birmingham but he would not,' Priscilla told John McLaren.[32] Under pressure Bright agreed to consider standing if he did not have to take up his seat until fully recovered. Sturge got back to Birmingham at two in the morning and relayed the message to the Liberal committee. Bright agreed under pressure from McLaren to travel south, but not to a maelstrom in Birmingham. Priscilla continued the story: 'So against all our convictions Papa and my brother have just started for Tamworth.

As there is both a Liberal (or a professed one) and a Tory in the field, I expect some trick will be played on the polling day – and the Whigs and Tories will go for one man and thus defeat the true liberals. I do not expect success and my brother seems very callous about it, or fancies he is so.' Her pessimism was unfounded. With Sturge's help a Tamworth manifesto was produced. The candidates already canvassing the constituency withdrew and at the age of 46 Bright became one of the two MPs for Birmingham, a seat he represented for over 30 years.

Testing his restored stamina, Bright prepared for a reform campaign in the country and a Bill in the Commons. His brother-in-law in Edinburgh would be his principal ally – a well-known figure to sit alongside him on public platforms and an experienced draftsman of detailed legislation. In November 1858 he wrote to McLaren proposing to spend a week at Newington House after addressing meetings in England. He would be happy to make a speech in Edinburgh or Glasgow, but he would come armed with documents and statistics necessary to frame a bill extending the franchise. The two men would work on these: 'I hope you are giving your mind to the question so that with your head and my tongue we may make something of it, as we are in strife.'[33] The last phrase is a reference to the attacks on Bright's initiative in the Whig press. A year later Bright was still praising McLaren's researches: 'You are a very "steam engine" for work at figures and arguments.'[34] Bright spoke to crowded meetings in both Edinburgh and Glasgow. At the Music Hall in Edinburgh's George Street McLaren, the chairman, struggled to keep order as the press of people at the doors and in the corridors brought a series of interruptions to Bright's speech. Although he included a populist attack on the power of the aristocracy, Bright concentrated on the nuts and bolts of his plans to extend the franchise. All proposals for reform until an Act was passed nine years later brought intricate discussion of enfranchisement by rates and rents because of widely held concerns to stop short of universal male suffrage. The detail is nowadays tedious. Bright nailed his colours to extending the vote to those who were liable for poor rates. He approved the extension of the 40-shilling freehold suffrage to Scotland. He proposed that small towns should lose their seats, which would be given to under-represented communities that had grown with the Industrial Revolution. McLaren, summing up the meeting, said that Bright's plans would double the Edinburgh electorate and triple that of smaller towns in Scotland. Reflecting on the Edinburgh and Glasgow meetings the *Edinburgh News* thought that Bright had struck a different note from that of his anti-corn law days. Then he had been impassioned. Now he appealed to the head more than the heart.[35]

McLaren followed up Bright's meetings with one in Perth where he spoke alongside a representative of the London Parliamentary Reform Committee and a young advocate and Edinburgh councillor, John Gorrie, who was a close friend of John McLaren. McLaren's was the speech of the evening, according to the *Edinburgh News*, as he laid in to James Moncreiff, now Dean of the Faculty of Advocates, who had just addressed his Leith constituents on the folly of a franchise based on rating.[36] *The Scotsman* sprang to Moncreiff's defence. The former Lord Advocate was working on a Bill for a rent-based franchise, and the newspaper accused McLaren of getting his figures wrong when he estimated the growth in the Scottish burgh electorate. It also started to refer to 'the family party', a description of the Bright-McLaren Radicals which it would continue to invoke when McLaren went into Parliament. The family comprised 'two godfathers and two or three exceedingly subordinate subalterns' who were orating their way round Scotland as if no one else had proposed franchise reform. Anyway, the public was 'utterly apathetic'.[37] Not so, McLaren thought. Aided by his son and by Gorrie, who were joint secretaries of the Parliamentary Reform Committee in Edinburgh, he called a meeting to rally support for the Bill that Bright had prepared. A petition was ready for signature and would be presented to Parliament by James Caird, MP for Dartmouth. McLaren said: 'The great thing was to unite the working classes and the honest portion of the middle classes who were disposed to go with them'.[38] That strategy was to serve well not just the 'family party' of Bright and McLaren but the new Liberal party that William Gladstone would soon emerge to lead.

Meanwhile Bright's measure was of significance at Westminster only as a comparison to the one being prepared by Benjamin Disraeli for the Tory Government led by Lord Derby that had taken office when Palmerston resigned after a Tory-Radical attack on his Conspiracy to Murder Bill. Disraeli's Bill was full of 'fancy franchises'. McLaren deployed his researches on Bright's behalf in a statistical pamphlet showing the inadequacies of Disraeli's measure when set alongside Bright's.[39] He went to Rochdale where Bright was still struggling with tiredness, an after-effect of his illness, and accompanied him to a public meeting in Bradford. Priscilla said he was useful to her brother because 'he has a head which can in a remarkable manner smooth difficulties – having a cool nervous system and a grasp of mind which not many can boast of'.[40] At Westminster Bright and Russell agreed to oppose the Tory initiative, with Bright demanding a better Bill from a future Liberal administration. The Government was defeated in March 1859 and went to the country. There were only eight contests in Scottish seats, none of them in the cities. But Moncreiff, who had become Dean of the Faculty after losing the Lord Advocacy with the change of Government, moved from Leith to Edinburgh on Cowan's retirement. Duncan McLaren junior, who was broadening his business experience with a company in Reading, wrote that it was unfortunate that Black and Moncreiff were likely to 'walk the course' unchallenged: 'It seems a great pity that you cannot get at least one thorough Liberal.'[41] His father did contemplate standing because the next Parliament would deal with reform. While in Stirling seeing about Caird's possible transfer to that seat from Dartmouth, he asked John to take private soundings in Edinburgh but without revealing his father's level of interest. In the same letter[42] he enclosed a note for Priscilla's eyes only. 'If wanted by Edinburgh generally' he might enter Parliament, where on a Reform Bill 'I might be of some use in getting justice for Scotland, by indirect influence and explanations to more influential men than myself. And the Parliament will be so short that I might return on a dissolution or not as I found convenient.' The Parliament was not short. It lasted six years and with Palmerston returned to head the Government and determined not to let reform onto the agenda, McLaren's advice on reform would not have been needed. Stability returned to politics as the uneasy and shifting coalitions of the 1850s gave way to a Liberal party uniting Whigs, Peelites and Radicals under a Prime Minister whose views were largely Tory but whose popularity in the country made him unassailable. Lord John Russell, in response to a letter from McLaren, agreed that there were still obstacles to amity: 'I regret the conduct of the editor of the *Scotsman*, and these exclusive friends of his, who are the enemies of union in the Liberal party.'[43]

For McLaren and the Independent Liberals a challenge to the Parliament House Whigs in 1859 was impossible. With Moncreiff as an MP for the city and again Lord Advocate in Palmerston's Government, applying pressure on him where there was a local grievance became the obvious tactic. Meanwhile McLaren's ceaseless activity continued in these years. He took up an interest in penal matters. In 1857 he occupied himself at the Ben Rydding preparing a paper about Scottish prisons which he wanted to read at a meeting in Birmingham, no doubt at Bright's behest. The hydropathic doctor dissuaded him from such strain.[44] He involved himself in a controversy about extending the number of reformatories in Scotland for juvenile delinquents with one in Edinburgh. The question was who would pay, the public or private purse. In a sign that cooperation was possible across a political divide, Adam Black proposed and McLaren seconded a proposal that £2,000 should be raised for a new institution, which the state should help to maintain. McLaren said that parents should be expected to contribute to the upkeep of inmates, a practice followed in England but not in other Scottish reformatories.[45]

Business organisations of which he had long been a member offered useful platforms for McLaren's views. He never took office in the Merchant Company after his spell as assistant master in the 1840s but he was increasingly influential in the Chamber of Commerce. Following Cobden's example, he used the chamber to promote political causes at home and abroad of significance to the business community. Local traders wanted easier movement of goods. A private member's Bill was introduced in 1858 to abolish county road tolls as an inhibition on trade. It failed to make progress but the Government set up a Royal Commission whose members included McLaren. They sat for two years and took evidence in various parts of Scotland. Moncreiff introduced a Bill to implement their recommendations but it did not succeed, and road tolls became an important matter for McLaren when he himself came to Parliament. The Royal Commission was the only public appointment he ever held, and it came from a Tory Government.[46] His political influence grew, however, in Radical circles as business trips south of the border gave the opportunity to visit a growing circle of acquaintances as well as Priscilla's extended family. In June 1858 during a stay in London they were forced to change their lodgings after being disturbed by nocturnal creatures. 'We went through some rich scenes with an obsequious landlord and his more shrewd wife which even Dickens might have enjoyed', Priscilla told John. Her sense of social nicety seems to owe more to another novelist of the age, Elizabeth Gaskell: 'Mrs J.B. Smith, Mrs Cobden and their daughters have called – and asked us to tea for Saturday evening. I think such an invitation very shabby, still we must take people as they are.'[47]

10. *A family at war*

From 1859 James Moncreiff was in a good position to rid Edinburgh of its great bugbear, the annuity tax. He was not only a new MP for the city but also Lord Advocate in Palmerston's Government. Throughout the 1850s refusal to pay towards the support of Church of Scotland ministers had continued to bring a procession of sales of goods at the Cross. McLaren and the Independent Liberals were at the heart of an Anti-Annuity Tax League. Moncreiff as leader of the Parliament House Whigs knew that a future political challenge would most likely come from the Independent Liberal Committee. Removing its most popular grievance would undercut its influence. His colleague Adam Black agreed but wanted the tax removed because he had opposed it on principle since the 1830s. He introduced Bills in the 1858 and 1859 sessions, carrying the second in the Commons. It never reached the Lords where he knew it would founder. Black took a different line from Moncreiff, who had earlier proposed a municipal tax for 12 years to create a fund that would then take over support of the city clergy. Black realised that any such tax was open to opposition as a levy to support a State Church; it merely took away the worst aspects of the annuity tax, not its principle. So his two Bills utilised seat rents, which were part of the city's revenues, to fund ministers' stipends but only until a minister died or left his parish. McLaren gave Black some help in framing his legislation.

In 1860 Moncreiff brought forward a Government Bill, and if he had adopted Black's principle, that would probably have resolved the matter. But he went back to the idea of a poundage rate – levied as part of the rate for financing the police, a necessity no one could object to. Allocating part of the revenue to the city churches for a period of 15 years would be the responsibility of Ecclesiastical Commissioners, who would comprise representatives from the Church of Scotland, the town council and the bodies representing advocates and solicitors.

Imprisonment for non-payment would be abolished. Moncreiff thought it sensible for householders to pay a single rate, and he expected the town to accede since it had supported a municipal replacement for the annuity tax. Black had his doubts. As a local businessman he was closer to opinion on the streets than the Lord Advocate but he accepted that Moncreiff had the standing and expertise to succeed where he had fallen short.

McLaren was at the centre of the opposition that soon expressed itself. At a public meeting he asked Black to reintroduce his Bill of the previous year: 'Mr Black's was a very good Bill and Mr Moncreiff's was a very bad Bill,' (cheers and hisses).[1] At Westminster Bright advised Moncreiff just to get rid of the tax: 'Nothing easier – the members of the Commons care not a straw about it, and if the inhabitants sign a solemn league and covenant that they will not pay a sixpence in future, you may depend it will be abolished in a month.'[2] Bright asked the Home Secretary, Sir George Lewis, to withdraw the Bill: 'I told him I thought the Lord Advocate was damaging the Government in Edinburgh very much, and that his party really were not in favor [sic] of anything liberal.'[3] *The Scotsman* was Moncreiff's strongest ally and argued that compromise was needed to end the long-running grievance. But 'indignation is got up in one very small but busy manufactory', which was 'the same little scheming, electioneering clique, consisting of our indomitable and inveterate friend, Mr Duncan McLaren, his family, and his very particular friends, or rather his friends who are not at all particular. First comes the Liberation etc Society – that is, Mr D McLaren, Mr J McLaren, Mr A Fyfe, Bailie T Russell, Mr J Gorrie. Then some committee of the Chamber of Commerce – Mr D McLaren and Bailie T Russell again. Then the 'public meeting' – Mr D McLaren, Mr J McLaren, Mr Gorrie, Bailie T Russell, Mr A Fyfe.'[4] McLaren certainly coordinated opposition to the Bill from the 'shopocracy' as well as his allies on the town council. He was particularly insistent that the amount that Moncreiff calculated could be raised from seat rents to meet the ministers' stipends – £1,600 – was too low. It should be at least £2,500, and why should people brought within the city boundaries by their extension in 1856 have to pay the levy for inner-city churches? A petition with 15,000 signatures was got up.

Making minor concessions Moncreiff got his Bill through Parliament before the summer recess. Scottish MPs voted 34 to 2 in favour on its third reading. That was not the end of the story. The town council teetered on the brink of refusing to implement it, thus raising the prospect of bankruptcy (a good weapon with which to attack McLaren).

Andrew Fyfe, identified by *The Scotsman* as a principal McLaren ally, challenged the Act in the Court of Session, and Moncreiff was forced to bring in another Bill clarifying the criteria for levying the tax. McLaren had a point when he wrote from London telling the council that their interference was 'unexampled in the legislation of the United Kingdom, its object being to legislate upon a matter now pending in a court of law'. The town council drew back from the brink of non-cooperation. Moncreiff told a meeting in December that he was proud of settling the 30-year-old controversy. He challenged his Voluntary opponents: 'Taking the highest Voluntary ground, I say there is not a shadow of pretence for saying that the penny put on the police rate, or the police rate itself, can by possibility raise a question of conscience which can affect them.' After all, in other towns and cities ministers were paid from a common good fund – and in Dundee from a duty on ale.

William Norrie, who wrote the history of the annuity tax 40 years after its final disappearance, was a young reporter on the radical *Caledonian Mercury* in 1860. Having covered the events day by day, he recalled the outcome: 'The result was certainly discouraging to the Dissenters of Edinburgh, and to the advanced Liberal party. A number of their leaders retired from the town council; and on the expiry of Lord Provost Brown Douglas's term of office, the combined Whig–Tory forces obtained a majority in the municipal parliament in favour of the finality of Mr Moncreiff's Act.'[5] Norrie's chronicle, however, was to continue for another decade. There was no finality: householders refused to pay the annuity-tax element of what was now known as the 'clerico-police tax'. The authorities demanded full payment and not just of the police rate, to which there was no objection. Sales of goods at the Cross continued and became alarmingly frequent, as *The Scotsman* noted in 1865, the year of the next General Election.[6]

McLaren and his supporters were determined not to let the town council slip from their grasp. According to *The Scotsman* the elections of November did not alter the balance of power. In mainly uncontested seats four candidates in favour of the new Act were returned, with four against it. The question was whether the council would sign bonds necessary to bring in its financial provisions. Former Bailie Russell, one of the paper's favourite targets, resigned his George Square seat on health grounds just after the elections – a 'ruse' in *The Scotsman*'s view since McLaren was immediately beseeched by electors in the ward to take his place. The next day at a public meeting he agreed and was elected unopposed, as was John Gorrie in another by-election for St Leonard's ward. The Independent Liberals had strengthened their position, but it was too late to prevent the annuity Act from taking effect because the council signed the bonds before McLaren and Gorrie joined. At his first meeting McLaren challenged the previous decision but lost 23–14. *The Scotsman* expected McLaren to become 'viceroy' to the Lord Provost, but 'if he is to be in the council, and to lead its majority, why should he not, in form as well as fact, be at its head, where he was before, and where he did the duties on the whole exceedingly well?' The compliment was backhanded but the paper was distinguishing between political motivation and administrative competence.[7]

McLaren said he intended staying on the council for only six months to voice opposition by voters in the southern districts to having to contribute to ministers in the inner city. He remained for a year, during which he claimed three successes – insisting that the Old Town should not have to pay a share of draining the Water of Leith, opposing the restoration of the Cross in the High Street because that would be vandalism and challenging the increased cost of becoming a burgess, which would exclude the poorer class from admission to Heriot's Hospital. *The Scotsman* said that his real purpose, to lead opposition to the annuity legislation, had failed. His campaign for the interests of the new districts was disingenuous since they would not have to pay 'and have no more to do with the matter than Southwark or Pimlico'. His party on the council was now split, the paper claimed, though McLaren said that opposition to the legislation was growing thanks to the lead given by councillors. The elections of 1861 saw contests in only five wards, all of which were won, according to *The Scotsman*, by candidates opposed to the fanatics 'bent on involving the city at once in moral and pecuniary bankruptcy, and quashing every useful or sensible scheme of municipal improvement'.[8]

McLaren's campaigning continued on other fronts. He clashed with Moncreiff at a meeting in April 1860 called to support the Reform Bill brought forward by Lord John Russell on behalf of the Government. Agnes attended with Priscilla and told the story: 'It was very exciting and stormy sometimes. The Lord Advocate was very angry at Papa's remarks and he spoke about them at great length, but was hissed and groaned down completely. It must have been very humiliating for him especially when Papa got up to say it was too bad not to give him a hearing. I think it was quite natural for him to say something, but Papa's remarks did not call for such an attack and such a lengthened one too. It was very unfortunate, for I am afraid it will take away from the influence the meeting would otherwise have had, and there will likely be a terrible article in today's *Scotsman* against Papa.'[9] She was right. The paper portrayed 'his ruling passion for making himself disagreeable'.[10] The problem was that the Lord Advocate had accepted an invitation to address a meeting organised by the Independent Liberals for mainly working men and to outline the proposals in the Bill, which he did straightforwardly, even congratulating McLaren for calculating the effect of the extended franchise. The rest of the Whig leadership stayed away because the event was not meant for them. McLaren, however, chose to denounce their absence, contrasting it with the Liberal unity that had brought reform in the 1830s. His comments occupied only a few moments of his 45-minute speech but Moncreiff had to defend his Parliament House colleagues. The result was uproar, and the point of the meeting was lost, despite the importance of Moncreiff's assurance that a £6 burgh and £10 county franchise would not mean 'that we are taking a step in what may be called a democratic, or what is meant to be a revolutionary direction'. *The Scotsman* thought that Moncreiff had fallen into a McLaren lure. Its leader began, 'Will you walk into my parlour said the spider to the fly?' John Gorrie as a young advocate felt the need to apologise to the leader of his profession for the conduct of the leader of his wing of the Liberal party – McLaren had had a 'momentary ebullition of feeling'. Agnes's account of the meeting to her brother John, who was Gorrie's friend, is too kind to their father. He had been unable to control his tongue, his attack was unnecessary and it played into the hands of his enemies and those of reform.

At the end of November McLaren spent two weeks in London with Priscilla.[11] Parliament was considering a proposed amalgamation of the Edinburgh and Glasgow Railway company with the Caledonian. It was a period when the economics of scale meant that the small companies that had opened up lines 20 years earlier needed to expand or disappear. The E and GR and Caledonian were in competition for traffic between the two cities, which was ruinous for their finances but welcome to the travelling public, who enjoyed cut-price fares. Parliament had to authorise amalgamations, and for several years the argument raged, with McLaren using his railway expertise to deploy facts and figures on the side of the Edinburgh and Glasgow and thereby on behalf of the citizens.

Eventually the Caledonian withdrew its bid and concentrated its resources on northern lines. The Edinburgh and Glasgow fell into the hands of the North British, which in turn was to cause concern to the public and to McLaren in the years ahead.[12]

Continued willingness to represent Edinburgh's interests in Westminster and Whitehall made McLaren a valued member of the city's two principal commercial organisations, the Merchant Company and the Chamber of Commerce. Manufacturers and merchants, while hostile to anything that reeked of a Chartist legacy, were eager for political change, as *The Scotsman* disapprovingly noted. Much of their agitation was directed to their own interests – improving commercial law, for example – but they were sympathetic to wider issues of reform, and McLaren and his allies both welcomed their support and rallied them to radical causes.[13] He was chairman of the Chamber of Commerce, almost 500 strong, from 1862 to 1865, during which time he took pleasure in having Gladstone made an honorary member for services to free trade. The Chancellor of the Exchequer had just removed duties on commodities like paper and had worked on a successful commercial treaty with France alongside McLaren's friend Cobden. In the autumn of 1862 Cobden and his wife took a long holiday in Scotland staying with well-heeled Radical friends at their Highland lodges and with the McLarens at Newington House. The American Civil War was a profound sorrow to Cobden both as a bloodstained affront to the peace movement and as a cause of economic distress in cotton-dependent areas like Lancashire. 'A very long ordeal of suffering and bad trade' was in prospect, he told McLaren. 'The great object of solicitude should be the working classes. They are not receiving sufficient to keep them in health and contentment.'[14]

Cobden was an enthusiastic supporter of chambers of commerce. He wanted to reform international maritime law to promote freer trade, and he was especially opposed to the blockade of commercial shipping imposed by the Northern states. He asked the Liverpool chamber to send a deputation to win the backing of the chambers in Edinburgh and Glasgow. 'For the interest of humanity and of all nations, especially England [*sic*] as the greatest commercial nation', the principle is 'that commerce should be as free as possible from interruption and violence in time of war.'[15] Unfortunately the Liverpool chamber fell prey to the local shipowners, who favoured a blockade and nullified Cobden's influence. The support of Edinburgh remained important, as the city rallied to raise money for the distressed cotton workers of Lancashire. 'To you I attribute much of this great and good work', he told McLaren.[16]

At the time of his Scottish holiday Cobden was predicting that the Government would come to an end in early 1863. After meeting Adam Black, who indicated an intention to retire, Cobden told McLaren: 'I shall hail any event that brought you into the House'. But in response to a disclaimer by his host he accepted that Edinburgh's 'religious divisions make it very difficult for a politician to estimate his chances'.[17] At this moment, too, McLaren was confronting a business and family crisis that diverted him from politics and put him under great stress. After the Cobdens left Newington House, Catherine McLaren wrote to her brother John: 'I think they enjoyed their visit here. And I hope it may have done good to Papa by diverting his thoughts a little – although there is no perceptible change in his feelings.'[18] The family had been rocked by Catherine's acceptance of a proposal of marriage from John Oliver and her father's unyielding opposition to the union. The partnership of McLaren, Oliver & Co. was in jeopardy. Before telling the story, it is worth noting that none of it appears in Mackie's authorised biography.

McLaren and his junior partner renewed their business agreement in 1861. Although their partnership dated back over a decade, its reconstitution was not without difficulty. Oliver sent a note to McLaren rejecting changes that would reduce his share of the business. He proposed instead a division of the profits into fourteen shares – eight for McLaren, four for himself and one each for the junior partners, young Duncan McLaren and John Towers, who managed one of the departments in the shop. He calculated that that would give McLaren £3,880, Oliver £1,940 and Duncan and Towers £485 each, but Oliver added: 'I should in case of your election for the city to Parliament, allow out of my share £100 annually for your extra expenses during the time you might remain an MP.' When the partnership eventually expired Oliver's share should be made over to him before McLaren's was paid because he would then be out of the business whereas McLaren would still have a pecuniary interest. Oliver claimed to have helped profits increase from £1,400 a year in 1847 when he joined as an employee to nearly £7,000.[19] The partnership was duly renewed, and Oliver's responsibilities remained considerable because his senior colleague was away so much on public commitments, family visits or trips to hydros and seaside resorts for the sake of the health of his wife and children. Duncan junior did not show the entrepreneurial spirit of his father, and Towers, though a trusted manager with a small share in the business, occupied the role that Oliver had had when Renton was still McLaren's partner.

Oliver was more than a business partner, however. For years he had been part of the family circle, taken under Priscilla's wing, and latterly he and John McLaren had shared a flat with a substantial library.[20] The arrangement made sense for both the young advocate striking out on his own and the older bachelor businessman with adequate means but no family base in Edinburgh. Oliver's roots were in Jedburgh, which he visited frequently, and despite the interruptions to his career for health reasons and the expense of his sojourns abroad, he was well provided for. In one letter he instructs his brother in New Zealand to invest £500 in a sheep farm. By 1862, when he was 44, it is not surprising that he wanted to settle down and start a family. He had long admired Catherine McLaren. When she was 17 in 1857 he gave her a gold watch and chain, 'but I scarcely like accepting it ... for it is quite too handsome a present for him to give me,' she told her brother Duncan.[21] In letters she frequently mentioned him, and by the spring of 1862 the relationship had developed into an intimate understanding whose progress would depend on her father's approval. McLaren was clearly taken aback. He claimed to have seen Oliver's 'unmistakeable attentions' to her for a long time but did not believe that because of the difference in their ages and Oliver's 'serious constitutional disease' he would entertain hopes of marriage. In fact he was blind to what was going on in his house, and it was a sense of betrayal and being made to look naive that drove his opposition.

In a bitter letter to Oliver from London in June he said that visits to Newington House had been to see her and not as a business partner and friend. He had behaved in a 'secret and unavowed manner' which was 'most unmanly'. He had failed to make his intentions clear to McLaren or Priscilla, which was made worse because of the disparity of age between him and Catherine – 24 years – 'causing great discomfort and distress to the family'. McLaren went on to justify his own actions. He had endeavoured to show his disapproval 'by my manner, when you came to the house and spent the evening playing chess with Catherine'. Having to behave in this way was 'galling' because 'my whole course of conduct has been to speak my sentiments openly, to every man, on every question, and frequently to my own hurt'. But if he had remonstrated, Oliver might have denied any untoward attention to Catherine. So since Oliver had acted in 'dumb show towards her and myself, I was obliged to act in dumb show towards you.'[22] He alleged that when he and Priscilla were away from home – which was for most of the spring and summer – Oliver had won Catherine's heart. Grant, Agnes and Duncan warned their parents about what was going on but they did not act until it was too late for McLaren's amour propre. Oliver offered to accompany Catherine to London to join her parents. McLaren immediately said no, and Duncan was substituted as a more fitting escort. The prospect of the relationship culminating in marriage still took McLaren unawares.

In most eyes the wedding would not have seemed objectionable. Oliver was well established in business and could offer Catherine as good a home as she had been brought up in. It was hardly unusual for a man to marry the boss's daughter. And Catherine was no gullible adolescent. Twenty-two was a normal age to marry, and it was common at the time for a young woman to marry a much older man. McLaren himself had been accepted by Priscilla as an older widower who already had a large family. Catherine in her stepmother's eyes was a presentable girl who had enjoyed the education afforded to middle-class daughters at the time. She thanked her brother John for taking an interest in her music, 'all the more as you are the only one at home, who does take any'.[23] Like most middle-class young women her life was comfortable but hardly fulfilling, an issue which her elder sister Agnes was later to confront head on. Visits, often extended, to family and friends broke the monotony of life at home, and all three adult daughters were helpmates to Priscilla and their father, taking responsibility for the younger children in the parents' absence. The servants were a perennial problem, squabbling and getting drunk. Catherine reported the incidents to her stepmother and no doubt gained practice in how she was likely to spend her life, as mistress of her husband's house. That husband was not to be John Oliver if her father had anything to do with it.

Over the summer of 1862 McLaren was the recipient of letters from both Oliver and Catherine. Oliver apologised for his conduct if it had embarrassed the McLaren family but it had been honourably meant. He asked for permission formally to 'pay her my addresses' and he concluded by clumsily stating that 'anything you can point out for to place everyone in a better and more agreeable, you will find me not slow in doing'.[24] Catherine wrote to her father from Glasgow, where she was staying with the Robson family. She was upset at his apparent 'want of confidence in her'. She had nothing to confide 'except that I love Mr Oliver which *you* knew before anyone else but Mama and that I have promised to be his wife, which I told you before anyone else'.[25] It is one of the characteristics of the months of arguments that they were conducted from so many places. In the spring Catherine was with her parents at Ventnor on the Isle of Wight, where they were visited by John Bright. Having returned to Edinburgh she then went with her brother Duncan to London and stayed with her parents in Bayswater. She asked her father when the marriage might take place, and he replied, 'Never'. By September she was living in Glasgow with the Robsons. Oliver's correspondence is from Edinburgh, Aberdeen, Jedburgh and London. McLaren and Priscilla spent part of August and September in Cheshire, at Cheadle and Alderley Edge, home of her brother Jacob.

Ever eager to bring computation to bear in a debate, even on so sensitive a matter, McLaren resorted to actuarial assessment of Oliver's life expectancy. Any insurance company, he claimed, would estimate Oliver's life expectancy at no more than half the usual for a person of his age, so poor had been his health record. Using his friend John McLaren as an intermediary Oliver assured McLaren that he was well and that the illness that had forced him to Madeira was not consumptive. An application to Scottish Widows for £500 life insurance was accompanied by a note from his physician Dr Begbie which attributed his earlier condition to stomach and bowel trouble brought on by overwork. Begbie termed it 'peritonitis'.[26] But now Begbie deemed his patient in good health and eligible for insurance, although the early death of his parents and brother from consumption might mean an extra five years should be added to his actual age for calculating the premium. Hearing this, McLaren retorted that £500 was a very small sum. His own life was insured for £11,000.[27] Catherine wrote to Oliver that Begbie's note would not change her father's mind 'but it must at any rate have the effect of preventing him from drivelling on what he formerly made his chief objection to me, and other people'.[28]

A casualty of the family conflict was McLaren's relationship with his son John. They had been close since his illness-afflicted boyhood. McLaren gave advice on John's legal career, burgeoning political aspirations and health. In the middle of 1862 the tone of their letters changed. John tried to make the case for his friend Oliver and for Catherine's future happiness. His father responded: 'As for Mr Oliver if I were forced to choose between being associated with him, and living in some secluded spot where no man knew me I would prefer the latter course. I consider his conduct most disgraceful and have already said to him all I mean to say.' He signed the letter, 'yours truly' instead of his usual 'yours affectionately'.[29] The next day, in another long letter, McLaren recounted how Oliver had wooed and won Catherine during her parents' absence earlier in the summer and upbraided John for continuing to discuss the matter with Oliver after being specifically asked not to intervene. He had always had 'a very poor opinion of your wisdom on any matter out of your own profession, and behind that all your meddling with him, and latterly with Catherine (after Mr Oliver came to London) was productive only of havoc'.[30]

But McLaren early in the argument knew he was powerless to stop the marriage and so he argued with John about the arrangements. John, presumably acting with Oliver and certainly in accordance with Catherine's wishes, argued for the wedding to be soon, 'indecently hurried', as McLaren called it, the inference being that people would assume haste was a necessity. It should not take place until next Whitsunday, 'as is usual with all reputable marriages'. That would allow

Catherine to spend the winter in England for her health: she was not at present physically fit to be married. He also laid down conditions for the ceremony itself. 'As to *your very foolish* remarks about people being at the marriage, all there is to say is that when I was married to Catherine's mother at Buccleuch Place there was no one present but the family; and when I was married at Rochdale there was no one present but the family; and if Catherine is to be married in my house she must be married in the same circumstances.' In a later letter making the same point he did add that after the ceremony in Rochdale he and Priscilla had had 'a handsome breakfast or lunch' at their home in Edinburgh. Although only relatives were present there were scores of other people who would have come if they had been invited. For Catherine, however, ten would be enough – including the minister and her brothers and sisters. He added: 'This sad affair has caused more bitter anguish both to [Mama] and myself than all the circumstances which have occurred during our married life, put together.'[31]

Priscilla was ill with inflammation of the nerves and head. She said she would succumb to the strain. But although she was indeed under pressure, her loyalties torn between her husband and her stepchildren, she was staying with her brother in Cheshire mainly to visit the dentist and have five teeth extracted. McLaren did not show her the letters from John, but she was grateful to him for getting his father to think of the date and details of the marriage.[32] Tensions in the family continued, however. In November John Bright wrote to his nephew John McLaren: 'I am grieved, deeply grieved whenever I think of the painful subject to which your refer. I fear I can do nothing in it that would not be likely to do harm rather than good. You lament for the trials of your sister – I grieve for them also, as I do for the much sorrow and anxiety which the matter has brought to the tender heart of my sister.'[33]

Early in the summer McLaren told Catherine that if she accepted Oliver's proposal he would never enter the shop again and would sell Newington House 'and leave Edinburgh for good and all'. John McLaren described the threat as 'intimidation'.[34] McLaren bitterly regretted having renewed his partnership with Oliver the previous year (when, as he admitted to John, he had reduced Oliver's share of the profits). If the marriage had been known about then, Oliver 'would have quietly dropped out of the business and ceased to visit our house a year ago.' John Towers would then have been promoted, 'just as I had to have Mr Oliver when Mr Renton's contract expired', or he would have found another partner.[35] At this point, in August 1862, McLaren's correspondence claims that Oliver had expressed willingness to leave the business but also that he would hold McLaren to the deed of partnership. If the latter was the case, 'I would as soon pay a thief who had stolen my watch as pay him for what he has, in this way, stolen from me by his low cunning, in addition to stealing my daughter.' He feared that Oliver would start up his own business in opposition to his father-in-law, which would be neither 'morally right [n]or seemly'. He told John that 'if our fortunes had been changed I would rather have worked for £60 a year as clerk or shopkeeper than have so forced myself upon him'.[36]

After a few weeks in which her husband threatened to turn away from the business, Priscilla reported from Cheshire that he was taking a renewed interest, spurred in part by comparisons he made with colleagues in the same trade in Manchester. At Falkner's, for example, the profits in the shawls and bonnets department were much the same as at McLaren's from the same amount of stock, but in prints and drapery their sales were double from a stock that was less extensive. Duncan junior back home in Edinburgh was the recipient of a stream of letters demanding changes in the business. On 4 September McLaren wrote, pointing out a fall in profit of £500 the previous month, although he accepted that there was a general slackness all over the city. He wanted changes in the dress department, which was Oliver's responsibility and which in Priscilla's view was much worse managed than the parts of the business run by John Towers. The next day he asked Duncan to look into re-employing Alexander Somerville who, having set up his own business, had gone bankrupt but had previously run the prints department well. Find out about his conduct, record and sobriety was the instruction. 'I intend continuing my care of the business by giving similar written directions in other matters, both when I am here and when I return to Edinburgh.' He did so relentlessly. He told Duncan that buyers were better judges of sales prospects than departmental salesmen and that he should try to find one for the dress department at not more than £200 a year. He himself would look in Manchester and if he was unsuccessful, Oliver and Duncan should advertise locally. McLaren's efforts were not immediately fruitful. There were eleven respondents to an advertisement in a Manchester paper, two of whom said they were Conservatives, presumably because it was a Conservative paper. He would try again in a Liberal paper. It was important to find someone for the dress department, which Duncan had rightly described as the 'mainstay of the house' and which was failing. Duncan was suspicious of new partners being brought into the business – 'which you seem to dread as inevitable,' his father said. By now McLaren was preparing the way for life after Oliver. All men should be judged by results, and Oliver's dress department was registering sales of only £3,919 compared with the upstairs area, which

163

brought in £7,301. So if Duncan's description of the 'mainstay' was right, bad management must be affecting the business. He should talk to Oliver and Towers and then come to Manchester 'because something must be done without delay'. Father and son would then interview candidates for the buyership. Ten days later, on 22 September, he issued his firm instructions. The dress department should have two or three buyers who would reduce unnecessary stock. If Duncan thought existing employees suitable they might be promoted and given £20 a year more, with further rises depending on profits and stock control. The existing situation could not go on, with dress sales languishing despite improvements in the layout of the shop and better window displays. On 1 October McLaren wrote to complain of slow progress in reorganisation and making appointments. He was prepared to come to the shop the next day 'and do the whole thing then and there'.[37]

Oliver reacted to McLaren's proposals cautiously. Similar changes in buying and departmental management had already been made in prints, stuffs and 'mournings', 'and not too successfully'. He did not object to being relieved of direct responsibility for three departments, and Duncan had chosen well-qualified hands to take over, but he pointed out that McLaren had no right to interfere with the details of the business under the terms of the partnership except by agreement.[38] Three days later McLaren's reply was uncompromising. The dress department had not been well managed and the changes had to be made; if they did not work he would lose £17 for every £7 lost by Oliver. It was an 'entire delusion' for Oliver to think he had management rights irrespective of McLaren's wishes. He and Duncan could manage only details, and as principal proprietor it was McLaren's right to be absent for as long as he liked, just as it was Oliver's duty always to be present: 'I gave you from a quarter to a third of the profits of my business already established', without conferring any privilege to manage it. For 11 years Oliver had not objected, and in the new contract the only change was to give Duncan a role in managing details of the business, with Towers having a similar role and a share of the returns in his own part of the shop. McLaren also pointed out that he had had to take over day-to-day management while Oliver was recuperating in Madeira but he had still given him a full share of profits for these two years.[39]

Three days later Oliver wrote from the house in Darnaway Street he shared with John McLaren acceding to McLaren's request that he leave the business on 1 January. Catherine, at home in Newington House, immediately sent a note to her fiancé hoping that he would not be downhearted at leaving. 'I am sure it must be a very great sacrifice but I hope you will be rewarded for your generosity and that it will help to bring about a reconciliation'.[40] Negotiations about the terms of separation continued for some time. The date of dissolution slipped to the end of January, and Priscilla hoped that by postponing a public announcement until after the wedding on 7 January, the need for a break-up might be averted.[41] The main difficulty lay in calculating the share of the profits that should pass to Oliver, taking also into account the cost of the extended premises. McLaren came up with a figure of £5,985 but said that if Oliver thought it should be more, based on an estimate of that year's profits, he should state a figure and McLaren would demand neither proof nor reasons. Then Oliver would walk away with 7/26ths of the business as the partnership provided.[42]

On 6 January, the eve of his wedding, Oliver stated that unforeseen circumstances such as the distress in the Lancashire mills caused by the American Civil War had postponed the financial benefits of alterations to the shop. If his calculations seemed generous to his own case, 'I feel it to be only justice that I should have taken the outside as I am sure the state Duncan, Towers and myself were in through his [McLaren's] own acting for the last six months to a certain considerable extent interfered with the prospects of the business'.[43] Oliver, pressed by Catherine, had for more than a month been trying to forge better relations with McLaren before the wedding. He sent a letter apologising for any annoyance he may have caused and recalling the fond parting with McLaren years earlier when embarking at Southampton for Madeira.[44] At Christmas 11-year-old Helen was a beneficiary of this friendly feeling. She sent thanks to Oliver for the locket and chain he had given her: 'We are very sorry to lose Kitty [Catherine], but we think you will be very kind to her because you have always been so kind to us'.[45]

Catherine and John Oliver were married at Newington House by the Rev. Henry Renton.[46] Apart from her parents and all her siblings, there were only four guests, all from the extended family. No one from Oliver's family in Jedburgh was present. Later in the day Catherine wrote to Priscilla from Newcastle, the first stop on their long honeymoon tour. She was sad to leave her home 'and not to know when I should ever come back'. In her hurry she had forgotten to say goodbye to the servants. She thanked her stepmother for her great kindness, 'always, but more especially lately', and said that it was through Priscilla's foresight that they had comfortable rooms awaiting them at the Station Hotel.[47] Priscilla's feelings were expressed the following week in a letter to her sister Maggie. Kitty had been 'the most beautiful bride I ever saw', and Oliver was also very well dressed and looked well. Everyone had done their best, 'even poor Papa'.[48]

Catherine and Oliver spent more than four months abroad, travelling from Paris to Rome, where they hired a language teacher, and then through northern Italy. On their way home they stayed at Jedburgh and finally at the Rentons' manse in Kelso. They were back in Edinburgh on 4 June when John, Grant and Duncan came to tea. The diary Catherine kept has conventional descriptions of the places they visited but it is punctuated by references to her bouts of illness. Sometimes Oliver had to take over the writing. McLaren's concern about Oliver's health was misplaced. It was his daughter who was increasingly sick with consumption.

While they were in Florence the couple heard of Priscilla's fears that Oliver might return to set up a business in direct competition with McLaren, which would prompt him to sell up in the High Street. The couple did return to occupy the first of a series of rented houses in Edinburgh's southern suburbs, but Oliver hoped for a post in England. Catherine told her brother John: 'An English manufacturing town does not seem a very agreeable place of residence after Edinburgh but I have got that I should not mind even going to New Zealand, if we were only sure of a settled and comfortable home.'[49] Oliver's brother was in New Zealand but her husband found initial employment closer to home with Clapperton's, another of Edinburgh's many drapery houses.

McLaren was still at odds with himself in May 1863. He had not been well, he told his son Charles in a letter marking the boy's 13th birthday. 'I have often suffered great distress and anguish of mind within the last 12 months about Catherine's marriage and other matters connected therewith, and have often felt so poorly in my bodily health that I thought I could not live very long.' But he had been sustained by thinking of the children, Charles, Helen and Walter.[50] If such an outpouring to a young boy seems odd it is all the more so since Charles himself had been seriously ill with liver and bowel trouble. Six weeks earlier Priscilla had written to her sister: 'I have a strong impression that this darling boy is not to be long ours.'[51] He survived and was told by his father: 'I have helped all your older brothers and sisters to the best of my ability, till they are now men and women, and I should like to help you, too, if it pleased God to spare me for a few years.'

Unflagging correspondent: the portrait of Duncan McLaren by Sir George Reid has him characteristically busy

Brother and sister: John Bright MP
and Priscilla Bright McLaren

John McLaren by the
well-known artist Sir
John Lavery

Newington House: for Priscilla it was
"very ugly outside but most commodious within"

Advertising the shop: entrance hall at
329 High Street

The hilltop memorial to
McLaren near Dalmally in
Argyll

George Hope, tenant farmer of Fenton Barns

Alexander Russel, combative editor

James Moncreiff, Lord Advocate and judge, clashed frequently with McLaren

Named after himself: the heart of McLaren's building enterprise

11. *In Parliament at last*

McLaren's attention was diverted from family and business problems in 1863 by the Social Science Congress which was held that year in Edinburgh and gave the city's leaders an opportunity to mix with academics and policymakers from across Britain and abroad. Founded in 1857 by Lord Brougham, the National Association for Promotion of Social Science set out to take the same role as the British Association had for the natural sciences.[1] McLaren had attended BA meetings and he went to the Glasgow Social Science Congress in 1860. The Edinburgh meeting attracted 2,830 participants, just a handful short of the number at Glasgow. Of these, 907 were women, although all the talking was done by men. After an inaugural lecture by Brougham in the presence of Prince Alfred, the congress divided into sections. John McLaren was on the local organising committee for two of these – on jurisprudence and on trade and international law. His father took part in a session on the effect of indirect taxation on the working classes, claiming that duties on tea, sugar and other necessities of life meant that the poor paid a higher percentage of their income in tax than the better off. He also told a discussion on civil procedure in Scotland that the judicial system in England offered speedier resolution than the cumbersome Scottish one. At the gala dinner for 400 that concluded the congress he responded as president of the Chamber of Commerce to the toast of 'the mercantile and manufacturing interests of Scotland'.[2] Many of the ideas floated by the Social Science Association came onto the agenda of Liberal politicians, especially during Gladstone's first Government. McLaren met some of the intellectuals with whom he would rub shoulders as an MP. He renewed his acquaintance with Henry Fawcett, a Cambridge University don whom he had first encountered at the Glasgow congress. In 1860 the young economist had set aside the handicap of blindness to fight a by-election in

Southwark. McLaren turned up unannounced and spoke warmly in his support, though unsuccessfully.[3]

During this period McLaren developed a new interest. The week after his daughter's wedding in January 1863 Priscilla reported that her husband, though ill, was a 'great deal amongst some houses that he is building in the hope of selling'.[4] It was the start of an enterprise that would occupy him for the rest of his life. He had been a banker and a railwayman. Now the self-made radical exercised feudal superiority and made growing profits. He was helped by Priscilla, who was comfortably provided for by the well-to-do Brights. She lent her husband sums of £2,000 and £3,000 secured on his domestic and business properties.[5] In the late 1850s he bought the feus of 32 acres of land to the south of Newington House for £16,000. This was sloping farmland bounded by low stone dykes stretching south of the modern Mayfield Loan and encompassing three hamlets – Powburn, Sharpdale and Echobank – which have been swallowed up in the city. In 1862 McLaren publishing his plan for feuing the area. It was drawn up by David Cousin, the city architect. Two years later the plan was considerably altered to give more open spaces. It is possible the change reflected McLaren's observation of the extensive building going on in London. Ladbroke Grove has a very similar layout to Cousin's second plan for the land now designated as the Waverley Park conservation area, about a mile south-west of the city centre. Typically, McLaren had firm ideas for the quality and detail of the land he was developing. Each new feuar had 18 months to build one or two villas worth at least £1,300 on his plot. The amenity of the houses would be ensured by insisting on a parapet wall between street and front garden, an average of 2 foot 6 inches above the pavement height, with a 3 foot 6 inch iron railing always to be kept open so that the 'flower-plot' could be seen from the street. He named the streets himself and for himself – McLaren Road and Burgess Terrace – which paid tribute to his status as a burgess of the city; Queen's Crescent as a loyal subject; Peel Terrace in memory of the man who repealed the corn laws; Cobden Road for his reforming friend (there is a Bright Crescent nearby); and Ventnor Terrace after the Isle of Wight watering place most in favour for the family's summer holidays. Waverley Park as a description of the whole development pays homage to Sir Walter Scott, like the similarly named railway station.[6] In 1872, when ownership of lands in Edinburgh, other than Crown lands, was tabulated, McLaren ranked as 14th largest proprietor in a list headed by Heriot's Hospital, the town council and the North British Railway. His 35 acres made him the eighth largest private owner, and the value of £43 an acre was second only to that of the smaller area owned by John Hope, a Tory legal grandee.[7]

McLaren's interest in building was not only personal. From his days as a councillor in the Old Town and as a campaigner against social ills stemming from abuse of alcohol, he knew that taking people out of crumbling slums in foetid closes was needed before morality would prevail. The middle classes comfortable in their New Town flats and suburban villas were able to close their eyes to living conditions in parts of the city they rarely visited. McLaren worked in the High Street in immediate proximity to families whose fecklessness and religious ignorance were deplorable to churchmen and councillors. It was obvious that only by rehousing such people could their behaviour be improved. But who would provide what nowadays would be called affordable housing? Certainly not, at this period, the State. Police rates and other sources of civic income were available to keep within bounds the ill effects of slum living but not to finance municipal housing. The Rev. James Begg, McLaren's colleague in the freehold movement, lectured on the problem in the 1850s. In developing his ideas for a cooperative movement to provide working-class housing, he had McLaren's active support, to which he paid tribute in his book *Happy Homes for Working Men and How to Get Them*, published in 1862.[8] The idea of 'happy homes' was an advance on evangelical injunctions to moral behaviour and measures of social control like the Forbes Mackenzie Act. Mutual help was replacing self-help, and the Edinburgh Cooperative Building Company, constituted in 1861, began developing terraces of modest but attractive housing in what are still regarded today as desirable 'colonies'. The leaders of the building company were skilled tradesmen. Begg says that McLaren gave them valuable advice on securing plots of land and handling lawyers. His involvement was altruistic, a response to conditions as he saw them in the city. But when he stood for Parliament he reaped the benefits, especially after the 1868 Reform Act enfranchised men who built the houses and those who now occupied happy homes.

McLaren, long the champion of a dependable water supply, continued to support schemes to improve sanitation and remove the worst of slums by opening up new streets and building along them. That project was led by another advocate of housing improvement, William Chambers, who, having retired from his publishing firm, became Lord Provost in 1865. McLaren attended Chambers's first public engagement after his appointment – the annual soiree of the 200-strong Edinburgh Sabbath School Teachers Union, whose secretary was Duncan McLaren junior. In vowing to tackle the sanitation problems of the Old Town, Chambers would be bound to run into criticism, McLaren senior told him. The one-time Lord Provost hoped that the new incumbent 'would be delivered from the woe of all men speaking well of him ... for it proved indisputably that he never did anything that was of much value to anybody'.[9] The sabbath school teachers joined in the laughter: they knew McLaren had never suffered from the handicap of universal praise.

Meanwhile back in the High Street the draper's business – whose breadth of stock by now qualifies it for the description of department store – flourished without John Oliver's participation. Duncan McLaren junior and John Towers were in day-to-day control of what had become McLaren & Son. The senior partner continued to exercise the right of unquestioned absence that he had made plain to Oliver. Much of his time from 1863 until his election to Parliament two years later was spent away from Edinburgh – on business, holiday or recuperation for himself and his family. In September 1864 Priscilla wrote from Clifton in Bristol to tell John that his father was thinking of wintering there because of the mild climate. Warmth 'seems life to him, and it is best for him to move about especially as he might feel annoyances more at home. I long to settle somewhere, but I have a horror of lodging houses and fresh beds, at least in strange houses.'[10] A month later they were in Brighton and preparing to spend four days with the Cobdens at Midhurst in the Sussex Downs. In March 1865 they were at Clifton when news came of the serious illness that had struck Richard Cobden. McLaren was in London by the time of their friend's death on 4 April. Priscilla wrote to him: 'I long to hear from thee for these sad things make me very nervous especially as evening comes on. I hardly remember when there were so many subjects pressing on one's mind to cause anxiety.'[11] She worried about the effect of Cobden's death on her brother John, who had visited the McLarens the previous week but who had also gone back to London, where the two men met tearfully. John Gorrie, now a journalist on the *Morning Star*, which Cobden had helped to found, was called in to hear their reminiscences and to write an obituary.[12]

By now the talk was of a General Election. The Parliament had lasted six years and the 80-year-old Prime Minister Lord Palmerston was determined to seek another term. For the Radicals this was both a drawback and an opportunity. They were the only parliamentary group who put electoral reform high up on their wish-list but they knew that as long as Palmerston was in charge, there was little or no chance of legislation. But they also appreciated that he would be unlikely to continue for many years and his probable successor, Lord John Russell, who was only 73, wanted to continue the work of the reformers of 1832. The election came in July 1865, and in the preceding months McLaren, under pressure and expectation that he would stand, had to make up his mind whether to challenge Moncreiff and Black. Since he was publicly at odds with the Lord Advocate and still resented Black's affiliation to the Whigs, the political impetus was there. If at the age of 65 he did not take his chance as the leader of the Independent Liberals, he might not get another. But would the Whigs, who had been unchallenged in 1857 and 1859, prevail as they had against him in 1852? Moncreiff was a prominent member of the Free Church, Black a Congregationalist who could make a pitch for Voluntaryist votes. Did such sectarian considerations count as they had a decade earlier? Would McLaren as the recognised (and by *The Scotsman*, reviled) leader of the Opposition to the clerico-police tax win enough support among the resentful? Should he stand alone, looking for second votes from Moncreiff or Black supporters, or should the Independent Liberals run two candidates? But above all, did he want to go to Westminster?

In April he voiced his doubts to John: 'Every month, I may say, and every new family incident, past, present or prospective, makes me less and less desirous of doing any thing else than living quietly as long as I may be spared, in some nice genial place, apart from many painful associations and from all contests.'[13] A month later Priscilla, who was still at Clifton, also told John and Grant that 'Papa is getting too old to go into Parliament now, broken down as he is in some respects by his own trials – tho' it might have contributed to his comfort to have had a more settled life in London.'[14] She asked for discretion in discussing the matter because she was wary of the pressure on her husband to stand. Some of those 'who come about Papa' were not very sincere. If he did stand he should do so alone since that would maximise his chances although these, she feared, were not too good. 'The Free Church people would send back the Lord Advocate, no matter what his political character and doings might be, but as Edinburgh is in reality represented according to the character of its inhabitants, saving a very small portion, I do not see why its present members should not be allowed to walk the course as I expect they will be.' In other words Edinburgh gets the MPs it deserves. At first McLaren's supporters thought he would take over from Black but despite rumours of retirement the 81-year-old was re-adopted by the Liberal Aggregate Committee alongside Moncreiff, who praised the outgoing Government for 'six years of singular repose and prosperity in the country'. Meanwhile a requisition had been dispatched to McLaren at Clifton asking him to be a citizens' candidate. Among the signatories were nine men singled out because their goods had been sold at the Cross for non-payment of the clerico-police rate. McLaren's leading supporters were from the Anti-Annuity Tax League but the committee that was formed to run his campaign contained his allies in the business community and the town council, including William McCrie, Bailie Andrew Fyfe, Hugh Rose, David Lewis, Josiah Livingston and John Millar of Sheardale, who would later become his son-in-law. *The Scotsman* thought that McLaren would again 'poison the atmosphere and exasperate the temper of Edinburgh as he has for 20 years'. It contrasted the narrow composition of the Independent Committee backing him with the 700–800 men of the Aggregate Committee among whom, it claimed, were some previous McLaren supporters.[15] The Independent Liberals challenged both MPs and chose John Miller of Leithen in Peeblesshire to fight alongside McLaren and, in the jibe of *The Scotsman*, to say 'ditto' to McLaren's remarks. Miller was a bit of an unknown. McCrie, chairman of the Independent Committee, said he met him only on the day of his adoption. He shared with McLaren experience of railway management, having been an engineer who made enough money laying out lines to retire in 1849. Three years later he fought Stirling burghs, a seat in which McLaren always took an interest, nominally as a Liberal but apparently with leanings to the Conservatives and loyalty to the Established Church. By 1865 he brought to the fight Radical pretensions and independence of means if not of mind.

John McLaren was very active in his father's support. He told his stepmother that he had spent the whole day from 12 o'clock canvassing in the New Town, first in Heriot Row and Abercromby Place and later at electors' places of business. He was joined by his friend William Robson from Glasgow, and they covered Castle Street and part of Queen Street, calling again on voters who had previously been out. In Castle Street nearly half of those canvassed promised to vote for McLaren but in Heriot Row (home to many lawyers) 'we have hardly any votes'. He summed up the prospects: 'We have not a majority in the New Town as a whole but I am told that in the Old Town the majority is overwhelming'. McLaren and Miller held a series of well-attended and rumbustious meetings. John described his father's speech to 'well to do' electors at Queen Street Hall as 'very good on the whole, and moderate' but he should not have predicted that Black would be bottom of the poll and he should have left the intricacies of cross-voting (for one Whig and one Independent Liberal) to the canvassers. He thought that his father would succeed and Miller would not. He was unhappy with their election committee, which lacked the influence of the Whigs'.[16] The main election issues were the clerico-police tax and the need for a Reform Bill that would fare better than those of previous years. Whereas in most constituencies in Scotland and England reform did not loom large in the campaigns even among Liberals who had supported earlier efforts, McLaren and Miller sought to discomfit the Lord Advocate, who was unwilling to make commitments, and Black, who had gone cold on the matter. But McLaren's prospects depended less on policy than on people's view of him. His reputation was well known. Some of the press supported him but he was attacked almost daily in *The Scotsman*, though such was the intensity of the invective that it probably helped him. The paper mocked the apparent self-deprecation of one of his statements: 'Many of my friends think that I have a talent for looking into details of bills and Scotch business.'

The election campaign jostled for attention with the trial in Edinburgh of Dr Pritchard for murdering his wife and mother-in-law. The verdict of guilty, condemnation to death and confession of his crime were more gripping than the accounts coming in from around the country that Lord Palmerston was strengthening his hold on Government. It was a vote of confidence in the old man rather than expectation of reforming legislation in the new Parliament. In Edinburgh, however, the contest on the streets as well as in the meeting halls was intense. In the absence of a Conservative representative the two factions of the Liberal party were happy to denounce each other. The difference from 1847, 1852 and even the 1856 by-election was that religious sectarianism had much less significance. The canvassers and leafleteers could be as annoying as they are today. 'Old Mally' complained: 'I am a small shopkeeper in the eggs and butter line and keep two or three cows; and my door being an open one, either my better half or myself lose half the day jawing about the election with all sorts of people – mostly McLaren and Miller's men – who must be out of work or on strike at their own trade.' These canvassers promised immediate abolition of the annuity tax and, improbably, utter extinction of the Roman Catholics. If he was out, his wife was being put into a tremor and he was seriously thinking of 'affixing a board to the door, to intimate to canvassers that call here, offenders will be dealt with as trespassers, and prosecuted according to law'. As a keen Dissenter he had been going to vote for McLaren and Miller but no longer.'[7]

Despite Old Mally's defection McLaren topped the poll with 4,354 votes. Moncreiff came second with 4,148. Black, with 3,797, lost his seat and Miller was last with 3,723. The open recording of votes throughout the day allowed the parties' tacticians to calculate where later voters could exercise the greatest influence on the result. It became clear that

McLaren was establishing an impregnable lead. So the aim of the Whigs – and of Tories looking for the least bad option – was to secure Black's seat at the expense of Miller but there were too many voters who rejected the Moncreiff/Black ticket and split their votes. Between the Old and the New Town the balance of support was as predicted during the campaign. *The Scotsman* was outraged. In defeating Black Edinburgh had behaved as it had to Macaulay; it was 'down in the dirt' like 1847, and for the same reason – a public impatient with truth-telling and hungry for flattery and division. In separating the New Town from the Old, McLaren, the paper alleged, had introduced class division as he had brought sectarianism 20 years previously.[18] McLaren could brush all that aside. At the declaration of the poll he said he would go 'free and independent' to Parliament 'as I told you I would, on the recommendation of Mr John Stuart Mill'. A paper more friendly to him, the *Weekly Herald and Mercury*, said that the defeat of Black and the 'virtual defeat' of Moncreiff were not attributable to the issue of reform. 'It is a protest against the iniquitous conduct of Mr Black and the Lord Advocate in the matter of the infamous clerico-police tax.' Reform had been of little influence, although the paper regretted that.[19]

McLaren entering Parliament for the first time at the age of 65 had achieved a long-held ambition even if he had usually disguised it from himself as well as from the supporters who wished he had realised it at a younger age. He was mentally and physically ready for the regime of the House of Commons – daytime committees followed by sessions that started at 4 p.m. and often went on until 2 or 3 in the morning. Nine years previously he had mocked Black for entering Parliament at an age when the business managers might excuse an MP committee work. McLaren had every intention of being a member diligent in the interests not just of Edinburgh but of all Scotland. The weariness brought on by upheavals in family and business had gone. With his usual determination he was ready to be always in his place on the Commons benches. Not that his services were immediately called upon. Parliament did not usually meet in the autumn when gentlemen were on their estates shooting game. Lord Palmerston was destined never to lead his new troops. He died on 18 October and was succeeded by Russell, who worked closely with Gladstone in forming an administration. Radicals had strengthened their position at the election at the expense of Whigs but only marginally so.

Bright pressed for an early Reform Bill but would he join the Government? From Rochdale he wrote to McLaren on 16 November doubting he would be asked and regretting that distance prevented him from talking over the possibilities with his brother-in-law. He added: 'I fear I should be miserable on the Treasury bench.'[20] He would keep up reform pressure from the back benches but confessed that he was 'lazy and tired of meetings'[21], by which he meant public rallies like one that was planned for Glasgow – 'not for me, as I do not go to Glasgow.' McLaren, however, retained an appetite for public meetings in the months before Parliament met. Aside from the sabbath school teachers there was the agitation about events in Jamaica to be addressed. Radicals were in the forefront of a campaign to bring home Eyre, the island's governor, who, they contended, should face a murder charge following too severe suppression of an insurrection. Agnes McLaren reported after a protest meeting in Edinburgh that 'I never heard Papa speak so well before, his manner was so good – more animated than usual – and he was received most enthusiastically.'[22] Election had increased his confidence and assurance. 'The two City Members seem to vie with each other in appearing and speaking at meetings,' Duncan junior pronounced.[23]

The issue of the moment was parliamentary reform. In the weeks before Parliament met and while ministers strove to frame an acceptable Bill, there were meetings in towns across Britain, Edinburgh included. On 16 January 1866 Agnes again praised a speech by her father at the Music Hall, contrasting it with a poor effort by John Miller, his recent fellow candidate.[24] Representatives of the working classes also made capital speeches, she said, but *The Scotsman* sneered that few people who mattered were at the meeting.[25] McLaren supported extending the vote to occupiers of houses worth £6 instead of £10. Opponents had said that this would put another 32,000 on the roll, but McLaren pointed out that of these 6,000 were female householders and, amid laughter, went on to say that 'as JS Mill's female franchise is not likely to be proposed in the forthcoming Reform Bill, we are therefore entitled to lay them to the one side'. He had analysed the statistics and the roll would increase by only 4,000. There were other meetings to address in Glasgow and Paisley, and Priscilla complained that he was exhausting himself instead of saving his energy for Westminster. They left Edinburgh on 2 February and after a couple of days at Alderley Edge arrived in London on the 6th, staying for a month in a hotel near St James's Street.[26] The new member took to parliamentary life immediately. On 24 February Agnes wrote: 'Papa seems from what I hear quite to enjoy his new life and has spoken twice on Scotch subjects but it was very late and so his remarks were not reported.'[27] He occupied a seat in the Chamber that had previously been Bright's, and he was surrounded by members of the Radical group, many of whom he knew as allies in the campaigns for free trade and peace.

Two other brothers-in-law of Bright – William and Edward Leatham – had also been elected, and among the large intake of 150 new MPs there were intellectuals whom McLaren admired, like John Stuart Mill, MP for Westminster, and Henry Fawcett. Liberalism was fashionable in the universities, and its young proponents were beginning to make their mark in the Commons, many as Radical challengers to the Whiggery of the great families.[28] Thomas Hughes, author of *Tom Brown's Schooldays*, sat with McLaren, as did J. D. Coleridge, a future Lord Chief Justice. Stirling Burghs were represented by Laurence Oliphant, an unlikely ally: he was a diplomat, traveller and author who resigned his seat in 1867 to join a commune of mystics in the state of New York. In Parliament he did little but annoy his own side,[29] which may be a characteristic of Radical individualism but defeated the purpose of parliamentary life for men like McLaren who wanted to effect practical change.[30]

The first benefit to Edinburgh from its new MP came in the form of a petition he presented on behalf of the Chamber of Commerce, which he had until recently chaired, complaining about the effect on business of delays in sending telegraphic messages. His first vote was derided by *The Scotsman*. He was accused of supporting Fenianism – a terrorist threat at the time – by backing a move to remove from the Queen's Speech reference to an Irish 'conspiracy'. He was supported by only four English MPs and fewer than one in five of the Irish.[31] It showed independence of mind and an interest in Irish affairs that went back to the 1830s and was often associated with his attempts to compare how the Government treated its westerly and northerly territories. McLaren was on safer ground when he intervened in the debate on the Cattle Diseases Bill. Mill also made his maiden speech on the subject, though neither MP had obvious connections with farming or veterinary science. Landowners were to receive compensation for cattle destroyed in the outbreak of plague. Radicals voiced the resentment of communities called upon to fund these payments. As the tale of Old Mally showed, the keeping of cattle was still an urban pursuit despite concerns about public health. McLaren successfully pressed for new inspection and regulation of cattle sheds in towns. Old concerns continued to dominate his new life. In April he received an Edinburgh deputation pressing for action on the clerico-police tax. They came to breakfast at the McLarens' hotel, where they were served a 'very fine salmon' that had arrived by way of Bright from Edward Ellice, the MP for St Andrews.[32] McLaren soon had a select committee established to look into the 1860 Act. He was also put on a committee looking into the condition of artisan dwellings.

The Government was now committed to a Reform Bill, having gone through tortures of indecision since the election and been berated by Bright for their tergiversations. Calculations about the number of men who would be enfranchised by the different sets of proposals being considered were regarded as crucial. Few MPs wanted the working classes to gain undue influence. In March as ministers at last reached agreement on a Bill based on a £7 borough franchise, the Commons debated a report on electoral statistics. McLaren repeated his claim that estimates of the effect of reform on Edinburgh's electoral roll were exaggerated, and he dismissed the anxiety of Scottish county members like Lord Elcho from East Lothian and Sir James Fergusson from Ayrshire about an extended franchise. The Radicals were unhappy that the Government's Bill avoided redistribution of seats. But they reluctantly supported Gladstone, who was responsible for the Bill in the Commons, and especially when there was a threat to its survival from within Liberal ranks. Beggars could not be choosers, Bright said, and he described its critics like Elcho as 'the political cave of Adullam', a phrase that became famous and helped boost his reputation in the country as well as make him still more of a bogey man to conservative Whigs. The Government survived an amendment to its Bill by only 5 votes as 35 Liberals voted with the Tories. McLaren was reinforced in his view that Whigs would endanger reform. A Redistribution Bill gave him the opportunity to show that Scotland was, in population terms, under-represented by 20 MPs. By the end of June the Government had fallen prey to Disraeli's tactics and been defeated on the borough franchise. The ministry resigned and Lord Derby became Prime Minister with Disraeli occupying the key role in the Commons that Gladstone was giving up. The cause of reform again appeared to have failed. Bright and his Radical allies decided that it was time to turn to the people. There was already in existence a Reform League and although its call for manhood suffrage was not Bright's policy (or McLaren's), it is little wonder that memories of the Anti-Corn Law League were stirred and a national campaign of rallies and petitions was set in train to put pressure on MPs. A huge meeting in London's Hyde Park was banned by the Home Secretary and ended in disorder. Government heavy-handedness gave strength to working men seeking the franchise, and Bright's oratory in a series of autumn rallies brought him new fame and gave the Radicals credibility in the country.

In late October 1866 McLaren reported to an Independent Liberal meeting on his first term at Westminster. His long speech concentrated on reform, the annuity tax and the need for a city improvement Bill to allow 4d in the pound to be levied to pay for Lord Provost Chambers's ambitious programme. He said that the defeat of the Reform Bill was not down to the Tories but to 'the treachery of a section of the old Whigs', without which the Tories would not have thought it expedient to oppose the Bill at all. For *The Scotsman* this was too much. In a leader insulting even by Russel's standards, it claimed that having McLaren in Parliament showed the reason for objecting to a much wider franchise: when a certain class of elector had rejected Macaulay and Black and returned men like McLaren, there must be a strong aversion to giving that class much power.[33] With a demonstration in the Queen's Park in Edinburgh planned for November, McLaren took steps to ensure that the authorities would not use the Hyde Park precedent to thwart it. He recalled being at a similar event in 1832 and was confident that a rally of the working classes would pass off peacefully and signal the inevitability of reform, as had happened 34 years previously. From a window in Princes Street he observed 'with great gratification' the procession making its way to the Queen's Park where between 30,000 and 40,000 people heard speeches from four platforms. *The Scotsman* did not deny the impressive effect but made the point that whereas in 1832 parliamentary reform had been promoted as opening the way to other great measures, in 1866 it appeared to be an end in itself.[34] In the evening there was a meeting with middle-class speakers at the Corn Exchange. Moncreiff sent his apologies. As many as 3,000 crammed in, forcing McLaren to apologise for the difficulty they had in hearing him. In answer to the Reform League call for manhood suffrage he defined his own position. He wanted a 'real, substantial measure of Reform' which would enfranchise 'a very large number of the working classes, in proportion to the wealth, the intelligence, and the power which they ought to have in the affairs of the country.'

This raised the question of education. Were the working classes well enough qualified to participate in electing their representatives? The Whig rebellion of the Adullamites had been given intellectual coherence by Robert Lowe, later to be Gladstone's Chancellor of the Exchequer, in whose view democracy was premature: the people had not attained a sufficient level of education to challenge the traditional balance between the interests of land and commerce on which the parliamentary system was based. McLaren was challenged at the Corn Exchange: did he think the working classes uneducated? He replied that the men of Edinburgh were ready for the franchise but that the Registrar-General had reported numerous cases in England of men unable to sign their own marriage certificates. From a professed Radical it was a barely satisfactory response, especially since McLaren had earlier pointed out that the Edinburgh electorate would rise from 10,343 to 38,284 with manhood suffrage and he did not think that the level of education was high enough yet to justify the increase. But he recovered by proclaiming that even Tories would accept that the time would come when, with the progress of education, every working man would have the vote. Meanwhile Bright was holding a series of huge demonstrations, including one in Glasgow where under the auspices of the Reform League 150,000 greeted him. Immediately after the Corn Exchange meeting McLaren hurried to Manchester to attend a banquet with Bright and other Liberal MPs. He spoke near the end of the evening and reported on the enthusiasm for reform at the meetings in Edinburgh, Glasgow and Dundee. Lord Derby's Government was likely to fall soon, he said, because it failed to follow the example of Sir Robert Peel and bring forward an honest measure. In a Liberal Government care should be given to appointing to the lesser offices men committed to reform, otherwise it would be found that some were using their influence and patronage to thwart legislation. McLaren raised another Radical (and Voluntaryist) flag by agreeing with an earlier speaker that something needed to be done about the established Irish Church. That was indeed to be on the agenda of a Liberal Government.[35] In December James Moncreiff, free from the constraints of office, explained what it meant to him to be a Whig. In so doing he showed the gulf between his Liberalism and that of his fellow MP for Edinburgh. 'The Whig party of which I profess to be a follower attaches more importance to the unseen tradition which mingles our political with our social constitution than to the line and plummet of hard logic.'[36]

For the parliamentary session beginning in February 1867 the Conservative Government could not avoid the question of reform but was undecided about what it should bring forward, hoping to delay legislation until the following year. With his party divided, Disraeli was faced with the prospect of a Bill from the Liberal benches. His response was rushed and the resulting Bill provided for household suffrage hemmed in by insistence on personal payment of rates, two years' residence, dual votes for property and other 'fancy' franchises. Gladstone set out to destroy the Bill, initially by seeking to remove the need for personal payment of rates. He calculated that if 'fancy' franchises disappeared, as he expected would happen during clause-by-clause debate, a £5 (or thereabouts) rating franchise would be substituted, which would satisfy him and Radicals like Bright. But when his amendment was put to the test, the Government had a majority of 21. Forty-five Liberals voted with the Government or were paired. It was 'a smash perhaps without example', Gladstone admitted. Disraeli, whose tactic was to outwit the Opposition leader and show his supporters that the Liberals no longer called the shots, accepted amendments that removed safeguards and produced the borough household suffrage that neither his party nor the Liberal leadership really wanted. He had been impressed by Bright's season of popular rallies and he used the Radicals to secure his own majorities and discomfit Gladstone.

McLaren was one of the MPs who were willing to be used but he saw through Disraeli's tactic, probably with greater clarity than Bright, and appreciated that the best chance for speedy and wide-reaching reform was to back the Government rather than to defeat it and wait for a Liberal measure which, in the hands of Gladstone and the Whigs behind him, was likely to be less favourable and would certainly mean more delay. Disraeli's Bill applied only to England and Wales. The complexities of personal payment of rates did not arise in Scotland. But as he awaited the Scottish Bill that would follow and the proposals for redistribution of seats across Britain (which engrossed him more than the details of qualification for the franchise) he was ready to vote against his own party. He rose from his sick bed to join the so-called 'tea-room party', Liberals of various hues who told Gladstone that he should not seek to wreck Disraeli's Bill and in all likelihood precipitate a General Election. On the subsequent key vote which led to Gladstone's 'smash', McLaren remained loyal but a month later, on 9 May, he sided with the Tories on an amendment by Gladstone about payment of rates which threatened to derail the Bill. His apparent disloyalty was vindicated when Disraeli capitalised on this victory and to avoid further confrontation removed all the restrictions on household suffrage in the boroughs, thus enfranchising about half a million occupiers. Just as Disraeli shamelessly used the Radicals, so McLaren had foreseen the possibility of Radicals using the Tories as early as March when he wrote to his son John: 'Mr Bright and Mr TB Potter [another Radical MP] ardently desire the Tories should not carry a Bill because they think it would be injured by many inconvenient provisions which the Whigs would not have in. My own desire is strong that the Government should be able to carry a Bill if at all good in principle.'[37] Disraeli's Bill was 'good in principle' even if that principle had not been the Government's first intention. At the moment of the key votes Priscilla noted that Papa 'thinks as in other past questions only the Tories can carry the present one'.[38] As with repeal of the corn laws, so with parliamentary reform.

McLaren knew he would be criticised for siding with the Tory enemy. He hastened to write a letter to McCrie, chairman of the Edinburgh Independent Liberal Committee, justifying his actions. 'No working man in England, being a householder, who is willing to take a little trouble to obtain the franchise, need go without it,' he declared.[39] Helping to achieve that end by his vote was in accord with the pledge he had given during the election campaign two years previously that he would vote for any Reform Bill candidly on its merits, regardless of whether it came from a Whig or Tory Government. He also expected that Disraeli's Bill for Scotland, on the point of being published, would provide for a more liberal burgh franchise than any so far proposed. So along with 52 other Liberals, 7 from Scotland, he was justified in helping to keep the English legislation on course. He had voted in the opposite lobby to Gladstone only twice.[40] The first time was on the rating franchise. The second was when John Stuart Mill proposed a simple amendment substituting 'person' for 'man'.[41] MPs were being called upon to consider female suffrage. McLaren's wife and daughter Agnes were by this time involved in campaigning for women's rights, as we shall see. Mill, whose mastery of written argument did not convert into assured parliamentary speech-making, was attentively heard but found only 72 supporters, including McLaren, Bright and Fawcett.

When the Government produced the Scottish Reform Bill McLaren praised it for extending the burgh franchise along the lines south of the border but he was unhappy about the treatment of burgh constituencies. Of the seven new seats on offer, two were to go to the universities, one each was added to the representation of Aberdeenshire, Ayrshire and Lanarkshire, and Glasgow got a third seat, while there was a new burgh district in Renfrewshire. McLaren continued to insist that Scotland merited at least 20 more seats, but he directed his criticism at the way the counties were protected at the expense of the growing urban areas. The power of landlords would be increased and should be resisted. The Bill was not tested beyond a first reading and was replaced by a similar one in 1868. McLaren wanted a third seat for Edinburgh but argued against the proposal for Glasgow which, he thought, would allow a Tory to be elected for the third seat (as was to happen in 1874). The city should be divided into three constituencies, which he knew would all go Liberal. While reducing his target for extra Scottish seats to 15, he directed his main fire at the way that the burghs were being regrouped. The aim of the Bill was to withdraw urban areas from county seats in order to strengthen the rural Tory preponderance. The Borders were a particular bone of contention. Putting Hawick, Galashiels and Selkirk in Haddington Burghs would make that seat unwieldy and reduce the Selkirkshire electorate from 7,000 to 3,000. During the debates, tedious in their detail, he was accused of ignoring local aspirations and ambitions. He explained to his son John, who was involved in the Liberals' on-the-ground jockeying for position: 'If it had been Gladstone's or Disraeli's seat that I thought should have been attacked I would not have been deterred from *directly* going at it, by a motion of my own just as I did in the case of Selkirk and Peebles, without knowing that any one member held the same views, or would support me.'[42] He was also a realist, repeating his opposition to university seats but accepting that when the two great parties united to promote the proposal, continuing the fight would be in vain.[43] On 28 May, after long evenings of debate, Disraeli addressed McLaren directly: 'The hon. Member for Edinburgh complains of the manner in which Scotland has been treated. I am not conscious that I have considered with any want of feeling the claims of Scotland ... and I think that Scotch members must be unreasonable if they are not satisfied too.' He pointed out that the Commons were coming towards the end of a second session devoted to Scottish representation. 'No doubt if we were to spend 50 years in devising a better electoral system we would arrive at a more perfect system than the one before us', but people ought to accept the progress that had been made.[44]

In autumn 1867, with the English Bill through Parliament and the Scottish one put to bed until the new session, McLaren gave his second annual address to the electorate. He was slightly miffed because Moncreiff had learned the tactic from his fellow MP and got in first this year while McLaren was on his way home from a Highland holiday. But McLaren's account of a momentous session was unambiguous as well as detailed. He had disliked Disraeli's Bill when it was published but soon recognised that the Government was willing to amend it in a way pleasing to Radicals. The changes, he claimed, had been achieved not by the Whigs, or Gladstone, or the Tories, but by Bright, which was true only up to a point. Bright, though listened to by Disraeli, had not been involved with the tea-room party which steered Gladstone away from wrecking confrontation. McLaren declared his own 'zealous' membership of that group, but, anxious to show that his support for the Government had been only limited and short term, he proclaimed to the Music Hall meeting, amid loud cheers, that his experience in Parliament showed him that 'by far the fittest man to be the future prime minister of this country' was Gladstone.[45] Nonetheless, 7,000 more working men were likely to obtain the vote in Edinburgh under Disraeli's Scottish Bill than would have been enfranchised by Gladstone's earlier effort. The rhetoric in McLaren's speech was a paean of praise for the working classes, who on the great movements of the age had been in the vanguard – campaigning against slavery, initiating the anti-corn law agitation, supporting the North in the American Civil War.

With a much enlarged electorate to face in the next General Election, McLaren was setting out his stall to be the candidate of the working man.

Throughout his first Parliament he was as assiduous an attender and speaker as his previous career would have indicated. In 1867 he addressed the House on East India revenues and Irish railways, on chaplains for prisons (he thought them unnecessary) and on the condition of agricultural children in England and Wales. He intervened over the regulation of parks, which became a favourite topic, forcing Gladstone to address a letter to him as Prime Minister in 1872 on the differing laws affecting parks in England and Scotland (Gladstone must surely have thought the matter outwith his immediate responsibilities). The Established Church in Ireland and that country's land laws interested McLaren, as they did many other MPs for British seats. There was also a Bill about Trinity College (in Edinburgh, not Dublin) to occupy him. And there was the continued vexed question of the annuity (or clerico-police) tax. He had been elected on a pledge to alter Moncreiff's 1860 Act. Around this time there was an increase in the number of warrants issued for non-payment. To Moncreiff, his Whig voters and *The Scotsman* the matter had already been settled and its continuation was merely irritating, but the persistent non-payers were among McLaren's supporters. Backed by the town council, he brought forward a Bill in 1867 guaranteeing payment of city clergy by using the income from seat rents but dependent on a reduction in the number of endowed ministers. It was opposed by Moncreiff and defeated by 107 votes to 74. Another McLaren Bill in 1868 was defeated by 86 votes to 59.

From February to August the strain of nightly participation in debates and votes took its toll on an MP in his late 60s who was, in his wife's phrase, 'straining every nerve for Scotland'.[46] Agnes, staying with her parents in London, wrote that he rarely returned home before two in the morning.[47] In the autumn there was time for holidays like the Highland jaunt during which Moncreiff stole a march on him with a public meeting in Edinburgh. McLaren's problem was that he had no leisure pursuit to look forward to. Bright stayed in Highland lodges and fished the rivers. McLaren spent his time in Oban in September 1867 waiting at the pier side to see who came off the steamer in the hope of bearing off an acquaintance for topical conversation. One day it was the editor of the Liberal paper in Kelso who was brought to the house. 'He was a clever man, but of such a dull, low, frightened, monotonous voice. I gave him a lecture about Uncle Henry's small income,' Priscilla recorded.[48] The inadequacy of the Rev. Henry Renton's

UP stipend was much deplored by the family. It is little wonder that the poor editor appeared frightened by the assault while on holiday. For McLaren and his young sons there was a diversion in Oban: the local MP came to make a speech, and they went to hear him, but Priscilla lamented: 'As we have the misfortune to wear petticoats we are not to go.'

After the 1868 session there was no relief. Parliament was prorogued on 31 July with an election on the new boundaries announced for November. McLaren almost immediately took seriously ill while in Harrogate. His son Charles reported on 10 August that he had had a feverish day and they were all anxious but he appeared to recover and took good turtle soup although he was still weak from diarrhoea. Priscilla's brother Jacob arrived and insisted on a doctor. Charles noted, as others in the family did whenever Papa was ill, that he was not an easy patient: 'He is hard to please generally and is very queer sometimes.'[49] As the illness continued (with more turtle soup ordered from London) the question arose: would McLaren be able to fight the election?

12. *The busy legislator*

In September 1868 John McLaren went to visit his sick father in Harrogate. The rumour was that he would return bearing McLaren's resignation. But that was not on the agenda. They discussed the election two months ahead by which time McLaren was confident he would be fit for the fray. In the period of uncertainty John took on responsibility for his father's political future. He was by now an established advocate, although his progress had stalled in 1865 when a renewed bout of ill health forced him to seek the sun in Algiers. Prolonged absence affected his practice but he was convinced that his political views and association with his father's attacks on Parliament House Whigs kept him out in the cold. He was torn between political aspirations of his own and professional advancement. Just before visiting his father in Harrogate he sent him a letter disapproving McLaren's intention of publishing a table drawn up by keen young Charles McLaren showing how Scottish MPs voted in the previous session and suggesting inattention to duties by some of them. While not attributable to the McLaren family, there would be obvious speculation and Moncreiff and his allies among the Bar leaders would say it was directed against them. John already felt excluded from cases where they were the senior counsel, 'not that they would do anything to make it unpleasant to act with them but that agents suppose we would not get on well together.'[1] In other words solicitors when instructing advocates would steer clear. John sought the security of a salaried legal position, and his search was long to continue, with his father and uncle John Bright exerting what pressure they could, especially when the Liberals returned to Government. He hoped for a legal post abroad, like the one obtained by his friend John Gorrie, who was embarking on a judicial career that led from the Indian Ocean to Pacific islands and the West Indies. But an early bid by John for a job in Mauritius brought disappointment. 'This state of suspense has been wretched and very bad for thee,' Priscilla advised.² He realised that he had talents other than courtroom pleading. He edited legal texts and in 1868, to his parents' pleasure and the approbation of colleagues, brought out two volumes entitled *The Law of Scotland relating to Wills*, which went through several editions and took its place as a leading textbook.³

He remained his father's political eyes and ears in Scotland during the parliamentary session and was involved in behind-the-scenes negotiations to find suitable Radicals to contest seats. In Clackmannan there were hopes of an Independent Liberal to challenge the Whig MP Adam. What about Brown Douglas, McLaren asked. Then there was speculation about Moncreiff's intentions. McLaren heard he was going to opt for Greenock, a 'safe seat'.⁴ John also briefed his father on legislation affecting Scotland, especially a Bill by Edward Gordon, the Tory Lord Advocate, to reform the Court of Session and create a court of appeal. Gordon also used John's expertise in drawing up his measure,⁵ and one of the rising stars on the Conservative side at the Bar, the splendidly named Badenoch Nicolson from Glenbervie in Kincardineshire, became a close friend of John's – another indication that it was easier to associate with recognised political opponents than with supposed allies among the Whigs. Nevertheless, politics still came in the way of advancement. Gordon overlooked him for an appointment in April 1868 and McLaren advised him to write declining any further consideration since the strain was too much. He should not have told people in advance of his 'expectations', certainly not Bright. 'If he should form part of a Liberal Government it will probably make him less friendly to you than he would have been had he not known of your application': Bright did not approve of seeking favours from the Tories.⁶ McLaren was conscious of tension between his son's hopes of Government preferment and his own activities in the Commons. If John was appointed and then McLaren voted against the Tory Government on the Reform Bill, 'it might [be] said that I had shown no gratitude or proper consideration.' On the other hand if John were appointed after McLaren went into the lobby against the Government no one could say anything disparaging against John, McLaren or the Government. 'On the contrary it will be considered complimentary to you, and as having no connection with my dealings in Parliament.'

As John endeavoured to hold the fort in Edinburgh while election preparations got under way, he had a pleasant surprise for his father and Priscilla. He announced his engagement to Ottilie Schwabe, aged 33, daughter of a Glasgow merchant. The family were known in Radical circles and she and her mother were associated with the growing pressure for women's rights. John told his parents that he had not had much opportunity to meet unmarried ladies, nor did he possess great prospects as a husband. Some years earlier Priscilla had suspected he was interested in Helen, John Bright's daughter, but nothing had come of that. Ottilie was an Episcopalian, and John said that he too had attended Episcopalian churches for some years, preferring them to Presbyterian worship.[7] In Harrogate Priscilla, 'according to a little peculiarity of mine', put on cheerful attire to tell her husband the good news. She had heard a great deal about Ottilie's mother, 'a very superior woman, and this is a strong recommendation to a daughter'. Papa heard the news 'with a calm pleasure', she reported.[8]

Before Parliament rose in July MPs talked informally about how they should campaign in an election with so many more voters. They were bewildered, McLaren concluded, telling John that in large English towns there appeared to be no plans for canvassing. 'The general impression is that any attempt at *universal* canvassing must be abandoned'. For Edinburgh he thought that ward meetings were the only way of reaching the working-class voters. As for the better off, who had had the franchise since 1833, 'they are better known and therefore more easily got at'.[9] McLaren cannot have been in much doubt about his re-election. The larger electorate was in his favour provided working men were registered and turned out on polling day. His Independent Liberal Committee was 900 strong, he claimed.[10] His fellow candidate was again John Miller, even although some prominent supporters such as Lyon Playfair, academic chemist and inventor of the postcard, thought he ought to have a stronger colleague. Playfair in fact wanted Moncreiff alongside McLaren.[11] But McLaren told John that he was 'bound to Mr Miller and the Liberal Committee, and I will always consider myself as in their hands and will cordially act with them in all circumstances, whatever they may be. I hold that my individuality is now merged in the committee'.[12] It could also be said, as his opponents did, that the committee was his creature. Men like William McCrie, Hugh Rose – a leading figure in both the Merchant Company and the Chamber of Commerce – and Andrew Fyfe, the solicitor, were ready to acknowledge McLaren's leadership and work in his interests. McLaren also noted that Miller would consider it a breach of the bargain governing their joint candidatures if anyone were admitted to the committee who would not support both candidates.

The question was, who would be their opponents? Moncreiff was in a difficult position in Edinburgh. His continued opposition to a new annuity-tax Bill made him unpopular in Radical circles, and McLaren was happy to allude to his fellow MP's voting record in the Commons. 'While my colleague was absent during the rest of the session the only thing he did ... was to go expressly to London for the purpose of speaking and voting against the Bill.'[13] Hugh Rose, a non-payer of the clerico-police tax, wrote that Moncreiff's attitude was reason enough to send him about his business if he should dare to stand again.[14] In the end the embattled Parliament House Whig stood in the newly created Glasgow and Aberdeen universities seat. In Edinburgh Moncreiff was concerned not just at the Radical threat but that the Tories would appear for the first time since 1852 and take middle-class professional votes from him.

The Tories were also targeting working men, partly in recognition of the party's role in enfranchising them. They realised that to make progress they had to start winning urban seats, and in 1867 they held a triumphant banquet for Disraeli in Edinburgh. Lord Stanley, Foreign Secretary and heir to the Earl of Derby, appeared ready to test the water. He was a liberal Conservative who later joined the Liberals and he would not have been seeking the seat if a proposal a few years earlier to make him King of Greece had come to pass. McLaren responded by asking his supporters to publicise Stanley's recent voting record – he had been against the Reform Act provision, by which 4,500 men had become eligible for the vote in the city. McLaren did not think Stanley would come to the poll but 'he may put us to great expense in preparing for a battle which will never be fought.'[15] Meanwhile McLaren instructed from his sick bed in Harrogate that Stanley's committee should be investigated for apparently offering to pay poor rates in order to enfranchise men who would vote the right way. That would be bribery and should be exposed. But if it was happening in only a few cases, better keep quiet, lest McLaren's committee be accused of depriving working men of their votes.[16] The Tories could hold their own in the public arena as well as in practising the black arts: a public meeting held by McLaren and Miller before McLaren fell ill was disrupted by Tory interventions. Later, the *Review*, which was friendly to McLaren, wrote that his absence ought to galvanise the Liberals against a well-funded Tory campaign. In the same issue of the paper John McLaren published a bulletin from Harrogate in which two doctors said it was essential that their patient avoid for six or seven weeks 'taking any active part either in the election or other business matters.'[17]

At the beginning of September McLaren was recovered enough to walk round a flower show without feeling the effects,[18] and by October he was back on the campaign trail. He spoke for an hour to an audience of almost 500 at the Queen Street Hall, touching on the 'abuse' that was the Irish Church, on the need for the secret ballot, on national education and on his promise to reintroduce his annuity Bill after the election. By this time Stanley's challenge had disappeared and he stayed with his long-term constituency of Kings Lynn. At the beginning of November John Bright arrived at Newington House for a week's visit during which he received the freedom of the city and struck a similar note to his brother-in-law when he spoke on reform, the ballot and Ireland. At a gathering of working men he cemented their alliance to Radical causes. Despite being away from his base in Birmingham during the election campaign Bright saw all three of the city's seats secured for the Liberals, and in Edinburgh McLaren and Miller were returned unopposed.

Thanking the electorate McLaren explained his approach to parliamentary duties. In the previous Parliament 'I did not feel great confidence in the general run of the Scotch Whig members, and therefore I took my place below the gangway in the midst of the English Radical members. I intend to go back to my old seat as soon as I get to London.'[19] He would devote himself to Scottish business but not exclusively. The MP 'who allows himself to be snubbed and told he is merely a Scotch member, or that a question is merely a Scotch question, is neglecting one of the great duties incumbent upon him – namely, to stand on his proper footing as a member having the same right to adjudicate on matters affecting the city of Cork or the county of Cornwall as on matters affecting the city of Glasgow or the county of Edinburgh.' He defended himself against the accusation in *The Scotsman* that his activities in the Commons had forced Moncreiff to decamp. They had differed in opinion only four times, but he added amid laughter that 'Mr Moncreiff was so seldom there that I had not the opportunity of bombarding him'. John McLaren, who worked hard in the election, may have thought back to a letter from his father two months previously about the difficulty of being an outsider at the Bar: 'These people have done everything spiteful and bad towards myself, and have been anything but friendly to you. I think by feeling my power over them, to a certain extent, and their humiliation in Edinburgh, that they will be less arrogant in future.'[20]

Before Parliament again took his time and energies McLaren celebrated John's marriage. At the time of his engagement John wrote to his fiancée Ottilie that 'ever since I have been old enough to enter with my father's ideas, there has subsisted between us a most intimate communion of thought and feeling – only once interrupted from a misunderstanding that has long since disappeared.'[21] The tension around Catherine's marriage and the rift to which John referred were absent on this happy occasion, although John had to endure a barrage of advice from his father on domestic arrangements. 'Housekeeping, for married people, is very expensive, unless great care and economy is exercised,' McLaren pronounced from his Harrogate sick bed. John's offer to Ottilie of £300 a year was 'altogether utopian and not belonging to the real life.'[22] He should not contemplate renting a four-storey flat for £165 a year. Two people, even a peer and a peeress, would never need such space. It would require four servants at £45 each for board and wages, a total of £180. Furniture and taxes etc would amount to £467. John's salary as counsel to Edinburgh council was only £500, and his practice brought in £400. All his income would be swallowed up, and, anyway, the house in Rutland Square that he was considering was too close to the railway. The wedding was fixed for December, which might be awkward for McLaren because the swearing in of MPs would require him to be in London if his health permitted, but the exact date of the ceremony was not for him (or even John) to pronounce upon. 'There is a rule *almost* universal, if not altogether, that all the gentleman has any reason to speak about is the *month* in which the marriage in his opinion should take place; and that for good or sufficient reasons the lady always fixes on the *week*; and you should never think of interfering with this part of her province.'[23]

John's was not the only family wedding that year. In January Catherine, in Bournemouth for her health, sent an excited letter to her husband seeking enlightenment on the suitor her sister Grant was boasting of. Apparently Grant had told her other sister Agnes that he was a 'man of sterling worth, godly, kind and considerate'. He had two houses – one in Edinburgh where he kept a biblewoman and the other, two years old, in the country where he kept a missionary establishment and a conveyance. He was tall, thin and for 20 years had been an abstainer; he was also aged 60, 'the only objection'. He held a Sunday class at 9 a.m. and a children's meeting every Sunday afternoon, 'and what I think should be Grant's real chief objection, he has worship every morning at half-past seven.'[24] The object of Grant's affections was John Millar, the rich, twice-widowed merchant who was a member of the Independent Liberal Committee. At 35 Grant was still often the butt of family comment. In a material sense Millar was a catch, with his houses in the New Town and at Sheardale near Dollar. The marriage also made her an immediate grandmother. The family jokes now were largely at Millar's expense. He sent Catherine a silver filigree bracelet, clumsily mended with some little pieces missing. She wondered if it had belonged to one of his previous wives and whether he really was rich. She had to stop Oliver sending it back to him. Later the newlyweds visited her in Bournemouth where Agnes was also staying. On Sunday it was too wet to go back to church for the evening service and Millar insisted on holding a service in the house and prayed for Oliver 'as the dear husband of this sweet family'. Catherine, a generous soul, commented: 'I do think he means to be very kind, though he is decidedly peculiar'. She and Agnes thought Grant tended to snub him, but Catherine agreed he had good taste in objecting to his wife's short dresses: 'She is far too little and broad to wear them'. Millar said of their wedding: 'Grant on the drawingroom at the marriage looked beautiful, but Grant in the lobby, dressed for her journey looked quite another person.'[25]

With half her year in London and with the Edinburgh house in her absence repeatedly plagued by servant problems, Priscilla felt the strain of leading two lives and leaving her own three children for such long periods. Staying again in lodgings for the 1869 parliamentary session, she confessed to her sister-in-law that she was going through 'that wretched state of nervous excitement and irritability that makes one a comfort to nobody. However, I have got a very patient husband'. The boys, recovered from their childhood illnesses, were doing well and showed signs of their father's entrepreneurial spirit by using the grounds of Newington House for a trade in poultry.[26]

McLaren had an over-riding aim in the 1869 session: to resolve the annuity-tax issue once and for all. Early in his first term as an MP he had been reluctant to push ahead, conscious that he had to learn the ropes and that electoral reform ought to be where his expertise could be most usefully deployed. His unsuccessful Bills to end the local tax came towards the end of the Parliament's life. There was now unfinished business, and he resolved to bring forward legislation as soon as the Commons met in February. The Liberals had a majority of 110, Gladstone was Prime Minister and John Bright had been persuaded to join the Government as president of the Board of Trade. Gladstone immediately tackled the anomalous position of the Church of Ireland, a minority Church with the status of an Established one. For McLaren the privileged position of Church of Scotland ministers in Edinburgh was another anomaly, albeit on a much smaller scale. In John Miller he now had a colleague similarly committed to action. Moncreiff, reinstated as Lord Advocate, was more accommodating than he had been as an MP for Edinburgh. Just weeks after McLaren introduced his revised Bill to the Commons, Priscilla commented on his new singlemindedness. 'Papa has changed', she told John. He could now go only 'in one path, as it were, just doing his political work – but nothing else ought to cross it – I feel this *myself* and have to learn to bear a more (shall I call it?) solitary life. I find this is the experience of most other wives and children when our men are in Parliament and take an interest in their work.'[27] The letter was written from the Ben Rhydding Hydro. Parliament was in session but she was for a time not with her husband in London.

The Bill provided £600 annual support for 10 ministers instead of the 13 supported under the 1860 Act. Seat rents and £2,000 from Leith harbour revenues ought to be enough to rid the citizens of the 3d in the pound levy dating from 1860, McLaren argued, and he reiterated his argument that the Church of Scotland was in a minority among Protestant worshippers and had too many empty pews. Among the opponents of change Archibald Orr Ewing, Conservative MP for Dunbartonshire, said that passing the Bill would deal 'a heavy blow' to the Church of Scotland. MPs who felt justified in supporting disestablishment of the Church of Ireland should realise that the Church of Scotland was in a different position since it could not be called an 'alien church'. The Conservatives exerted themselves in support of the city clergy but the Bill passed its second reading by 151 votes to 142. Some MPs, including Gladstone, made themselves late for the Lord Mayor's dinner by waiting for the division. McLaren reckoned that without the dinner another 30 MPs would have voted with him. Among Scottish members 25 Liberals supported the Bill, and it was opposed by 5 Liberals and 7 Conservatives.[28] Leading members of the Independent Liberal Committee whom John met the next day thought the result a 'great triumph'.[29] But it meant only the start of long and frustrating negotiations. These involved Moncreiff, who was no longer an MP having become Lord Justice Clerk, and the town council. But it was the Church of Scotland clergy who proved the obstacle despite being promised a payment of £53,000 guaranteed by the Government and repayable in ten years by the council.

In 1870 McLaren resolved to introduce a new Bill which aimed to replace the tax with seat rents worth £4,300, £2,000 from Leith and £1,200 from sums raised to support the poor. He said the Church of Scotland should be happy that he had listened to its arguments during the negotiations.[30] However, the new Lord Advocate, George Young, knew that a private member's Bill, especially from a member as divisive as McLaren, was likely to run into the buffers again. The Government had to intervene to end the matter once and for all. The upshot was a Bill sponsored by Young superseding McLaren's own. It was more generous to the clergy, offering support to the tune of £60,000. The town council and the Annuity Tax Abolition Association, successor to the League, came out in opposition. John McLaren suggested that his father was off the hook since it was the Lord Advocate who had to deal with the town council and Young had rashly taken up a matter he did not understand. John, however, wanted the council to make a small concession to achieve a settlement since the annuity tax was standing in the way of considering a larger matter, disestablishment of the Church of Scotland, whose clergy might prefer the Dissenters to continue the tax battle for another few years rather than have the Church being forced 'to consider, what next?'[31] By the end of April a compromise had been arranged, thanks in the main to the Lord Provost, William Law. The man who was now McLaren's ablest civic supporter, David Lewis, voiced the objections to settling so much on the clergy. McLaren himself was for the time being sidelined but at a meeting of the Independent Committee on 28 April he turned partial success into a claim of outright victory. He realised that compromise, unattainable when Moncreiff legislated in 1860, had to be achieved. *The Scotsman* mercilessly mocked him for moving from initial disparagement of Young's Bill to taking credit for it on the basis that it followed his own proposals.[32] His speech was hailed by the Independent Committee but in truth a settlement that depended on continuing for ten years payment of a tax of 3d in the pound, albeit buried in the general police rate, was not the stunning victory he was claiming. The Church of Scotland clergy still received public money, £56,000 being the final figure, that was not available to ministers of the Free Church and United Presbyterian communions.

McLaren, ignoring the niceties of the compromise, said that a great burden had been lifted from his shoulders. He was careful to heap praise on the Dissenters who had led the campaign and suffered imprisonment and distraint. 'Many of you know that I have never made the non-payment of the tax a matter of conscience, as very many of my brethren have done ... I have paid the tax for 46 years without resistance, legal or passive. I cannot therefore claim the merit of any great sacrifice in the cause.' But he said that he had written pamphlets, letters and newspaper articles, and made speeches 'I do not know how many times against this odious tax.' He hoped there would be no further disagreements before the Bill became law, and his hope was justified when after further negotiations it passed its last parliamentary stage on 1 August. Although McLaren was not the author of the final settlement and although his tactics since 1860 had prolonged the controversy by making it a test of strength within the Liberal party, he deserved from his supporters the credit he took for himself. As a young councillor he gave intellectual substance to the anger of Dissenters by setting out the history of the tax and showing its indefensibility in an age of denominational pluralism. For decades he campaigned for a resolution of the dispute while resisting the temptation to be a martyr himself. The animus between himself and Moncreiff probably delayed a settlement but it allowed the Independent Liberals to maintain cohesion and common cause in their opposition to the Whig leadership of the party to which they were all supposed to belong. On the back of the clerico-police tax he became an MP and then saw off Moncreiff. His persistent campaigning kept him at the head of his sect of Liberals just as his successes over the city's debt and as Lord Provost gave him the wider constituency of approval without which he would not have turned the sect into the dominant political force that it became by 1868.

Along the way, however, he lost a supporter who turned against him in public distress. James Robie, former editor and proprietor of the *Caledonian Mercury*, published a letter in February 1870 condemning McLaren and all who put their political trust in him. Bitter experience had taught him that 'changes in representation, municipal and parliamentary, are not always improvements, and that under the guise of liberty and independence there can be as thorough tyrants and abject slaves as ever wielded a sceptre on the one hand, or crouched ignobly at the foot of coarse, imperious power on the other.'[33] Robie could handle rhetoric and his outburst was only one of a series that had troubled McLaren for years past. The charge was that having used Robie's paper to promote his causes – opposition to the annuity tax and election to Parliament – McLaren had bankrupted him and left his family in distress. The *Mercury* had a history dating back to 1729. One of its editors fought a duel with Charles Maclaren, editor of *The Scotsman*. By the 1860s *The Scotsman* was only too happy to publicise the falling out between the *Mercury* and McLaren. Anything that cast him and the Independent Liberals in a bad light was worth supporting, and by that time *The Scotsman* was so dominant that it could discount commercial threat from a rival in financial difficulty. The years after taxes on knowledge were reduced and newspapers went into daily cut-price competition brought changes on the Edinburgh scene as in other newspaper centres. The *Daily Express* ceased publication in 1859 and its copyright and that of its sister *Weekly Herald* passed to the *Mercury*, which added the prefix 'Caledonian'. In the same period the Free Church *Witness* disappeared and the *Daily Review* was founded to respect civil and religious rights – largely but not exclusively associated with the Free Church. McLaren looked for and often found support from the *Review* but he (and especially Priscilla) were often disappointed by its choice of news which in their opinion undervalued the significance of McLaren's initiatives. In later years McLaren and the *Review* came closer but in the 1860s the Independent Liberals looked for a dependable voice. In 1862 the proprietor of the *Caledonian Mercury*, under pressure of competition, wanted to sell it. McLaren, on holiday at Ventnor, took the lead in persuading the editor, Robie, to buy the paper with financial support from himself and others, mainly Independent Liberals. Robie later claimed that he agreed to the proposal reluctantly, but his editorship was vigorous and controversial, his strong support for the North in the American Civil War putting him at odds with opinion largely Southern in its loyalty. The annuity tax and the seizure of goods from non-payers were his main targets. William Norrie, historian of the tax, was at the time a young reporter on the paper and in his book he recalled the meetings of anti-tax campaigners in the editor's room.[34] When McLaren stood for Parliament in 1865 the *Mercury* gave him strong backing.

Soon relations turned sour. The paper continued to lose money. McLaren and others dipped into their pockets but Robie, reducing his own pay to invest in the paper, said he could not continue to 'go home every day broken-spirited to my family'. In 1865 500 men subscribed £700 as a testimonial to Robie's efforts. He claimed that McLaren said he owed his election to the editor's 'energetic co-operation'. But the MP's initial reluctance to sponsor a Bill to end the annuity tax upset Robie. In 1866 he realised that financially the paper was unviable. It had drained his resources and when he told McLaren and other backers, he was informed that the £700 testimonial must be counted among the paper's assets and was lost. Andrew Fyfe, McLaren's lawyer and spokesman for those who had invested, showed little sympathy with Robie, who accused the Independent Liberals of selfishness, meanness and ingratitude once McLaren's election had been achieved. 'I was left in broken health, with a large family, without a situation, and with just five shillings between me and immediate ruin.' The question of selling Robie's furniture was especially emotive. Fyfe and McLaren said that legally it should be included to meet the debt but McLaren said the creditors would not take payment from that source. Robie poured out his grievances in a damaging pamphlet, *The Representative Radicals of Edinburgh: their Professions and Practices Described.* In great detail and with a journalist's command of the telling phrase, the Independent Liberals and their leader were excoriated. McLaren, realising the damage to his reputation for probity and straight dealing, immediately responded with a *Reply to the Attempt made by Mr James Robie to extort £1100 by means of a threatening letter.*[35] He turned the disagreement into one of resisting an ill-founded claim for compensation. During the negotiations to wind up Robie's involvement McLaren was in London, but in view of the accumulated liabilities he thought the creditors had been generous at settling for five shillings in the pound.

The financial details are of little significance now but the relationship shown between politics and the press is of interest. McLaren agreed he had met regularly with Robie, who should have known that McLaren did not follow the 'extreme views you inculcated' on resistance to the annuity tax. He had always paid without legal enforcement but he respected those who practised passive resistance. On the role of the *Mercury* in his election McLaren wrote: 'Of the 4300 electors who voted for me, I greatly doubt whether one-third part of them were readers of the *Mercury*'. Nonetheless he was grateful for the paper's support, as he was to the *Review* with its larger circulation and to the working-class paper the *North Briton*. For years Robie continued to publicise his grievance against the McLarenites, as he termed them. The truth is that he took the proprietorship of the paper on an insecure basis and, despite vigorous journalism, was unable to turn round a loss-making enterprise. The McLarenites supported him financially for several years but when they realised his cause was a constant drain they abandoned him in a way that looked like political ingratitude. And their attitude to the loss of his £700 testimonial was insensitive and hard-hearted. McLaren continued to use the press to promote his political causes and in later years he contributed to the *Review*. But he would never again seek to bind a paper to him financially and he was to be concerned when his son Charles risked involvement in an English newspaper in the mid-seventies.

McLaren began his second Parliament with a Bill on parochial schoolmasters, which is discussed along with national education in the next chapter. He also tried to abolish church rates in Scotland. This was a follow-up to legislation passed for England and Wales where the payment of church rates had long been a major grievance for Dissenters. The problem, as MPs pointed out to McLaren, was that there were no church rates as such in Scotland. So his Bill was misnamed and easily derided. It was aimed in fact at the sums that could be charged to the owners of properties for the upkeep of churches and manses in their neighbourhood. McLaren was supported by town councils in his effort to remove such historic imposts, but the Bill was heavily defeated on its second reading. Undaunted he reintroduced the Bill in 1871, and this time extracted a promise from the Lord Advocate to look at the problem with a view to legislating. On that basis – and on McLaren's own promise not to proceed with his measure this session or to bring it back next year – he secured a second reading. The matter is minor except in two points. First, the support for the measure in Scotland, if not much reflected at Westminster, showed the first stirrings of agitation for disestablishment of the Church of Scotland, the issue that was to dominate Scottish politics and divide the Gladstonian Liberal party. Second, George Young in answering the debate in July 1871 pointed out that as the Government's business manager for Scottish affairs 'not a single hour of any Government day since the commencement of the session has been at my disposal for the despatch of Scotch business except briefly one evening'.[36] Little wonder that assiduous Scottish MPs like McLaren used private members' time for Bills of their own,. These were unlikely to surmount the many parliamentary hurdles but were expressions of frustration at the Government's attitude to Scottish affairs. Reform of the system was and remained one of McLaren's pressing causes.

Despite his earlier membership of the National Association for the Vindication of Scottish Rights, McLaren's concern was not to wave the Saltire. He sought efficiency and economy, those watchwords of Radical Liberalism. The fact that Whiggery, not least north of the border, was based on family connections and patronage was an incentive to prune from the national Budget posts which were shared among (usually) worthy beneficiaries of these connections but which were unnecessary for good administration. McLaren gained a reputation for scrutinising civil service estimates and pouncing upon waste. In this at least he was as Gladstonian as his party leader and former cheese-paring Chancellor of the Exchequer. To give one example, in 1870 he demanded to know why it cost £6,000 to run the Lunacy Board in Scotland but only £3,800 in Ireland and £20,000 for the whole of England.[37] Inefficiency extended to the Palace of Westminster where Scottish MPs grew increasingly frustrated at the lack of time for Scottish business, which was ignored or pushed to the middle of the night and the fag-end of the parliamentary session. McLaren spoke for a majority of his colleagues when on 5 August 1869 he asked the Prime Minister to consider 'the propriety of providing some additional means for the transaction of public business connected with Scotland'. Gladstone distinguished two threads to the argument. He praised the hard work of Lord Advocates past and present but said there was a feeling that a great deal of non-legal business might be more appropriately lodged in hands not legal. Second, MPs had suggested that improvements and economies could be made in various administrative bodies in Edinburgh. The Prime Minister announced a commission to take evidence, headed by the Earl of Camperdown, a junior minister at the age of 28.

Gladstone, having been personally lobbied by McLaren before announcing the inquiry, asked him to put his ideas in writing. His main proposal was to create a Scottish Secretaryship (or some such title) which would take over the non-legal responsibilities of the Lord Advocate for Government business. He should be paid £1,200, his staff would be minimal and he would take on areas of administration, thus saving the pay of some officials. Under this limited form of devolution Scotland would have a minister much like the Chief Secretary for Ireland. The other aspect of McLaren's advice to the Prime Minister concerned the plethora of administrative boards whose wasteful unaccountability he expanded on when giving evidence to the Camperdown Commission. The 'public light never shines on them,' he argued, and it would be better for their functions to come within Government departments and thus be accountable to Parliament. The Fishery Board attracted his special scorn. Its insistence that every barrel of herring be branded by red-hot iron with the royal insignia before being sent for export was not only unnecessary but an affront to free trade. McLaren's detailed and costed case was not well received, certainly not by public employees whose livelihoods he threatened (even John McLaren's legal post might go, it appeared). In May 1870 the Earl of Airlie asked in the House of Lords for a Government statement on the outcome of the inquiry, prefacing his question with a denunciation of Radical witnesses. Their evidence contradicted that of conveners of counties and magistrates of burghs who expressed confidence in the boards. The earl claimed that McLaren under questioning admitted 'that he was not familiar with the working of the boards, but asserted that the people of Scotland disapprove of boards – an assertion he [the earl] would leave the hon. Member to fight out with the town councils'.[38] The Duke of Argyll answered for the Government. The Lord Advocate might not always be accessible to Scottish MPs as they would like on account of his private practice in Edinburgh but that was no reasons for appointing 'a Chief Secretary for Scotland similar to the Chief Secretary for Ireland ... A Chief Secretary would not have enough proper business to occupy his time, and he would be likely to fill it up by meddling with things which he had better leave alone.' The parallel between Scotland and Ireland was not exact anyway, since the Irish Chief Secretary was responsible to the Viceroy. The Government intended no serious change in Scotland, only a few economies recommended by the commission.

Gladstone was interested in legislating for Ireland, not Scotland (sometimes not even for England either). His first Government dealt with the Irish Church, land laws and (unsuccessfully) the universities.

In the parliamentary recess of autumn 1869 he wrestled in private over the complexities of Irish land holdings, which he thought were at the heart of the island's discontents. Bright was told that the Prime Minister could not accept McLaren's invitation to a banquet in Edinburgh. He had three reasons – the need to spare his strength, 'the inappropriateness of the present juncture for crowing' and recognising that 'the hard and heavy work of every day does not admit of it [acceptance] without injury to that study of the Irish Land question which I am pursuing *daily* with all the patience I can'. Bright agreed and was left to thank his brother-in-law for the kind offer.[39] McLaren was always ready to intervene in Irish affairs but like other Scottish MPs he deplored the neglect of one part of the United Kingdom because of obsession with another. As Lord Advocate, Young worked hard for Scotland, as had Moncreiff, but McLaren found him a hard man to deal with. To a determination greater than his predecessor's to get his own way he added sharp sarcasm, and Priscilla's distaste for him was visceral. She told John that when the Lord Advocate took her down to dinner in her own house, never had she shrunk so instinctively from any man, as if foreshadowing his conduct to Papa.[40]

She voiced her distaste at the moment in March 1870 when her husband was at his busiest, trying to push through his annuity-tax and church rates Bills in the face of the Lord Advocate's opposition. In a bad-tempered debate Young accused McLaren of divulging private correspondence between the Lord Advocate and a Wigtown constituent. Just before the vote McLaren interrupted the Speaker to protest that the correspondence, far from being private, had appeared in the *Wigtown Free Press*.[41] It may be to this passage of arms that Priscilla referred in her letter: 'When Young had done his worst, I shall never forget how he looked round with a fixed look upon Papa to see how he bore it – and Papa looked so grand I thought, like a fine old lion. I never saw *such* a picture of "dignity and impudence". She claimed the Government's plan was to ignore McLaren and Miller, but, referring to the church rates argument, she went on, 'If the Scotch people are true to themselves, the Church may be disestablished in three years,' another indication that the legal obscurities of church rates in Scotland, whose irrelevance was much mocked by Young and his supporters, were recognised as significant in the growing agitation for disestablishment. Priscilla was also concerned about Gladstone's attitude – 'I can believe that gross lies are told him against Papa'. Gladstone voted against the church rates Bill, not surprisingly since the opposition was led by his Lord Advocate. The recently promoted rising star, W.E. Forster, however, took time from his wrestling with reform of English elementary schools to support McLaren and the Radicals. Jacob Bright, MP for Manchester, voted with McLaren but his brother John was absent, 'prostrate and helpless' with nervous dyspepsia, as he told the Prime Minister.[42] His long absence from Westminster culminating in resignation from the Government in December was another reason why Priscilla thought that Gladstone was being turned against her husband, John being the vital link between the Cabinet and the Radical benches.

Illness, which so disrupted Victorian private and public life – even Gladstone, that strongest of men, was frequently laid low – had recently taken heavy toll in the McLaren family. Catherine died in October 1869 aged 29. Since before her marriage she had battled tuberculosis. She and John Oliver spent their six years together seeking a place where he might find permanent employment fitting his talents and experience, and where her health would most benefit. The two needs did not coincide. Catherine spent time in Cannes and in Bournemouth. Together in the year she died the couple went to Madeira, which had previously benefited Oliver. In December 1867 McLaren and Priscilla visited them in Bournemouth. Catherine could not understand their motive, 'but past experience does not tend to make me very charitable. However, we are exchanging civilities in the most amicable manner. Papa looks very much older.'[43] He took his daughter out in a carriage, and Freddy, the elder of his two little grandsons, cried because he could not go too; so granddad took him to the stables to see the carriage being made ready. Priscilla thought Catherine looked very frail, and added in a letter to John, 'If she was not a Renton, I should be more sad about her perhaps than I am.'[44] The tribe of Rentons, who seem to have been omnipresent – the Rev. Henry Renton was in Bournemouth just before Catherine died – were clearly a trial to Priscilla's Quaker patience and she could share the thought with John, son of the pre-Renton period. In March 1869 Oliver wrote from Madeira to 'My dear Mr McLaren' that his wife was very ill. Agnes wanted to go out to help her. McLaren first forbade the trip on account of Agnes's own health but must have relented because by the beginning of May she was in Funchal helping to teach Freddy. In July Catherine was installed again in Bournemouth and wrote to Agnes, who was helping her find a nurse or teacher for the boys. 'I hope the Irish nurse [one of the candidates] is not a Roman Catholic. I have an impression (prejudice it may be) that they are not so truthful, and for many other reasons I should not like one to be with the children.'[45] On 6 October Priscilla told Grant that Catherine's death was imminent and that it would be a release. Oliver and Agnes recorded her last days as she was given drinks including gin and brandy and lots of arrowroot to soothe her. On 17 October, in a note typical of Victorian desire to record last moments, Agnes wrote that she was agitated and frightened. Attacks of black, watery sickness weakened her further and she said: 'I would never stand another attack like this.' Then she quietened, thanks to the opiates she had been given. Her last act was to ask Agnes to rub her and put her in a warmer nightdress.[46] The next day McLaren telegraphed to Oliver: 'Agnes letter received saying funeral to be in Edinburgh if so as your house is let we wish you would bring remains to our house and have funeral from there.' The list of those invited included John Bright and George Hope, the Radical farmer from East Lothian. Despite McLaren's offer, the cortege proceeded to the Grange Cemetery not from Newington House but from an address in George Street.

13. School reform, women's rights

In the last days of the 1871 parliamentary session an exasperated McLaren protested to the Prime Minister about the level of consideration given to Scottish MPs and Scottish measures.[1] Lack of time and common courtesy meant that Scotland was either ignored or treated offhandedly. Pressure on the parliamentary timetable, especially as MPs chafed at being kept in London to endure the oppressiveness of late July and August, meant that Bills were summarily discarded or brought in and passed without Scottish MPs knowing what was going on. McLaren instanced a single-clause Bill about the Register of Sasines: 'The legal profession in Edinburgh knew nothing about it. It passed the House before they had seen it, and it was found to be a most objectionable Bill'. It was stopped in the House of Lords. Scotland was being treated like 'a conquered province of the Roman Empire,' he said. Scottish MPs could not be expected to sit into the early hours night after night to keep watch lest legislation affecting their constituents come up without notice. Gladstone replied that in the busy session just ending Scots had had an interest in many of the measures debated – an army Bill, the Bill introducing a secret ballot for elections, a trades union Bill, a merchant shipping Bill and a Bill repealing the Ecclesiastical Titles Act (McLaren was one of a small minority of MPs against the repeal of this sectarian legacy from Russell's first Government, on the ground that no clergyman of any denomination should be designated a territorial bishop).

Two years earlier Lord Advocate James Moncreiff had expressed exasperation just like McLaren's. The last of his attempts stretching back 15 years to reform Scottish education was running into the sands of the parliamentary timetable. Knowing the futility of a measure doomed to fail, he complained: 'While our Bills are brought in and lost, education stands still, but crime, intemperance and poverty make rapid strides.'[2] By 1869 support for some form of legislation to bring an orderly pattern to the muddle of education provision was all but universal. Since the embarrassing sectarian failures of the 1850s there had been only an Act in 1861 opening up the posts of parish schoolmaster to candidates not of the Established Church. But in both England and Scotland there had been commissions of inquiry whose series of reports showed the need for action by Parliament. Among Gladstone's ministers eager to make their mark while their leader concentrated on drafting new laws for Ireland were Moncreiff and the most recent recruit to Whitehall, W. E. Forster, vice-president of the council, which in effect meant minister for English education. The question was whether Scottish or English schools legislation would come first.

Scotland looked better placed. In February 1869 the Government introduced a Parochial Schools Bill in the House of Lords. Although that tactic was to prove misplaced because it allowed Tory peers to distort it beyond later rescue, it seemed appropriate that the Duke of Argyll, who had chaired the long-running commission of inquiry that identified shortcomings in education provision and made recommendations largely adopted by Moncreiff in framing the Bill, should introduce the measure to Parliament. The details of the Argyll reports and of Moncreiff's proposals have been thoroughly examined by educational historians and need not detain us[3] but it is worth noting that the wake-up call was the claim that up to 92,000 children had no schooling. This made the connection with crime, intemperance and poverty that Moncreiff spoke of. Moral and social evils rather than the rights of children were still the prompt to action. McLaren, who had experience of providing through the Heriot's schools for children who might otherwise be part of the statistic of neglect, was convinced of the need for legislation but he took issue with the way the numbers had been calculated. The Argyll Commission arrived at its figure of one in six children remaining unschooled by taking the population of school-age children, deducting the number registered as at school and thus arriving at the shortfall. The commission had also relied heavily on statistics from Glasgow which had provided the fullest urban figures but also faced one of the most serious problems of school provision and attendance. So extrapolating the Scottish figures from Glasgow's probably exaggerated the national problem. McLaren pointed out that 'the commissioners assumed that every child should be ten years at school – that was from 3 to 14 years of age. It might well happen that a child had been only five years at school, but they were all set down by this mode of calculation as if they had not been at school at all'.[4] When in mid-July the House of Commons got its opportunity to debate Moncreiff's Bill, barely recognisable after the Lords' amendments, McLaren declared support for its intention but not its form. In particular he challenged the creation of a Board of Education in Edinburgh; it would be another of the 'secret' boards he had been denouncing. The Bill would set up a national system of schools supervised by local boards and would put a charge on ratepayers, which McLaren saw as saving well-heeled heritors, who had always contributed to the costs of parish schools, the unnecessary sum of £48,000. He looked ahead to the day, not provided for in the Bill, when education would become compulsory with 'either very low fees or no fees at all, in order to make the compulsion practically operative in the case of the humbler classes, as was the rule in the United States and in some other countries'.[5] He could not support the Bill as it stood, and at the end of July he argued that it should fall, as it was to, for lack of time to debate it properly. He urged the Government to try again next session.

The 1869 Bill would have provided Scotland with in effect a dual system of rate-aided national schools on the one hand and, on the other, grant-aided schools under the aegis of the various churches. That was what lay in store for England under the Bill brought forward by Forster in 1870. There was no chance of a Scottish measure being debated at the same time. This had the advantage of reducing English MPs' interest in any future Scottish measure. In both Houses they had intervened in the 1869 debates because they feared a Scottish Act might set undesirable precedents for the English Bill. When the time came to look again at Scotland, Moncreiff had given way to the less accommodating George Young, whose proposals in 1871 went under the straightforward title of Education (Scotland) Bill. It dispensed with the idea of a Board of Education in Edinburgh, controversially substituting a Scottish Education Department under the Privy Council in London. The emphasis was now heavily on rate-supported national schools, downplaying the role of denominational ones. As in 1869 there was no mention of the place of religious instruction in classrooms, an issue that much bothered denominations of all hues. There were 200 amendments tabled. McLaren, who thought the Bill was on the right lines, sensibly proposed that the amendments be dealt with in a select committee rather than on the floor of the House. Gladstone refused but recognised the high claim of Scotland to an important measure 'when one session and a half [had] been almost exclusively given to the consideration of important measures for the sister island'.[6] The Lords were causing trouble over the ballot and the army Bill, and so the Government abandoned the Scottish education Bill.

Everyone knew the Government would try again; so the following months saw intense debate across Scotland, with the religious denominations in the forefront and the United Presbyterians strengthening their opposition to any religious teaching in the schools. Young realised, however, that unlike in the 1850s the churches would not have the power to stifle reform. Public opinion, bored with the neverending arguments and frustrated by Parliament's inability to see reform through, especially after the English Act, wanted a decisive outcome when Young introduced his Bill in February 1872 – early enough in the session to allow adequate debate in the Commons and time to face down amendments from the Lords. Knowing that he had only to stick to his guns, the Lord Advocate made no fundamental changes to his previous Bill, and the concessions he made during its passage did not undermine its principles, as had happened in 1869. One successful amendment provided for a board in Edinburgh, but only for a fixed term. McLaren reiterated his opposition but accepted that his was a minority voice; public opinion preferred the Government's controlling hand to be in Edinburgh rather than London. At all stages in the Bill's passage he was an assiduous participant. He was happy to ally himself with the Tories' main spokesman, Edward Gordon, former and future Lord Advocate, who did not want the new school boards to dictate whether and how religious instruction would be provided in their schools. For Gordon and for most of his countrymen the matter should be left to the good sense of schoolmasters, as it always had been. In the end Parliament agreed that the national schools should be allowed to continue religious instruction according to 'use and wont'. McLaren approved of the conscience clause, which allowed parents to withdraw their children, a proviso made easier through another amendment by which RI was to be timetabled for the beginning and/ or the end of the school day. McLaren had argued for that in the 1850s.

An important question was the content of religious teaching. McLaren moved an amendment proposing that the Bible should be read and taught. That was defeated. He had never been keen on the Free Church's emphasis on the Catechism in schools, and an attempt to put it on the curriculum was also defeated. Everything was to be left to the discretion of school boards. While preparing his amendment McLaren explained to his son John that '"religious instruction" is not defined, and there is nothing therefore to prevent the Koran from being taught or any Roman Catholic book, as the Bill stands. The religious instruction being thus *optional* they may say there shall be none given. In that case my amendment cannot apply. If they say religious instruction must be given *then* my amendment comes in, and says it shall be given from the Bible and not from any catechism. If the parent does not desire Bible instruction the child does not attend the class, and is exempted from any harm by the conscience clause.'[7]

McLaren saw rightly that the days of schools owned by Presbyterian denominations were coming to an end, and most of the small and often inefficient adventure and dame schools were also destined to be swallowed up. He told the Commons: 'Much harm arose when there was a multitude of small schools in the place of one larger one under efficient management.'[8] Despite previous hostility McLaren and Young argued their cases with mutual respect, the Lord Advocate accepting some of McLaren's detailed points, courteously rejecting others. The passage of the Bill in August was a triumph for Young, who had shown determination accompanied by readiness to compromise when the force of argument was against him. The Scottish MPs who followed the long process to its successful end emerged with credit, too. Some were spokesmen for local interests such as those of parish heritors or of the various churches, but unlike in the 1850s and even in 1869 they did not turn special pleading into wrecking. Compromise by Voluntaryists like McLaren was as necessary as for members of the Established and Free churches who had most to lose as their schools were turned over to the new boards. Scotland escaped the division south of the border between national secular and denominational schools. There was a greater break with the past than would have been the case if the 1869 Bill had gone through.

It has been argued[9] that the egalitarian tradition of Scottish parish school education, especially in preparing able boys for the universities, was lost in 1872. But by producing a common form of elementary schooling across the country, Young and the Scottish MPs who created the 1872 Act avoided the continuing resentment about Protestant denominational education that plagued English politics into the twentieth century. The Act did not treat the curriculum in any detail (apart from religion), nor did it provide for more than a small number of secondary or higher schools and therefore for entry to universities. Filling these gaps soon engaged university leaders and MPs like McLaren in deep argument. For the time being a fitting comment on the events of 1872 was the appeal by the acknowledged spokesmen of both the Free and United Presbyterian Churches to Dissenters from south of the border, led by Robert Dale, a Birmingham Congregationalist, to call off their speaking campaign in Scotland against any form of religion in schools.[10] Their extremism was an unwelcome distraction, just as for McLaren the necessity of a national education system had taken precedence over Voluntaryist aspirations as far back as the early 1850s.

Funding secondary education was now a major problem, especially for the middle classes and for the universities, which expected incoming students to show reasonable academic grounding. The 1872 Act transferred burgh schools to school boards but prevented them from becoming a charge on the rates. The focus of attention was on unlocking funds held by charitable endowments. The Government had acted in 1869 by bringing forward the Endowed Hospitals (Scotland) Act which, with the backing of the Edinburgh Merchant Company, allowed holders of charitable funds to prepare for Government approval schemes to turn the hospitals they ran into day schools for the middle classes. McLaren, as a member of the Merchant Company, supported the legislation but agreed to speak in favour of amendments brought forward by the company and the town council.[11] The Merchant Company and the governors of hospitals elsewhere in Scotland had plans ready to present when the Bill became law. Moderately priced day schools like George Watson's, Daniel Stewart's and the Young Ladies' Institution were soon up and running and attracting increasing numbers of pupils, to the dismay of teachers at dearer schools whose livelihood was affected. Heriot's Hospital needed time to prepare its plans. With its outdoor schools and council-dominated management it was in a peculiar position. Lyon Playfair, distinguished academic and now MP for Edinburgh and St Andrews universities, poured scorn on the standards achieved by boys in the hospital and especially the outdoor schools. The Principal of Edinburgh University, Sir Alexander Grant – a product of Harrow, Balliol and Indian administration – cast envious eyes on the hospital building, which he believed would make an excellent hall of residence for his students. The delay in deciding Heriot's future played into the hands of those who thought hospitals out of date, inefficient and expensive and not the best way to provide for the offspring of the poor. In 1871 the Home Office refused Heriot's governors permission to reform the hospital because the plan they put forward went beyond the powers of the 1869 Act. Further progress was time-barred by the terms of the Act, and the Lord Advocate proposed a new Bill, but after McLaren and Miller objected, that was not proceeded with. The Home Secretary, Henry Bruce, said that only McLaren's persistent opposition had killed the Bill but admitted that his own lack of knowledge of education in Edinburgh had prevented him from reaching agreement with the Heriot's governors. The result, McLaren declared, was to encourage the university's hope of swallowing up the hospital and thus to 'rob the poor for the benefit of the middle classes'.[12]

The following year a Royal Commission was set up to investigate how all endowed institutions could be made more useful and efficient. Chaired by Sir Thomas Edward Colebrooke, its membership was denounced by McLaren as all Whig and ignorant of Edinburgh and Scotland. He refused to give evidence, which was a mistake. He should have stated his political objection and gone on to speak for the cause he embraced, not least because he aimed to represent working-class opinion whereas the commissioners, he claimed, were fearful of the working class and would not work with them. The absent witness had unrivalled knowledge of the Heriot foundation, was instrumental in the creation of the outdoor schools (now 11 in number, with 3,500 pupils), had chaired the governors as Lord Provost and in addition had experience of being vigorously cross-examined by many commissions over nearly 40 years. Without McLaren the town council witnesses, led by his close ally David Lewis, were given a hard time. The commissioners were more sympathetic to Principal Grant when he spoke about using endowments to fund secondary education and claimed that it cost £41 to educate a boy at Heriot's Hospital, from which no pupil had gone on to university in the previous year. Lyon Playfair and Fleeming Jenkin, professor of engineering, were also listened to when they outlined a scientific and technical curriculum for a reformed Heriot's fee-paying school.[13] The Colebrooke Commission did not report until 1875 by which time the Government was Conservative.

McLaren on the sidelines mounted a press campaign. In December 1872 he gave (and published) a major address to the Literary Institute on the history and importance of the hospital and outdoor schools.[14] He showed that the problem of restricting hospital admission to the sons of burgesses would be solved if any man resident in the city for three years thereby qualified as a burgess. He was later to sponsor an Act of Parliament to that effect. The bulk of his address was a direct attack on Sir Alexander Grant and the 'rubbishing evidence' with which the Principal sought to denigrate the hospital and schools. The next day Grant responded with a letter to *The Scotsman*, affecting not to be concerned by the attention he had received but wondering if it had merited virtually a whole lecture. McLaren's 'long diatribe against myself seems to me to play in the air as innocuous as summer lightning'. The MP's criticisms would be better voiced to the commissioners whom he was ignoring.[15] McLaren, however, knew that if Parliament was to be roused to support reform of Heriot's in the interests of the poor, the pressure against urbane academics had to come from the city's working class, whose views he sought to represent directly, and through his followers in the town council, which also provided the majority of the Heriot's governing board.

In spotting the opportunities and demands of the dawning age of democratic politics, McLaren did not shun the old ways of the despised Whig system where necessary. He sought to use his contacts among ministers and Whitehall officials to obtain for his son John the professional advancement that continued to elude him despite years at the Bar and widely praised legal writings. Expertise in the laws of inheritance brought a part-time appointment as sheriff of chancery in 1869 worth £500 a year but that was only a spur to ambition. The family correspondence for the late 1860s and throughout the 1870s is full of references to sheriffdoms and other judicial appointments sought by and denied to John. At first when Gladstone brought Uncle John Bright into the Cabinet, the prospect of a successful word in the right ear seemed good, but Bright soon left the Government. In July 1870, however, Bruce, the Home Secretary, who was ultimately responsible for Scottish affairs, was making appointments and according to John, 'seems to be really desirous of giving me a step in advance, and I must wait and see what is intended'.[16] But his father urged him not to jump the gun by making application for posts not yet vacant: 'I am as strongly of this mind as it is possible for anyone to be on any subject'.[17] John should be ready to alert the Lord Advocate to his availability if a sheriffdom was to be filled, as was likely in the case of Dumbarton and Bute. McLaren would then back up his claim. Nothing happened, and Bruce had already told McLaren that there were other competent candidates. Political realism also came into the matter, exactly as John frequently lamented and as his father now explained: 'Even if I were Home Secretary I would not appoint you now, nor for some time; for I don't believe public opinion would satisfy the act in present circumstances'.[18] John always felt the hindrance of his father's position and reputation.

The following year he was reassured by his old friend John Gorrie that he would certainly get 'a considerable step' before very long. Gorrie was by this time in Mauritius and embarked on his career in colonial justice. It was John's own failure to make such progress that was galling. Gorrie pointed out that 'Mr Bright, although no longer of the ministry, is still the second man in the liberal party, and Bruce would willingly do anything he asked. They cannot doubt your competence after what you have achieved, and your father is no doubt assured although for a time the old Whig exclusiveness may have its dying day.'[19] Bruce wrote to McLaren: 'I can assure you that your son's claims have been, and are being considered with reference to vacant professional appointments, and they shall receive full justice.'[20] Bright kept up the pressure in 1872, telling his nephew that he had written to

Bruce urging 'that you should be offered the next vacancy in the office of sheriff of a county'.[21] The following year, however, he offered further advice now that John was swithering between a legal and a political career. An election was in the offing but Bright counselled: 'You are right where you are, and your prospect is good, and with fair health, I should say it is certain.' Being adopted as a candidate would be risky: 'You might miss your election – you might get into Parliament and not get appointed one of the law officers – the Government might be thrown out, and you might miss your judgeship. Your present position might be lost and it would not be easy to recover. You are doing well – and are prosperous – don't throw away a good certainty for an uncertainty which is not much better ... You are not in body or in health equal to the demands which House of Commons life might and would make upon you, and I advise you not to try it.'[22] John did indeed enjoy a comfortable lifestyle, but legal reforms which the Government was bringing in might take away his post as sheriff of chancery.[23] He and Ottilie had a daughter Kitty, and in 1871 a son Hernie was born, who turned out to be sickly and needed care. Ottilie's father died and the Schwabe family business was in trouble. John spent time and energy supporting his in-laws. McLaren, who was in the habit of giving his daughter-in-law's family £50 a year, said that their new claim for £400 a year was excessive, much above the average for a minister's stipend. They should move to a smaller house, as he would do in similar circumstances. As for John, he should learn the lesson of prudent economy, 'for if you were taken away it would be a sad change for her [Ottilie]; as it would also be for you both if disabled by impaired health from practising at the bar'.[24]

When Ottilie gave birth to Kitty in 1870, Priscilla wrote: 'She has come at a moment of considerable intellectual excitement connected with women, and I take it as an omen that she will shine in the future amongst many emancipated and highly educated women.'[25] Much of the 'intellectual excitement' about women's rights was generated by the extended Bright connections. Priscilla's two MP brothers gave support in Parliament – Jacob ardently, John with some reluctance. Jacob's wife Ursula was active in Manchester. John Bright's sisters-in-law founded female suffrage societies in Bristol and Bath, and Priscilla's favourite niece, Helen, who married into the west-country Clark shoemaking firm, was active too. In Glasgow Ottilie's mother was prominent in the cause. Priscilla herself took the lead in Edinburgh, becoming president of the local branch of the National Society for Women's Suffrage, which was created in the wake of Mill's failure to amend the 1867 Reform Bill and which sought the parliamentary franchise 'on a par with men'. Agnes was one of the joint secretaries; the other was Eliza Wigham, a family friend, Quaker and longstanding activist in the anti-slavery movement. McLaren was president of the New Edinburgh Anti-Slavery Association, and it was easy for the women in his family and many others to transfer to the feminist cause their skills in organising emancipation meetings and petitions.[26] McLaren at his wife's instigation sent out what would now be called a press release about an Edinburgh petition with 2,000 signatures in favour of women's votes.[27] Priscilla had the advantage of spending half her year in London where she met like-minded women and those MPs open to the arguments for women's rights.

When Mill was defeated in the 1868 General Election – partly because of his support for the female franchise – Priscilla wrote on behalf of the Edinburgh branch of the National Society expressing her deep regret. The *Times* wondered why these Edinburgh women had arrogated to themselves this initiative and mocked 'the "coming woman"' in general and Priscilla in particular. Mill said that despite his defeat and that of several other prominent Radicals 'the cause has a sufficient number of supporters among the best men in the House of Commons to carry on as much of a contest as can be conducted there. It remains for the intelligent women of the country to give their moral support to the men who are engaged in urging their claims.'[28] How much support was needed became clear to Priscilla as she observed the Commons in action. In 1869 she told Agnes of her disappointment that it might be a reformed House as far as the Irish Church question was concerned, and possibly even for the ballot, but 'how little conscience there is about other things and the House never will take things up until there is a tremendous force outside to push it on'.[29] A public meeting was needed to focus attention on women's rights, in particular married women's property rights. McLaren knew many of the members of ladies' committees campaigning for change. He shared their objection to the recently introduced Contagious Diseases Acts which in poor areas could force medical examination on women in an attempt to reduce venereal disease in the armed forces. In September 1870 he wrote to Gladstone following a mass meeting in Newcastle of mainly working men which he had travelled from Edinburgh to address. It called for the repeal of the legislation, and McLaren wanted the Government to listen to these voices of the people as well as to experts in the field.[30]

Early in the same year an Edinburgh ladies' committee organised a crowded meeting on the franchise, chaired by McLaren and addressed by Jacob Bright. McLaren emphasised that the aim was votes not for all women but specifically for those who were unmarried and had a house or lands of their own – in other words on the same property basis as men. In backing the case made by Bright and other speakers, including the universities MP Lyon Playfair, he said he 'never held a stronger opinion on any subject'. A *Scotsman* leader, while patronisingly friendly to the aims of the meeting, pointed out the anomaly that married women would not be enfranchised.[31] The following year Mill was persuaded to come to a meeting in Edinburgh at which he said 'the cause owes an immense debt to Scotland and in Scotland to Edinburgh'.[32] McLaren, again in the chair, took pleasure in the fact that all the MPs from burgh and county constituencies in the area supported the cause, and Edinburgh town council was the first public body to petition for women's suffrage. Mill, who had recently published his book *The Subjection of Women*, was at the height of his enthusiasm for reform, though by the time of his death in 1873 he was dismayed by tensions in the movement between moderates and Radicals like Jacob Bright who wanted to keep up pressure on Parliament by Bills every year. The level of activity in Scotland to which he referred was largely due to the energy of Jane Taylour from Stranraer, who organised and spoke at a formidable number of meetings, taking in the Highlands and Orkney. Agnes McLaren was her frequent companion on her travels. Despite their campaigns and Mill's commendation, Scotland lagged behind England in giving women the vote in local elections and in letting married women own and control their own property. The new school board elections, however, were contested by both sexes. For Priscilla women's causes were a lifelong concern. In 1873 her daughter Helen expressed exasperation at the burden: 'She would go to a stupid women's rights meeting yesterday, just got out of bed to go.' Fortunately, other aspects of her regimen were beneficial: 'She has taken to mutton chops and champagne, which seem to have done her good.'[33]

Sir Alexander Grant had graced the platform at the Queen Street Hall meeting in 1871 and he supported the gradual opening of classes in his university to women. But when the university community became deeply split over extending the right to the medical lecture rooms and the wards of the Royal Infirmary, he was on the side of the conservatives. The McLaren family were firm supporters of the group of women led by Sophia Jex-Blake in their efforts to become doctors. The principal opponents were medical professors, though many male students were hostile too, especially when Jex-Blake and her colleagues proved more than an academic match for them. During the long and bitter struggle McLaren said he saw no reason why a female medical student should not pay her fees and walk into the classroom with her male counterparts, sit the same examinations and be awarded a degree to practise. The strongest argument was that many women wanted a female practitioner.[34] Jex-Blake appreciated the significance of the McLarens' support, especially their friendship with senior members of the university like Professor David Masson, who were trying to convince sceptical colleagues. Jex-Blake was a close friend of Agnes. From her home in Buccleuch Place she wrote in 1872 to John McLaren expressing alarm at her friend's exertions. Agnes 'is utterly unfit to be rushing about the country as she does. But I fear it is the old story of the "willing horse". She says the work must be done and it appears that no one else is able or willing to do it. All of which does not by any means reconcile me to her knocking herself up habitually, but one does not know how to prevent her doing it. I wish I did.'[35]

Agnes was developing her own ambition to join Jex-Blake in becoming a doctor. The problem was that neither her father nor her stepmother wanted her to fulfil her ambition: their feminist views did not encompass the family at Newington House. For them Agnes was a dependable housekeeper in their absence and a minder of the younger children. Perhaps it is as well that Edinburgh University held out against female medical students. To realise her ambition Agnes had to leave home. She tried and failed to persuade her father to change his mind. In 1873 she was studying Latin and mathematics as preparation for admission to a medical course. Her brother John, with whom she shared her frustrated hopes, reported that she thought no one could object to her learning such subjects, which could be useful anyway, 'but she did not seem to care to undertake this study unless she were assured that she could make it available as a pass to Medical'.[36] After a short period at the new London School of Medicine for Women which Jex-Blake was helping to found, she decided on the medical school at Montpelier, apparently on the advice of Cardinal Manning.[37] She travelled there via Cannes, escorting John's sick child Hernie, who was being sent for treatment in the Mediterranean sun. She told John she needed a certificate from a previous anatomy teacher testifying for the Montpelier authorities that 'I have gone over the whole body'.[38] It took time to be accepted as a full student and allowed to go into hospitals but she attended classes and took private instruction.[39] Eventually she qualified, and Jex-Blake did so too in Switzerland. They were among the first ten British female doctors.

Medicine and public health dominated politics in McLaren's constituency for several years. In early 1871 he delayed his return to London for the opening of Parliament because the arrangements for removing the Infirmary from its home in the heart of the Old Town to a site bordering the Meadows and opposite George Heriot's School were at risk of foundering. There had been debate for some years about the wisdom of a move. McLaren supported professorial opinion that the old buildings were outdated and inadequate. He was on the side of the modernisers, although he drew the line when medical research involved vivisection. Value for money was for him of prime importance in any public transaction. Therefore when he heard that the managers of the Infirmary had agreed to an offer by the university to buy the old buildings for £20,000 when independent valuation said they were worth £30,000, he sprang into legal action. With some of his friends he brought the deal to a halt. Like many prominent citizens he was a member of the Infirmary's court of contributors, made up of those who supported it financially. McLaren did so personally and as an employer. Together with Kennington & Jenner, a leading competitor in the household furnishing trade, McLaren & Son made subscriptions to ensure that a total of 200 hands were protected medically. He stated that it was the duty of employer-subscribers to attend meetings and work with the Infirmary managers to ensure that there was efficient provision 'in order that their hands may be restored to health, for the pecuniary advantage of the firm as well as on moral grounds'.[40] McLaren was chairman of a committee set up by the court of contributors to liaise with the hospital's managers. He was determined to make the funders see sense and he asked his son John to give an immediate opinion on the legality of the proposed sale. From his own reading of his son's textbook it appeared that Court of Session authorisation was needed for trustees to make a sale by private bargain. Would that apply in the case of the Infirmary, he asked John, whose legal opinion turned out sceptical.[41]

The Principal of the university used a speech at the Royal Scottish Academy to turn a commercial disagreement into an assault on the narrow-mindedness of the Infirmary, the town council and McLaren. Sir Alexander Grant was addressing the dinner before the opening of the gallery's annual exhibition. The Lord Provost and other guests protested at the inappropriateness of his theme. McLaren tore off a letter to *The Scotsman* condemning the 'outrage'.[42] Grant had said the difference between £20,000 and £30,000 was paltry: that was no argument to place before a professional economiser like McLaren. In the court of subscribers doubters about the wisdom of the sale were influenced more by Grant's intemperance than by McLaren's minute computations. The new Infirmary was under construction from 1872, opened seven years later and was to remain beside the Meadows until its successor opened on the city outskirts in 2003. But the university was thwarted in its hopes of a quick and advantageous land deal. It had to bide its time before it could expand on the old Infirmary site.[43]

The other contentious health-linked issue of the age was the city's water supply. It is strange that McLaren, who had so prominently represented the people's interest in the arguments of the 1840s – to the point of seriously irritating Lord Cockburn (see Chapter five) – was hardly to be seen when the inadequacies of the system again prompted calls for a new source of supply to meet the needs of an expanding city. The water company had dithered for years, offering only dribblets, as one commentator described its proposals to lay new pipes from the hills to the south.[44] New tenements were being built, and there the supply was at best intermittent. One letter-writer to *The Scotsman* asked if he was expected to remain up until midnight to fill a bath when the water came on. The matter became political. At Westminster there were private Bills and select committees from both Houses. A board of trustees replaced the water company and legislation was proposed to bring water from St Mary's Loch in the Borders. The town was divided between supporters of the scheme and its bitter opponents who, by and large, were middle-class Whigs and Tories – and Russel of *The Scotsman*. The town council elections of November 1871 were dominated by the issue. The quality of the water in St Mary's Loch had been questioned. It was supposed to be polluted by a species of flea, and throughout the city posters displaying a much-magnified insect were directed at the promoters of the scheme, including leading councillors. At the polls only 2 supporters were elected against 11 opponents, 8 of them new councillors. A year later, however, continuing lack of progress brought a reversal of fortune with opponents of the St Mary's project losing their seats. In the end, after further delays it was hills near Edinburgh that brought an adequate supply, encouraging the growing movement for public health and, for a century, taking water out of the political arena.

'Since the celebrated Disruption of the Church of Scotland in 1843, party feeling in Edinburgh had never been so high, nor was it so embittered, as in this great water struggle,' later wrote James Colston, having been involved in the controversies of the 1870s.[45] Yet McLaren, usually so eager for a scrap and the self-appointed spokesman for the working men who were most affected by the poor water supply, remained on the sidelines. He had written many letters to the press about water over the years, but when the arguments reached Westminster he gave no lead. He was not a member of the Commons select committee that examined expert witnesses, which was understandable since the MPs nominated were expected to bring a detached view. But whereas in the Commons hearings of 1843 he had spent up to 15 hours a day briefing and lobbying, he now attracted no attention. Press coverage of the select committee records on one occasion that Mr McLaren and Mr Miller had been in the room for a while, and on another day Miller alone attended. But that was all. The shoemaker and bailie David Lewis, McLaren's loyal lieutenant, was a strong advocate of the St Mary's Loch scheme and later wrote a long and immensely detailed account of its fortunes.[46] He mentions McLaren only twice. It appears that the MP left Lewis and other supporters to fight their own corner. He no longer felt the need to take the lead on every pressing issue. That he believed in their cause is not in doubt. The Radical majority on the council – undermined in 1871, restored a year later – were largely his men. Bailie Lewis had a stern and expensive fight to retain his seat in 1872 against a Liberal opponent of the St Mary's scheme. McLaren offered to help defray his costs, which Lewis gracefully declined.[47] For once it was not McLaren who took flak from *The Scotsman*, which deplored Lewis's election 'in the interests of peace, truth, and decency, especially truth'.

At Westminster much of McLaren's work in the public eye involved scrutiny of Government estimates. He regularly pounced on what he deemed profligacy – or discrimination against Scotland. Foreign entanglements and the military spending they produced were anathema to disciples of Cobden and Bright. Gladstone's Government steered clear of the Franco-Prussian War, and his Minister of War Edward Cardwell set about modernising the army at a time of little external threat to the United Kingdom. McLaren, veteran of Peace Society congresses, showed a surprising interest in military strategy and a concern for the defences of Scotland and the Forth estuary in particular. In a debate in 1871 initiated by Robert MacFie, MP for Leith, who thought Britain was more exposed to attack on its eastern than its southern coast, McLaren painted a picture of Edinburgh under bombardment.[48] There was 'nothing to prevent a man-of-war sailing at any time within three miles of the city, to bombard it, or exact a ransom as the price of forbearance'. The funds of all the Scottish banks were kept in Edinburgh – £3–4 million in gold. So the capital needed shore defences, but not of the type proposed for the south coast, with foundations laid on sandbanks under water. Nature had provided Edinburgh with an island, Inchkeith, commanding the approaches, and all that was needed was to embed a few long-range guns. Recalling a past threat, he ended by saying: 'The success which attended the attempts of Paul Jones in former times without the advantage of steam should not be forgotten.' What Priscilla as a Quaker made of her husband's military planning is not recorded, but he returned to the matter in 1878.

In 1872 at the end of the parliamentary session there was a family holiday abroad for the first time. McLaren and Priscilla were joined by Helen and Walter on a visit to France and Switzerland. The cheapest tickets from London to Paris were secured. 'We shall travel very slowly,' Walter wrote, 'much the best way, as three of our party are in a tired condition.'[49] The 19-year-old university student meant everyone except himself. His sister Helen was not a robust girl; at times she had to be carried in a chair. The itinerary was open to change: 'We shall very likely meet some one Papa knows and get some idea of our future plans from other travellers' advice.' When they reached Chamonix, McLaren defied his years with a hard walk. He was very tired in the evening but the next day was ready for more.[50] In Lausanne there was trouble with their accommodation. Helen later recorded that Papa became very angry and nearly fought the man because they were told they could have rooms only on the fourth floor. When it was explained that Helen could not climb the stairs she got a first-floor room, with her parents on the third floor and Walter 'somewhere in the roof'.[51]

In July 1873 McLaren and Priscilla celebrated their silver wedding at their London lodgings in Cornwall Gardens. John could not be at the party, but along with his present sent congratulations for their 25 years 'in harmony of opinion and sentiment'. Duncan would speak for the family and his elder brother hoped that he would 'throw off some of his usual reserve in honour of the occasion'.[52] The Commons were debating a Bill on arbitration sponsored by a Radical friend, Henry Richards, and so no MP could be at the celebrations, not even John or Jacob Bright.[53]

14. *At odds with the unions*

A two-mile procession wended its way across Edinburgh in August 1873 towards a mass rally in the Queen's Park. Forty craft unions from Scottish towns and cities were represented, and forty thousand people, brought in by special trains, were estimated to have heard speeches from four platforms in the park. *The Scotsman* praised the organisation of the day by Edinburgh Trades Council and the quality of the speeches from working-class leaders.[1] Duncan McLaren wandered about the park listening to attacks on his betrayal of the men whose interests he claimed to represent. His sin was to have supported the Criminal Law Amendment Act passed two years previously. It outlawed picketing of employment places and so exposed men on strike to the risk of prosecution. Since the Government purported to support the rights of working people, the Act was regarded as retrograde. And in the view of trade unionists other pieces of legislation needed amendment, too.

McLaren, a veteran of large outdoor demonstrations dating back to the one that preceded the first Reform Act, recognised that this was bigger than any. But he was not daunted by the threats of a withdrawal of support if he stood at the next General Election. He wrote a letter to the joint chairmen of the Independent Liberal Committee, Hugh Rose and William McCrie. It was published in *The Scotsman* on 29 August and in it he pledged to seek re-election if his health permitted (he had had a bout of ill health in March).[2] He was unrepentant about his support for the Criminal Law Amendment Bill when it was passed by Parliament with almost no dissent and when even MPs who acted as spokesmen for trade unions accepted its provisions. If trade disputes were accompanied by no threats, violence or intimidation it was in effect a dead letter, he said. It also had to be viewed alongside an Act of the same year that gave unions legal status and protection of their funds. 'The restrictions imposed by the second Bill were the price to be paid for the passage of the first,' McLaren wrote. He argued that union leaders seeking repeal were no friends of the working classes, who accepted the legislation and opposed intimidatory strikes. Interestingly, he emphasised that at the next election he would trust to the protection of the new secret ballot, 'with full confidence in the intelligence of the great body of the working classes equally with other classes'. Working men could vote without fear of intimidation – just as the disputed Act was intended to prevent intimidation at the factory gate. McLaren wrote to make a political point but even in private he was confident about the forthcoming election. He described the size of the march and demonstration in a letter to his son Walter and yet concluded: 'I would be returned at the head of the poll. I do not in the least fear the result.'[3]

His relationship with organised labour was generally good bearing in mind that he was an employer of up to 200 whose genuine interest in the welfare of his 'hands' was paternalist. He told a public meeting in 1867 that unions ought to have legal protection for their funds but he thought that the many provident and friendly societies should embrace unions willing to accept the terms of registration. During the 1868 election campaign he was interviewed and approved by trades council representatives. He had no sympathy with the growing interest in socialism – whatever that meant in practice – on the part of some working men and a few middle-class intellectuals. The Edinburgh trades council asked him to become an honorary president, but he declined. He defended himself against complaints of bad faith by Dundee-based campaigners from the Nine Hour Factory Association, claiming he could not recall ever meeting their lobbying deputation in London and pointing out that he had been in favour of short working hours all his life, with his firm having been the first draper's to give a Saturday half-day.[4]

The trade unionists sought to press their discontents at the annual meeting of the city MPs with the electors. It took place two days before Christmas in the Queen Street Hall, which was not fully filled but at which there was a strong representation of union members.[5] McLaren as usual gave an inordinately long account of the parliamentary session that had ended months ago, dwelling particularly on the Irish University Bill whose defeat had almost brought down the Government. It gave him the opportunity to dilate on the differing financial treatment of Ireland and Scotland, one of his favourite themes but not one that many in the audience had come to hear about. Before he reached his peroration there were shouts of 'time' and he had to come to a rushed conclusion. His colleague John Miller was received with great cheers because he had already pronounced in favour of repealing the Criminal Law Amendment Act and of paying working men who were elected as MPs. A leading trade unionist, William Paterson, whose career started as a joiner and would end as firemaster of Glasgow, proposed a motion condemning McLaren and thanking Miller. Storming onto the platform he contrasted the attendance records of the two MPs in the Commons. Miller had voted more than twice as often as McLaren, but Paterson had to withdraw his criticism when it was pointed out that the older MP had been ill for part of the session. The vote easily went Paterson's way after McLaren gave a direct refusal of support for a private member's Bill to repeal the contentious Act. One of Paterson's supporters stated: 'We wished the franchise only as a means of raising ourselves to a position of equality with others in the social scale, and to that end we are determined to use it.' This was the impending question. Would working men be able to, or even want to, attain a position of equality by returning one of their own to Parliament? McLaren, denying that he was hostile to working men, pointed out that the hall held no more than 1,000 and the electorate in Edinburgh was 25,000. It was significant that one of the Radical town councillors present said he was in favour of repealing the Act but recognised the services that McLaren had given to the city in Parliament.

On Christmas Day *The Scotsman* appeared with good cheer towards its old enemy. It wrote 'in kindliness and reconciliation' while accepting that McLaren was not its admirer. His stand had been right. 'If it is a stand for property, [it] is as much a stand for honesty, and, more than all, for freedom.' The paper had no time for the threats and violence that accompanied some strikes. As for Miller 'the less said the better', but he received anyway a dose of the vitriol directed in the past at his colleague: 'Mr McLaren took Mr Miller from the horrible pit of obscurity, and the miry clay of Toryism, and set his feet on the rock of Radicalism from which the *protege* seems now trying to shove his rescuer.'

Could the two MPs fight the next election as allies? A year previously McLaren had no doubt. From his holiday in Montreux he sent not a postcard but a long political letter to his son John.[6] It was primarily an admonition against secret 'negociations' [sic] in which John appeared to be involved concerning parliamentary candidates. But it indicates the influence of on-the-ground political organisation, at least in Edinburgh, in the years immediately before national party structures took modern form. The Independent Liberal Committee was not a transient coming together of like-minded individuals when an election was on the horizon. Like its counterpart and rival, the Liberal Aggregate

Committee, it had permanent being. Parliamentary elections might happen only every seven years – the 1868 Parliament lasted almost six – but there were annual elections to the town council. Ward committees and meetings decided on councillors seeking re-election and found new candidates for vacancies. The water supply controversy focused their attention. The Independent Committee and the Radical councillors – McLaren's allies – were closely associated. The committee itself was almost 1,000 strong, as McLaren reminded his son, and

> I feel bound to stick by them as they have stuck by me, and not to be a party, in present circumstances to any secret understanding ... While Mr Miller stands I intend to stand with him, and if he gives up it will be for the public voice to decide who should be brought forward to succeed him; and in that decision I will heartily concur whoever the party may be. I dare say that you will remember that this is the stand I took up at my first election. I said 'let the Committee fix on any man of similar politics – I will stand along with him'; and they fixed on Mr Miller without any intervention on my part. I never had any communication on the subject till I met him in Edinburgh on the evening of the public meeting.

The possibility of attracting Gladstone as a running mate for McLaren had been mentioned. The Prime Minister was not happy representing Greenwich, which had rescued him after his defeat in South Lancashire in 1868.[7] But McLaren thought that the former Rector of Edinburgh University was not suited: 'I think he is the most liberal man of his Cabinet,[8] but I don't think the working men of Edinburgh would accept him. Remember the election is now practically in their hands. There are 23,000 electors and the Whig party might muster about 3,000 or 4,000 votes, and the Tories as many. The Tories would all go against him, merely as a political move to damage the Government, or refrain from voting at all. Why then should 3,000 or 4,000 electors choose one candidate when there are 16,000 or 17,000 other liberals who might not approve of their nominee.' Gladstone's reputation as the 'people's William' came later. He had not yet taken his campaigns beyond Westminster and so, in McLaren's view, the Prime Minister had nothing special to commend him to the recently enfranchised.

Fifteen months later, with Miller being cheered by trade unionists and McLaren denounced, the situation had changed. A new force appeared in Edinburgh parliamentary politics – the 'Advanced' Liberals. The grouping appears to go back to 1868 and the founding of the weekly *Reformer*, edited by David Lewis and dedicated to working-class expression of Liberal causes such as the extension of the new burgh franchise to the counties and, as events played out in Parliament, to trade-union rights.[9] Miller's commitment to repeal of the objectionable legislation gave Advanced Liberals hope of a spokesman in Parliament and provided Miller with an organisation – albeit inferior to that of the Independent Liberals – to run his campaign when Gladstone called a snap election at the end of January 1874. The fact that there were now three Liberal factions is testimony less to inherent fissiparousness than to longstanding dominance by 'Liberalism' in a city where Tories might appear on the town council but had no chance at parliamentary level. It is not surprising, however, that when three Liberals fought for the two votes of electors, Tory hopes of profiting were aroused. Their candidate, J. H. A. Macdonald, the prominent advocate who had jeered the McLaren campaign as a schoolboy in 1852, was early in the field. Three days after news of the dissolution reached the city, John McLaren wrote to his brother Charles that Macdonald had posted a circular to all electors, whereas the McLaren camp was still preparing its leaflet and reply card. The only consolation was that Miller and Lord Provost James Cowan, brother of the former MP for the city and candidate of the (Whig) Aggregate Liberals, were further behind still.[10] McLaren played his hand skilfully. When the Independent Liberal Committee met, he said that it existed to return two MPs, but he and Miller now disagreed on 'a chain of questions which had been raised into prominence by a section of the constituency', and so it could not act as it had in previous elections. Some of its members, especially at ward level, had allied themselves with Miller, who had sent a letter to the Independent Liberals declaring his candidacy.[11] The committee declared strongly for McLaren and agreed to dissolve and re-form at ward level with new conveners where there had been defectors. Meanwhile the Advanced Liberals, by a majority of nine to seven, determined to seek a running mate with Miller but were unable to do so. *The Scotsman* characterised the new faction as a body 'lying to the left of the extremist Left of the "Independent Liberals"'.[12] Its ward office bearers included six councillors.

The election campaign across the United Kingdom lasted barely ten days. In Scotland it was overshadowed by a railway accident at Manuel junction near Linlithgow which cost 17 lives. The appalling number of such accidents in recent years became a minor election issue on which Miller, as a former rail engineer, could claim some authority. McLaren, confident of victory, depicted himself as tried and trusted – a tactic aimed at securing second votes from both the Miller and Cowan camps. Miller's supporters sought to run a double ticket with McLaren but were rebuffed. Miller therefore resorted to claiming that McLaren was now back with the Whigs. The two former allies had broken the neck of the Aggregate Committee in 1868, he said, but it had been allowed to recover by the alliance of Cowan and McLaren, who 'now rested in the bosom of Mr Russel of the *Scotsman*, and he [Miller] wished Mr McLaren joy of his bed.'[13] The newspaper certainly gave McLaren a much easier time than in any previous election and was happy to provide extensive coverage to his claims that Miller had reneged on shared election expenses in the 1865 campaign. The Radically-inclined *Daily Review* favoured Miller as McLaren's colleague and, while paying due respect to the office of Lord Provost, thought that its holder Cowan would make only 'a good average member' of Parliament.[14] But the momentum was with McLaren and Cowan, and it is a symbol of their joint appeal that the Master of the Merchant Company, John Clapperton, publicly endorsed both. McLaren disclaimed any alliance with Whigs but benefited nonetheless.

The first General Election with the secret ballot passed off unremarkably but the count in the Oddfellows' Hall in Forrest Road, which began at 4 p.m., was marred by rioting among those deprived of the former ruckuses on the hustings. At 1.40 a.m. the result was declared: McLaren 11,431, Cowan 8,749, Miller 6,281, Macdonald 5,713. For McLaren the magnitude of his success was reduced by the realisation that he was joined by a Whig in place of an Independent Liberal and by the triumph of Disraeli's Tories across the country. In Scotland they gained thirteen seats, including one in Glasgow where electors had two votes for three MPs and a Tory was able to exploit Liberal divisions and grab the third seat. In Great Britain as a whole the Tories had a majority of 83, although that had to be reduced to 48 if the first success of an Irish home rule party was taken into account. From Manchester came a blow to the McLaren family: 'I grieve especially over the rejection of Jacob Bright,' wrote John, 'which almost neutralizes Papa's great success.' He also regretted George Young's defeat at Wigtown because the Lord Advocate – replaced of course by a Tory – decided to become a judge and so removed John's own immediate hope of elevation to the bench.[15]

Gladstone's Government was beaten because it ran out of steam and suffered heavy losses partly because the Liberals were slower than the Tories in learning how to organise and rally the much extended electorates and in particular how to appeal to working men. It now took the Liberals years to adjust – for the first time since Peel's premiership – to a lengthy period in opposition. Gladstone reacted by going off for months to Europe and then resigning the leadership of the party. For Radical MPs like McLaren there was some solace in Opposition. They no longer struggled against their own ministers' reluctance to embrace Radical ideas. The party, in theory at least, should be more united in the face of the Tory enemy. On the other hand backbench Liberals no longer had access to ministers to press favourite causes or plead for patronage. John Bright's brief restoration to the Cabinet in late 1873 had brought John McLaren new hopes. Just a week before the election was announced, his father wrote three letters in one day to Uncle John, though not just about John's career. At issue was the sheriffdom of Renfrewshire to which John thought he had a prior claim. McLaren held out some hopes but said John must accept that 'all Scotch appointments are *jobbed*', and he should not feel too much disappointment if he did not immediately get one since as an aspirant judge he still had youth on his side.[16] After the election John was still useful in Westminster and Whitehall for legal advice. He even had a new contact in high places. His Tory advocate friend Badenoch Nicolson was appointed secretary to the Lord Advocate and valued John's opinion on measures that Edward Gordon brought forward to reform Scottish legal practice. But the doors to preferment were closed.

At the beginning of 1874 news of David Livingstone's death in Africa, months earlier, reached Britain. For Presbyterian Scots of all denominations his mission was a symbol of dedication and fortitude. The funeral at Westminster Abbey in April was a national occasion. Parliament had recently opened, and McLaren was in London. Priscilla told him to stay for the funeral rather than travel to Keighley in Yorkshire where Walter, who was learning business at shopfloor level, was due to celebrate his 21st birthday. She recalled 'asking Livingstone to shake hands with Walter when he was a child'.[17] The funeral cortege comprised 12 carriages. McLaren and Cowan occupied the seventh. Back in the Commons McLaren busied himself with the scrutiny of Bills and Government spending as before. He did not confine himself to Scottish affairs. Priscilla recorded the events of one evening during a debate on an Irish coercion Bill. The Opposition front bench was empty when McLaren was speaking and 'the liberties of a nation were being discussed'. He had originally given his notes for a speech to an Irish MP who, unable to weave them into his own contribution, passed them to another Irishman. 'Papa saw this MP could not manage it, so proposed to say his own say himself, which was most warmly responded to ... Such a set of grateful faces turned up to him.'[18] Scottish affairs, however, remained his main occupation: 'I have taken such a large share in Scotch matters that I have reason to believe some of the Scotch members are a little jealous of me, thinking I take too prominent a part,' he told John in 1875.[19] He worked hard on the details of legislation, recording for example the Home Secretary's immediate concession to a point he made about Scottish judges in a new appeal court: 'By this declaration of his I think I have gained a great deal; but I wish I had gained more. The carelessness and apathy, and even hostility of Scotch members you will see exemplified in the votes enclosed,' he complained in a letter to John with the lists of how MPs had voted.[20] The debate had begun at 1 a.m. and the vote was at almost 2. McLaren spent time in the Commons library beforehand preparing notes with which to prime another MP, who then made an excellent speech. The 74-year-old did not get to bed until 2.30 and had to be at the Commons at 2 p.m. the next day.

This was a period in which John and his father worked very closely. The son's own political ambitions were beginning to overtake his hopes of speedy promotion within his own profession. The Government's Scottish legal reforms, taking over those initiated by Young before the election and continuing until 1876, allowed John to feed advice to his father, who was often then in the position of voicing the opinions of Parliament House – a sea-change indeed. On the need for a Scottish judge to be appointed to the proposed new Court of Appeal, McLaren asked John to send a private circular to all Scottish MPs.[21] The judges had to be kept within bounds, however. They should not be agitating about their own salaries – 'a private huxtering kind of correspondence, as if it were a matter that concerned them only'. It was not very dignified and, anyway, judges had accepted office on their present salaries, and to McLaren's knowledge many men had declined an office because it was not in their pecuniary interest.[22] Contacts with William Adam, the Liberal Chief Whip, and with Badenoch Nicolson added to the influence John now exerted among his fellow advocates. He also began legal contributions to the *Daily Review* at a guinea a column.[23]

At Westminster Scottish church affairs came to the fore for the first time since English parliamentarians had burned their fingers in seeking to head off the Disruption. The issue was disestablishment of the Church of Scotland – and linked to that, abolition of patronage in appointing the Church's ministers, the issue which had largely contributed to the creation of the Free Church. Why did a new Tory Government promote a Patronage Bill and why did so many Liberals embrace calls for disestablishment that had previously been heard only from Voluntaries like the United Presbyterians but which were now to bring the Liberal party in Scotland close to fatal division in what has been described as a 'violent' campaign?[24] The background is both political and denominational. Gladstone disestablished the Church of Ireland in 1869. Attention then turned to Scotland (and Wales). Because of the Disruption and the strength of the Free and United Presbyterian churches, the Established Church no longer enjoyed the allegiance of a majority of Scots, although the parallel with Ireland, where the division between the creeds was so much starker, is hard to press. In 1873 a Radical MP, Edward Miall, unsuccessfully moved a motion to disestablish the Church of England, and his seconder was his friend McLaren, who devoted his speech entirely to Scotland. He referred to a disestablishment petition he had presented from the Edinburgh presbytery of the United Presbyterians and, amid hostile shouts from fellow MPs, detailed the numerical strength, activity and fund-raising success of the Free and UP churches compared with the Church of Scotland.

It may be surprising that McLaren was now a voice for the Free Church, with which he had such sticky relations in the past. But a majority of Free Churchmen had moved in a direction welcome to the United Presbyterians. Their previous insistence that they were a Church in favour of State Establishment had been widely abandoned. Their earlier confidence in sidelining the Church of Scotland had also largely disappeared as the Established Church under a new generation of able leaders won back adherents and restored its prestige. Above all a majority of Free Church leaders had sat down year after year with UP colleagues in the search for a formula by which they could form a union. In 1873 the talks were given up because a Free Church minority, largely in the Highlands, refused all compromise. 'So far as Christian charity was concerned, the United Presbyterians came out with an unblemished record, but otherwise they were the losers.' That modern verdict[25] is based on the UP's shedding of congregations, especially in England, to other English Presbyterian churches. Free Church and UP leaders, however, had found common cause and fellow feeling, and the two Churches were soon collaborating in a campaign for disestablishment based on converting the Liberal party. The Free Church Assembly in 1875 carried a pro-disestablishment motion by 397 votes to 84. The United Presbyterians were no longer voices in the wilderness.

Since the foundation of the UP Church in 1847 McLaren had kept away from the level of involvement in church politics he had shown as a young man. He continued to be a voice for Voluntaryism, especially in the endless debates on state education. He was a committed member of his local church in the suburb of Newington and a contributor to its good causes. For example, in 1859 he instituted a Sunday-morning service for the children of non-churchgoing parents, the first of its kind in Edinburgh.[26] He maintained close personal and family ties with leading members of his church, through the Rev. Henry Renton in Kelso and the family of the Rev. Dr John Robson in Glasgow, the city which through its strong and wealthy congregations was the powerhouse of the denomination.[27] His reputation as a UP parliamentarian is clear from a story told by Ottilie McLaren. She was on holiday with her children in Highland Kingussie when they came across Mr Arris, a 'toothless and inoffensive old gentleman' who chuckled that one day he might meet 'the member' if McLaren happened to join the family. Mr Arris said that he often read the MP's speeches and he was a wonderful man and that he (Mr Arris) was a staunch United Presbyterian as he supposed all the McLarens were (they all weren't, as we shall see).[28]

Around the time that Miall and McLaren flew their disestablishment kite another Liberal MP, Sir Robert Anstruther, asked the Government to consider abolishing lay patronage in the Church of Scotland. McLaren was the first to rise to oppose the resolution on the grounds of its vagueness and to dispute the desirability of state intervention in the affairs of a church that could no longer be called pre-eminent in Scotland.[29] Gladstone refused to commit himself to abolition and called for a parliamentary inquiry. Edward Gordon, speaking for the Tory Opposition, was much more supportive, arguing that removal of an old grievance might speed reunion of the churches. Since the Tory party had good support among Church of Scotland members, it is unsurprising that Disraeli's Government brought forward a Bill in its first session. To a large extent abolition of the rights of lay patrons was symbolic as it had long been in decline. The Church of Scotland had been steadily moving to the position where members chose their minister, as in the Free and UP churches. But these two churches objected to the Bill, ostensibly because they had not been consulted by the Government but actually because they feared that removal of the patronage grievance would enhance the status of the Church of Scotland in the country and put pressure on the other Presbyterian churches.

McLaren's speech in the second-reading debate on the Bill, which had originated in and been commended by the House of Lords, was specifically made as a representative of the 'Nonconformist' churches. The UP minister Henry Renton was at the Commons lobbying MPs against the Bill.[30] Quoting the views of the Synod, their Church's highest governing body, McLaren said that the issue was not abolishing patronage but 'disestablishment and disendowment'.[31] MPs who adopted the same line were easily dismissed as partisan and the Bill passed into law. Nonetheless, discontent had been building up in assemblies, synods and presbyteries for a decade and was about to be expressed in a campaign for disestablishment. Sectarian politics, which had been at their height in the 1840s and 1850s and which appeared to be on the wane, not least because of the settlement of the education question, were now alive once more. Men of McLaren's generation turned back to the religious controversies on which they had cut their political teeth. The role of the State in religion was more intellectually and emotionally absorbing than its role in ameliorating the social problems of the Scottish people. In Parliament McLaren returned session after session to his Bill abolishing church rates. His indefatigability won him admirers but his purpose was denominational – to end the levy in support of Church of Scotland buildings, a benefit denied to other churches. He carefully distinguished his measure from the issue of disestablishment but his hope of removing the anomaly, while popular in non-Establishment pews, was lost amid fears of that he was opening a Pandora's box.[32]

McLaren felt that as a representative of ordinary people his interest in religious matters (and for that matter in the evils of intemperance) was as relevant as support for their material concerns. In the same busy month of March 1876 that he launched his annual attack on church rates, he was successful with one of his longstanding projects – to change the conditions under which a citizen could qualify for the benefits of becoming a burgess. The restrictions had bothered him since he first joined Edinburgh town council. Now he won cross-party support for bringing Scots law into harmony with English law and thereby making payment of rates the sole qualification for becoming a burgess. The only objectors were MPs for a few burghs that feared loss of revenue. On this matter the young Radical member for Stirling and future Prime Minister, Henry Campbell-Bannerman, was at odds with the old Radical of Edinburgh.[33]

The state of the roads and obstacles in the way of trade were another of McLaren's bugbears. Near the end of his life he would reflect that his achievement in helping commerce as well as ordinary travellers by removing road tolls was down to working with Conservative Governments. It was the Tories who put him on the ambulatory Royal Commission that took two and a half years of evidence in the late 1850s (see Chapter nine). It was Disraeli's Home Secretary who listened to him and others and promoted legislation in 1878 whilst Liberal ministers had promised action and achieved nothing. In 1873 he had struggled even to convince fellow Scottish MPs that progress could be made. One evening he fell asleep on the sofa at his Queen's Gate house because he had to go out again at 11 p.m. to support a Bill aimed at removing turnpikes and had failed before dinner to convince some of his colleagues of its necessity. 'He says he must go back at whatever cost to look after it. Alas! We would rather have the turnpikes doubled in number than lose him – and he is far too reckless with his health,' complained Priscilla.[34] With the Tories in power, McLaren led a delegation from the Convention of Royal Burghs to meet Richard Cross, the Home Secretary, who at first thought burgh representatives were simply out to gain free access to the county roads that were kept up by toll revenues. McLaren retorted that if the burghs gained free access, so did county travellers in towns. He also pointed to the great changes in townsmen's travel: 'In the old days we travelled over the county roads, by coaches to London and Manchester and elsewhere in England, and to country towns and districts, and it was then equitable that we should pay for them by the tolls on these coaches. But now we use the railways, and there is no longer any equitable claim on us to pay for these roads.'[35] For McLaren finding a way of replacing toll-levying turnpike trusts was an extension of the work he started in the 1830s to reduce the burdens on trade between country suppliers and town consumers. The turnpike trusts largely comprised local landowners whose stranglehold on development of through routes offended his social convictions as well as his commercial sense. But it was as a burgh representative that he took issue with the details of the Roads and Bridges Bill, which the Lord Advocate introduced in 1878. He applauded its aim of removing tolls, but it was ill thought out in the way turnpike trusts were replaced with road boards comprising elected representatives as well as the commissioners of supply (the local landowners who traditionally administered county life and who were to give way to county councils from 1889).[36] McLaren peppered the debates with amendments to protect the interests of Edinburgh and other urban areas. There was a toll on the road from Midlothian close to his home in Newington. On 15 May 1879 all tolls in Scotland came to an end, an event marked in some places by shots fired from the windows of toll houses.

With Disraeli in his pomp and Gladstone retired from leadership of the Liberals, the political prospect was hardly encouraging for the Opposition in the years from 1874. Hard graft on the details of legislation and in committees scrutinising Government spending was the response of dedicated MPs like McLaren, while the Liberal party nationally began to confront the fact that its organisation had been inferior to the Conservatives' in choosing candidates and supporting them in the constituencies. There were consolations as by-elections began to go against the Government of the day just as they had when Gladstone's ministry was running out of steam. One victory brought joy to the McLaren family. In February 1876 Jacob Bright won back a seat in Manchester. His sister Priscilla could hardly contain herself in reporting the result to Helen McLaren. As the count reached its climax she heard cheers mingled with 'groans such as only Tories can utter and which make one think there must be a Hell somewhere'.[37] With partisan fervour which made her a campaigner to rival her husband, she pronounced: 'The nation is not dead, it only requires to recognise virtue in its leaders – God was with this candidate. *He* has done the great work. *He* has stopped the march of the enemy.'

In Scotland a couple of months earlier things had not gone so well for Radical Liberalism. There was a by-election in East Aberdeenshire, and tenant farmer George Hope was chosen as standard bearer in the predominantly rural constituency. Following his early days as a proponent of free trade, Hope was now a popular symbol of resistance to landlordism, having been ejected from his long-held tenancy at Fenton Barns in East Lothian. Technically, it was a matter of non-renewal of the lease but that was depicted as ejection because Hope had dared to stand against Lord Elcho in 1865.[38] After winning comfortably, Elcho proclaimed that if Hope, friend of poachers, had come out on top 'he would have found himself sitting with Mr Duncan McLaren on his right hand, and John Bright on his left'. Ten years later – and after Elcho and McLaren had frequently clashed in the House – Hope argued the case for tenants' rights to the voters of East Aberdeenshire. While many welcomed his championing of the right to shoot rabbits on landlords' ground, they were distressed by his call for disestablishment of the Church of Scotland (he himself was a Unitarian) and for querying the Queen's change of church allegiance when she crossed from her English to her Scottish kingdom. In a poorly run campaign he was defeated by a Conservative member of Lord Aberdeen's family. Bright dissected the result in a letter to McLaren: 'Our friend George Hope is a great man in agriculture – but a child in the political world I fear. His religion is against him in Scotland – but allow himself to be entrapped about the religion of the monarch is a wonderful matter of simplicity ... I suppose too that Mr Hope's readiness to swallow 'women's suffrage' – or his great frankness and too little caution must have injured him with some of the electors.'[39]

In 1876 McLaren had an awkward encounter in the lobby of the

Commons. His old foe Alexander Russel had by now passed much of the day-to-day business of *The Scotsman* to his assistants, and in fact he had only months to live. Observed by those who knew of the decades of bad blood between them, McLaren went over and shook Russel's hand. Although *The Scotsman* had latterly approved McLaren's resistance to trade-union pressure, the old editor maintained his reputation for acerbity, at least in private. His successor Charles Cooper received a letter following the handshake in the Commons: '*Entre nous*, the gracious Duncan came to me in the lobby last night, made a pretty little speech, and insisted on shaking hands. More when we meet.' Cooper added the gloss: 'The "more" was not praise of Mr McLaren.'[40] McLaren got on better with Cooper, an English-born Roman Catholic, than with Russel, who was as flinty a Scot as himself and a member of his own United Presbyterians. Cooper and McLaren were united in determination to see Liberalism reasserted.

15. Father and son in and out

In January 1879 McLaren felt compelled to write a letter to the Tory-supporting *Edinburgh Courant* denying its claim that he was on the electoral register for Midlothian solely to influence what was likely to be a crucial battleground between the Liberals and Conservatives at the next election. He explained that 'nearly twenty years ago I purchased the estate of Mayfield and Powburn for £16,000, which is partly in the county, but chiefly within the city boundaries, and my name was put on the electoral roll as owner of that property, on which (as far as within the county) I have paid all county rates ever since. *Literally,* I am, as you say, a non-resident voter, but in spirit I am not, for my residence is within a few hundred yards of the land on which I am registered.'[1] The newspaper said he was a 'faggot' voter, one of the hundreds whom both Liberal and Conservative agents were trying to include on the register as non-resident voters who qualified by virtue of paying the charges on a property. Since property-holding was still the basis of the franchise the qualification was defensible, but contentious in that a close contest could turn on non-resident voters. In the case of Midlothian faggot voters were not necessarily possessors of a country cottage. The county constituency included suburbs of the rapidly expanding city and one of the contested claims concerned Liberals (organised by John McLaren) staking an electoral claim on new flats at Tynecastle, which is now within the inner suburbs and is the Heart of Midlothian only as home to the football club.

For a time John had his eye on the Midlothian nomination. In December 1878 Lord Rosebery, a Midlothian magnate as well as a rising star in the Liberal party nationally, wrote to James Reid, the party's principal agent for Scotland, that McLaren had made a tentative offer.[2] But already William Gladstone was being talked of as the ideal candidate. If the former Prime Minister could be persuaded to take on and defeat the sitting MP, son of the Duke of Buccleuch, Scotland's leading Tory nobleman, it would send a signal to the tens of thousands of his admirers that he and his party were about to topple Lord Beaconsfield (as Disraeli had become) and end the reign of jingoist imperialism. Whether Gladstone would then be reinstalled as party leader and Prime Minister in place of Lord Hartington, who had borne the burden of re-establishing a shaken Opposition, was a matter for the future. Gladstone was also talked about as a possible candidate for the city of Edinburgh but Midlothian was the bigger challenge and prize. Not that success was guaranteed. In July 1879 John McLaren agreed with Reid that Gladstone must visit his new seat soon: 'All the enthusiasm will die away unless the great man comes down, and *we* can't revive it.'[3]

Reid's job, working closely with William Adam, the Chief Whip and MP for Clackmannan and Kinross, was to prepare the party in Scotland for the next election. The Conservatives had campaigned much more effectively than the Liberals in 1874. Reid wanted to ensure that Liberal associations chose suitable candidates who were not then challenged by other Liberals when the election came. For there to be more than one Liberal in the field, even where Liberals normally easily outnumbered Conservatives, was to open the way to defeat and also to highlight political differences within the party. The Tories had won one of the three Glasgow seats in 1874 because of an excess of Liberal candidates. In his electioneering work Reid had the support of aspiring politicians, including advocates like John McLaren. As articulate presenters of the Liberal case they addressed Liberal meetings, and they amassed intelligence about affairs in the fiercely independent local parties. From 1877 there were two national associations – one in the West and South of Scotland, the other in the East and North. Adam and Reid corresponded regularly about possible candidates, but as late as January 1880, only three months before the election, Adam told the East and North Association annual meeting that no constituency had taken up his offer of advice.[4] Nonetheless as Chief Whip he, with Reid, knew which budding MP might be suitable where, and the process of matching available men and local sensitivities went on for many months. John McLaren was one of the hopefuls – and a possible Lord Advocate in the next Government.

John's problem was that he could not make up his mind whether to make his mark within the Faculty of Advocates or to seek a winnable parliamentary seat. The more he was publicly associated with Liberal party organisation, the less he was likely to commend himself to fellow advocates when office as dean or vice-dean of the faculty became a possibility. The more, too, his practice suffered from lack of time. He received unhelpful advice from his father and John Bright. In January 1878 McLaren sent his son a note summarising a long conversation they had had. John's principal rival among Liberals at the Bar was John Balfour, whose credentials for influence and promotion were enhanced when he married Lord Moncreiff's daughter. McLaren suggested that John and Balfour should reach an agreement by which John would allow Balfour to become Lord Advocate in the next Liberal Government while Balfour used his influence to help John become dean of the faculty. Or the two could agree to swap the posts. If such an accord could not be reached, John should stand as dean, since even defeat would be better than remaining on the sidelines and allowing his public and professional character to be seriously damaged.[5] McLaren also passed on Bright's advice that John should not seek a political position where he would lose half of his professional income and face the increased expenditure of living in London. 'If our party were in power we might do something for him by making him Lord Advocate.'[6] When McLaren said that a General Election was two years away, Bright suggested that Irish MPs would not assist the Liberals in forming a Government.

John was enjoying one piece of relative good fortune. At Parliament House he was no longer so damaged by being his father's son. In part that was because Duncan McLaren worked tirelessly to improve Government legislation reforming the courts, legal training and salaries, and defining the role of the Scottish jurisdiction in new appellate procedures in London. He relied on copious advice from John, who framed the views of his fellow advocates. At the same time John's politics were not those of his father in earlier days. His contribution to the efforts of Adam and Reid in presenting a united Liberal front commended John to moderates in the party. He was a bridge between Parliament House Whigs and the Independent Liberals. In January 1877 he was the principal speaker at the launch of a Liberal Association in Edinburgh's West End. The idea was to attract working class members and appeal to a wider constituency than comprised the ward committees whose representatives formed the very large committees that Duncan McLaren knew how to handle. The *Daily Review*, which supported Radical Liberals, commended the idea and hoped it would be repeated elsewhere in the city.[7] But McLaren was concerned at John's activities since it would be assumed that the son was speaking for the father.

Matters came to a head in March. By this time John was taking the initiative along with other leading Liberals in setting up a united Liberal Association for the city, with the aim of ending the decades of squabbling between Whigs and Independent Liberals and of presenting a common front against the Conservatives at the next election. McLaren in London expressed scepticism amounting to hostility. On 16 March he sent John a letter enclosing cuttings from the *Courant* about the united association and John's prominent role. 'The members of the Liberal independent committee, I am satisfied, will never unite with the old Whig Committee, called the Aggregate,' he warned.[8] His supporters would assume that he was of the same mind as his son and many 'will become incensed at me' and say that he was falling away from his old opinions. John and his associates appeared to be doing a good deal to strengthen the Tories 'by causing men who formerly supported me to hive off in disgust and rather vote for a popular Tory, like McDonald [*sic*], than for another Whig.' In 1874 McLaren had secured right-wing Liberal votes that in future might slide away to the Whiggish Cowan and a Conservative. He was against all attempts at formal union but in favour of friendly cooperation where possible. If John were to contest Edinburgh upon his father's retirement he would be 'a Government official' like Moncreiff in the old days. And if George Harrison, town councillor and former chairman of the Chamber of Commerce, were the other Liberal he would be an old Whig 'of the true *Scotsman* type' like Adam Black. But Harrison was not Black's equal and 'I do not rate you as equal to Mr Moncreiff with his 15 years experience in Parliament, when he was turned out.'

Not surprisingly, John felt stung, as did Ottilie. Two days later he responded with an eleven-page letter.[9] He began by pointing out that until the last year or two he had kept away from publicly expressing his political opinions, partly so as not to stray into his father's territory but also because he had felt estranged from other Liberals at the Bar, 'not being admitted to their confidence or been recognized as belonging to their party, and that simply because a former generation of lawyers (who are all gone or on the Bench) took up an attitude of hostility to the citizen party of that time' and because the citizen party was indeed hostile to Parliament House. But now he knew of no Liberal advocate who would not vote for his father and many thought that he (John) should be in Parliament and the next Government. Liberal lawyers and commercial leaders like Harrison and John Clapperton (a draper like Harrison) thought that the old Liberal Committee had lost its influence and they would be glad to join the Independent Committee to show that a union was on equal terms. If, however, John's father felt that a united association would cause dissension, the plan would be abandoned since its proponents esteemed the MP and his knowledge of the constituency. John himself would maintain his habit of not interfering in local matters 'except in concert with you', but he must make public his commitment to a political life or he would be passed over. At a dinner to formulate the plan for union, it had been agreed that the new association would comprise committees nominated at public ward meetings and that there would be no 'platforms' or declarations of principle. Among leaders of the Independent Committee the feeling was 'that it was so long since the wards had been consulted that we could not depend on it being accepted by the electors as a properly elected body'. But it would now be strengthened by going back to the wards for 'an infusion of fresh members' and so become prepared for the next General Election. The only obstacle, John claimed, lay in the Whig Committee's opposition to any element of popular election to the united association because of fears that meetings 'packed by promoters of the permissive Bill [on availability of alcohol] might elect a ward committee consisting entirely of themselves'. John warned his father against holding a meeting of his large committee in the near future while negotiations were going on. He sought not his father's commitment to the plan but only his consideration of it. And in a reference to McLaren's speculation about candidates, he said that Harrison had given up the idea of Parliament. Ottilie, on being shown this long epistle, remarked that it would be strange if John was now to be told he was a Whig and be rejected by the voters on that ground.

Ten months later, at the beginning of 1878, John took the plunge and put himself forward for a by-election in the safe seat of Leith. He was first in the field and attacked the Government's jingoism in the Near East. He and the two Liberal rivals who entered the contest were agreed on issues that commended them to advanced opinion among working-class voters. All three professed support for a permissive Bill that would allow a local option in the provision of public houses, and all were for disestablishment of the Church. *The Scotsman*, however, distinguished between McLaren as 'a quiet and leisurely disestablisher' and his main opponent, Andrew Grant, who was 'a raving disestablisher'. The third candidate withdrew and a meeting of the Leith Liberal Committee voted for Grant. This posed a problem to McLaren. The committee had not invited to its meeting representatives from the burghs of Portobello and Musselburgh, where McLaren had spoken well and had support. Should he listen to his backers and go to the poll, or should he follow his own advice elsewhere as well as that of national party organisers and avoid having two Liberals on the ballot paper? McLaren withdrew. Priscilla expressed surprise, saying she had expected him to stick to his guns and that Grant's success exemplified the past experience of her husband that Tories and Whigs would unite round a

Whig.[10] In fact Grant's views were not Whiggish but he did have appeal as a son of Leith and successful businessman, whereas the constituency did not want to resume its former role of providing the seat for a future Lord Advocate. Everyone, including his father, approved John for not splitting the party and for making his mark for the future. But behind the scenes there was sign of discord. In two letters to his brother Charles, 'confidential to you and Laura [Charles's wife] only', John wailed: 'I have been "wounded in the house of my friends", and such wounds burn deep. I feel that I shall never be the same man again.' His father had encouraged him to stand but on going to London for the parliamentary session had met Bright, who thought the prospects for the party were so uncertain that John should not become an unpaid MP now. In duty to his family he should withdraw and stick with his legal practice. 'They did it for the best and from the kindest feelings to me; but I do not think the advice sound though I felt bound to follow it.'[11] In other words it was family pressure that undermined his venture.

Still, he continued to seek a seat and even contemplated crossing the Irish Sea, though England appeared a better prospect. Bright, however, was pessimistic. 'As a rule they [English boroughs] do not like Reform Club candidates. I mean those chosen by W. Adam or any one who is supposed to be active in London for the party.' That was especially the case with northern towns. Lawyers were not much liked either. Constituencies would find 'a great disadvantage with a lawyer and a Scotch man'. They preferred someone they knew either as a neighbour or by public report. Scotland offered a much better prospect, as John's father would confirm. Bright concluded: '*I* want to get out of Parliament, which seems as difficult for me as it is for *you* to get in.'[12] John turned his attention to Kilmarnock burghs but his colleague Dick Peddie, who had tested the water at the Leith by-election and withdrew, was already in the field. So what about a county seat in Scotland? He told Ottilie that 'I have been thinking that my proper course would be to contest some county with a Tory where I have no Liberal opposition. Even if I didn't get in it would give me a claim on the party.'[13] He lit upon Peebles and Selkirk which Reid thought would meet with Adam's approval, but McLaren senior was hostile to the idea, 'backing his opinions as usual by Mr Bright's' for 'the ridiculous reason that it would offend Tory agents and lose me business. I have replied that I have no Tory professional connection.'[14] Meanwhile Alexander Asher, a Liberal advocate friend and another potential Lord Advocate, was ready to chance his arm in Tory Inverness-shire, where a contest expensive to the candidate was inevitable. 'I am sure it would go against me if I declined a cheap seat while other advocates are willing to contest dear ones. Therefore I must keep to Peebles etc as a *pis aller* if no better occurs.' The maximum John thought he should offer to fund a county campaign was £500, leaving local agents to find the rest.

In February 1879 John listened to Bright's fresh advice. Wigtown burghs were a possibility. Adam told Bright he could not interfere with the selection – there were apparently four other Liberals interested – but he could help once the selection was made. That probably meant financial help since Adam had a war chest with which to fund Liberal campaigns. John's father had said earlier, when Kilmarnock seemed a possibility, that he would lend money and add to his son's income if he became an Opposition MP (that is, without chance of paid office) but that he could not help with election expenses as he was overdrawn![15] On 19 February John wrote to his parents that he had been unanimously invited to contest Wigtown. Friends in Edinburgh and Glasgow had recommended him on the basis of his speeches in Leith. He was asking Bright to secure the backing of the Earl of Stair, whose influence maintained a long Whig tradition in the area.[16] John had been told by the earl's factor that whoever was chosen by the local committee would receive his lordship's blessing. The irony was surely not lost on Duncan McLaren and John Bright: noble Whig suzerainty, which they had spent their lives fighting, was being called in aid of their son and nephew.

John was now established as a future MP. He dismissed a Tory accusation that he was a faggot voter by virtue of being on the electoral register in Glencarron, Ross-shire, where he had a house. John replied that the property was rented at more than £50 a year, was open all year round and was used by his family. Fittingly for his Galloway constituency, he brushed up his knowledge of rural affairs, using his professional expertise in land law to address a meeting of the Farmers' Alliance, a Liberal-inclined national pressure group that sprang up in the wake of the depression which was devastating the agricultural economy and was being blamed on the Government.[17]

In November 1879 when Gladstone arrived in Midlothian for his first campaign of speeches in the towns and villages, John was given the honour of proposing the vote of thanks at the opening rally in the Edinburgh Music Hall. His father was among the throng at an evening party held by Lord Rosebery to welcome his distinguished guest. Only days before, McLaren, accompanied by Priscilla, had been in Inverness to receive the freedom of the burgh in recognition of his many campaigns for Scotland. The ceremony had been postponed from an earlier date during the couple's two-month holiday in the Highlands because McLaren was ill. Recovered, he recalled to the provost and councillors the freedom which as Lord Provost of Edinburgh he had conferred on Gladstone a quarter of a century ago – in absentia as it turned out since the great man had been unable to call in on Edinburgh during a journey down from the Highlands. McLaren now pronounced Gladstone 'the greatest statesman that this century has produced', an interesting testimonial in view of his disagreements with his former and future leader on various aspects of policy.[18]

A recent candidate for the freedom of Edinburgh did not meet with McLaren's approval. The claims of Richard Cross, the Conservative Home Secretary, were strongly supported by the *Courant* but in *The Scotsman* McLaren said that Cross had blocked the progress of Scottish Bills. No more so than previous Liberal Home Secretaries, riposted the *Courant*, but since the town council agreed with McLaren nothing came of the proposal.[19] Cross posed a challenge for Scottish Liberals because he was not content to leave the law officers in charge of business north of the border. By elevating the importance of the Home Office and emphasising his seniority to the Lord Advocate, he challenged the established Whig way of conducting Scottish business. Further, because he represented the Conservative minority (in terms of Scotland), he fed the discontent voiced by McLaren and other Liberal MPs about governance of the northern kingdom. In August 1878 there was renewed outcry about Scottish matters being consigned to the end of the parliamentary day and the fag-end of the session. McLaren was especially upset that the committee stage of a Scottish Education Bill, with which he wanted to take issue, began at almost 3 a.m. Worse, the parliamentary business managers had not forewarned Scottish MPs, most of whom were tucked up in bed.[20]

Foreign affairs were now at the heart of the political battle, and in November 1878, when McLaren and Cowan made their annual reports to constituents, McLaren unusually devoted the bulk of his address to the war that had drawn British troops into Afghanistan, not for the first or last time. The aim was to contain Russian ambitions which, it was claimed, had been heightened by recent victory over the Turks. The Liberals in Parliament were divided on the prominent diplomatic role played by Beaconsfield in refereeing between the Porte and St Petersburg, and they feared the domestic political consequences of the Prime Minister's success. Radicals who wanted Britain to stay away from Near Eastern entanglements saw only further evidence of Tory jingoism in the expedition into Afghanistan. For McLaren it was 'neither a just nor a necessary war'.[21] He did not possess Gladstone's soaring rhetoric in making the same case a year later to the people of

Midlothian that 'the sanctity of life in the hill villages of Afghanistan, among the winter snows, is as inviolable in the eyes of Almighty God as can be your own'. But as with the slaughter of Zulus at British hands in South Africa, Liberals of all stripes came together to turn the Government's overseas adventurism into an election issue.

With the benefit of hindsight the victory that followed the adulation of Gladstone in the months leading up to the election in April 1880 seems inevitable. But that was not evident at the time. In London and the south of England Beaconsfield's exercise of imperial power was popular, and despite setbacks at home his administration did not run out of steam like the Liberals' in 1874. During the election campaign the keenly Liberal Charles Cooper, as *Scotsman* editor, was several times in the London headquarters of the Liberal Central Association, where confidence was low.[22] His own optimism, based on Scottish opinion and a knowledge of how sentiment in the north of England was very different from that in the Home Counties, was shared, however, by Adam, who as principal officer was seeing the reports from constituencies. As well as overseeing the adoption of suitable candidates and (on the whole) successfully avoiding contests where rival Liberals would split the vote, Adam was determined that divisive issues should be avoided in party caucuses. In Scotland he and Reid tried to prevent local associations from talking about disestablishment of the Church. Another Scottish 'crotchet' – that is a policy dear to the heart of zealots but troublesome to a party leadership seeking unity – was the introduction of the permissive Bill that worried some Whigs when the Edinburgh United Liberal Association was being planned. The long search for an answer to the moral and social consequences of intemperance now focused on the idea, borrowed from North America, that local communities should decide on the number and location of licensed premises. A succession of Bills since the 1860s had failed to make progress but led by Sir William Lawson, MP for Carlisle, the campaign became more optimistic and ardent in 1878–9.[23] In many Liberal associations permissive legislation and Church disestablishment were badges of Radical faith to be worn by candidates. But as indication of a divided party, the Liberal *Scotsman* was as dismissive of both policies as the Liberal *Daily Review* was in favour.

The Edinburgh United Liberal Association, which Harrison in particular had steered into existence and of which he was the first chairman, fulfilled its role of keeping tensions within bounds. On 18 January 1880 when, 150 strong, it met to consider candidates for the election now imminent, McLaren was absent ill but had already made clear his willingness to stand again. His failing powers, however, had been noticed by journalists. Henry Lucy, the leading lobby correspondent of the day, wrote in 1878 that 'there are times when McLaren's voice sinks below the key at which it is audible throughout the House. The inconvenience is increased by a habit he has contracted of confidentially addressing the blue book or report he holds in his hand.'[24] The *Daily Review* now considered the issue of his age and health and recognised that he was no longer able to go out in severe winter weather and so was 'compelled to withdraw of late from active participation in the duties of citizenship, of which he is one of the best upholders, and of which his whole life has afforded an admirable example to other and younger men.'[25]

The United Liberals had no hesitation in backing him. He no longer faced trade-union opposition because the Conservative Government, with its strategy of appealing to the working man, had changed the law and removed the grievance of 1873–4. But a final decision on candidates was postponed because of doubts over McLaren's running mate. John told the meeting that his father had no wish to influence the committee but in six years he had had no difference of opinion with Cowan and would be happy to continue cooperation. McLaren was now showing a willingness to compromise that had not been present in previous elections dating back to 1852. Cowan had been elected in 1874 as a Whig in preference to Miller, whose opinions were closer to McLaren's except on the matter of trade-union rights. Now Radicals in the United Association pointed to Cowan's lukewarm attitude to both disestablishment and a permissive Bill. The *Daily Review* said that his speaking and voting record in Parliament was poor compared with that of his older colleague. An attempt was made to promote the candidature of John Traynor, a prominent advocate (soon to be made a Court of Session judge) who was active in the Scottish Permissive Bill Association. He had support from some trade unionists, but only three weeks before the election was rejected by the United Association in favour of Cowan by 146 votes to 43.[26]

Liberal candidates across the country notched up victories, reversing the 1874 outcome and in Scotland restoring almost total dominance over the Conservatives. Midlothian was won with a small majority: ensuring Liberal strength among faggot voters paid off. The contest was not just a highminded matter of Gladstone's oratory and a clash of the aristocratic houses of Buccleuch and Rosebery. During the campaign the partisan *Daily Review* was concerned about the effect of Tory tactics and spending power: 'The assiduous Tory education of the constituency during the past two years, by frequent lectures and the profuse distribution of Tory literature – to say nothing of the frantic endeavours being made to secure a circulation for a new Tory halfpenny paper by offering free advertising to working men and servant girls in want of situations, and bribes of gold brooches and silver watches to street arabs who can dispose of the greatest number of the new journal – probably means more than appears on the surface.'[27] In Glasgow all three seats went Liberal this time, and in Edinburgh John Macdonald's second attempt at maximising the Tory vote was less fruitful than his first six years earlier. The result conveyed to an enthusiastic crowd of 15,000 in Forrest Road was: McLaren 17,807; Cowan 17,301; Macdonald 5,651. McLaren's last election victory was his most convincing, and he took much pleasure from it. The old man was at long last seen as a unifier. His daughter Helen, now married in Bradford, wrote congratulating him but regretting that Cowan's vote had been so close to his. She went on: 'I trust your health will long be spared to work for the city to whom, as well as to all of us, your life is so valuable.'[28] In the new Parliament McLaren would be joined by two sons. John won Wigtown burghs, where with an electorate of only 1,400 he increased the Liberal majority from 1 to 12, and Charles secured a seat at Stafford.

Helen, in a letter to her mother, expressed delight at John's success and expressed the hope that John Balfour would be defeated in Ayrshire, in which case John would be without a rival as the new Lord Advocate.[29] Her wish came true. Ayrshire remained one of the few Tory bastions. During the election campaign John wrote from Stranraer in his constituency to tell his father that he would be going to dinner the following Sunday at Dalmeny House as Rosebery 'has asked me to come to meet Gladstone any time I like.'[30] After the election he had to wait an anxious time while the Prime Minister formed his Cabinet before attending to the junior appointments and making John Lord Advocate. Ambition was realised but John's troubles were just beginning. His first problem was his seat in the Commons. Like other ministers entering on an office of profit he had to seek re-election. Often ministers were either not challenged or easily saw off opposition. John, however, had narrowly defeated a former Tory member, Mark Stewart, who, only weeks after the first poll, won back the seat with a similar majority in his favour. John McLaren could not lead on Scottish business without a seat and he immediately had to divert his attention from ministerial matters to chasing a suitable by-election. The MP for Berwick-on-Tweed retired, which Gladstone described as a 'kindness' to McLaren, though there could be no obligation on the Government to find him a seat.[31] He again lost despite his father speaking for him at a public meeting 'We cannot go on losing seats for him' was the exasperated view of the party's business managers.[32] A challenge to the legitimacy of the poll was raised, but unsuccessfully. The Liberal Chief Whip, Lord Richard Grosvenor, reported to John Reid: 'Our little friend has been booted out of Berwick so he is on our hands again. Is a Glasgow seat possible?'[33] It was not, nor could any other vacancy be created in Scotland despite John's increasingly feverish requests and machinations.

He had the advantage but also the handicap of being a party leader in Scotland as well as the Government's legal and parliamentary business manager. On 28 November John told Reid that he had no desire to interfere in seats but there had to be a flow of information between Scotland and London. William Adam, disappointed in the lowly post that Gladstone had given him despite his electoral triumphs, was off to govern Madras, and John felt he had to take on an organisational role. 'As the Government have at present no special parliamentary whip for Scotland I feel that a certain responsibility rests with me, independent of any interest which I may have in the activities of the constituencies.'[34] Adam's own seat of Clackmannan and Kinross was a concern to John. The favoured successor was John Balfour, now Solicitor-General. If he entered Parliament at the by-election in John's absence, how long would it be until Balfour assumed the senior post of Lord Advocate? The departing Adam knew the score: 'He will have to give up the Lord Advocate soon if he does not get a seat and the knowledge that this is the case ought to act as a turn of the screw on his unfeeling parent.'[35] John himself had wondered as long ago as June about whether his father might make way for him. He told Ottilie that he had spoken to his stepmother 'about my father resigning, but from what she says, I fear there is no chance of his doing so at least this session.'[36]

As John's mood darkened, he had little help from his father. They clashed on educational policy, as we shall see. McLaren suggested that John give up and become a judge, which he was not ready to contemplate although he admitted that honourable exile to a colony would be a relief, impractical as it was because of his young son's health. Gladstone said that he wanted to keep John as Lord Advocate but 'the seat I must find myself', as he told Ottilie.[37] Meanwhile his sensitivity to slights showed up under the strain. He felt excluded from social invitations by other members of the Government. He crossed swords with Reid, who had been appointed an advocate depute and in John's view should therefore resign as secretary of the East and North Liberal Association. Rosebery thought that was unnecessary.[38] John would have experienced difficult relationships in Government even if he had been in the

Commons. He was unlucky that the Cabinet minister to whom he was responsible was the Home Secretary William Harcourt, who gained a reputation for being difficult and domineering, and politicians stronger than John McLaren were to suffer the consequences until the end of the century.

The problem was not that Harcourt wanted to run Scotland himself. He pled ignorance of its peculiar ways. 'Nobody but a Scotchman can manage Scotchmen,' he told John at one point, exasperated by self-interested representations from the Faculty of Advocates and Edinburgh Town Council.[39] He would have been happy for Scottish business to be removed from the Home Office but where would it go? In John's view the transfer of Harcourt to another Cabinet post would help, and John would give up all private practice to become a Scottish Secretary as well as Lord Advocate. 'The difficulty is I must be secretary to someone and who is that to be?' Harcourt and he could not establish a working relationship. 'Personal intercourse becomes less,' John complained, and he lacked the easy access to Cabinet ministers that Moncreiff had enjoyed. Harcourt occasionally interested himself in Scottish legal business where the Lord Advocate's autonomy ought to have been obvious, such as a prisoner's appeal for commutation of a long sentence. The Prime Minister himself valued and sought John's legal opinions. During the election campaign he had expressed thanks for John's advice on the controversial law of hypothec affecting landlords' and tenants' rights, in Midlothian as elsewhere. Two months later, in May, a letter from Downing Street expressed the Cabinet's desire for a verbal account by the Lord Advocate of game law from a Scottish perspective.[40]

It was unfortunate that a Bill for Scotland decided upon by the Cabinet put the Lord Advocate at odds with his father. The Educational Endowments Bill was not generally controversial but it undermined the position of the Heriot Trust and its schools. The threat was identified by Duncan McLaren and the town council before John joined the Government, and Duncan was to take the fight for the schools into his years of retirement from Parliament (see next chapter). Even the old man's detractors in the matter – *The Scotsman* in particular – had to admire his dogged determination, and it put him on a course of clear disagreement with his son, who welcomed the Cabinet's readiness to legislate. 'I am glad of this, though I am afraid it hits on my father. Still he deserves to be taken down a little. He really has been too extreme and disagreeable about his objections, and instead of calming down the deputations has encouraged them in all their extravagant demands.'[41] If the old man retired John's chances of succeeding him in

Edinburgh would be adversely affected 'by, I will not say encouraging, but identifying himself with the pitiful opposition to me in connection with the Education Bill'. He wrote to the editor of the *Daily Review* complaining about sneers appearing in its columns.[42] By December 1880 John was having to justify himself to Priscilla: he had sought to protect the Heriot schools and blamed Harcourt for standing in the way of a compromise which might have been secured if John had been in Parliament in the summer. 'Harcourt is not easy to deal with when he takes the bit between his teeth, and without a Parliamentary position I am not strong enough to oppose him even in matters where my opinion ought to be decisive.'[43]

John faced another threat. John Balfour replaced Adam as MP for Clackmannan and Kinross. Would the Solicitor-General now be promoted to Lord Advocate? Pressure grew on Duncan McLaren to retire. On 10 January John wrote: 'I have a notion that at the last, my father would retreat rather than see me replaced by Balfour. But he is curiously blind to the real state of things. He took Balfour all over the House of Commons to show his good feeling!'[44] Bright, once more in the Cabinet, became involved. On 14 January he called on the Prime Minister, at McLaren's request, to discuss a transfer of the Edinburgh seat to John. Gladstone, suffering from a cold, listened to the arguments from his sick bed. Two days later Bright's diary records: 'Evening to Buckingham Palace Hotel with dear Priscilla and McLaren. Conversation on the position of the Lord Advocate and the suggestion that his father resign his seat to allow him to come in for Edinburgh. McLaren very quiet as usual, and disposed to make a sacrifice for his son's interests.'[45] The next day McLaren told the Chief Whip that he was retiring and he sent a letter to his constituency.

For almost 16 years, from middle age to 80, he had diligently served Edinburgh and Scotland. By now the designation 'member for Scotland' was widely used. His departure was not a surprise though it came sooner than expected, right at the start of the parliamentary year. It might have been postponed had John not been in need of a seat because McLaren felt himself able to perform his parliamentary duties despite increasing deafness. But political and family pressure pointed in one direction, and by-elections aimed at transferring a family seat were unexceptional. On 30 March his fellow members for Scottish constituencies assembled to recognise his seniority and services by presenting him with an album containing their signatures. The event was held in a Commons committee room and was attended by Priscilla, her two brothers in Parliament and the McLarens' two sons who were now MPs, Charles and John. The Lord Advocate had easily won the

Edinburgh by-election despite supposed dislike among the city's Radicals of a Government member as their representative. The Prime Minister could not be present, nor had he added his signature to those of his Scottish colleagues for the reason he explained in a letter read to the gathering: 'In conformity with the general rule, to which I am obliged pretty strictly to adhere, I have refrained from subscribing a document framed on behalf of the Scottish Members, but I cannot refrain from writing a few lines to state with what sincere regret I subscribed, according to my official duty, another document which opened the door for your exit from the House of Commons at a time when all the qualities you possess have so wide a field for employment in that assembly. Your ability, your application, your stout heart, your facility of clear exposition, will be long and well remembered by your parliamentary comrades; and your great courage in the discharge of laborious duty amidst advancing years will, I trust, have many admirers, even if few imitators.' As the retired MP addressed the gathering, the division bell rang, signalling a vote. He stopped and urged the MPs to hurry off. But no one stirred, and he was asked to continue. He said that he had come to the Commons as a Liberal but was 'unsupported by any prestige or any political party, for I got in by fighting and beating the dominant party at the time. I had no aristocratic or other privilege. I can truly say that, from my earliest youth, I never had a patron of any kind.' With emotion that revealed something of his nature, he added that 'I am always more easily overcome by kindness than by opposition.'[46]

In Parliament his son John now found little kindness and much opposition. He brought forward Bills, some on matters which his legal experience made him especially fitted to handle – the law of entail and reform of teinds, for example. He also went ahead with the Educational Endowments Bill in the teeth of his father's opposition. But his fellow Scottish MPs were in rebellious mood about the lack of time and regard for Scottish measures – the complaint Duncan McLaren had voiced since the days of the Camperdown inquiry. Had the old man still been in the House he would certainly have signed the request of 33 Scots MPs led by Peter McLagan of Linlithgowshire that the Government appoint a political minister for Scotland as well as a legal one. This memorial, as it was called, circulated only weeks after John McLaren took his seat; a copy is lodged among his letters. As the parliamentary session wore on, the familiar problem of lack of time for Scotland appeared again. Cooper of *The Scotsman* wrote to John to find serious fault with the practice of bringing forward or promising so many Bills without any chance of passing them. Criticism in the newspaper might be annoying,

Cooper accepted, but in time John would come to agree.[47] Meanwhile Lord Rosebery was becoming the influential spokesman for reform. He wrote to Gladstone's private secretary: 'If things go on as they are, you will have Scotland as well as Ireland on your hands',[48] a reference not just to the discontents across the Irish Sea but also to the disruption of Commons business by Irish Nationalist MPs which had a knock-on effect on the prospects for Scottish Bills. Rosebery's own ambitions were involved. With the brittle fastidiousness that marked his character, he had turned down two junior posts when Gladstone formed the Government. Now he made clear his hope for a place in the Cabinet, for which the Prime Minister felt he was not ready. However, in July an undersecretaryship in the Home Office became vacant. It offered a solution to several problems. Harcourt, tired of wrestling with the complexities of the 'land of brown heath and shaggy wood' (his depiction) and with a Lord Advocate in whom he had little confidence, wanted a deputy political minister for Scottish business. Rosebery was the obvious candidate, despite being in the Upper House. On 1 August, the earl, admitting to Gladstone that he might have been 'crotchety' about offices previously offered, accepted the post, which it was agreed would have Scotland as a main responsibility.[49] Harcourt's hopes of getting another deputy in the Commons were, however, disappointed. Importantly, Scottish opinion had confidence in Rosebery's connection with Gladstone and in his potential as a national leader.

The victim was John McLaren. He made the mistake of annoying Gladstone at this sensitive moment by demanding to be made a Privy Councillor. The Prime Minister replied that only three of the previous ten Lord Advocates had been in the Privy Council and none until they had been much longer in office than John. 'The fact that future Scotch arrangements are at present in suspense, affords another reason against action'.[50] On 3 August Harcourt wrote that he had the Prime Minister's authority to offer John a judgeship. Changes at the Home Office 'in Mr Gladstone's view as well as my own point to the expediency of a change in the office of Lord Advocate'. Sententiously, Harcourt added that he almost envied the tranquil dignity of the Court of Session compared with the House of Commons, 'at least such as it now is'.[51] A footnote explained that Rosebery was about to become undersecretary. John immediately wrote to Gladstone resigning from 'a Government under which I had looked forward to some years of useful public life, and a Prime Minister for whom, if you will allow me to say so, I have felt so high a regard'.[52] Gladstone regretted the speed of his going but accepting his judgment in preferring no delay. The letters of sympathy were many. Lord Hartington at the India Office wished there had been a chief justiceship available in the sub-continent, for which he would have considered John's claims.[53] John Albert Bright, son of Uncle John and later an MP, wrote condemning the actions of Gladstone and Harcourt, who, he added, should never become Liberal leader. 'I fear such treatment of the member for Edinburgh will not strengthen the seat of the member for Midlothian – if the latter were anybody else.'[54] John's successor as member for Edinburgh was Thomas Buchanan, a Scots-born London barrister who had fought Haddingtonshire the previous year. The successor as Lord Advocate was the Solicitor-General John Balfour, whose Whiggish family connections made him a congenial companion to the party grandees. 'The Home Secretary, the Lord Advocate (regnant), and I have been like lambs and lions and cockatrices', Rosebery wrote to Gladstone's daughter following a house party at Dalmeny that included Harcourt and his wife as well as young Balfour.[55]

John's brother Walter, in blaming Gladstone, Harcourt and the greater subordination of the Lord Advocate to the Home Secretary, told him that 'you will be remembered as the last political Lord Advocate and the good Liberal Bills which you attempted to pass will be a proof that so long as the Lord Advocateship was in the hands of an earnest and conscientious Liberal there was no need to degrade the office and trust Scotland to the tender mercies of the House of Lords.' He found Rosebery's conduct deceitful.[56] There is no evidence that Rosebery schemed against John although he knew of the Lord Advocate's difficulties. John fell victim to circumstances and was blind to the weakness of his position until it was too late. John Bright offered only sympathetic noises rather than intervention with the Prime Minister. At one moment John was telling Ottilie: 'I have not a single enemy among the Scotch MPs and I think a few warm friends, who would make their feelings known if anything to my disadvantage were proposed.'[57] Then, on the bleak day when Harcourt signalled the end, he wrote: 'I fear if things come to the worst it will be known in Scotland that I have resigned against my will, and what a nice position for a judge to be in.' He asked his wife: 'Would you not think that my old proposal of going to India would be preferable? I should prefer it, but one cannot always do what one would like.'[58]

16. Campaigner to the end

One reason why Duncan McLaren was willing to retire from Parliament in favour of his son was his belief that the future of Heriot's Hospital and the outdoor schools was becoming secure. The Government – pressed by the Scottish middle classes in search of wider and better secondary education, followed by entry to the universities – wanted to revisit the question of endowments. In 1870 the Merchant Company in Edinburgh had used the first round of legislation to turn charitable foundations into fee-paying day schools. There were hundreds of other benefactions that remained unchanged, and for more than 15 years argument about their future raged in different parts of the country, though nowhere as virulently as in Edinburgh. It was a clash of the classes. The changes to charitable trusts in 1870 had served the middle class. By the end of the decade the pressure was to secure the interests of the artisan class, and the future of Heriot's was the point of keenest conflict.[1] At issue was not just the hospital, where the number of resident foundationers was reduced and the curriculum altered to reflect the needs of commerce and the industries in which the boys were expected to make their careers. Classical studies aimed at sending the brightest boys to university via the High School were downgraded and Greek abandoned. The future of the outdoor schools catering for 5,000 poor boys and girls was also in doubt, because reformers thought that the flourishing revenues of the Heriot Trust could be put to better educational use than running free schools that existed alongside those now under the auspices of the school board.

McLaren was four-square against changes that he regarded as robbing the poor to help middle-class families who could look after themselves. When a Heriot's Trust Defence Committee was formed in 1875 and held a public meeting, McLaren's pledge of support won a rousing reception. A commission under Lord Moncreiff was set up by an Act of 1878 to advise the Government on 32 endowment schemes across Scotland, of which Heriot's was the most controversial. McLaren did not repeat the mistake he had made with the Colebrooke Commission. He gave evidence and showed his own position had changed. Previously he had doubted the value of retaining the hospital but now he favoured it on grounds of educational efficiency and cost. He also came out firmly for free education, linking the day schools to the hospital, which would be 'a great civic school for the clever boys and girls selected from the elementary schools, to be educated along with the boys placed on the hospital foundation'[2] Free education was the practice in other advanced countries, he argued, and a halfpenny on the rate would remove fees from the city's schools. His case was based on interpretation of what George Heriot had intended way back in the seventeenth century. *The Scotsman* was unimpressed: 'It is really difficult to know when the [Heriot] Trust is being administered according to the Will of George Heriot, and when according to the will of Duncan McLaren.'[3]

McLaren's evidence supported the most recent proposals by Heriot's board of governors – that is, in effect, by the town council, which filled most of the seats. Under the only proposal acceptable to the Moncreiff Commission Heriot's became the funder of the Watt Institution, which provided technical education. McLaren, remembering his own youthful benefit from vocational education, was committed in support of the new Heriot-Watt College, nowadays a university strong in technology and business. The commission was not happy at the influence of electoral politics on the hospital's board of governors and counselled the Government not to accept changes to the hospital and schools until the governing body was reduced in size and made less the creature of the town council. McLaren saw off two threats. The first concerned the purpose George Heriot had had in mind when founding his trust. Was he providing for the merchant class or the poor? Those who wanted to increase the trust's contribution to middle-class student bursaries argued the former. McLaren said that by the terms of his Burgess Act of 1876, sons of the poor now qualified for entry to the hospital in accordance with Heriot's will. The second threat lay in the claim that the Heriot benefaction should benefit education beyond Edinburgh – with bursaries at St Andrews University suggested. McLaren comprehensively demolished that argument.

In June 1880 Harcourt as the new Home Secretary and John McLaren as Lord Advocate thought they had a compromise acceptable to the governors and Parliament. The governors would remain in place but would reduce the number of foundationers to 60 and provide more bursaries for students. No more free schools would be founded. But a Bill introduced in the Lords ran into trouble and had to be withdrawn. John, who prided himself on knowing more than anyone about the history of the matter, blamed Harcourt for allowing the provisional order setting out the terms of the new arrangements to be undermined by the Moncreiff Commission. The Home Secretary, who found the whole business increasingly tiresome, made two mistakes in John's eyes. He yielded to pressure and let the commission interfere with the provisional order; and he offended Moncreiff with the tone of a 'Harcourtian' letter, that is, one exemplifying the Home Secretary's tactlessness.[4] John remained hopeful of a compromise: 'I should be so sorry to see the Free Schools interfered with that I would gladly do anything to get the matter settled before Parliament meets.' A compromise would have been achieved months previously had he been in the Commons, but Harcourt was not an easy man to deal with. Bright agreed that John had a right to be involved in framing educational endowments legislation and other Bills since he was, in practice, the Secretary of State for Scotland.[5] It was at this point, just as Parliament met, that Duncan McLaren agreed to leave the outcome to his son. During the subsequent by-election, in which Heriot's was the main local issue, John agreed to maintain the popular element in the board of governors (through the annual town council elections). But the new Bill replacing the one withdrawn the previous summer was in the hands of Anthony Mundella, vice-president of the Board of Education, who knew the history of English endowments but not sensitivities north of the border. He ran into opposition from Scottish MPs, who accused him of bullying tactics. John was accused of going back on his word to the Heriot's governors, and there matters unhappily stood when he left Parliament. Buchanan, his successor as MP, declared that Heriot's was the 'burning question' and vowed to retain a two-thirds majority for councillors on the board.

For Duncan McLaren there could be no contented retirement with Heriot's under threat. His emotional commitment is understandable. He had been on the board of governors since 1833. He saw the steady increase in the wealth of the trust and he put it to good use by being the principal founder of the outdoor schools for the poor of the old town. Forty years later his fellow MP, Lyon Playfair, may have been ironical in calling them the 'McLaren schools',[6] for as an academic he wanted university access to Heriot's money, but he was only speaking the truth. McLaren's reputation as a friend of the poor was associated with the schools more than through any other of his campaigns. Because the schools were eventually brought under the wing of the

Edinburgh school board, we easily forget them and their chief supporter. In the first years of his retirement from Parliament he kept up a campaign to protect the Heriot's board and its schools. He proposed amendments to Mundella's Bill but of course was hampered by not being able to argue for them in the Commons. The Heriot cause and that of other endowments under threat of what was called 'spoliation' was taken up by the Glasgow Radical Liberal MP Charles Cameron, who wanted to protect foundations in his own city as well as Edinburgh. Delays in getting the Bill to and through Parliament led Rosebery as a minister for Scottish affairs to complain to Gladstone in June 1882. A similar Bill had twice before been rejected 'by a combination of what I fear our enemies would term indifference on the part of the Government, and very unscrupulous lobbying on the part of a small and corrupt clique which opposes it.' Rosebery claimed that no more than eight Scottish MPs were against the Bill, and he advised that a letter in the press by McLaren – who was certainly regarded as part of the 'clique' – should be answered by decisive action.

After much argument the Bill emerged with some safeguards for Heriot's. Governing bodies had to include a minimum representation from town councils or school boards, and in cases like Heriot's that representation would amount to at least two-thirds of the members. McLaren supported female education at elementary as well as university level and won the support of MPs for imposing on a new commission the need to ensure equal provision for girls. Making decisions under the Act fell to commissioners led by a Tory peer, Balfour of Burleigh. He and his colleagues, who included the Lord Provosts of Edinburgh and Glasgow, cannot be accused of shirking an immense labour. By 1889 they had reviewed 379 schemes involving 821 endowments.

McLaren and the town council – derided as the 'Heriot ring' – fought a rearguard action until 1885. In his last years the former MP re-cemented the radical alliance with councillors that had launched his career almost half a century previously. Gone were the accusations of 1873–4 that he had abandoned the working classes. He was again the people's champion in the city as Gladstone was in the country as a whole. McLaren's own respect for the Prime Minister was by now in steep decline for other reasons, but it is a signal of his renewed radical reputation that prominent among his opponents was that voice of the middle class, *The Scotsman*. McLaren sprayed the press with letters about Heriot's and spoke occasionally at public meetings. With Cooper as editor the paper was measured in its criticism compared with the days of Russel. But the divisions highlighted by Heriot's were on class lines. The fragile unity among Liberals that had been constructed before the 1880 election was stretched to breaking point, although of course there were other factors at work beyond the fate of a hospital and elementary schools.

When the Balfour Commission turned its attention to the trust responsible for Fettes College, McLaren opened a new front in his campaign, alleging that the boarding school, founded as recently as 1870, betrayed the intentions of Sir William Fettes, its benefactor, by catering for professional-class products of English and Scottish preparatory schools rather than children of the disadvantaged. McLaren wanted to turn Fettes into a Heriot-style hospital and won the support of the town council and MPs. But the commission and the Government made only minor changes to the composition of the Fettes board and provided for a few scholarships.[8] The tide was flowing in favour of secondary education part funded by endowments. Heriot's, because of its outdoor schools, was a special case but it fell victim to the prevailing orthodoxy. In 1885 the last negotiations between governors and commissioners led to a petition with 42,000 signatures to stave off the inevitable. Buchanan's final defence of Heriot's in Parliament was backed by Charles McLaren, MP for Stafford, but change when it came was sweeping.[9] The outdoor schools were transferred to the Edinburgh school board and the hospital followed the examples of others in Edinburgh and other cities by becoming a fee-paying day school. There was still provision for foundationers but most of the scholarships and bursaries established with trust money were competitive and therefore unlikely to be won by candidates from the poorer classes.

McLaren, his health now uncertain, had lost his dearest fight. The writing had been on the wall for years. In 1882 Priscilla turned her rage (evident in her loss of syntax) on all who opposed her husband's campaign, not least the 'so called' Liberal Government:

> I hardly know how to write my heart aches so for thee and this sad result of so long and patient faithful work – and recently at thy age, of almost super-human work on behalf of that noble and nobly wrecked Heriot Trust – and that it should thus be broken by a so called Liberal Government. Well, I am thankful my brother John was out of the Government at the time – but I do feel that the Edinburgh people have not done their part – the *whole people*, tho' the *Review* has. But I can't help thinking the Scottish MPs might have hindered this cruel ending ... I feel that the town should be placarded as suggested yesterday and the words added 'by a so

called Liberal Government.' It would delight me to know that the *Scotsman* office was mobbed. But the people seem to have nothing of impulse about them. I wish I was with thee at home ... oh, it's a sad and a tyrannical act.[10]

The demands of the grown-up family and of campaigning causes – Priscilla's for women's rights as much as McLaren's – frequently kept one or other of the couple away from home. In 1883 Helen, now a doctor's wife in Bradford, wrote to her mother about a visit by her father which had lasted only two minutes. He looked well, 'but it is queer how he seems always to want to be moving about.'[11] Not that Priscilla was a home bird either. While McLaren was in Yorkshire she was in Droitwich. Helen had married Andrea Rabagliati, who was born in Edinburgh to a family of political refugees. Helen was still showing signs of her early ill-health when they became engaged in 1876 but Priscilla approved of the match – she now had three sons! 'I would rather he had been less of a metaphysician and more of a politician, but Helen is not political and so it suits her.'[12] McLaren settled £10,000 on her. Of Priscilla's two real sons, Charles, academically gifted, was a London barrister who also dabbled in newspaper journalism and proprietorship before finding the road from the Bar to Parliament less perilous than his elder stepbrother. Largely thanks to his new father-in-law he landed one of the two seats in Stafford in 1880 as colleague of Alexander Macdonald, the miners' leader. Charles appealed to the middle-class electors, Macdonald to the working men. Charles's wife Laura was the daughter of Henry Pochin, a rich businessman whose home was at Bodnant, North Wales, and who had unsuccessfully contested Stafford three times on a thoroughly Radical platform. As for Walter, a career in Yorkshire textiles, branching out into other business enterprises, was accompanied by political hopes that might have secured him a Liberal nomination in 1880 and were to do so by the next general election. Like Charles he found a wife involved in women's rights. Eva, a Quaker with strong views on temperance, came on her father's side from Chile. Helen thought the newcomer 'such a very low squat body', who, however, improved on acquaintance. The engagement, she suggested, did not 'seem at all to have lessened his extraordinary liking for the society of all the other young ladies of his acquaintance', and she hoped her brother would restrain his flirtations in Eva's presence.[13]

For Priscilla the arrival of daughters-in-law of like mind to herself was a spur to increasing prominence in the women's movement. Her absences from home included taking a prominent role at women-only

Grand Demonstrations in the large cities. The spate of marriage alliances shows the close connections between well-to-do radically minded (and high-minded) families with whom the elder McLarens mixed as well as those to whom they were already related. In addition to numerous Brights, there were Priestmans, Lucases, Ashworths, Thomassons and the shoemaking Clarks of Somerset.[14] The men of the younger generation, John Albert Bright as well as Charles and Walter McLaren, encouraged by their wives, were more reliable recruits to women's causes than Duncan McLaren and John Bright. But for politicians seeking to reconcile the desirable with what was feasible in law, the demands of woman campaigners could not be fully met, as John McLaren discovered. He largely wrote a Bill to give the property of married women in Scotland the same protection as south of the border. But as Lord Advocate in charge of the legislation he did not go far enough. Jacob Bright's wife told Priscilla that she had given up on John and his boss, the Prime Minister, who said he was too busy with public business to become involved. 'The safety and honour and lives of married women are not a matter of public business in his eyes.' Women had to make themselves into prostitutes 'before they can be concerned worthy of public concern or be entitled to any protective legislation from him, or his Government.'[15] Gladstone's well-known interest in the welfare of prostitutes on the London streets did not equate with the demands of propertied ladies.

While Charles and Walter embarked on political careers, McLaren's other two sons moved away from his influence in different ways. John, free of politics, proved an able judge, his opinions reflecting the clarity that had gone into his earlier legal writings.[16] In autumn 1881 John Bright reflected on a difficult year for both uncle and nephew: 'Let us try to forget the past and dwell rather in the present, if there is any good in it. This rather for you than for me – for my present is desolate at home, and has cause for imitation in regard to public matters from which as yet, I cannot see my way to escape.'[17] Bright's wife had died three years previously, and he was increasingly conscious of being old. The rupture with Gladstone's policy that was soon to take him out of the Cabinet was looming: the Government seemed to be following the aggressive imperial policy of its predecessor, while he was still the acknowledged leader of the 'peace party'. Bombardment of Alexandria and subsequent defeat of Arabi Pasha in Egypt led to his resignation in 1882. For John McLaren that year brought public recognition – an honorary LLD from Edinburgh University – but private tragedy. His son Hernie, sickly since a baby, died aged ten. The elder McLarens were on English travels at the time, and Priscilla wrote to John and

Ottilie regretting that she could not come to Edinburgh because McLaren needed her by his side: 'I can only yield to his decision and be with you in spirit, but it is a decision I shall never cease to regret.'[18]

One reason why McLaren was so constantly on the move was that his retirement from Parliament had been preceded by retirement from business. In June 1880, the year that Duncan junior married Elizabeth Struthers,[19] he took over the large department store, at a cost of £10,500 for the goodwill. That sum, payable over a period, was later reduced to £6,000 in view of Duncan's expenditure and circumstances. To be his own man at last must have been welcome. In 1875 he had turned down a suggestion that he stand for the town council, pleading pressure of business and adding: 'There are some questions which will probably come before the council, in which my opinions differ from our father's; and I would not like publicly to speak and vote against his expressed views.' One point of disagreement was the Heriot's endowments.[20]

On the female side of the family Agnes continued to prove that self-reliance brought its satisfactions. She divided her time between a medical practice in Cannes, where she had tried to ensure the best treatment for Hernie, and working in Edinburgh at a medical mission dispensary in the Canongate. Her sister Grant found no such fulfilment. The death of John Millar, her elderly husband, left her well provided for, with houses in Kinross-shire and Edinburgh, but discontented. She blamed her brother John for legal problems with her family's trust fund and inexplicably complained about lack of accommodation for visitors at Sheardale, her large country home. She asked him for a bed in Edinburgh so that she could attend a prayer meeting: 'I would not think of going to Newington House. I have never at any time been asked to stay a night in the house since I was married ... Indeed I am unwilling to be indebted more than I can help to any member of my own family. It is from Mr Millar's relations that I have received increasing delicate kindnesses and attention since my husband's death.'[21]

For McLaren himself there were numerous relations as the result of his three marriages. The Renton connection remained strong and in 1882 became a subject for adverse comment. James Cowan retired from Parliament, and the Edinburgh United Liberal Association, far from taking a strong lead, was content to sit on its hands until Liberals of whatever hue emerged as candidates. Eventually two contested the by-election, which the Conservatives kept out of. The favourite, who commended himself greatly to *The Scotsman*, was a former MP, Samuel Waddy, an English barrister. McLaren proposed James Hall Renton, a stockbroker who also lived south of the border. His Scottish heritage was not in question, since he was the youngest brother of Christina, McLaren's second wife. McLaren openly acknowledged the relationship in speaking at a Renton campaign meeting. The contest touched on disestablishment of the Church of Scotland, but the outcome hardly turned on that topical issue since both candidates pled support for the campaign. *The Scotsman* wrote: 'If a peer ... had put first his son forward, and then his brother-in-law, what would have been the outcry from Newington House?'[22] When Waddy comfortably won, McLaren was declared the main loser.

In the women's movement with its grand demonstrations Priscilla rallied the family. So many ladies flocked to a meeting in Manchester in 1880 that her sister Margaret Lucas had to preside over an overflow meeting while Priscilla chaired the main demonstration. Two years later she spoke to between 5,000 and 7,000 at St Andrew's Hall in Glasgow, an event ignored by *The Scotsman* although fully reported in the *Glasgow Herald*. Another speaker was Laura McLaren, wearing what was regarded as the dress outfit for reformers – a divided skirt. By the time of Edinburgh's turn for a great rally in March 1884, campaigning was directed towards securing votes for women householders in Gladstone's Reform Bill. Priscilla coupled the claim with that of another topical campaign. There was a need 'to disestablish from men's minds, and from women's also,' she was sorry to say, 'the idea that the rights of citizenship must always be associated with physical power.'[23] Mention of disestablishment brought a few hisses amid the applause. Walter McLaren had seconded a motion demanding votes for women at the 1883 Liberal conference, but the Prime Minister was not to be convinced. In July that year Priscilla wrote from Bradford to her husband expressing disgust at the attitude of MPs to women.[24] Four months later, in better humour, she was at a meeting to found an International Society for Women's Suffrage when she was informed that Edinburgh Liberal Association had passed a suffrage resolution: 'My dear old husband of 84 sent me the telegram at 11 o'clock at night.'[25]

Gladstone's second Government proved a disappointment not just to campaigning women and to John Bright. Wrestling with the intractable problem of Ireland and the disruption Nationalists caused to the business of Parliament, he slipped into decisions abroad that smacked of Palmerston or Disraeli. Emotions roused by the plight of General Gordon in Sudan turned politics away from causes dear to moralising Liberals – the bad state of trade, temperance and, in Scotland, disestablishment of the Church and land reform, especially in the Highlands. Gladstone himself was still a demi-god to the masses but his preoccupations were not those of activists in the Liberal constituency associations, which came under pressure from the leadership to steer clear of contentious commitments. Curiously, John McLaren, though a non-partisan judge, remained an unofficial adviser to Lord Richard Grosvenor, now in charge of Government patronage, and supplied him with a 'character' of Renton before the by-election. Grosvenor was irritated by the way Cowan's resignation had wrongfooted the party: 'A Tory,' he told John, 'never gives up his seat without consulting his party, and resigning at exactly the proper moment, and so helping the interests of the party nationally, but Liberals appear to consult their own convenience, and no one else's.'[26] Lord McLaren also maintained a relationship with Gladstone. When the Prime Minister announced a trip to his constituency for January 1883, the first since the election, John sent an invitation to visit. Regrettably 'his friends' in Midlothian would take up all the MP's time and leave no opportunity to spend time in Edinburgh.[27]

For McLaren senior the pressing issue was disestablishment. Separation of Church and State was rapidly gaining support beyond the ranks of United Presbyterians. In 1875 the Free Church Assembly overwhelmingly voted for disestablishment, and leaders of the UP and Free churches thenceforth frequently shared public platforms. But only a Liberal Government might be persuaded to contemplate legislation. In Opposition Lord Hartington, leader during Gladstone's 'retirement', was non-committal when he spoke at the inauguration of the East and North Liberal Association in 1877. He wanted Scottish or even Scottish Liberal opinion to be more fully formed before making a commitment. Gladstone in Midlothian and then in Government was similarly unsure of the ground despite pressure from Liberal associations, Glasgow's in particular. The Prime Minister said in 1880 that disestablishment was not occupying 'nearly the first place' in his mind.[28]

The next year McLaren chaired a disestablishment meeting in Edinburgh at which some divinity students formed a chorus of opposition to the reformers. McLaren accepted that the Government was not going to act immediately but he rejected the suggestion that in Parliament and the country there should be no debate. Only by discussing the matter would public opinion be formed, and so there should be meetings 'carried on in a Christian spirit'. Ministers needed to be convinced of the weight of the argument, he said, as they had been through agitation against the corn laws and before the Irish Church was disestablished. He explained that for more than 40 years he had believed that disestablishment, with proper safeguards for Church of Scotland ministers, 'would not only be just and beneficial to the people of Scotland, but would ultimately prove to be for the benefit of the present congregations of the Church of Scotland'.[29] McLaren won a response the next day from Gladstone, praising his moderation: 'Were the cause of disestablishment sufficiently powerful and mature to force its way to the front in defiance of all competition, its friends need not be deterred from bringing it into activity and prominence at head quarters. But if it has not reached that very advanced stage, my opinion is that the measure is more likely to be thrown back than pushed forward by endeavours to bring the Government or Parliament prematurely to entertain it ... My observation has no reference to any proceedings taken in Scotland.'[30]

Proceedings in Scotland included an increasingly active and strident campaign for disestablishment embracing Free Churchmen and United Presbyterians; and on the other side an association to defend the Established Church and fear on the part of Church Liberals that grassroots pressure might swing the party irrevocably towards disestablishment. With hindsight we can see that the Liberal leadership in Scotland, still Whig dominated, was not going to let that happen, and when Dick Peddie, MP for Kilmarnock, brought forward disestablishment Bills in the Commons he was in a small minority (though encouraged by some English Radicals who saw a gateway to disestablishment of the Church of England, too). Gladstone was petitioned by the disestablishers to be bold and from the other direction counselled by Church Liberals and his own Scottish advisers to avoid splitting the party and letting the Conservatives gain seats. Matters came to a head at the start of the 1885 election which was fought under the newly passed Reform Act that gave the vote to all male householders, sweeping away the distinction in qualifications between counties and burghs, and creating more seats for the cities – seven in Glasgow, four in Edinburgh and two each for Aberdeen and Dundee.

By now the Irish MPs had been seduced into defeating the Liberals and installing a Tory Government led by Lord Salisbury. On 11 November when Gladstone, as Leader of the Opposition, arrived in Edinburgh to launch his Midlothian campaign he was given the rare privilege of making a speech within the Free Church Assembly Hall. This was the electioneering opportunity for him to commit to disestablishment – or so its advocates hoped. In a front-page advertisement in *The Scotsman* 1,475 ministers signed a petition in favour, and McLaren was due to chair a disestablishment meeting in the Synod Hall. He had to send his apologies having caught a cold on his way south from the Highlands, but in his letter he took the opportunity of striking a radical political note: 'I greatly lament the disunion caused in the Liberal ranks by coalition of old Whigs with the Tories in order to oppose the return of advanced Liberals, because they include disestablishment in their political creed.'[31] Gladstone disappointed the disestablishers, going no farther than in his letter to McLaren four years earlier. Disestablishment was still 'at the end of a long vista' and 'if the Church question is not to be a test question in England, it ought not to be in Scotland'. Two days later Priscilla commented: 'It would serve Gladstone right if some disestablishers refrained from voting, but there is no doubt there are more pressing questions than disestablishment.'[32] Most Liberals, including Free Churchmen and United Presbyterians, were willing to accept that the time was still not right, but for the determinedly committed minority, a demonstration of strength at the polls would convince Gladstone that Scotland spoke with a clear voice. One of the seats where a Church Liberal and a disestablisher clashed was Inverness Burghs. Robert Finlay, an Edinburgh-educated English barrister, defended the Church of Scotland. Assailing its privileged position was McLaren's son Walter. The contest for the future direction of Liberalism in Scotland is well depicted in McLaren family correspondence from the campaign.[33]

In his last years Duncan McLaren lived for extended periods in the Highlands. His son John had a house at Lochcarron in Ross-shire, and in 1884 McLaren visited him there during a stay of several months at Strathpeffer, a spa centre of the kind much appreciated by the family. When a by-election occurred in the county, McLaren inevitably became involved, speaking at meetings for 24-year-old Ronald Munro-Ferguson of Novar, a Liberal candidate challenged both by a Conservative and by Roderick Macdonald as a representative of the crofters, whose campaign for Highland land reform was gaining in strength. McLaren said that once the Reform Bill was through Parliament, where it was being bad-temperedly batted between Lords and Commons, the Government would look at the plight of crofters.[34] While McLaren was glad his man won, he welcomed the election the following year of Macdonald, who benefited from the newly extended electorate to unseat the landlord Munro-Ferguson and accompany three other crofter members to Westminster. The 1885 election marked the end of Whig landlord domination of Highland county seats, and McLaren's radicalism was stirred by the change.

In the burgh constituency of Inverness, which took in Nairn, Forres and Fortrose, Walter had no Conservative opposition, and so the two Liberals could battle over disestablishment. Walter's pitch was to working men, and when the campaign was at its November peak and his rival Finlay was receiving powerful support from Church of Scotland pulpits and the Church Defence committee, Walter wondered if his own meetings were too much about disestablishment. At morning service the minister of the Gaelic church had earnestly denounced Walter for 'dishing the church' and so, accompanied by a Gaelic-speaking supporter as interpreter, Walter went to the afternoon service to hear for himself, and to fear a loss of votes among older electors. Free Churchmen who opposed their denomination's adoption of disestablishment were also against him. His father was drawn into controversy. Although a freeman of the burgh, he had once tried, it was alleged, to block Government money from being used to build the suspension bridge across the River Ness. Kept at home in Edinburgh by a persistent cough, McLaren eagerly searched among his papers to refute the charge. Priscilla on the campaign trail was proud of her son's efforts. He reminded her of her brother John at the same age. She wrote to her husband that 'he is such a mixture of thyself and John. May both mantles fall upon him.'[35]

By the time Invernessians went to the poll there was good news and bad for Priscilla to comment on in her daily letters to Newington House. Charles comfortably held his seat in Stafford, and Priscilla excused him for distancing himself from the local Liberation Society on the ground that Church disestablishment was not yet a pressing issue in England. But Edinburgh, where Liberals took all four seats, was 'once more in the hands of the Whigs, only they dare not be exactly what the Whigs of old were.'[36] In the newly drawn South constituency the candidate whom McLaren had proposed, Thomas Raleigh, was beaten by Sir George Harrison, the former Lord Provost. John McLaren had sent his carriage to Newington House so that his father could go out to vote.[37] The radical Liberals alleged that Harrison had won on Tory as well as Liberal votes. Worse for Priscilla, her brother Jacob lost in Manchester. She blamed the Irish vote there although she said that he had risked his life by consistently opposing the Government's policy of coercion across the Irish Sea. By the eve of the Inverness vote she wrote that 'the tide has been so strongly against the advanced Liberals and indeed Liberals of every shade, that one may well doubt the result.' On a 92 per cent poll Walter won 1,546 votes to Finlay's 1,709, a defeat attributed by Priscilla to Church, Tory and public-house influence. She detected bribery and thought Finlay might be turned out on petition, but she was advised to keep quiet, and she turned her ire on *The Scotsman*'s view of the result: 'That paper deserves the gallows, if a paper could be punished.' Her last letter from Inverness concluded: 'I shall be very glad to get home to be with thee once more darling.'

There were 27 seats like Inverness where Liberals fought each other, a failure of the unity strategy of five years earlier. But such divisions were not punished; only 8 Tories were returned from the 70 Scottish seats provided for in the Reform Act, compared with 6 from the 58 seats in 1880. Priscilla's complaint at the retreat of advanced Liberalism was based largely on candidates' attitudes to the religious question. More significant was the failure of the new radical Liberalism of the party's rising star, Joseph Chamberlain, to create an institutional base in Scotland with the influence of his National Liberal Federation south of the border. He did help found a National Liberal Federation of Scotland in 1885, in rivalry to the Scottish Liberal Association. The NLFS talked policy while the SLA remained the more powerful body by overseeing the party's organisational work. Scottish radicalism remained in the mould of McLaren rather than of Chamberlain's Birmingham caucus. It was, however, Chamberlain's populism, appealing in particular to the newly enfranchised agricultural workers of England, that allowed the Liberals to prevail over the Tories in the election, though the Irish Nationalists still held the balance. An agrarian motion for 'three acres and a cow' moved by Chamberlain's followers brought down Salisbury's Government in January 1886 and re-installed Gladstone. He immediately turned his recent speculations about resolving the Irish problem into a Home Rule Bill that split his party. The old loyalties, Radical as well as Whig, were shattered. McLaren in the last few weeks of his life abandoned the Gladstone Liberals. In Scotland Gladstone's 'end of the long vista' for disestablishment stretched over the horizon. Symbolically, Walter's conqueror, Robert Finlay, immediately on taking his seat introduced a Bill declaring the spiritual independence of the Church of Scotland, which seemed to ask Parliament to repent for having caused the Disruption. It was defeated, as was a motion by the Glasgow MP Charles Cameron for disestablishment. The arguments stuttered on while Irish home rule was being passionately debated and defeated. There followed a General Election in July 1886 that threw the Liberals out of office.

In the mind of advanced Scottish Liberals the party in 1885 was divided because of unwillingness to commit to disestablishment. How severe or permanent that division would have become we will never know because it was lost in the much deeper fissures over the Irish Home Rule Bill. McLaren's last election was in his own South Edinburgh constituency. Harrison died only weeks after his success at the General Election. The party leadership with allegedly indecent haste installed Hugh Childers as the by-election candidate. He was a close associate of Gladstone's, having served as Chancellor of the Exchequer in the previous Government. But to advanced Liberals he was unsound on disestablishment, and in the first days of January 1886 there were desperate attempts to find a challenger from the radical wing. Even McLaren himself was asked to consider a return to Westminster. Among others who turned down the opportunity were Jacob Bright and the swashbuckling Robert Cunninghame Graham. No one could be persuaded, and the inadvisability of having two Liberals in the field was underlined when a Tory, Walter Hepburne-Scott, the Master of Polwarth, cast his hat in the ring. The South Edinburgh Liberal Association voted by 80 to 3 against Childers' candidacy on the grounds of haste and his views on disestablishment, but the result of the by-election in a straight Liberal–Tory contest was not in doubt. McLaren explained in a letter to a friend that Childers' religious policy was only one reason for staying on the sidelines. He also wanted leading Liberals to be aware of the dangers of committing to sweeping changes in the Government of Ireland, which Gladstone was clearly contemplating. Childers, as a former colleague in the Commons, called on McLaren, although the candidate knew that the old man did not want a representative of Government Whiggery as the MP. McLaren was out but next day returned the visit and told Childers of his worries about Irish policy. Despite assurances that ministers would not allow an Irish Parliament to have charge of an armed police force – one of McLaren's main concerns – he concluded his account of the meeting: 'I am still by no means satisfied that an Irish Parliament will not be proposed with plausible guarantees so-called, which would be swept away in a short time, and separation or civil war, or both, be the result.'[38]

McLaren was concerned not only at the principle behind a Parliament in Dublin and the withdrawal of Irish MPs from Westminster but at the manner in which Gladstone sprang such far-reaching change on his party and the country. The contrast between the headlong dash to Irish legislation in the first months of 1886 and the procrastination over Church disestablishment was offensive to those who, wisely or not, laid such emphasis on the latter. McLaren in his correspondence at this time professed still to venerate Gladstone as the greatest man of the age but in common with many radical Liberals he distrusted the Prime Minister's judgment. For Chamberlain and his followers the problem was Gladstone's unwillingness to embrace their programme of social reform. For the 'peace party' it was the entanglements in east and southern Africa. For many Scottish Liberals it was his failure to embrace their pressing cause of disestablishment. Yet none of these upsets explains the immediate wave of hostility to the Irish Home Rule Bill and the accompanying assumption that it would sunder the party for ever. In McLaren's case the depth of his opposition is, on the surface, the more puzzling because he was a constitutional reformer who accepted the justice of Irish grievances. As an MP he was recognised as a friend of Ireland who frequently contributed to debates on its affairs. He did so, however, as a believer in equal treatment for the three kingdoms of Scotland, England and Ireland. Often that meant sticking up for Ireland as well as Scotland but he also sometimes caused offence. His calls were for efficient as well as fair government.

In 1883 Lord Rosebery, exposed as a junior Home Office minister to the inefficiencies of handling Scottish business, peremptorily demanded action by the Prime Minister, and McLaren approved the emphasis on administrative tidiness. Harcourt brought forward a Bill for a Scottish local government board, which, to indignation north of the border, was thrown out by the Lords. Rosebery then petulantly resigned from the Government, adding to the discontent. In January 1884 a great national meeting was called in Edinburgh at the instigation of the Convention of Royal Burghs, whose members continually suffered the frustrations of doing business with Whitehall departments. Chaired by the Marquess of Lothian, it brought together peers and commoners of both parties, as well as provosts up and down the land. McLaren was among those contributing to its debates and to the call for a separate department of state for Scotland. Change had to come, he said, not as 'a matter of favour, not cringing', but by right of equality with England and Ireland.[39] He set to work on drafting a Bill better than the failed Government one. A month later he was in London as part of a large delegation presenting the results of the Edinburgh meeting to the Prime Minister. It was agreed five members would speak, among them McLaren, not because of his venerability but because he was master of the detailed case for change. No greater compliment could be paid by the cream of the Scottish political establishment which had spent so much time denigrating him. The delegation emphasised that on behalf of the Scottish people they were seeking not to interfere with the Union or look for home rule but to ensure better government. Gladstone thanked McLaren for his work and remarked that in 'green old age' he looked fresher than he had years before in the atmosphere of Parliament.[40] It took more than a year for legislation to reach the statute book, and it was Lord Salisbury's short-lived Government that finally enacted the bipartisan measure and appointed the Duke of Richmond and Gordon the first Scottish Secretary. But while Scotland took a significant step to administrative devolution, Ireland was soon presented with the prospect of its own legislature almost wholly divorced from the Imperial Parliament.

In joining the National Association for the Vindication of Scottish Rights 30 years earlier, McLaren was not seeking a Parliament in Edinburgh. He was no romantic mourner of the loss of independence. He sought not more legislatures but better government. And so there was in his mind no illogicality in seeking change for Scotland while condemning home rule. He had contempt for Parnell and his Nationalist MPs, who habitually rendered Westminster ineffective. He did not trust them with government of their disturbed country where neither coercion nor concession made a lasting difference – hence his opposition to Irish control of armed police. He also, like many Liberals, could do the electoral arithmetic. A Liberal Government might be hobbled by dependence on Irish Nationalist support, but without the presence of the Irish a Conservative majority looked like becoming permanent. In his last illness he poured out his concerns to his brother-in-law Bright. Unable to write, he dictated to Priscilla his worries for the country and the Liberal party. The possibility of 'home rule all round' with a Parliament in Edinburgh as well as Dublin was no solution. 'This, I think, would be a great calamity for Scotland; and if I had the health and strength which I possessed in Anti-Corn-Law times, I would be prepared to do what you and other noble patriots did, and do what our ancestors used to call "to testify" against the proposed injustice.'[41] Priscilla added a note to her brother that 'his voice assumed a solemnity such as I have never heard in him before. And when he had finished he broke down and wept.' McLaren, like the whole of the Liberal party, wanted to know what line Bright would take. Priscilla recalled the atmosphere in a letter to a friend months after her husband's death: 'He [McLaren] was greatly concerned at the silence maintained by my brother John Bright on the matter, when there were so many wishing to know his opinion, for really few men think for themselves and Gladstone never had become the Shibbolith [sic] of the Liberal party.'[42]

McLaren's own position was clear and robust. He had recently been made honorary president of Edinburgh South Liberal Association, which came out in support of Gladstone's Irish policy. At once he resigned, stating that if there were an early election and 'if in our district a candidate comes forward for an Irish Parliament and another against it, if I should be spared in health and strength, I should vote for the candidate against the Irish Parliament, whatever his other political opinions might be, whether Radical, Whig, or Tory, so strong is my conviction of the ulterior evil consequences which would flow from such a measure.'[43] Influential Unionists used McLaren's name to bolster their cause. Their side of Liberalism was especially strong in Glasgow, led by men as diverse as the tea merchant Thomas Lipton and the scientist Sir William Thomson (later Lord Kelvin), who, not knowing that McLaren was in his last illness, wrote to ask him to speak at a Unionist rally in St Andrew's Hall. McLaren's explanation for declining but affirming support was read to and acclaimed by the meeting.

In March McLaren was asked by the Convention of Royal Burghs to comment on a memorandum it had commissioned about local government. A speedy reply was sought, and he responded in four days, laying out a complex system by which local Bills could be considered in Scotland instead of expensively at Westminster. It involved electing a second tranche of representatives to sit alongside half of the Scottish MPs when local Bills were being examined. Cumbersome, wrongheaded and ignored the plan might have been, but its attempt to deal in detail with a real problem was typical of McLaren in his last days as throughout his public life. He addressed the challenge head on, but at a price. Priscilla appended a note to the correspondence between her husband and the Convention: 'His compliance with this request was the last effort which broke him down.'[44]

Despite the cough that troubled him towards the end of 1885 McLaren was fit enough to go out and about – visiting Childers for example – until the following March. Affliction when it came was to his heart and brought increasing bouts of pain. Priscilla, who was in England on a visit when he took ill, became his amanuensis as well as his nurse. She recorded in the letter to a friend mentioned above: 'The *spirit within* must have known that the end had come – every letter he had received, mine amongst the rest up to the last day, he sate [sic] where I am now sitting, he had carefully tied up, and written on the cover what each was docketted [sic], as he termed it.' Business-like orderliness was maintained. In April he was mainly confined to bed: 'His sufferings were very great but when the attacks of pain in the heart were over he could enjoy the intervals of ease. I sometimes think that the Doctor encouraged too much the hope of recovery – but the dear patient once or twice or oftener said "when I use judgment and look at my case as tho' it were that of another man I see how serious it is" and once he called me to him and said, "Seeing this, do not let anything occur if you can help it to annoy me, I wish to keep very quiet preparing for the end. I am willing to meet whatever comes."'

The family, including grandchildren, made welcome visits. His daughter Grant gave him a book of scriptural extracts from which he took comfort. Charles, arriving from Parliament, took a more optimistic view of Irish home rule than his father, and the two amicably discussed the pros and cons. Dr Rabagliati, his son-in-law, came from Bradford and could only observe the patient's decline. On 26 April, after a night of pain, the old man was more relaxed. He asked Charles to write a letter to someone who had been a source of irritation in the past, and remarked: 'That is all past. I feel no irritation now none.' Priscilla described the end to her friend who was also recently widowed: 'His noble life closed in one of those attacks of pain but it was soon over.'

The funeral, on the afternoon of Saturday, 1 May, was a public one and a solemn spectacle of the kind at which Victorian Edinburgh excelled.[45] A service was held in Rosehall United Presbyterian Church, in whose recent foundation close to his home McLaren had taken a keen interest. Bright sunshine greeted the procession as it went from Newington House to St Giles' Cathedral headed by office bearers of the High Constables and the Merchant Company, the Lord Provost, magistrates and councillors, mostly in open carriages. Shops on the route were closed, and crowds grew in the High Street long before the cortege arrived. Representatives attended from the many bodies with which McLaren was associated, including 330 boys from the 11 Heriot day schools who joined the procession, which after the service involving Principal Rainy of the Free Church and Dr Alison of Newington Church of Scotland made its way by Princes Street to St Cuthbert's churchyard. The family grave is against the wall dividing the grounds from Princes Street Gardens and only yards from the bridge across the railway line. The tombstone already contained a memorial to McLaren's mother, his wives Grant and Christina, and four-year-old Anne. Priscilla commented later: 'His grave is not where I would like it to be – but he bought it when it was a lovely spot. Now trains with their shrieking whistle pass near it every hour under our grand Castle rock.' She placed on the stone a testament to his fight for the underprivileged and especially for the Heriot schools: 'He considered the poor, he understood righteousness and judgment and equity. Yea every good path.' Among the pall-bearers were John Oliver, his son Fred and John Bright, whose attendance allowed him to escape making a speech in the tortured Commons debate on Irish Home Rule – he gained a little time before having to take a stance.

Among the many tributes Gladstone recorded: 'A remarkable life has closed – his age 86 – a life of continuous, devoted and honourable labour and service to Edinbro', to Scotland, and to the whole country.'[46] Churchmen sent letters and gave sermons. Among them was Cardinal Manning, who wrote to Agnes McLaren, soon to join the Roman Catholic Church as a medical missionary. Newspapers carried full and fulsome obituaries. Most revealing is the tone of *The Scotsman*, which noted that as recently as 17 April it had published a long letter from McLaren on the Irish question.[47] 'He had the true and valuable restlessness of the Scotsman which will not allow him to be quiet when he thinks he should speak out and act.' The paper said it fought against McLaren when it thought him wrong, but did not fail to give him credit when it believed him to be right. 'Never was there a more tenacious controversialist.'

17. Envoi

In October 1887 the Earl of Breadalbane gave Priscilla McLaren permission to build a stone monument to her husband on his land near the Argyll village of Dalmally. Because the plot was small there was to be no charge.[1] The site chosen was as close as possible to the cottage in which McLaren had spent much of his boyhood with his grandparents. When he visited the area in 1867 he struggled to find buildings he recognised such were the effects of rural depopulation over the previous half-century. Nowadays the site of the memorial is isolated, off a little used road from Dalmally up Glen Strae. It impressively commands a hillock looking south towards Loch Awe and is a peaceful spot, though prone to midges.

Besides a monument in stone, Priscilla and the family commissioned a two-volume biography. When a life of Adam Black was published in 1885, McLaren read it with enthusiasm, disputing parts of its account of his relationship with his mentor and rival. Priscilla remarked that her husband was a greater man than Black and that he should set down his own story. In his last months he spent many hours looking out and meticulously arranging papers in Newington House. Even before he died it was clear that a biography and not an autobiography was needed. The choice of a sympathetic writer fell upon John Beveridge Mackie. This Dunfermline-born journalist was one of three brothers looking after the editorial and business affairs of the *Daily Review*, McLaren's most loyal Edinburgh paper. The *Review*, however, was on its last legs and when it folded in 1886, John Mackie had to find another job as leader writer on the *Newcastle Daily Leader*. He was flattered to be asked to undertake McLaren's life and was given access to the papers at Newington House. Inevitably the task took longer than planned and the family correspondence reflects irritation at the delay. Already by July 1887 Priscilla was complaining to her stepson John about the slow progress on 'this sacred work'. Then there were hold-ups in production.

As Christmas 1888 approached, she wrote that it was 'as tho' some Old Whig Spirit had been let loose to try to hinder the Book from coming out in time for sale'. John was underwriting the cost, and there was debate about whether some copies should be dispatched free or whether that would detract too much from sales. In the end between 200 and 300 copies were sent out by the family, 36 of them reserved by Grant. Although, in the tradition of Victorian hagiography, Mackie's depiction is of a hero almost unblemished, John Bright complained that 'not one quarter of the praise due to McLaren has been given him'.[2] His brother-in-law's last campaign against Irish home rule was especially in Bright's mind. The old Radical was now firmly in the Liberal Unionist camp. He died in March 1889.

Priscilla stayed on in Newington House. 'It is rather a white elephant, but I feel as though no other place ever could be *home* to me, and all the older children are very anxious for me to remain here, but I often wish it had not so happened that my younger ones were all in England.[3] Her husband's estate was valued at £33,013 14s 4d. She was left an annuity worth at least £1,000 plus life-rent of the house, its contents and two carriages. The trust set up to administer the estate was directed to fund the annuity from the lands which McLaren had developed and which offered ample income from feu duties.[4] She survived for 20 years during which, aside from conducting a voluminous correspondence with her extensive family, she worked tirelessly for women's causes, especially the vote. She spoke at meetings, collected signatures for petitions, raised money, served on committees and wove her way through the divided politics of the movement. As an executive member of the National Union of Women's Suffrage Societies, she believed, as many did not, that the Liberal party held the key to success. She was on the side of radical campaigners and in 1906, just weeks before her death, she signalled acceptance of suffragette militancy by sending a letter of sympathy to activists who had been imprisoned.

John McLaren served almost 30 years as a judge respected for his courtesy, fairness and conciseness. He showed a geniality and wit absent in his earlier public dealings. Clearly he was a man happier out of politics, though he made no secret of his preference for Liberal Unionism. He looked after a Highland estate as well as his Edinburgh home, and he dabbled with some skill in both astronomy and meteorology. The boy too delicate for the Scottish climate survived until he was almost 79, outliving his sister Grant by a month. John's daughter Katharine was by then long married to her cousin, Frederick Scott Oliver (1864–1934), son of Catherine and John Oliver (who died in 1903). Fred, a great favourite of Priscilla's, was a precocious Cambridge student who became a successful director of Debenham and Freebody in London and then a writer on military and diplomatic affairs. He told his grandmother that he had become a Conservative but also spoke of his continuing admiration for John Bright. He bought an estate near his father's family home in Jedburgh, and it is the Frederick Scott Oliver papers in the National Library of Scotland that open the door to the McLaren family story over three generations.

Duncan McLaren junior remained in charge of the family business after his father's death, eventually moving it from the High Street (where its premises were absorbed in the expanded City Chambers) to join the Rentons in their Princes Street shop, and the McLaren name finally disappeared from the retail trade. He overcame his previous reluctance and served for a time as a town councillor, but his principal interest and that of his wife lay in the foreign missions of the United Presbyterian Church and latterly of the United Free Church. Chairman of the UP Foreign Mission Board, his tact and unassuming manner were regarded as helpful in the negotiations that led to the union of the UP and Free churches in 1900. He had spent the winter of 1879–80 in India studying mission work and he made many overseas visits, especially after his retirement. Twice he and his wife journeyed to Manchuria, and he went to South Africa as the Boer War was coming to an end. He lived until 1920.

Priscilla was right in that her three children never returned to Scotland except on visits. As an MP Charles followed Gladstone on Irish home rule and lost his seat in the 1886 election but came back six years later as MP for Bosworth, while retaining his practice at the Bar. Increasingly, he was involved with the coal, iron, steel and other businesses that his wife Laura inherited from her father, and he took on chairmanships and directorships. As chairman of John Brown and Co. on the Clyde he was responsible for launching a succession of warships and passenger liners. He wrote a book called *The Basic Industries of Great Britain*. Asquith as Prime Minister made him Lord Aberconway, and at Bodnant in North Wales he and the Pochin family led a life on whose luxury Priscilla commented with a touch of disapproval as early as 1885. The garden for which the estate is now famed was Laura's inspiration. Their elder son Henry succeeded his father as MP for Bosworth and in 1934 inherited the Aberconway title. His brother Francis, Liberal MP for Spalding, was killed in the First World War but Francis's son Martin continued the Westminster tradition by serving as Conservative MP for Bristol North-West from 1959.

Walter McLaren won the Crewe seat for the Liberals in 1886 and gave up his interest in the Yorkshire spinning firm of Smith and

McLaren in 1890. Out of Parliament from 1895 until 1910 he developed other business interests but was MP for Crewe again at the time of his death in 1912. Influenced by his wife Eva more than by his mother, he was a prominent parliamentary advocate of women's rights. In 1886 Eva became first national organiser of the Women's Liberal Federation.

Helen Rabagliati, mother of five, spent her life in Yorkshire exemplifying the belief that equality was best attained through involvement in public affairs. She and her doctor husband were pioneers of the hospice movement, founding a home in Bradford as early as 1893. She promoted education for girls and her work during the First World War won her a medal from the King of the Belgians. Andrea Rabagliati was a leading practitioner and medical writer, especially regarding the treatment of children. He was a convinced vegetarian who favoured only two meals a day with eight hours between them. His wife's politics moved to the Right: for the last 28 years of her life until 1934 she was president of the Ben Rhydding Women's Unionist Association.[5]

It is fitting for the spotlight to fall last on Agnes McLaren, for hers was the most unlikely of careers. Her struggle to complete medical studies brought her into contact with Catholic doctors, priests and nuns in France. For 20 years while still a Presbyterian and practising physician, she made an annual retreat under the guidance of a priest from Lyons, and at the age of 60 she became a Roman Catholic, associating herself with the Dominican order. Her interest turned to India where Hindu and Muslim women alike sought treatment from a female doctor. Finding that there were no Catholic woman doctors in the sub-continent, she organised a medical mission committee in London in 1906. Four years later in failing health she went to India to help found a hospital for women and children in Rawalpindi. She badgered the Vatican to allow nuns to study and practise medicine, and the legacy after her death in 1913 was the Society of Catholic Medical Missionaries, a religious community trained in all areas of medicine. Following a papal decree in 1936 religious orders were urged to educate sisters as doctor missionaries.[6]

For over 30 years Newington House was associated in the Edinburgh public mind with Duncan McLaren. After Priscilla's long widowhood the house passed out of the family. It was not the most beautiful of buildings but it did not deserve to be knocked down in the 1960s and be replaced by a particularly hideous Edinburgh University hall of residence. McLaren's memory is perpetuated only in a couple of streets bearing his name. A portrait by George Reid hangs in the City Chambers. McLaren is in civic regalia and it makes him forbidding as well as formidable even by the standards of nineteenth-century official portraiture. The majesty of office was more important than conveying the man behind the robes. So we are left still wondering what made him such a significantly greater man than most other civic dignitaries. John Mackie's two volumes are a starting point. They do not lack detail of his achievements in both Edinburgh and Parliament. Praise is heaped upon him at every turn. With the family looking over his shoulder there is barely a hint of criticism. Aspects of his life that reflected badly on him or were still sensitive to his widow and children, such as Catherine's marriage to John Oliver and the dissolution of the business partnership, are wholly ignored.

From a modern historical perspective there is an unwitting tribute to one of Duncan McLaren's skills in John Vincent's groundbreaking study, *The Formation of the British Liberal Party 1857–68*.[7] Vincent discusses John Bright's limitations as a self-made man and argues that the university-educated men who dominated Government had little to fear. He quotes a letter by Bright showing that the details of drafting a Reform Bill were beyond him: 'Mr McLaren has worked hard on the statistics of the question, and during my stay there [Newington House], he arranged the schedule of the proposed Bill. We also went through [former Bills] ... and found that many of the clauses would meet our case now by filling up the blanks differently.' Vincent clearly did not appreciate that some non-university men, like McLaren, had mastered skills assumed to belong only to the expensively educated. Analytical reading and computational skills learned in Edinburgh's nascent evening classes and at the shop counter furnished McLaren's keen mind. Self-help, given popular appeal by Haddington's Samuel Smiles, made him rich and allowed him the freedom to mould the politics of religion, the administration of Edinburgh and the developing Liberal party according to his beliefs and ambitions.

He was a controversial figure, of course. But he was also trusted by a large section of the Edinburgh populace, and in later life he had many admirers across Scotland – hence the accolade of freeman of Inverness. The breadth and persistence of his parliamentary endeavours won him the description 'member for Scotland', even though it may first have been used by irritated opponents of his indefatigability. Much of the hostile testimony quoted in this book came from men of social and political prominence who found him an awkward intruder on their territory. Their allies in the fractious press heaped on the abuse. The correspondence of hostile Whig magnates and Parliament House leaders survives; the opinions of working people died with them. Of course McLaren could be a good hater, like his arch-opponent Russel of *The Scotsman*. But in abrasively going over the top as he sometimes did, and in never letting a cause lapse, he was guided by beliefs, not by personal malice. He gave voice to the concerns and complaints of the unprivileged and the downtrodden, and he won their loyalty even when they disagreed with him, as over trade-union legislation. His language could be moralistic and sententious, though no more so than was the convention, especially when dealing with problems like public drunkenness. Better housing, purer water, parks and museums open to the public – these were causes he embraced, though he shared the conventional opinion that the state should not be the provider. A national framework of free education, however, he embraced earlier than most and against the views of co-religionists.

His early forays in politics coincided with debilitating sectarianism. He entered public life as a spokesman for Dissenters who felt discrimination within the Protestant communion. He built a power base that carried over into secular causes such as free trade and franchise reform. New allies like Bright and Cobden recognised his abilities. Urbane Macaulay saw only intolerance. Yet the truth is that McLaren, unlike many of his time, was no bigot. He disliked rule by bishops, especially the bishop of Rome, but he had a Dissenter's fellow feeling for Episcopalians and Catholics complaining of discrimination. He repeatedly emphasised that he was a Dissenter in religion, not in politics (though the political support of Dissenters was always important to him).

McLaren would not have become Scotland's leading Radical without looking south. From church rates to voting reform, the radicals of England fought causes akin to his. When his cooperation with John Bright turned into family alliance, an important contribution was made to the Liberal party that found its modern form in 1859. Most Scottish MPs remained Whig but it was the radicalism of Bright and McLaren that ensured the support of the new urban voters from 1868 on. He was crucial in building the Liberalism that brought thousands on to the streets to mob Gladstone in the Midlothian campaigns.

So why was he so quickly forgotten after his death? His last campaigns were unsuccessful. In Edinburgh his Heriot schools disappeared or were transformed. In Scotland the agitation for disestablishment of the Church of Scotland faded away. He embraced Liberal Unionism just before his death and so as the Gladstonian Liberals struggled to reassert themselves, it was without the McLaren legacy. Anyway McLaren's causes were those of his century. State intervention by the Governments of Asquith and Lloyd George, much less the socialism that displaced Liberal domination of Scotland, signalled a different political era. McLaren had fought for more efficient and sensitive government of Scotland without the expense of a Parliament in Edinburgh. The creation of a Secretary for Scotland appeared to answer the challenge for decades ahead.

Applying talents in biblical fashion was McLaren's commitment, as apprentice shopkeeper and deathbed provider of advice to the Convention of Royal Burghs. His correspondence makes no mention of interest in the arts or sport. His public writings are formidable arguments, but in style forbidding. In religion he found a moral code more than a spiritual life. Emotion was not to be exposed, and so he needed to feel always in control. When confronted by the challenge of his daughter Catherine's romance with his business partner, he could not go beyond a sense of betrayal. Yet he was a loving soulmate for Priscilla, and by Victorian standards an enlightened father who judged his children's education by more than their place in class. His grandchildren saw him at his fondest. One of his last letters was to Charles's son Henry on the boy's seventh birthday:

> I want to explain about the difference between old age and young children like you, if you will do what I tell you. First take seven little pebbles from the lawn and lay them down in a row thus: You would think 'That's myself Harry'. Then you would lay down another row opposite it, and you would say, 'This for the first seven years of grandpapa's life, when he was as old as I am now'. Then you would put down another and another, till you had put down ten rows altogether, and you would see that ten rows of seven would make seventy. That would represent me as ten times older than you are now, when I was seventy; and people often talk as if men when they are seventy would soon die, as that is the general expectation. But to complete the picture by the little stones, of comparing my life with yours, you must lay down other two rows of seven, and that would be twelve times as old as you are, and show me to be eighty-four. But you cannot stop here. You must begin another row and lay down two stones and then stop. That will represent my age, eighty-six. That will show what a long distance in age there is between us, and how old I am; and that I cannot expect to live long. Now, my dear boy, be good and affectionate and kind to everybody, but especially to your little sisters, and fear God in all your doings, and that the blessing of God may rest on you is the sincere prayer of your loving grandfather.[8]

The farewell is pious, thoughtful and kind – and displays the painstaking computation that buttressed so many of Duncan McLaren's arguments.

References

CHAPTER 1
1. Macleod, D., *Historic Families, Notable People and Memorabilia of the Lennox.*
2. Cockburn, H. (Lord), *Memorials of his Time*, p. 67.
3. Ibid., p. 185.
4. Youngson, A.J., *The Making of Classical Edinburgh 1750–1840*, p. 226.
5. Quoted in Robertson, D. and Wood, M., *Castle and Town.*
6. From a lecture by Duncan McLaren at the founding of the Edinburgh Cobden Club, *The Scotsman*, 19 December 1868.
7. NLS MS7373. Combe Papers. Duncan McLaren to George Combe, 16 January 1858.
8. Winstanley, M.J., *The Shopkeeper's World 1830–1914.*
9. Marwick, W.H., 'Shops in eighteenth and nineteenth century Edinburgh'.
10. Marwick, J. (Sir), *Edinburgh Crafts and Guilds.*
11. Winstanley, *The Shopkeeper's World*, p. 7.
12. *The Scotsman*, 20 September 1834.
13. NLS MS24782. Frederick Scott Oliver Papers. Grant Aitken to McLaren, 12 May 1829.
14. NLS MS24783. Nicol McIntyre to McLaren, 27 April 1833.
15. NLS MS24782. McLaren to John (friend), 24 April 1833.
16. NLS MS24782. McLaren to John, 24 April 1833 (second letter).
17. Smith, R.M., '"Auld Licht, New Licht" and Original Secessionists in Scotland and Ulster'.
18. Obituary of Duncan McLaren, by Henry Calderwood, Editor, *United Presbyterian Magazine*, June 1886.
19. Peddie, J., *The Hand of God in Public Calamities*; Thin, J. (ed.), *Memorials of Bristo United Presbyterian Church.*
20. Brown, S.J., 'Religion and the rise of Liberalism: the first disestablishment campaign in Scotland 1829–1843.'

21. Brown, S. J. and Fry, M., *Scotland in the Age of Disruption*.
22. McKerrow, J., *History of the Secession Church*.

Chapter 2

1. Mackie, J.B., *The Life and Work of Duncan McLaren, Vol. 1*.
2. Gordon Pentland's *Radicalism, Reform and National Identity in Scotland, 1820–1833* is the most recent study. See also Michael Dyer's '"Mere detail and machinery": the Great Reform Act and the effects of redistribution on Scottish representation'.
3. Brash, J.I. (ed.), *Scottish Electoral Politics 1832–1854*. Among the other co-purchasers were Adam Black, McLaren's senior council colleague, and Charles Maclaren, editor of *The Scotsman*.
4. Cockburn, *Memorials*, pp. 70–1.
5. Fry, M., *The Dundas Despotism*, p. 356.
6. *The Scotsman*, 6 November 1833.
7. Ibid., 16 November 1833.
8. Moir, D.G. (ed.), 'Extracts from an Edinburgh journal, 1823–1833, part 2 (1829–1833)'.
9. Cockburn, H. (Lord), *Journals*, vol. 1, p. 54.
10. *The Scotsman*, 14 August 1833.
11. Russell, T. ('lately a prisoner in the Calton Jail, at the instance of the Edinburgh clergy, for non-payment of the tax'), *The Annuity Tax or Edinburgh Church-Rate, Opposed to the Law of God, and Therefore Not Binding on Man*.
12. Norrie, W., *The Annuity Tax*. The 98-page pamphlet which Norrie found hard-going is entitled *History of the Resistance to the Annuity Tax under each of the four Church Establishments for which it has been levied, with a statement of its Annual Produce since 1690* (Edinburgh, 1836).
13. Robertson and Wood, *Castle and Town*. The chapter 'The Old City Debt' (pp. 221–56) is useful for untangling the finances of the bankrupt city. It was written by Robertson when he was Edinburgh's depute town clerk. He became town clerk in 1934.
14. The figures are those arrived at in two reports: that of the Committee of the Trustees for the Creditors of the City (1835) and Henry Labouchere's *Report to the Chancellor of the Exchequer regarding the Affairs of the City of Edinburgh and Port of Leith*.
15. Black, A., *View of the Financial Affairs of the City of Edinburgh with Suggestions for a Compromise with the Creditors*.
16. *The Scotsman*, 20 February 1836.
17. *Report of the Treasurer's Committee to Consider the Reasons of the Trustees for the Creditors for Declining the Proposal of Settlement with the City, on the*

Plan Proposed by the Rt Hon Henry Labouchere (Edinburgh, 1836).
18. Town Council minutes, 4 April 1837.
19. Ibid., 11 April 1837.
20. Ibid, 20 June 1837.
21. Quoted in Mackie, *Life and Work of Duncan McLaren*, Vol. 1, pp. 105–6.
22. NAS GD45/14/642 Dalhousie Papers. Letter to Fox Maule from Andrew Rutherfurd, Edinburgh, 20 November 1837.
23. McLaren, D., *Letter to the Members of the Town Council of Edinburgh on the Recent Discussions Regarding the Proposed Settlement with the Creditors of the City*.
24. *Edinburgh Weekly Journal*, 13 December 1837.
25. *The Scotsman*, 20 December 1837.
26. Ibid., 9 March 1836.
27. NLS MS1045 Melville Papers. McLaren to second Viscount Melville, 19 March 1838.
28. Robert Cadell at public meeting, Edinburgh, 3 October 1838. Quoted in Mackie, *Life and Work of Duncan McLaren*, Vol. 1, p. 116.
29. Mackie, *Life and Work of Duncan McLaren*, Vol. 1, p. 115.
30. *Report by the Treasurer's Committee to the Town Council Regarding the Future Revenue and Expenditure of the City of Edinburgh* (Edinburgh, 1838).

CHAPTER 3
1. Reported by Adam Hope, brother of George, whose biography *A Sketch of the Life of George Hope of Fenton Barns* was compiled by his daughter.
2. Brown, S.J., *Thomas Chalmers and the Godly Commonwealth in Scotland*.
3. Montgomery, A.B., 'The Voluntary controversy and the Church of Scotland 1829–1843'.
4. McKerrow, J., *History of the Secession Church*.
5. *The Scotsman*, 7 January 1835.
6. Clason, P., *Strictures on the Statement of the Central Board of Scottish Dissenters in a Series of Letters to Bailie McLaren*.
7. NAS GD/45/14/648 Dalhousie Papers. James Miller to Fox Maule, 13 March 1835.
8. McLaren, D., *The Working of the Established Church in Edinburgh Explained*.
9. NLS MS27282. Henry Renton, Kelso, to McLaren, 14 April 1837.
10. NAS GD45/14/642 Dalhousie Papers. Andrew Rutherfurd to Fox Maule, 20 November 1837.
11. Hutchison, I.G.C., *A Political History of Scotland 1832–1924*, p. 39.
12. Montgomery, 'The Voluntary controversy'.

13. NAS GD45/14/642. Rutherfurd to Maule, 25 June 1838.
14. Brown, 'Religion and the rise of Liberalism'.
15. McLaren, D., *Facts Regarding the Seat Rents of the City Churches of Edinburgh in Seven Letters to the Creditors of the City*.
16. NAS GD/45/14/648. McLaren to Fox Maule, 15 September 1839.
17. NLS MS3441 John Lee Papers. McLaren to Lee, 30 September 1836.
18. Ibid., 28 September 1839.
19. McLaren, D., *Substance of a Speech Delivered at a Public Meeting of Dissenters held in Edinburgh on the 14th July 1841*.
20. Bone, T.R., *School Inspection in Scotland 1840–1966*.
21. The National Library of Scotland acquired in 2005 a sumptuously bound Holy Bible presented to William and Agnes Renton by their family on their golden wedding anniversary, 7 July 1852. NLS Bdg. 1.48.
22. Renton, H., *Memorials of the Rev. Henry Renton MA*.
23. NLS MS24782. Duncan McLaren to Christina, from 14 Cecil Street, Strand, 4 July 1838.
24. Ibid. Two letters, 29 June 1838.
25. Quoted in Mackie, *Life and Work of Duncan McLaren*, Vol. 1, pp. 43–4.
26. NLS MS24784. Duncan McLaren to John McIntyre, 14 April 1840.
27. NLS MS24791. Duncan McLaren to John McIntyre, 17 August 1841.
28. NLS MS24782. Janet McLaren to Duncan, 26 November 1841.
29. Renton, H., *Memorial of Mrs Agnes Renton*, p. 25.
30. Rodger, R., *The Transformation of Edinburgh: Land, Property and Trust in the Nineteenth Century*, Chapter 3: Victorian Feudalism.
31. Lockhart, B.R.W., *Jinglin' Geordie's Legacy: a History of George Heriot's Hospital and School*, p. 114.
32. McLaren, D., *Suggestions for the Consideration of the Committee of Heriot's Hospital in Support of the Motion of Bailie McLaren*.
33. Town Council minutes, 10 October 1837.
34. Marwick, *Edinburgh Crafts and Guilds*.
35. *Report of the Burgh Commissioners examined by the Town Council* (Edinburgh, 1835).
36. *The Glorious Privilege: the History of 'The Scotsman'*, p. 28.
37. NLS MS27482. Charles Maclaren to editor of the *Morning Chronicle*, 26 April 1838.
38. NLS MS7235. Combe Papers. McLaren to George Combe, 17 December 1835.
39. NLS MS 27482. Charles Maclaren to McLaren. Two letters, undated.
40. Quoted in Mackie, *Life and Work of Duncan McLaren*, Vol. 1, p. 154.
41. McLaren, D., *Proposed Heads of Agreement to be Submitted to the Treasurer's*

References

Committee of the Town Council of Edinburgh by the Committee of Farmers and Traders for a Commutation of the City's Customs.

CHAPTER 4
1. Sturrock, J.B., *Peter Brough – a Paisley Philanthropist*.
2. Brent, R., 'The Whigs and Protestant Dissent in the decade of reform: the case of church rates 1833-1841'.
3. *The Scotsman*, 17 January 1837.
4. NAS GD/45/628 Dalhousie Papers. Sir James Gibson-Craig to Fox Maule, 17 May 1839.
5. Ibid., 21 May 1839.
6. NLS MS9694. James Ivory to Andrew Rutherfurd, 15 May and 24 May 1839.
7. NAS GD/45/628. Gibson-Craig to Maule, 29 May 1839.
8. NLS MS9694. Ivory to Rutherfurd, 31 May 1839.
9. Pinney, T. (ed.), *The Letters of Thomas Babington Macaulay*, Vol. 3. To Adam Black, 15 May 1839.
10. Ibid., to Lord Melbourne, 20 September 1839.
11. Quoted in Williams, J.C., 'Edinburgh Politics, 1832–52'. The references are to letters of 26 May and 31 May 1839 in Rutherfurd MSS.
12. Brash, *Scottish Electoral Politics*.
13. NAS GD45/14/628. Gibson-Craig to Maule, 29 May 1839.
14. NLS MS9694. Ivory from Glencorse to Rutherfurd, 26 May 1839.
15. Ibid., 17 January 1840.
16. NLS MS9698. Maule to Rutherfurd, 26 November 1840, *31* October 1840.
17. *The Scotsman*, 31 October 1840.
18. McLaren, D., *Bailie Johnston Refuted by Attested Statements of Facts*. This was in response to W. Johnston's *Letter to Sir James Gibson Craig Bart*.
19. Nicolson, A. (ed.), *Memoirs of Adam Black*, p. 107.
20. NAS GD45/14/628. Sir James Gibson-Craig to Fox Maule, 5 November 1840; and Maule to Gibson-Craig, 7 November 1840.
21. Ibid., Gibson-Craig to Maule, 6 December 1840.
22. Ibid., Gibson-Craig to Maule, 16 October 1840.
23. *The Scotsman*, 28 November 1840.
24. HWUA. Gibson-Craig Papers. Sir James Gibson-Craig to William Gibson-Craig, 20 May 1841.
25. NLS MS9392. John Hill Burton Papers. McLaren to John Hill Burton, 19 May 1841.
26. Gibson-Craig Papers. Sir James Gibson-Craig to William Gibson-Craig, 22 May 1841.

The Member For Scotland

27. Ibid., William Gibson-Craig to his father, 10 May 1841.
28. Ibid., Sir James Gibson-Craig to William, 1 June and 11 June 1841; NAS GD45/14/628. Sir James Gibson-Craig to Maule, 11 June 1841.
29. NAS GD45/14/628. Sir James Gibson-Craig to Maule, 9 June 1841.
30. Ibid., Gibson-Craig to Maule, 10 June 1841.
31. Ibid., Gibson-Craig to Maule, 24 June 1841.
32. *The Scotsman*, 17 July 1841.
33. Marwick, W.H., 'Municipal politics in Victorian Edinburgh'.
34. A copy of 'Duncan MacLaren - a New Song' (1842) is held by the National Library of Scotland.
35. Pinney, *Letters of Thomas Babington Macaulay*, Vol. 3. Macaulay to Macvey Napier, 10 August 1840.
36. Pinney, *Letters of Thomas Babington Macaulay*, Vol. 3. Macaulay to McLaren, 1 January 1840.
37. *The Scotsman*, 22 January 1840.
38. Pinney, *Letters of Thomas Babington Macaulay*, Vol. 3. Macaulay to McLaren, 15 June 1840.
39. Ibid., to McLaren, 5 December 1840.
40. Ibid., to McLaren, 11 December 1840.
41. Ibid., to McLaren, 31 January 1841.

CHAPTER 5
1. Pickering, P.A. and Tyrell, A., *The People's Bread: a History of the Anti-Corn Law League*.
2. A useful account of the organisation of and campaigning for corn-law abolition in Scotland is contained in Pickering and Tyrell, The People's Bread..
3. Quoted in Robbins, K., *John Bright*, p. 46.
4. Cameron, K.J., 'William Weir and the origins of the "Manchester League" in Scotland, 1833-9'.
5. *The Scotsman*, 23 January 1839.
6. West Sussex Record Office Cobden Papers No. 71, Richard Cobden to McLaren, 4 March 1842.
7. Cameron, K.J., 'Anti-Corn Law agitation in Scotland with particular reference to the Anti-Corn Law League'.
8. *The Corn Laws condemned, an account of their injustice and immoral tendency by upwards of five hundred ministers of different denominations, resident in Scotland*, 2nd edn (Edinburgh, 1842).
9. *The Scotsman*, 15 January 1842.
10. *The Scotsman*, 12 January 1842.
11. Hope, G., *George Hope of Fenton Barns*.

12. Extracts from several letters in Cobden Papers No.71 and 1–8 (MF1–8).
13. Cobden Papers 1–8 (MF1–8). Cobden to McLaren, 14 March 1842.
14. Cobden Papers No. 71. Cobden to McLaren, 21 November 1842.
15. *The Scotsman*, 25 January 1843.
16. Mackie, *Life and Work of Duncan McLaren*, Vol. 1, p. 229.
17. Robertson, W., *Life and Times of the Right Hon. John Bright*. The references are to meetings on 10 November and 11 November 1844.
18. The view of Cameron in his doctoral thesis, 'William Weir and the origins of the "Manchester League" in Scotland, 1833–9'.
19. Quoted in Mackie, *Life and Work of Duncan McLaren*, Vol. 1, pp. 240–1.
20. Mackie, *Life and Work of Duncan McLaren*, Vol. 1, pp. 247–8.
21. Pinney, *Letters of Thomas Babington Macaulay*, Vol. 4. Macaulay to McLaren, 28 December 1842.
22. Ibid., Macaulay to Adam Black, 22 February 1843.
23. Ibid., Macaulay to McLaren, 24 February 1843.
24. Ibid., Macaulay to McLaren, 1 March 1843.
25. Ibid., Macaulay to McLaren, 13 March 1843.
26. Ibid., Macaulay to William Gibson-Craig, 19 April 1843.
27. Ibid., Macaulay to Sir James Gibson-Craig, 24 November 1843.
28. Cobden Papers No.71. Cobden to McLaren, series of letters, March–May 1843.
29. Ibid., Cobden to McLaren, 25 May 1843.
30. Ibid., Cobden to McLaren, 3 December 1843.
31. Gibson-Craig Papers. Archibald Davidson to William Gibson-Craig, 7 March 1843.
32. *The Scotsman*, 13 January 1844.
33. *The Scotsman*, 17 April and 24 April 1844.
34. Letter from Macaulay to John Wigham reprinted in *The Scotsman*, 11 May 1844.
35. Mackie, *Life and Work of Duncan McLaren*, Vol. 1, p.274 is wrong to state that the interchanges at this period between Macaulay and McLaren did harm only to the former.
36. NLS MS7273. McLaren to George Combe, 21 August and 24 August 1844.
37. Gibson-Craig Papers. Macaulay to William Gibson-Craig, 5 September 1844.
38. Mackie, *Life and Work of Duncan McLaren*, Vol. 1, p. 45.
39. Cobden Papers 1–8 (MF1–8). McLaren to Cobden, 14 March 1842.
40. NLS MS7273. McLaren to Combe, 21 August 1844.
41. NLS MS7286. McLaren to Combe, 3 March 1847. He claimed that

even in the last years of Maclaren's connection (though his editorship formally lasted till 1849), the paper had lost ground as 'a moral engine'. Since then 'the downward velocity has been accelerated'.
42. Cooper, C., *An Editor's Retrospect*, p. 252.
43. NLS MS24782. John Bright to McLaren, 10 November 1844.
44. McLaren, D., *A Visit to Madeira and Teneriffe*. The pamphlet appears to have been reprinted from a magazine.
45. NLS MS24795. Grant McLaren to John, 29 December 1845.
46. Cobden Papers 1–8 (MF1–8). McLaren to Cobden, 1 January 1846.
47. Ibid., 31 January 1846.

Chapter 6

1. Morris, R.J., 'Death, Chambers Street and Edinburgh Corporation'.
2. Colston, J., *The Edinburgh and District Water Supply*.
3. Gibson-Craig Papers. McLaren to William Gibson-Craig, 13 April 1843.
4. Pinney, *Letters of Thomas Babington Macaulay*, Vol. 4. Macaulay to William Gibson-Craig, 19 April 1843. Pinney, the editor, states that the correspondence and McLaren's publicising of it show his 'self-righteousness in an unpleasant light'. Others might see it as a politician's pre-emptive strike.
5. *The Scotsman*, 15 April 1843.
6. Gibson-Craig Papers. Henry Cockburn to William Gibson-Craig, 29 March 1843.
7. *The Scotsman*, 16 August, 20 September and 24 September 1845.
8. Ibid., 11 October 1845.
9. Robertson, C.J.A., *The Origins of the Scottish Railway System, 1722–1844*.
10. The Incorporation Act was 8 & 9 Victoria, cap. 75, 1846.
11. NLS MS7276. McLaren to George Combe, 17 December 1845.
12. *Tait's Edinburgh Magazine*, n.s., XVI. June 1849.
13. Mackie, *Life and Work of Duncan McLaren*, Vol. 1, p. 58.
14. Thomas, J., *The Railways of Great Britain*.
15. Manchester Central Library MS923.2 S343 J.B. Smith Papers. Smith to McLaren, 3 May 1849.
16. Ibid., 14 May 1849.
17. Nottingham University Archives Priscilla Bright/Duncan McLaren Papers, Vol. 1. John Bright to McLaren, 11 July and 14 July 1850.
18. Cockburn, *Journals*, p. 161.
19. Millar, G.F., 'Maynooth and Scottish Politics: the role of the Maynooth Grant issue 1845–1857'.

20. Hinde, W., *Richard Cobden: a Victorian Outsider*, p. 162.
21. Marwick, J. (Sir), *A Retrospect*.
22. Trevelyan, G.O., *The Life and Letters of Lord Macaulay*, Vol. 2., p. 472.
23. Cowan, C., *Reminiscences*.
24. NAS GD45/14/642. Andrew Rutherfurd to Fox Maule, 28 July 1847.
25. Marwick, *A Retrospect*.
26. Pinney, *Letters of Thomas Babington Macaulay*, Vol. 4. Letters to Hannah (Mrs Charles) Trevelyan, 30 July 1847; Andrew Rutherfurd, 26 December 1848; Adam Black (?), 11 August 1847.
27. *List of Voters in the City of Edinburgh who voted for Mr Charles Cowan MP (1847)* (Edinburgh, 1848).
28. Williams, 'Edinburgh Politics'.
29. Letters from Lord John Russell to Queen Victoria, August 1847, quoted by John Prest in *Lord John Russell* (London, 1972), p. 262.
30. Hutchison, *Political History of Scotland*, p. 65.
31. *Report of the Speeches delivered at the public meeting of the inhabitants of Edinburgh opposed to the Government scheme of education, held in the Music Hall, March 31 1847* (Edinburgh, 1847).
32. Withrington, D.J., 'Adrift among the reefs of conflicting ideals?: Education and the Free Church 1843–55'.
33. NLS MS7235 Combe Papers. McLaren to George Combe, 17 December 1835.
34. NLS MS7273. Combe Papers. Copy of letter by McLaren to Horace Mann, and letter from McLaren to Combe, 16 August 1844.
35. Ibid., McLaren to Combe, 21 August 1844.
36. Manchester Central Library MS923.2 S343 J.B. Smith Papers. Smith to McLaren, 12 June 1847.
37. Myers, J.D., 'Scottish Nationalism and the antecedents of the 1872 Education Act'.
38. Eadie, Rev. Prof. and McMichael, Rev. Prof., *The United Presbyterian Church*.
39. Cockburn, *Journals*, p. 179.
40. Drummond, A.L. and Bulloch, J., *The Church in Victorian Scotland 1843–1874*, p. 46.
41. Robson, G., *Mission of the United Presbyterian Church: the Story of the Jamaica Mission with Sketch of the Mission in Trinidad*.
42. NLS MS24791. McLaren to John, 15 March 1848.
43. Robbins, *John Bright*.
44. Mills, *John Bright and the Quakers*, p. 269.
45. Mackie, *Life and Work of Duncan McLaren*, Vol. 1, p. 50.
46. Mills, *John Bright and the Quakers*, p. 153.
47. Walling, R.A.J. (ed.), *The Diaries of John Bright*, 5 April 1849.

48. ECA McLaren Papers. Box 2. McLaren to Priscilla, 1 April 1849.
49. Ibid., 3 April 1849.
50. Letter from Priscilla McLaren to Martha Holdsworth, 17 March 1849, quoted in Mills, *John Bright and the Quakers*.
51. NLS MS24782. Priscilla to McLaren, 25 April 1849.
52. MCA MS923.2 S343 Smith to McLaren, 11 July 1847.
53. ECA McLaren Papers. Box 1. McLaren to Priscilla, 10 March 1849.
54. ECA McLaren Papers. Box 2. McLaren to Priscilla, 15 November 1849.
55. NUA Bright/McLaren Papers, Vol. 1. Priscilla to Agnes, 8 January 1849.
56. NUA Bright/McLaren Papers, Vol. 1. Priscilla to Agnes and Catherine, 4 September 1851.
57. NUA Bright/McLaren Papers, Vol. 1. Priscilla to McLaren, 9 January 1849.

Chapter 7

1. McLaren, D., *Evidence given before the Select Committee of the House of Commons Respecting the Annuity Tax.*
2. NLS MS7295 Combe Papers. McLaren to George Combe, 23 September 1851.
3. See Chapter two, page 23.
4. *Edinburgh News*, 11 November 1851.
5. *The Scotsman*, 8 November 1851.
6. Ibid., 22 October 1851.
7. NLS MS9689 Rutherfurd Papers. William Gibson-Craig to Andrew Rutherfurd, 10 April 1852.
8. Hutchison, *Political History of Scotland*, p. 67.
9. NLS MS12342. Minto Papers. Combe to Melgund, 7 May and 10 May 1852.
10. MCL MS 923.94 J.B. Smith Papers. McLaren to Smith, 19 April 1852.
11. *The Scotsman*, 12 May 1852.
12. Trevelyan, *The Life and Letters of Lord Macaulay*, p. 562.
13. Pinney, *Letters of Thomas Babington Macaulay*, Vol. 5. To Frances Macaulay, 16 June 1852.
14. NLS MS12342. Minto Papers. McLaren to Lord Melgund, 18 June 1852.
15. Johnston had himself suffered from a sneering description during the row over his role in the Lord Provost election of 1840. He was called a mere 'scratcher on copper'. The map-engraving firm he founded had a long and distinguished history. Its records are in the

References

National Library of Scotland and contain several of the squibs from the 1852 election (ACC 5811/1).

16. *Caledonian Mercury*, 12 July 1852.
17. NLS MS7327. McLaren to George Combe, 19 June 1852.
18. NLS MS24781. John McLaren to McLaren, no date but he had just arrived in Southampton having left Madeira in early June 1852.
19. NLS MS12342. Minto Papers. James Simpson to Lord Melgund, 2 June 1852.
20. Macdonald, J.H.A. (Lord Kingsburgh), *Life and Jottings by an Old Edinburgh Citizen*.
21. *The Scotsman*, 14 July 1852.
22. NUA Bright/McLaren Papers, Vol. 1. Priscilla to Maggie, 16 August 1852.
23. J.R. Vincent included the 1852 Edinburgh election in his study *Pollbooks: How Victorians Voted*. The most detailed examination, which I draw on heavily, is a chapter entitled 'Edinburgh's Subscriber Population' in *Unionist Nationalism: Governing Urban Scotland 1830–1860* by Graeme Morton.
24. NLS MS24793. Priscilla to John McLaren, 8 January 1852.
25. NLS MS7334. McLaren to Combe, 5 July 1853.
26. ECA McLaren Papers. Box 1. McLaren to Priscilla in Blackpool, 27 July 1853.
27. *Edinburgh News*, 4 March 1854.
28. Marwick, *A Retrospect*, p. 94.
29. *Edinburgh News*, 26 June and 8 July 1854.
30. *Edinburgh News*, 16 September 1854.
31. Mackie, *Life and Work of Duncan McLaren*, Vol. 1, p. 303.
32. *Edinburgh News*, 29 January 1853.
33. ECA McLaren Papers. Box 2. Robert Jameson to McLaren, 29 December 1851 and 8 March 1852.
34. *Report by the Lord Provost's Committee on the opening of Princes Street (West) Gardens to the Public* (Edinburgh, 1854). The tale of gaining access to the gardens is told by Connie Byrom in *The Edinburgh New Town Gardens* and by David Robertson in *The Princes Street Proprietors and other chapters in the History of the Royal Burgh of Edinburgh*.
35. NLS MS24793. Priscilla McLaren to John, 8 January 1852.
36. McLaren, D., *Substance of a Speech Delivered to the Meeting of the Edinburgh Anti-Corn Law Association on the 9th May 1844*; McLaren, D., *Facts about Trinity College Church*.
37. Mackie, *Life and Work of Duncan McLaren*, Vol. 1, p. 305.
38. Checkland, O., *Philanthropy in Victorian Scotland*, p. 94.
39. McLaren, D., *The Rise and Progress of Whisky-Drinking in Scotland*.

40. Mackie, *Life and Work of Duncan McLaren*, Vol. 1, p. 306.
41. McLaren, *Rise and Progress of Whisky-Drinking*; McLaren, *One Year's Experience of the New Public-House Act in Edinburgh*.
42. Mclaren, *One Year's Experience*.
43. *The Scotsman*, 13 April 1853.
44. *Edinburgh Evening Courant*, 26 March 1853.
45. *Edinburgh News*, 23 May 1853.
46. 'An Old Councillor' conveniently lists what McLaren did as Lord Provost in *Mr M'Laren's Services to the City of Edinburgh'* (Edinburgh, 1863).
47. *Edinburgh Evening Courant*, 9 November 1854.

CHAPTER 8

1. NLS MS21241. John Wilson Papers. McLaren to Wilson, 14 April 1852.
2. Quoted in E. Swann, *Christopher North*, p. 225.
3. NLS MS24810. Requisition from the committee of inhabitants that a public meeting be called by the Lord Provost, who fixed it for October 28 1852 at Queen Street Hall.
4. Horn, D.B., *A Short History of the University of Edinburgh 1556–1889*, p. 152.
5. NLS MS2623. John Stuart Blackie Papers. McLaren to Blackie, 4 March 1852.
6. Ibid., McLaren to Blackie, 26 October 1866. There are two principal biographies of Blackie a century apart: Anna M. Stoddart's two-volume *John Stuart Blackie: A Biography* and Stuart Wallace's *John Stuart Blackie: Scottish Scholar and Patriot*.
7. Davie, G.E., *The Democratic Intellect*, p. 292.
8. *The Scotsman*, 9 June 1852.
9. Davie cites professorial appointments in the Scottish universities as evidence of the (losing) battle to retain the broad undergraduate curriculum rooted in philosophy in the face of pressure from supporters of specialist studies favoured in England and Germany. For a different interpretation, see R.D. Anderson, *Education and Opportunity in Victorian Scotland*.
10. New College MSS CM/A4. Lord Aberdeen to McLaren, 20 July 1858.
11. Kelland's appointment to the mathematics chair is evidence for Davie (see The Democratic Intellect) of a victory for Cambridge algebra over Scottish emphasis on geometry. How far McLaren and his fellow councillors appreciated the significance of their choice

is hard to say. Sir William Hamilton (another McLaren-backed appointee) was champion of the rival candidate, the Scottish-educated Duncan Gregory, and he warned the councillors of the danger of being 'frightened into voting for a stranger by the dread that local influence may be imputed' (The Democratic Intellect, p. 119). In discussing university reform Davie concentrates on the intellectual preferences of professors to the detriment of discussion about the governance and financing of universities – matters which were of significance to practical men like McLaren faced with Government initiatives and legislation.

12. ECA McLaren Papers. Box 2. George Combe to McLaren, 12 January 1852.
13. NLS MS12342. Minto Papers. McLaren to Melgund, 19 June 1852.
14. *The Scotsman* and *Daily News*, 13 March 1854.
15. *Daily News*, 13 March 1854. The Puseyites were the influential section of the Church of England who favoured ritual and were accused of being too close to Roman Catholicism.
16. Myers, 'Scottish Nationalism'.
17. There is a good account of the National Association for the Vindication of Scottish Rights in William Ferguson's *Scotland: 1689 to the Present*.
18. NLS MS4004 Blackwood Papers. McLaren to John Blackwood, 28 May 1851.
19. *Report of the first meeting of the National Association for the Vindication of Scottish Rights* (Edinburgh, 1853).
20. Cockburn, *Journals*, Vol. 2, pp. 300–1.
21. *Reasons for Declining to Join the National Association for the Vindication of Scottish Rights* (Edinburgh, 1854). Its author, 'a Scotchman', was the Rev. Sir Henry Moncreiff.
22. NLS MS14303. Charles Rogers Papers. McLaren to Rogers, 11 November 1856.
23. Anthony Howe, in the introduction to A. Howe and S. Morgan (eds), *Rethinking Nineteenth-Century Liberalism* (Aldershot, 2006).
24. WSA Cobden Papers CP29. Cobden to McLaren, 19 September 1853.
25. WSA Cobden Papers CP107. J.B. Smith to McLaren, 6 October 1853.
26. WSA Cobden Papers CP29. Cobden to Fred Cobden, 11 October 1853.
27. Ceadel, M., *The Origins of War Prevention: the British Peace Movement and International Relations, 1730–1854*.
28. McGilchrist, J., *The Life of John Bright MP*.
29. *The Times*, 17 October 1853.

30. WSA Cobden Papers CP29. Cobden to Fred Cobden, 16 October 1853.
31. NUA Bright/McLaren Papers, Vol. 1. Priscilla to sister Maggie, 7 February 1852.
32. NLS MS24808. Priscilla to Grant and Agnes, 6 May 1857.
33. NLS MS24802. Two letters from Grant to John; neither is dated but from internal evidence they must be from 1852.
34. NLS MS24793. Priscilla to John, 21 April 1857.
35. NLS MS24786. Catherine to Priscilla, 21 May 1857
36. NUA Bright/McLaren Papers, Vol. 1. McLaren to Priscilla, (n.d.) 1858.
37. NUA Bright/McLaren Papers, Vol. 1. Priscilla to Maggie, 16 August 1852.
38. NLS MS24809. Priscilla to Maggie, 21 March 1858.
39. Heiton, J., *The Castes of Edinburgh*.
40. *The Scotsman*, several issues in December 1853.
41. NLS MS7355. Combe Papers. McLaren to George Combe, 2 May 1856.
42. NLS MS24782. Sales and stock figures for McLaren, Oliver & Co.
43. NLS MS24782. John Oliver to McLaren, 21 February and 13 March 1855.
44. NLS MS24782. Oliver to Priscilla, 1 March 1856.
45. Trevelyan, *The Life and Letters of Lord Macaulay*, pp. 593–4.
46. NLS MS7355. McLaren to Combe, 26 January 1856.
47. Pinney, *Letters of Thomas Babington Macaulay*, Vol. 6. Macaulay to William Gibson-Craig, 7 February 1856.
48. Stalker, J., *Francis Brown Douglas*. Privately printed for his grandchildren (Edinburgh, 1886).
49. The view of the *Aberdeen Herald* newspaper quoted by *The Scotsman*, 11 February 1856.
50. *Courant*, 8 February 1856.
51. *The Scotsman*, 9 February and 11 February 1856.

CHAPTER 9

1. Record of action of damages, McLaren against Ritchie etc, Second Division, 5 July 1856.
2. NLS MS7349. Combe Papers. McLaren to George Combe, 14 April 1856.
3. Cooper, *An Editor's Retrospect*, p. 258.
4. ECA McLaren Papers. Box 2. Combe to McLaren, 1 May 1856.
5. NLS MS7349. McLaren to Combe, 17 April 1856.

6. ECA McLaren Papers. Box 2. Combe to McLaren, 21 April 1856.
7. NLS MS7349. McLaren to Combe, 14 April 1856.
8. Cowan, R.M.W., *The Newspaper in Scotland 1815–1860*.
9. NLS MS24791. McLaren to John, 29 August 1856.
10. WSA Cobden Papers MF4. McLaren to Cobden, 11 August 1856.
11. Lockhart, *Jinglin' Geordie's Legacy* and Marwick, *A Retrospect*.
12. *The Scotsman*, 2 August 1856.
13. *The Glorious Privilege*, pp. 31–2.
14. *The Scotsman*, 5 August 1856.
15. The circulation figures are taken from *The Waterloo Directory of Scottish Newspapers and Periodicals 1800–1900* (Waterloo, Ontario, 1989).
16. NLS MS7366. McLaren to Combe, 16 February 1858.
17. Fraser, D., 'Edward Baines', in P. Hollis (ed.), *Pressure from Without in Early Victorian England*.
18. Brown, D., 'Cobden and the Press', in Howe and Morgan, *Rethinking Nineteenth-Century Liberalism*.
19. NLS MS24791. McLaren to John, 18 June 1857.
20. NLS MS15911. Murray, editor, *Daily Express and Weekly Herald*, to McLaren, 20 July 1857.
21. NUA Bright/McLaren Papers. Priscilla to John and Elizabeth Bright, 11 October 1856.
22. James Mushet wrote 'A Dissenter's Reasons for Not Voting for Bailie Brown Douglas'. Referred to by Millar, 'Maynooth and Scottish Politics'.
23. WSA Cobden Papers CP107. Cobden to McLaren, 6 March 1857.
24. Ibid., 11 March 1857.
25. NLS MS24808. Priscilla to Grant and Agnes, 18 March 1857.
26. *The Scotsman*, 21 March 1857.
27. Ibid., 5 November 1856.
28. NLS MS24793. Priscilla to John, 22 December 1856.
29. *The Scotsman*, 27 December 1856.
30. New College MSS CM/L3. Samuel Laing to McLaren, 6 March 1857.
31. NLS MS24793. Priscilla to John, 18 April 1857.
32. Ibid., 7 August 1857.
33. Mackie, *Life and Work of Duncan McLaren*, Vol. 2, pp. 147–8.
34. ECA McLaren Papers. Box 2. Bright to McLaren, 28 December 1859.
35. *Edinburgh News*, 18 December 1858.
36. Ibid., 25 December 1858.
37. *The Scotsman*, 29 December 1858.

38. Ibid., 2 January 1859.
39. *Information for reformers respecting the Cities and Boroughs of the United Kingdom, classified according to the Schedules of the Reform Bill proposed by John Bright, Esq., MP; and also showing the Results of the Government Bill* (London and Edinburgh, 1859).
40. NUA Bright/McLaren Papers. Priscilla to 'a Friend', 17 January 1859.
41. NLS MS24795. Duncan junior to McLaren, 15 April 1859.
42. NLS MS24791. McLaren to John, 4 April 1859.
43. New College MSS CM/R35. Lord John Russell to McLaren, 1 July 1859.
44. NLS MS7866. McLaren to Combe, 24 November 1857.
45. *Edinburgh News*, 18 December 1858.
46. Mackie, *Life and Work of Duncan McLaren*, Vol. 2, p. 110.
47. NLS MS24793. Priscilla to John, 17 June 1858.

CHAPTER 10
1. *Edinburgh News*, 18 February 1860.
2. Ibid., 10 March 1860.
3. New College MS CM/B107. John Bright to McLaren, 4 March 1860.
4. *The Scotsman*, 18 February 1860.
5. Norrie, *The Annuity Tax*, p. 225.
6. *The Scotsman*, 22 April 1865.
7. Ibid., 8–21 November 1860.
8. Ibid., 10 October and 6 November 1861.
9. NLS MS24796. Agnes to John, 16 April 1860.
10. *The Scotsman*, 16 April 1860.
11. NLS MS24796. Agnes to John, 30 November 1860.
12. See Ransom, P.J.G., *Iron Road: the Railway in Scotland* and Nock, O.S., *The Caledonian Railway*.
13. Harrison, G., *A Brief Account of the Rise, Progress and Present Position of the Chamber of Commerce and Manufacturers in the City of Edinburgh*.
14. WSA Cobden Papers 71. Cobden to McLaren, 21 October 1862.
15. Ibid., 25 October 1862.
16. Ibid., 8 May 1863.
17. Ibid., 21 October and 25 October 1862.
18. NLS MS24796. Catherine (spelt on this occasion with an 'a') McLaren to John, 15 October 1862.
19. NLS MS24817. Draft of letter by John Oliver to McLaren, 19 February 1861.

20. NLS MS24808. John McLaren to Duncan, 6 December 1858.
21. Ibid., Catherine to Duncan, 23 December 1857.
22. NLS MS24817. McLaren to Oliver, 24 June 1862.
23. NLS MS24796. Catherine to John, 12 June 1861.
24. NLS MS24782. Oliver to McLaren, 26 June 1862.
25. Ibid., Catherine to McLaren, 2 September 1862.
26. Confirmation that John Oliver's illness was digestion-related, possibly ulcers, comes in a note he wrote in 1869 to John McLaren, who was suffering stomach problems, saying that he (Oliver) had had the same problem in Madeira and alleviated it by taking half a tumblerful of new milk with two tablespoonfuls of lime water before meals.
27. NLS MS24818. McLaren to Oliver, and Oliver to McLaren, several letters from 3 July to 1 August 1862.
28. NLS MS24816. Catherine to Oliver, 21 December 1862.
29. NLS MS24791. McLaren to John, 22 August 1862.
30. Ibid., 23 August 1862.
31. Ibid., 25 August 1862.
32. NLS MS24793. Priscilla to John, (n.d.) September 1862.
33. NLS MS24796. John Bright to John, 22 November 1862.
34. NLS MS24791. McLaren to John, 23 August 1862.
35. Ibid., 26 August 1862.
36. NLS MS24791. McLaren to John, 26 August 1862.
37. NLS MS24808. McLaren to Duncan, eight letters, 4 September to 1 October 1862.
38. NLS MS24818. Draft letter by Oliver to McLaren, 1 October 1862.
39. Ibid., McLaren to Oliver, 4 October 1862.
40. NLS MS24816. Catherine to Oliver, 8 October 1862.
41. Ibid. Referred to by Catherine in an undated letter.
42. NLS MS24782. McLaren's statement of proposed terms of dissolution of the partnership.
43. Ibid., Oliver's statement on terms, 6 January 1863.
44. NLS MS24818. Oliver to McLaren, 30 November 1862.
45. Ibid., Helen to Oliver, 27 December 1862.
46. NLS ACC7662. Box 207. From Catherine's diary of her honeymoon tour.
47. NLS MS24786. Catherine to Priscilla, 7 January 1863.
48. NLS MS24808. Priscilla to Maggie, 16 January 1863.
49. Ibid., Catherine to John, 8 August 1863.
50. NUA Bright/McLaren Papers. McLaren to Charles, 12 May 1863.
51. Ibid., Priscilla to Maggie, 27 March 1863.

Chapter 11

1. Goldman, L., *Reform and Politics in Victorian Britain: the Social Science Association 1859–1886*.
2. *The Scotsman*, 8–15 October 1865.
3. Goldman, L. (ed.), *The Blind Victorian: Henry Fawcett and British Liberalism*.
4. NLS MS24809. Priscilla to Maggie, 16 January 1863.
5. NLS MS24782. McLaren's will.
6. Waverley Park Conservation Area character appraisal: edinburgh.gov.uk/caca/cacaWaverley_Park.pdf
7. Table from Parliamentary Papers 1874, Owners of Lands and Heritages, 1872–3, quoted in Rodger, *The Transformation of Edinburgh*.
8. Begg, J., *Happy Homes for Working Men and How to Get Them*.
9. *The Scotsman*, 21 November 1865.
10. NLS MS24793. Priscilla to John, 29 September 1864.
11. ECA. Box 2. McLaren Papers. Priscilla to McLaren, 5 April 1865.
12. Walling, *The Diaries of John Bright*, 25 March and 2 April 1865.
13. NLS MS24791. McLaren to John, 22 April 1865.
14. NLS MS24793. Priscilla to John and Grant, 23 May 1865.
15. *The Scotsman*, 5 May and 7 May 1865.
16. NLS MS24785. John to Priscilla, 11 June 1865 and undated letter.
17. *The Scotsman*, 4 July 1865.
18. Ibid., 14 July and 15 July 1865.
19. *Weekly Herald and Mercury*, 15 July 1865.
20. NLS MS24782. Bright to McLaren, 16 November 1865.
21. Bright to McLaren, 4 November 1865, quoted by Robbins, John Bright, p. 177.
22. NLS MS24797. Agnes to John McLaren, 13 December 1865.
23. Ibid., Duncan to John, 12 December 1865.
24. Ibid., Agnes to John, 16 January 1866.
25. *The Scotsman*, 17 January 1866.
26. NLS MS24793. Priscilla to John, 26 January 1866.
27. NLS MS22797. Agnes to John, 24 February 1866.
28. See Harvie, C., *The Lights of Liberalism: University Liberals and the Challenge of Democracy 1860–86*.
29. The verdict is that of Oliphant's entry in the *Dictionary of National Biography*.
30. F.B. Smith in *The Making of the Second Reform Bill* states that 'rarely can such a brilliant group of new members have entered the Commons at an election', all with reform at the head of their programmes. He cites as members of this band of the intelligentsia Mill, Hughes, Fawcett, Oliphant, Coleridge, George Otto Trevelyan – and

McLaren. The last – a self-made man – might have been flattered to be in such company but he was happier finding messages in statistics than in the speculation of the lecture room or the quarterly reviews.
31. *The Scotsman*, 12 February 1866.
32. NLS MS24797. Charles McLaren to John, 16 April 1866.
33. *The Scotsman*, 23 October and 24 October 1866.
34. Ibid., 19 November 1866.
35. Ibid., 21 November 1866.
36. From an 'Address on the Extension of the Suffrage', quoted in Bain, W.H., 'The life and achievements of James, First Baron Moncreiff 1811 to 1895'.
37. NLS MS24791. McLaren to John, 9 March 1867.
38. NLS MS24793. Priscilla to John, 10 May 1867.
39. NUA J.B. Smith Papers. Copy of letter from McLaren to McCrie. The text is in *The Scotsman*, 12 May 1867.
40. Mackie, *Life and Work of Duncan McLaren*, Vol. 2, p. 167.
41. Reeves, R., *John Stuart Mill*, p. 367.
42. NLS MS24791. McLaren to John, 3 June 1868.
43. Ibid., 5 June 1868.
44. The details of the Scottish Reform Bills of 1867 and 1868 are dealt with in Smith, *The Making of the Second Reform Bill*, and in Dyer, M., *Men of Property and Intelligence: the Scottish Electoral System Prior to 1884*.
45. *The Scotsman*, 23 October 1867.
46. NLS MS24791. Priscilla to John, 9 June 1868.
47. NLS MS24803. Agnes to John. No date but from internal evidence 1867.
48. ECA. Box 3. Priscilla to Agnes, 12 September 1867.
49. NLS MS24808. Charles to Agnes, 10 August 1868.

CHAPTER 12
1. NLS MS24781. John to McLaren, 1 September 1868.
2. NLS MS24793. Priscilla to John, (n.d.) 1868.
3. Walker, D.M., *The Scottish Jurists*, p. 334.
4. NLS MS24791. McLaren to John, 7 June and 25 June 1868.
5. NLS MS24798. John McLaren's letters of 3 June and 10 June 1868.
6. NLS MS24791. McLaren to John, 25 March and 4 April 1868.
7. NLS MS24781. John to McLaren and Priscilla, 3 September 1868.
8. NLS MS24793. Priscilla to John, 4 September 1868.
9. NLS MS24791. McLaren to John, 24 July 1868.
10. *Weekly Review*, 7 October 1868.

11. NLS MS24798. Lyon Playfair to John, 20 November 1868.
12. NLS MS24791. McLaren to John, 25 June 1868.
13. Mackie, *Life and Work of Duncan McLaren*, Vol. 2, pp. 201–2.
14. From Rose, H., *Hugh Rose – A Sketch of his Life by One of his Daughters*.
15. NLS MS24792. McLaren to John, 3 July 1869 (should be 1868).
16. Ibid., 19 September 1868.
17. *Weekly Review*, 23 August 1868.
18. NLS MS24792. McLaren to John, 3 September 1868.
19. *Weekly Review*, 18 November 1868.
20. NLS MS 24792. McLaren to John, 3 September 1868.
21. NLS MS24805. John to Ottilie (n.d.).
22. NLS MS24792. McLaren to John, 4 September and 9 September 1868.
23. Ibid., 21 October 1868.
24. NLS MS24816. Catherine to John Oliver, 6 January 1868.
25. Ibid., 20 April 1868.
26. ECA. Box 3. Priscilla to Elizabeth Bright, 4 June 1869.
27. NLS MS24794. Priscilla to John, 25 May 1869.
28. Mackie, *Life and Work of Duncan McLaren*, Vol. 1, p. 203.
29. NLS MS24781. John to McLaren, 1 July 1869.
30. *The Scotsman*, 15 February 1870.
31. NLS MS24785. John to Priscilla, 25 March 1870.
32. *The Scotsman*, 30 April 1870.
33. Ibid., 14 February 1870.
34. Norrie, *The Annuity Tax*.
35. The pamphlets by Robie and McLaren were published in Edinburgh in 1867. The quotations are from them.
36. Hansard, 5 July 1871.
37. Ibid., 22 July 1870.
38. Ibid., House of Lords, 20 May 1870.
39. Matthew, H.C.G. (ed.), *The Gladstone Diaries*, Vol. 7, 30 November 1869. 'He ruled Scottish MPs with a verbal rod of iron.' Entry in *Dictionary of National Biography*.
40. NLS MS24794. Priscilla to John, 15 March 1870.
41. *The Scotsman*, 10 March 1870.
42. Robbins, *John Bright*, p. 207.
43. NLS MS24798. Catherine to John, 13 December 1867.
44. NLS MS24793. Priscilla to John, 16 December 1867.
45. NLS MS24808. Catherine to Agnes, 11 July 1869.
46. NLS Acc. 7662. Box 208. 'Some particulars relating to Catherine's last illness.'

CHAPTER 13

1. Hansard, 18 August 1871.
2. Ibid., 12 July 1869.
3. See Withrington, D.J., 'Towards a national system, 1867–72, the last years of the struggle for a Scottish education system' and Lenman, B., 'The beginnings of state education in Scotland, 1872–1885'. Anderson, *Education and Opportunity in Victorian Scotland*, not only examines the politics of the pre- and post-1872 periods but also analyses the data and statistics from studies by the churches' education departments, the Government inspectors and the Argyll Commission.
4. Hansard, 12 February 1872.
5. Ibid., 12 July 1869.
6. Ibid., 13 June 1871.
7. NLS MS24792. McLaren to John, 11 May 1872.
8. Hansard, 14 June 1872.
9. Myers, 'Scottish Nationalism'.
10. Dale, A.W.W., *The Life of RW Dale of Birmingham*.
11. ECA. Box 4. Telegram from joint committee, Royal Exchange, to McLaren, 21 June 1869.
12. Hansard, 14 August 1871.
13. The debate about Heriot's future before the Colebrooke Commission is extensively covered by Lockhart, *Jinglin' Geordie's Legacy*.
14. *The Scotsman*, 17 December 1872.
15. Ibid., 18 December 1872.
16. NLS MS24781. John to McLaren, 19 July 1870.
17. NLS MS24792. McLaren to John, 24 July 1870.
18. Ibid., 1 March 1870.
19. NLS MS24799. John Gorrie to John, 6 April 1871.
20. NLS MS24782. Henry Bruce to McLaren, 16 July 1871.
21. NLS MS24799. John Bright to John, 4 July 1872.
22. Ibid. 23 June 1873.
23. NLS MS24799. Draft of letter by John to J. Delves Broughton, 17 February 1873.
24. NLS MS24792. McLaren to John, 30 October 1871.
25. NLS MS24794. Priscilla to John, 4 April 1870.
26. See Leneman, L., *A Guid Cause: the Women's Suffrage Movement in Scotland*. Eliza Wigham figures prominently in Knox, W.W., *Lives of Scottish Women: Women and Scottish Society 1800–1980*. The family connections that were important in the women's movement are discussed in Holton, S.S., *Suffrage Days*.

27. ECA. Box 1. McLaren Papers. Priscilla to McLaren, 9 April 1867.
28. See Kinzer, B.L., Robson, A.P. and Robson, J.M., *A Moralist in and out of Parliament: John Stuart Mill at Westminster 1865–1868*.
29. ECA. Box 3. Priscilla to Agnes, 10 March 1869.
30. Mackie, *Life and Work of Duncan McLaren*, Vol. 2, p. 162.
31. The *Scotsman*, 18 January and 20 January 1870.
32. Quoted by Leneman, *A Guid Cause*.
33. ECA. Box 3. Helen to Charles, 15 April 1873.
34. Mackie, *Life and Work of Duncan McLaren*, Vol. 2, p. 72.
35. NLS MS24799. Sophia Jex-Blake to John, 26 September 1872.
36. NLS MS24785. John to Priscilla, 11 August 1873.
37. See *The Pioneer in Medical Mission Work: Dr Agnes McLaren*. Society of Catholic Medical Missionaries (Philadelphia, n.d.).
38. NLS MS24802. From Agnes to John, (n.d.) 1875.
39. Ibid., 3 December 1875.
40. NLS MS24792. McLaren to John, 19 January 1872.
41. Ibid., 12 January and 14 July 1871.
42. The *Scotsman*, 15 February and 16 February 1871.
43. See Turner, L.A., *Story of a Great Hospital: the Royal Infirmary of Edinburgh 1729–1929*.
44. The comment is by Colston, Edinburgh and District Water Supply.
45. Colston, Edinburgh and District Water Supply, p. 135.
46. Lewis, D., *Edinburgh Water Supply*.
47. Ibid., p. 422.
48. Hansard, 21 April 1871.
49. NLS MS24799. Walter to John, 11 August 1872.
50. NLS MS 24794. Walter to John, 18 September 1872.
51. ECA. Box 2. Helen to Charles, 15 April 1873.
52. NLS MS24781. John to McLaren and Priscilla, 4 July 1873.
53. NLS MS24794. Priscilla to John, 10 July 1873.

Chapter 14

1. The *Scotsman*, 21 April 1871.
2. ECA. Box 2. Priscilla to Helen and Walter, 17 March 1873.
3. ECA. Box 3. McLaren to Walter, 25 August 1873.
4. See MacDougall, I. (ed.), *Minutes of Edinburgh Trades Council 1859–1873*.
5. The *Scotsman*, 24 December 1873.
6. NLS MS24792. McLaren to John, 20 September 1872.
7. Greenwich 'aroused neither his affection nor his interest' was Roy Jenkins's verdict in *Gladstone*, p. 377. He held his seat in the two-

member constituency in 1874 – behind a Tory gin-maker.
8. John Bright did not rejoin the Cabinet until September 1873.
9. See Gray, R.Q., *The Labour Aristocracy in Edinburgh*, p. 153.
10. NLS MS24808. John to Charles, 28 January 1874.
11. The *Scotsman*, 26 January and 27 January 1874.
12. Ibid., 3 February 1874.
13. Ibid., 30 January 1874.
14. *Daily Review*, 28 January 1874.
15. NLS MS24808. John to Charles, 6 February 1874.
16. NLS MS24792. McLaren to John, 18 January 1874.
17. NLS MS2794. Priscilla to John, 16 April 1874.
18. ECA. Box 3. Priscilla to Walter, 30 April 1875.
19. NLS MS24792. McLaren to John, 10 June 1875.
20. Ibid., 17 July 1874.
21. Ibid., 11 July 1874.
22. Ibid. Another letter, 11 July 1874.
23. NLS MS24800. *Daily Review* office to John, 24 November 1874.
24. See Kellas, J.G., 'The Liberal Party and the Scottish Church disestablishment crisis'.
25. Drummond and Bulloch, *The Church in Victorian Scotland*, p. 327.
26. Goodfellow, J., *The Print of His Shoe: Forty Years' Experience in the Southside of Edinburgh*.
27. John Robson was married to Agnes Renton, sister of Henry and of Christina, McLaren's second wife.
28. NLS MS24790. Ottilie to John, 18 May 1875.
29. Hansard, 17 June 1873.
30. Renton, *Memorials of the Rev Henry Renton MA*.
31. Hansard, 13 July 1874.
32. Ibid., 15 March 1876.
33. Ibid., 9 March 1876.
34. NLS MS24794. Priscilla to John, 10 July 1873.
35. Mackie, *Life and Work of Duncan McLaren*, Vol. 2, p. 113.
36. See Gordon, A., *To Move with the Times: the Story of Transport and Travel in Scotland* and Whetstone, A.E., *Scottish County Government in the 18th and 19th Centuries*.
37. ECA. Box 1. Priscilla to Helen, 18 February 1876.
38. Nisbet Hamilton, Hope's landlord, dismissed his ability to do more than 'grow turnips and potatoes'. From Hope, *George Hope of Fenton Barns*.
39. NLS MS24784. John Bright to McLaren, 26 December 1875.
40. Cooper, An Editor's Retrospect.

Chapter 15

1. *Edinburgh Courant*, 24 January 1879.
2. NLS J.J. Reid Papers. MS19623. Rosebery to Reid, 12 December 1879.
3. Ibid., John McLaren to Reid, 27 July 1879.
4. *Daily Review*, 29 January 1880.
5. NLS MS24792. McLaren to John, 6 January 1878.
6. Ibid., McLaren to John, 18 January 1878.
7. *Daily Review*, 10 January and 17 January 1877.
8. NLS MS24792. McLaren to John, 16 March 1877.
9. NLS MS24781. John to McLaren, 18 March 1877.
10. NLS MS24803. Priscilla to John, 21 January and 24 January 1878.
11. NLS MS24809. John to Charles, two letters (n.d.).
12. NLS MS24801. Bright to John, 25 December 1878.
13. NLS MS24803. John to Ottilie, 9 July 1878.
14. Ibid., John to Ottilie, 11 July and 18 July 1878.
15. NLS MS24805. John to Ottilie, three letters (n.d.).
16. Hanham, H.J., *Elections and Party Management: Politics in the Age of Disraeli and Gladstone*, p. 164.
17. *The Scotsman*, 13 October 1879.
18. Ibid., 24 November 1879.
19. *Edinburgh Courant*, 19 November 1878.
20. *The Scotsman*, 1 August and 12 August 1878.
21. *Edinburgh Courant*, 29 November 1878.
22. Cooper, An Editor's Retrospect.
23. Checkland, Philanthropy in Victorian Scotland.
24. Lucy, H.W., *A Diary of Two Parliaments: the Disraeli Parliament, 1874–1880*, p. 430.
25. *Daily Review*, 16 January 1880.
26. Hanham, *Elections and Party Management*, p. 168.
27. *Daily Review*, 4 March 1880.
28. ECA. Box 2. Helen to McLaren, 2 April 1880.
29. ECA. Box 1. Helen to Priscilla, 3 April 1880.
30. NLS MS24781. John to McLaren (n.d.).
31. NLS MS24801. William Gladstone to John, 20 August 1880.
32. NLS MS19623. Craig Sellar to John Reid, 29 July 1880.
33. Ibid., Lord Richard Grosvenor to Reid, 20 October 1880.
34. Ibid., John to Reid, 28 November 1880.
35. Ibid., William Adam to Reid, 3 November 1880.
36. NLS MS24801. John to Ottilie, 1 June 1880.
37. Ibid., John to Ottilie, 21 August 1880, two letters.
38. NLS MS19623. John to Reid, 15 May 1880.
39. NLS MS24803. John to Ottilie (n.d.).

References

40. NLS MS24801. Gladstone to John, 11 March and 5 May 1880.
41. NLS MS24803. John to Ottilie, 5 July 1880.
42. Ibid., John to Ottilie, 21 August 1880.
43. NLS MS24785. John to Priscilla, 5 December 1880.
44. NLS MS24804. John to Ottilie, 10 January and 18 January 1880.
45. Walling, *The Diaries of John Bright*, 14 January and 16 January 1881.
46. Mackie, *Life and Work of Duncan McLaren*, Vol 2., pp. 229–31.
47. NLS MS24801. Charles Cooper to John, 9 June 1881.
48. McKinstry, L., *Rosebery*, p. 95.
49. Crewe, Marquess of, *Lord Rosebery*, Vol. 1, p. 144.
50. NLS MS24801. Gladstone to John, 23 July 1881.
51. Ibid., Harcourt to John, 3 August 1881.
52. Ibid., John to Gladstone, draft letter, August 1881.
53. Ibid., Hartington to John, 7 September 1881.
54. Ibid., John Albert Bright to John, 14 August 1881.
55. Crewe, *Lord Rosebery*, Vol. 1, p. 145.
56. NLS MS24801. Walter to John, 14 August 1881.
57. NLS MS24804. John to Ottilie (n.d.).
58. Ibid., John to Ottilie, 3 August 1881.

Chapter 16

1. The reference to class is made by Brian Lockhart (in *Jinglin' Geordie's Legacy*), who charts every twist and turn of the arguments involving the Heriot's governors, the several commissions of inquiry and the Government. The relationship between educational endowments and the development of secondary education is the subject of a chapter in Anderson, *Education and Opportunity in Victorian Scotland*.
2. Mackie, *Life and Work of Duncan McLaren*, Vol. 2, p. 192.
3. *The Scotsman*, 10 June 1879.
4. NLS MS24785. John to Priscilla, 5 December 1880.
5. NLS MS24803. John Bright to John, 2 July 1880.
6. Hansard, 9 July 1875.
7. Crewe, *Lord Rosebery*, Vol. 1, p. 154.
8. McLaren, D., *Fettes College Trustees and the Rights of the Citizens of Edinburgh*.
9. Anderson, *Education and Opportunity in Victorian Scotland*, p. 189.
10. ECA. Box 1. Priscilla to Duncan, 24 July 1882. John Bright had left the Cabinet in July 1881. Priscilla notes that their son Charles missed a key vote on the matter and hopes 'there was some unavoidable reason'.
11. ECA. Box 1. Helen to Priscilla, 5 August 1883.

301

12. ECA. Box 3. Priscilla to Elizabeth Bright, (n.d.) 1876. There is also a note about Helen's marriage settlement.
13. ECA. Box 1. Helen to Priscilla, 13 November and 12 December 1882.
14. Crawford, E., *The Women's Suffrage Movement – a Reference Guide 1866–1928* includes a genealogy of connections on p. 767.
15. ECA. Box 1. Mrs Jacob Bright to Priscilla, 16 June 1880.
16. Walker, The Scottish Jurists, p. 175.
17. NLS MS24801. John Bright to John, 7 November 1881.
18. NLS MS24794. Priscilla to John and Ottilie, 16 May 1882.
19. NLS MS24787. Frederick Scott Oliver to Priscilla, 18 July 1880. John Oliver's son, aged 16, presumptuously described Duncan's fiancée as not pretty but pleasant looking and vivacious, though not clever.
20. NLS MS24800. Duncan to John, 13 August 1875.
21. Ibid., Grant to John, 28 July 1875.
22. *The Scotsman*, 2 November and 4 November 1882.
23. Ibid., 24 March 1884.
24. ECA. Box 2. Priscilla to McLaren, 9 July 1883.
25. Ibid., Priscilla to Jacob and Ursula Bright, 20 November 1883.
26. NLS MS24802. Lord Richard Grosvenor to John, 20 October 1882.
27. Ibid., Gladstone to John, 7 December 1882.
28. Kellas, 'The Liberal Party and the Scottish Church disestablishment crisis.'
29. *The Scotsman*, 21 December 1881.
30. Matthew, The Gladstone Diaries, Vol. 10. Gladstone to McLaren, 22 December 1881.
31. Daily Review, 11 November 1885.
32. ECA. Box 1. Priscilla to McLaren, 13 November 1885.
33. The letters are among the McLaren papers in the Edinburgh City Archive.
34. *The Scotsman*, 19 August 1884.
35. ECA. Box 2. Priscilla to McLaren, 19 November 1885.
36. From letters Priscilla wrote every day, sometimes twice a day from 18 November to 2 December (ECA. Box 2).
37. ECA. Box 1. McLaren to Priscilla, 24 November 1885.
38. From a letter to David McLaren, a longstanding Edinburgh friend, quoted in Mackie, *Life and Work of Duncan McLaren*, Vol. 2, p. 250. Hutchison, *Political History of Scotland*, p. 162 exaggerates the influence McLaren exercised by this time: his name was still useful to employ but he had little direct involvement by the end of 1885.
39. *The Scotsman*, 17 January 1884.
40. Ibid., 20 February 1884.

41. Mackie, *Life and Work of Duncan McLaren*, Vol. 2, pp. 251–4.
42. ECA. Box 3. Priscilla to a friend, Mary, 28 November 1886.
43. Mackie, *Life and Work of Duncan McLaren*, Vol. 2, p. 258.
44. ECA. Box 2. Note by Priscilla, written after McLaren's death.
45. *Daily Review*, 3 May 1886.
46. Matthew, The Gladstone Diaries, 26 April 1886.
47. *The Scotsman*, 27 April 1886.

CHAPTER 17

1. ECA. Box 1. Earl of Breadalbane to Priscilla, 27 October 1887.
2. NLS MS24794. Priscilla to John, 7 July 1887, 16 December 1888, 17 February and 25 February 1889.
3. ECA. Box 3. Priscilla to Mary, 28 November 1886.
4. NLS MS24782. McLaren's will of 1883 with codicils to 1885. Walter McLaren intended bequeathing to his godson Neil Ferguson a portrait of McLaren by Edward John Gregory, which was exhibited at the Royal Academy in 1877. But in 1910 Walter changed his mind: Ferguson was not being educated in a way that would make him venerate McLaren, and so the portrait was to be handed down to Walter's nephew Francis McLaren who had just become Liberal MP for Stafford (ECA Box 4).
5. Report of Bradford University lecture by Dr Jo Stanley, *Bradford Telegraph and Argus*, 19 April 2007.
6. *The Pioneer in Medical Mission Work: Dr Agnes McLaren*.
7. Vincent, *Pollbooks: How Victorians Voted*, p. 198. The parenthesis referring to Newington House is my own.
8. Mackie, *Life and Work of Duncan McLaren*, Vol. 2, pp. 271–2.

Bibliography

Adelman, P., *Radicalism: The Middle-class Experience* (London, 1984)
Anderson, J., *History of Edinburgh from the Earliest Period to 1850* (Edinburgh, 1856)
Anderson, R.D., *Education and Opportunity in Victorian Scotland* (Edinburgh, 1983)
Anderson, R.D., *Education and the Scottish People 1750–1918* (Oxford, 1995)
Bain, W.H., 'The life and achievements of James, First Baron Moncreiff 1811 to 1895', Glasgow University MLitt thesis (1977)
Begg, J., *Happy Homes for Working Men and How to Get Them* (Edinburgh, 1862)
Bell, G., *Day and Night in the Wynds of Edinburgh* (Edinburgh, 1849)
Biagini, E.F., *Liberty, Retrenchment and Reform: Popular Liberalism in the Age of Gladstone, 1860–1880* (Cambridge, 1992)
Black, A., *View of the Financial Affairs of the City of Edinburgh with Suggestions for a Compromise with the Creditors* (Edinburgh, 1835)
Blake, R., *Disraeli* (London, 1966)
Bone, T.R., *School Inspection in Scotland 1840–1966* (London, 1968)
Bradley, I., *The Optimists: Themes and Personalities in Victorian Liberalism* (London, 1980)
Brash, J.I. (ed.), *Scottish Electoral Politics 1832–1854* (Edinburgh, 1974)
Brent, R., 'The Whigs and Protestant Dissent in the Decade of Reform, the case of church rates 1833–1841', *English Historical Review*, 102 (1987)
Brereton, B., *Law, Justice and Empire: The Colonial Career of John Gorrie 1829–1892* (Kingston, Jamaica, 1997)
Brooks, D., 'Gladstone and Midlothian. The background to the first campaign', *Scottish Historical Review*, 64 (1985)
Brown, S.J., *Thomas Chalmers and the Godly Commonwealth in Scotland* (Oxford, 1982)
Brown, S.J., 'Religion and the rise of Liberalism: the first disestablishment campaign in Scotland 1829–1843', *Journal of Ecclesiastical History*, 48 (1997)

Brown, S.J. and Fry, M., *Scotland in the Age of Disruption* (Edinburgh, 1993)
Byrom, C., *The Edinburgh New Town Gardens* (Edinburgh, 2005)
Cameron, K.J., 'Anti-Corn Law agitation in Scotland with particular reference to the Anti-Corn Law League', Edinburgh University PhD thesis (1971)
Cameron, K.J., 'William Weir and the origins of the "Manchester League" in Scotland, 1833-9', *Scottish Historical Review*, 58 (1979)
Ceadel, M., *The Origins of War Prevention: the British Peace Movement and International Relations, 1730-1854* (Oxford, 1996)
Checkland, O., *Philanthropy in Victorian Scotland* (Edinburgh, 1980)
Checkland, S.G., *Scottish Banking – a History, 1695-1973* (Glasgow, 1975)
Cheyne, A.C., *Victorian Scotland's Religious Revolution* (Edinburgh, 1983)
Clason, P., *Strictures on the Statement of the Central Board of Scottish Dissenters in a Series of Letters to Bailie McLaren* (Edinburgh, 1835)
Cockburn, H. (Lord), *Journals*, 2 vols (Edinburgh, 1874)
Cockburn, H. (Lord), *Memorials of his Time* (Edinburgh, 1946)
Colston, J., *The Edinburgh and District Water Supply* (Edinburgh, 1890)
Cooper, C., *An Editor's Retrospect* (London, 1896)
Cowan, C., *Reminiscences* (Privately published, 1878)
Cowan, R.M.W., *The Newspaper in Scotland 1815-1860* (Glasgow, 1946)
Crawford, E., *The Women's Suffrage Movement – a Reference Guide 1866-1928* (London, 1999)
Crewe, Marquess of, *Lord Rosebery* (London, 1931)
Dale, A.W.W., *The Life of RW Dale of Birmingham* (London, 1898)
Davie, G.E., *The Democratic Intellect* (Edinburgh, 1961)
Drummond, A.L. and Bulloch, J., *The Scottish Church 1688-1843* (Edinburgh, 1973)
Drummond, A.L. and Bulloch, J., *The Church in Victorian Scotland 1843-1874* (Edinburgh, 1975)
Drummond, A.L. and Bulloch, J., *The Church in Late Victorian Scotland 1874-1900* (Edinburgh, 1978)
Dyer, M., '"Mere detail and machinery", the Great Reform Act and the effects of redistribution on Scottish representation', *Scottish Historical Review*, 62 (1983)
Dyer, M., *Men of Property and Intelligence: the Scottish Electoral System Prior to 1884* (Aberdeen, 1996)
Eadie, Rev. Prof. and McMichael, Rev. Prof., *The United Presbyterian Church* (Glasgow, 1852)
Ferguson, W., *Scotland: 1689 to the Present* (Edinburgh, 1968)
Fraser, D., 'Edward Baines', in P. Hollis (ed.), *Pressure from Without in Early Victorian England* (London, 1974)

Fry, M., *Patronage and Principle: a Political History of Modern Scotland* (Aberdeen, 1987)
Fry, M., *The Dundas Despotism* (Edinburgh, 1992)
Fry, M., *Edinburgh: a History of the City* (London, 2009)
Gibbon, C., *Life of George Combe* (London, 1878)
Goldman, L., *Reform and Politics in Victorian Britain: the Social Science Association 1859–1886* (Cambridge, 2002)
Goldman, L. (ed.), *The Blind Victorian: Henry Fawcett and British Liberalism* (Cambridge, 1989)
Goodfellow, J., *The Print of His Shoe: Forty Years' Experience in the Southside of Edinburgh* (Edinburgh, 1906)
Gordon, A., *To Move with the Times: the Story of Transport and Travel in Scotland* (Aberdeen, 1988)
Gracie, J., *Stranger on the Shore: a Short History of Granton* (Glendaruel, 2003)
Gray, R.Q., *The Labour Aristocracy in Edinburgh* (Oxford, 1976)
Gray, W.F., 'The lands of Newington and their owners', *Book of the Old Edinburgh Club*, 24 (1942)
Hanham, H.J., *Elections and Party Management: Politics in the Age of Disraeli and Gladstone* (London, 1959)
Hanham H.J., 'The creation of the Scottish Office 1881–87', *Juridical Review*, 10 (1965)
Harrison, G., *A Brief Account of the Rise, Progress and Present Position of the Chamber of Commerce and Manufacturers in the City of Edinburgh* (Edinburgh, 1861)
Harvie, C., *The Lights of Liberalism: University Liberals and the Challenge of Democracy 1860–86* (London, 1976)
Heiton, J., *The Castes of Edinburgh* (Edinburgh, 1859)
Heron, A., *The Rise and Progress of The Company of Merchants of Edinburgh 1681–1902* (Edinburgh, 1903)
Hinde, W., *Richard Cobden: a Victorian Outsider* (London, 1987)
Holton, S.S., *Suffrage Days* (London, 1996)
Hope, G., *A Sketch of the Life of George Hope of Fenton Barns (Compiled by his Daughter)* (Edinburgh, 1879)
Horn, D.B., *A Short History of the University of Edinburgh 1556–1889* (Edinburgh, 1967)
Howe, A. and Morgan, S. (eds), *Rethinking Nineteenth-Century Liberalism* (Aldershot, 2006)
Hutchison, I.G.C., *A Political History of Scotland 1832–1924* (Edinburgh, 1986)
Isichei, E., *Victorian Quakers* (Oxford, 1970)
Jenkins, R., *Gladstone* (London, 1995)

Johnston, W., *Letter to Sir James Gibson Craig Bart* (Edinburgh, 1841)

Kaufman, M.H., *Edinburgh Phrenological Society: a History* (Edinburgh, 2005)

Kellas, J.G., 'The Liberal Party and the Scottish Church disestablishment crisis', *English Historical Review*, 79 (1964)

Kellas, J.G., 'The Liberal Party in Scotland, 1876–95', *Scottish Historical Review*, 44 (1965)

King, E., *Scotland Sober and Free* (Glasgow, 1979)

Kinzer, B.L., Robson, A.P. and Robson, J.M., *A Moralist in and out of Parliament: John Stuart Mill at Westminster 1865–1868* (Toronto, 1992)

Knox, E., 'Between capital and labour – the petite bourgeoisie in Victorian Edinburgh', Edinburgh University PhD thesis (1986)

Knox, W.W., 'Whatever happened to Radical Scotland? The economic and social origins of the mid-Victorian political consensus in Scotland', in R. Mason and N. Macdougall (eds), *People and Power in Scotland* (Edinburgh, 1992)

Knox, W.W., *Lives of Scottish Women: Women and Scottish Society 1800–1980* (Edinburgh, 2006)

Koss, S., *The Rise and Fall of the Political Press in Britain* (London, 1981)

Labouchere, H., *Report to the Chancellor of the Exchequer regarding the Affairs of the City of Edinburgh and Port of Leith* (Edinburgh, 1836)

Larsen, T., *Friends of Religious Equality: Nonconformist Politics in Mid-Victorian Britain* (Woodbridge, 1999)

Leneman, L., *A Guid Cause: the Women's Suffrage Movement in Scotland* (Aberdeen, 1991)

Lenman, B., 'The beginnings of state education in Scotland, 1872–1885', in *Scottish Educational Studies*, 4 (1972)

Lewis, D., *Edinburgh Water Supply* (Edinburgh, 1908)

Lockhart, B.R.W., *Jinglin' Geordie's Legacy: a History of George Heriot's Hospital and School* (East Linton, 2003)

Lucy, H.W., *A Diary of Two Parliaments: the Disraeli Parliament, 1874–1880* (London, 1885)

McCaffrey, J.F., *Scotland in the Nineteenth Century* (Basingstoke, 1998)

Macdonald, J.H.A. (Lord Kingsburgh), *Life and Jottings by an Old Edinburgh Citizen* (Edinburgh, 1915)

MacDougall, I. (ed.), *Minutes of Edinburgh Trades Council 1859–1873* (Edinburgh, 1968)

MacEwen, A.R., *Life and Letters of John Cairns D.D., LL.D.* (London, 1895)

McGilchrist, J., *The Life of John Bright MP* (London, 1868)

Machin, G.I.T., *Politics and the Churches in Great Britain 1832 to 1868* (Oxford, 1977)

McKerrow, J., *History of the Secession Church* (Glasgow, 1841)

Mackie, J.B., *The Life and Work of Duncan McLaren*, vol. 1 (Edinburgh, 1888)

McKinstry, L., *Rosebery* (London, 2005)

McLaren, A., *The Pioneer in Medical Mission Work: Dr Agnes McLaren* (Philadelphia, n.d.)

McLaren, D., *Suggestions for the Consideration of the Committee of Heriot's Hospital in Support of the Motion of Bailie McLaren* (Edinburgh, 1835)

McLaren, D., *Letter to the Members of the Town Council of Edinburgh on the Recent Discussions Regarding the Proposed Settlement with the Creditors of the City* (Edinburgh, 1837)

McLaren, D., *The Working of the Established Church in Edinburgh Explained* (Edinburgh, 1837)

McLaren, D., *Proposed Heads of Agreement to be Submitted to the Treasurer's Committee of the Town Council of Edinburgh by the Committee of Farmers and Traders for a Commutation of the City's Customs* (Edinburgh, 1839)

McLaren, D., *Facts Regarding the Seat Rents of the City Churches of Edinburgh in Seven Letters to the Creditors of the City*, 2nd edn (Edinburgh, 1840)

McLaren, D., *Substance of a Speech Delivered at a Public Meeting of Dissenters held in Edinburgh on the 14th July 1841* (Edinburgh, 1841)

McLaren, D., *Bailie Johnston Refuted by Attested Statements of Facts* (Edinburgh, 1841)

McLaren, D., *Substance of a Speech Delivered to the Meeting of the Edinburgh Anti-Corn Law Association on the 9th May 1844* (Edinburgh, 1844)

McLaren, D., *Evidence Given Before the Select Committee of the House of Commons Respecting the Annuity Tax* (Edinburgh, 1852)

McLaren, D., *Substance of a Speech Delivered at a Meeting of the Town Council of Edinburgh on 6th December 1853 Respecting the Trinity College Church by the Lord Provost* (Edinburgh, 1853)

McLaren, D., *One Year's Experience of the New Public-House Act in Edinburgh* (Glasgow, 1855)

McLaren, D., *Facts about Trinity College Church* (Edinburgh, 1858)

McLaren, D., *Report to the Edinburgh Chamber of Commerce Proposing a Just and Simple Mode of Laying on the Income and Property Tax* (Edinburgh, 1862)

McLaren, D., *Reply to the Attempt Made by Mr James Robie to Extract £1100 by Means of a Threatening Letter* (Edinburgh, 1867)

McLaren, D., *Speech by Duncan Mclaren MP on the Abolition of Tolls ... delivered on 1st November 1873* (Edinburgh, 1873)

McLaren, D., *Fettes College Trustees and the Rights of the Citizens of Edinburgh* (Edinburgh, 1883)

McLaren, D., *A Visit to Madeira and Teneriffe* (n.p., n.d.)

McLaren, D., *The Rise and Progress of Whisky-Drinking in Scotland* (Glasgow, n.d.)

Macleod, D., *Historic Families, Notable People and Memorabilia of the Lennox* (Dumbarton, 1891)
Marshall, J.S., *The Life and Times of Leith* (Edinburgh, 1986)
Marwick, J. (Sir), *A Retrospect* (Glasgow, 1905)
Marwick, J. (Sir), *Edinburgh Crafts and Guilds* (Edinburgh, 1909)
Marwick, W.H., 'Early adult education in Scotland', *Journal of Adult Education*, 5 (1932)
Marwick, W.H., *Economic Developments in Victorian Scotland* (London, 1936)
Marwick, W.H., 'Shops in eighteenth and nineteenth century Edinburgh', *Book of the Old Edinburgh Club*, 30 (1959)
Marwick, W.H., 'Municipal politics in Victorian Edinburgh', *Book of the Old Edinburgh Club*, 33 (1969)
Matthew, H.C.G. (ed.), *The Gladstone Diaries* (Oxford, 1968–94)
Maver, I., *Glasgow* (Edinburgh, 2000)
Miall, A., *The Life of Edward Miall, Formerly Member of Parliament for Rochdale and Bradford* (London, 1884)
Michie, R.C., *Money, Mania and the Markets: Investment, Company Formation and the Stock Exchange in Nineteenth-Century Scotland* (Edinburgh, 1981)
Millar, G.F., 'Maynooth and Scottish politics, the role of the Maynooth Grant issue 1845–1857', *Records of the Scottish Church History Society*, 27 (1997)
Miller, K., *Cockburn's Millennium* (London, 1975)
Mills, J.T., *John Bright and the Quakers* (London, 1935)
Milne, D. (Sir), *The Scottish Office* (London, 1957)
Mochrie, R.I and Sawkins, J.W., 'A bibliography of sources of quantitative data for studies in the economic history of the Scottish churches in the mid-nineteenth century', *Records of the Scottish Church History Society*, 38 (2008)
Moir, D.G. (ed.), 'Extracts from an Edinburgh journal, 1823–1833, part 2 (1829–1833)', *Book of the Old Edinburgh Club*, 30 (1959)
Moncreiff, Rev. Sir H. ('a Scotchman'), *Reasons for Declining to Join the National Association for the Vindication of Scottish Rights* (Edinburgh, 1854)
Montgomery, A.B., 'The Voluntary controversy and the Church of Scotland 1829–1843', Edinburgh University PhD thesis (1953)
Morris, R.J., 'Death, Chambers Street and Edinburgh Corporation', in A. Cooke et al. (eds), *Modern Scottish History 1707 to the Present*, vol. 4. (East Linton, 1998)
Morton, Graeme, *Unionist Nationalism: Governing Urban Scotland 1830-1860*. East Linton 1999
Munn, C.W., *The Scottish Provincial Banking Companies 1747–1864* (Edinburgh, 1981)

Myers, J.D., 'Scottish Nationalism and the antecedents of the 1872 Education Act', *Scottish Educational Studies*, 4 (1972)
Nenacic, S., 'The Victorian Middle Classes', in Fraser, W.H. and Maver, I. (eds), *Glasgow*. Vol. 2. 1830 to 1912 (Manchester, 1996)
Nicolson, A. (ed), *Memoirs of Adam Black* (Edinburgh, 1885)
Nock, O.S., *The Caledonian Railway* (London, 1963)
Norrie, W., *Edinburgh Newspapers Past and Present* (Earlston, 1891)
Norrie, W., *The Annuity Tax* (Earlston, 1912)
Omond, G., *The Lord Advocates of Scotland*. 2nd ser. (Edinburgh, 1914)
Parker, C.S., *Life and Letters of Sir James Graham 1792–1861* (London, 1907)
Parry, J., *Democracy and Religion: Gladstone and the Liberal Party 1867–1875* (Cambridge, 1986)
Peddie, J., *The Hand of God in Public Calamities* (Edinburgh, 1824)
Pentland, G., *Radicalism, Reform and National Identity in Scotland, 1820–1833* (Woodbridge, 2008)
Pentland, G., 'The debate on Scottish parliamentary reform, 1830–32', *Scottish Historical Review*, 85 (2006)
Pickering, P.A. and Tyrell, A., *The People's Bread: a History of the Anti-Corn Law League* (Leicester, 2000)
Pinney, T. (ed.), *The Letters of Thomas Babington Macaulay* (Cambridge, 1976)
Ransom, P.J.G., *Iron Road: the Railway in Scotland* (Edinburgh, 2007)
Read, D., *Cobden and Bright: a Victorian Political Partnership* (London, 1967)
Reeves, R., *John Stuart Mill* (London, 2007)
Renton, H., *Memorial of Mrs Agnes Renton* (Kelso, 1866)
Renton, H., *Memorials of the Rev. Henry Renton MA* (Kelso, 1877)
Ridley, J., *Lord Palmerston* (London, 1970)
Robbins, K., *John Bright* (London, 1979)
Robertson, C.J.A., *The Origins of the Scottish Railway System, 1722–1844* (Edinburgh, 1983)
Robertson, D., *The Princes Street Proprietors and other chapters in the History of the Royal Burgh of Edinburgh* (Edinburgh, 1935)
Robertson, D. and Wood, M., *Castle and Town* (Edinburgh, 1928)
Robertson, W., *Life and Times of the Right Hon. John Bright* (London, 1883)
Robie, J., *The Representative Radicals of Edinburgh: their Professions and Practices Described* (Edinburgh, 1867)
Robson, G., *Mission of the United Presbyterian Church: the Story of the Jamaica Mission with Sketch of the Mission in Trinidad* (Edinburgh, 1894)
Rodger, R., *The Transformation of Edinburgh: Land, Property and Trust in the Nineteenth Century* (Cambridge, 2001)
Rose, H., *Hugh Rose – A Sketch of his Life by One of his Daughters* (Privately printed, 1893)

Russell, T., *The Annuity Tax or Edinburgh Church-Rate, Opposed to the Law of God, and Therefore Not Binding on Man* (Edinburgh, 1836)

Savage, D.C., 'Scottish politics 1885–6', *Scottish Historical Review*, 40 (1961)

Scotsman, The, The Glorious Privilege: the History of 'The Scotsman' (Edinburgh, 1967)

Searle, G.R., *Morality and the Market in Victorian Britain* (Oxford, 1998)

Shannon, R., *Gladstone: Peel's Inheritor 1809–1865* (London, 1999)

Simon, S., 'Church disestablishment as a factor in the General Election of 1885', *Historical Journal*, 18 (1973)

Smith, F.B., *The Making of the Second Reform Bill* (Cambridge, 1966)

Smith, R.M, 'The United Secession Church in Glasgow 1820–1847', *Records of the Scottish Church History Society*, 34 (2004)

Smith, R.M., '"Auld Licht, New Licht" and Original Secessionists in Scotland and Ulster', *Records of the Scottish Church History Society*, 36 (2006)

Stalker, J., *Francis Brown Douglas* (Edinburgh, 1886)

Stoddart, A.M., *John Stuart Blackie: A Biography* (Edinburgh, 1895)

Sturrock, J.B., *Peter Brough – a Paisley Philanthropist* (Paisley, 1890)

Swann, E., *Christopher North* (Edinburgh, 1934)

Taylor, M., *The Decline of British Radicalism 1847–1860* (Oxford, 1995)

Thin, J. (ed.), *Memorials of Bristo United Presbyterian Church* (Edinburgh, 1888)

Thomas, J. (revised Paterson, A.J.S.), *The Railways of Great Britain*, vol. 6. Scotland (Newton Abbot, 1984)

Thompson, D.M., 'The Liberation Society 1844-1868', in P. Hollis (ed.), *Pressure from Without in early Victorian England* (London, 1974)

Trevelyan, G.O., *The Life and Letters of Lord Macaulay* (London, 1931)

Turner, L.A., *Story of a Great Hospital: the Royal Infirmary of Edinburgh 1729–1929* (Edinburgh, 1937)

Tyrrell, A., *Joseph Sturge: the Moral Radical Party in Early Victorian Britain* (Bromley, 1987)

Urquhart, R.M., *The Burghs of Scotland and the Burgh Police (Scotland) Act 1833* (Motherwell, 1989)

Vincent, J.R., *Pollbooks: How Victorians Voted* (Cambridge, 1967)

Vincent, J., *The Formation of the British Liberal Party 1857–1868* (London, 1972)

Walker, D.M., *The Scottish Jurists* (Edinburgh, 1985)

Wallace, J.M., *Traditions of Trinity and Leith* (Edinburgh, 1997)

Wallace, S., *John Stuart Blackie: Scottish Scholar and Patriot* (Edinburgh, 2006)

Walling, R.A.J. (ed.), *The Diaries of John Bright* (London, 1930)

Whetstone, A.E., *Scottish County Government in the 18th and 19th Centuries* (Edinburgh, 1981)

Whyte, I., *Scotland and the Abolition of Black Slavery* (Edinburgh, 2006)
Williams, J.C., 'Edinburgh politics, 1832–52', Edinburgh University PhD thesis (1972)
Wilson, G.M., *Alexander McDonald: Leader of the Miners* (Aberdeen, 1982)
Wilson, J., *CB – A Life of Sir Henry Campbell-Bannerman* (London, 1975)
Winstanley, M.J., *The Shopkeeper's World 1830–1914* (Manchester, 1983)
Withrington, D.J., 'Towards a national system, 1867–72, the last years of the struggle for a Scottish education system', *Scottish Educational Studies*, 4 (1972)
Withrington, D.J., 'Adrift among the reefs of conflicting ideals? Education and the Free Church 1843–55', in S.J. Brown and M. Fry (eds), *Scotland in the Age of the Disruption* (Edinburgh, 1993)
Wohl, A.S. (ed.), *The Victorian Family – Structures and Stresses* (London, 1978)
Youngson, A.J., *The Making of Classical Edinburgh 1750–1840* (Edinburgh, 1966)
Zimmerman, K., 'Liberal speech, Palmerstonian delay, and the passage of the second Reform Act', *English Historical Review*, 108 (2003)

Index

Abercromby, James (Lord Dunfermline) 20, 26, 39, 46, 54, 105, 172
Abercromby, Ralph 105
Aberdeen 20, 33, 53, 63, 92, 112, 114, 120, 122, 123, 136, 160, 188, 230, 259, 276
Aberdeen, Earl of 33, 63, 112, 114, 123 136, 230
Aberdeenshire East by-election 230
Aberdeen University 120, 123
Adam, William 225, 233, 243
Advanced Liberals 92,154,221, 222, 260,261, 263, 263
Advertiser (Dundee) 142
Afghanistan 239,240
Aggregate Committee (Whig) 55, 57, 62, 104, 107, 135, 171, 172, 220, 222, 223, 235
Airlie, Earl of 198
Aitken, Grant (McLaren) 6, 16, 267
Ale duty 27, 30, 35, 36
Alexander, Lindsay 93
Alison, Sir Archibald 126, 128
Alloa 53
American Civil War 157, 165, 182, 195
Annuity tax 22, 24, 29, 33, 42, 53, 54, 98, 101,103, 110, 112, 116, 152, 154, 173, 177, 192,196
Anstruther, Sir Robert 227
Anti-Corn Law League 42, 68, 69, 80, 85, 87, 90, 128, 131, 177
Anti-Annuity Tax League 101, 152, 172, 313
Argyll, Duke of 198
Asher, Alexander 237
Ayrshire 177, 181, 242
Aytoun, James 56, 57

Baines, Edward (sen and jun) 94, 95, 144
Baines, William 54
Balfour, John 234, 242-245, 248, 253
Balfour of Burleigh, Lord 252
Ballot 56, 104, 106, 121,122, 133, 189, 202, 204, 211, 219, 223, 236
Begbie, Dr 161
Begg, James 146, 147, 169

Ben Rhydding Hydro 97, 99, 100, 144, 192, 272
Berwick-on-Tweed 85-87, 242, 243
Bible Board 43,44, 56
Birmingham 147,148, 150, 189, 206, 262
Black, Adam 14, 15, 26-29, 38, 45, 54-62, 66, 75, 77, 80, 82, 90-92, 100, 107, 116, 120-123, 127, 129, 135-138, 141, 145, 146, 150-153, 157, 171-174, 178, 188, 201, 235, 269
Blackburn, Peter 91, 92
Blackie, John Stuart 120-123
Blackwood's Magazine 120, 127
Board of Education 204, 251
Bodnant 254, 271
Bosworth 271,
Bournemouth 190,191, 200
Bouverie, Edward 105-107
Bradford 149, 242, 254, 257, 267, 272
Breadalbane, Earl of 269
Brewster, Sir David 95
Bright Crescent 168
Bright Helen (Clark) 98
Bright, Jacob (sen) 97,98
Bright, Jacob (jun) 200, 211, 212, 217, 223, 255, 263
Bright, John 8, 69-73, 77, 81, 82, 96 107 129-131, 146-150, 153, 160, 162, 168-170, 176-191, 199-201, 209-212, 216, 217, 223, 224, 230-234, 237, 238, 245, 248, 249, 255-257, 263-267, 270-274
Bright, John Albert 248, 255
Bright, Ursula 210
Bristol North-West 271
British Association for the Advancement of Science 72
Brough, Peter 53, 85
Brougham, Lord Brougham 11, 167
Bruce, Henry 207
Bruce, Thomas 108, 110-112
Buccleuch, Duke of 26, 27, 34, 39, 119, 232, 241
Buchanan, Thomas 248, 251, 253
Burgess 15, 48,49, 119, 155, 168, 208, 228, 250,

313

Burgess Act 250,
Burgess Terrace 168
Burgh Commissioners on municipal corporations 49
Burgh Reform Act 21, 22
Burton, John Hill 61

Caird, James 149
Caledonian Mercury 109, 154, 194,195
Cameron, Charles 252, 262
Campbell of Monzie, Alexander 107-111
Campbell, Sir John 48, 61
Campbell-Bannerman, Sir Henry 228
Camperdown Commission 198
Cannes 200, 213, 256
Canongate 256
Cardwell, Edward 216
Cattle Diseases Bill 176, 314
Central Board of Dissenters 40, 56, 60
Chalmers, Thomas 25, 38-41, 44, 58
Chamberlain, Joseph 262, 263
Chambers, William 169, 177
Chamonix 217
Chartism 8, 54, 57
Childers, Hugh 262, 263, 266
Church Liberals 106, 259
Church of Scotland 17,18, 24, 38, 40, 42,44, 58, 60, 63, 88,90, 121, 124,125, 144, 152, 191,193, 197, 215, 225,228, 230, 257,262, 267, 274
Church rates 54, 98, 196, 199, 228, 274
City Agreement Act 43
Clackmannan 186, 233, 243, 245
Clapperton, John 223, 235
Clapperton's (drapers) 166
Clarks (of Street) 210, 255
Clerico-police tax, 154, 171, 172, 174, 176, 183, 188, 194
Clason, Patrick 39
Clifton (Bristol) 170, 171
Cobden, Fred 131
Cobden, Richard 69-73, 76, 77, 80, 82, 85, 90, 99, 128-131, 142, 144-146, 151. 157, 158, 168, 170, 216, 274
Cobden Road 168
Cockburn (Henry), Lord 11, 12, 21, 22, 56, 84, 89, 116, 215
Colebrooke, Sir Thomas Edward 208, 250
Coleridge, JD 176
Collins, William 117
Combe, George 13, 51, 78-81, 86, 93, 94, 102, 105, 106, 110, 112, 124, 125, 139, 140, 144
Commission on Municipal Corporations 25, 49
Committee of Farmers and Traders 52
Conference of ministers 70, 71
Congregationalism 18, 54, 92, 171, 206
Contagious Diseases Acts 211

Convention of Royal Burghs 147, 229, 264, 266, 275
Cooper, Charles 80, 139, 231, 240, 246, 247, 252
Corn laws 64, 68, 71, 74, 78, 80, 82, 168, 180, 258
Coronation of Queen Victoria 45
Cousin, David 168
Cowan, Charles 90-92, 102, 104, 106-112, 127, 145, 146, 150
Cowan, James 222-225, 259, 241, 242, 256-258
Crewe 271,272, 301, 305, 314
Crieff 53
Criminal Law Amendment Act 218, 220
Cross, Richard 239

Daily Express 142, 145, 194
Daily News 125, 142, 148, 149
Daily Review 194, 223, 225, 234, 240, 241, 245, 269
Dale, Robert 206
Dalkeith 72
Dalmally 9,10, 269
Debenham and Freebody 271
Derby, Lord 103, 149, 177, 179, 188
Deuchar, Robert 32, 33, 38
Disestablishment 54, 192,193, 197, 199, 225, 228, 230, 236, 240, 241, 257, 263, 274
Disraeli, Benjamin (Lord Beaconsfield) 149, 177, 179-182, 188, 223, 227-229, 233, 257
Disruption of churches 18, 42, 63, 67, 88, 101, 121, 215, 225, 226
Dissenters 18, 21, 24, 28, 38, 44, 50, 54, 56, 63, 65, 67, 70, 71, 74, 80, 89, 91, 93, 96, 106, 110, 118, 136, 143, 154, 193, 196, 206, 274
Douglas, Francis Brown 135-139, 141, 145, 154, 186
Dunbar 10, 14, 16
Dundee 20, 53, 70, 142, 154, 179, 259
Dunlop, Alexander Murray 146

East and North of Scotland Liberal Association 243, 258
Edinburgh Academy 110, 121
Edinburgh and Glasgow Railway 156
Edinburgh Anti-Corn Law Association 75,77
Edinburgh Anti-State Church Association 106
Edinburgh Chamber of Commerce 69, 77, 104, 134, 151, 157, 167, 176, 187
Edinburgh Cooperative Building Company 169
Edinburgh Directory 73
Edinburgh Evening Courant 28, 118, 119, 144, 232, 239
Edinburgh Industrial Museum 114

Index

Edinburgh Merchant Company 15, 104, 151, 156, 207, 249, 267
Edinburgh News 125, 142, 148, 149
Edinburgh Review 11, 51, 54, 65
Edinburgh Sabbath School Teachers Union 169
Edinburgh South Liberal Association 265
Edinburgh town council 15, 19, 23-25, 28, 33, 35, 39, 40, 43, 47-50, 64, 83, 101, 103, 113, 116, 119, 123,124, 134, 135, 145, 152-154, 168, 172, 183, 192, 193, 196, 198, 207, 208, 212, 214, 220-222, 228, 235, 239, 244, 250-253, 256, 271, 279-20
    Act to regulate debt (1838) 35
    police commission 113
    water supply 65, 83, 84, 99, 169, 215, 221
Edinburgh Trades Council 218, 219
Edinburgh United Liberal Association 240, 256
Edinburgh University 7, 121, 207, 213, 221, 255, 272
    professors' salaries 27, 36, 49
    elections to chairs 49, 51, 95, 120-125
Educational Endowments Bill 244, 246
Education, national 8, 65, 66, 93-95, 124, 126, 140, 144, 196, 206
    Acts 11, 20, 22, 60, 84, 211
Eglinton, Earl of 126
Elections, Edinburgh parliamentary
    1832 19, 21, 26, 56, 63, 146,147, 170, 178
    1835 21, 24, 26,27, 38, 40, 48, 49, 51, 83, 95
    1837 15, 21, 27, 29, 41, 44, 45, 49, 54
    1839 (by-election) 54, 56, 63
    1841 21, 42, 44, 47, 61, 63, 64, 66, 74,75, 78
    1846 (by-election) 89, 90
    1847 18, 86, 90, 92, 93, 95, 98, 105, 109, 133, 135, 143, 158, 173, 174, 226
    1852 96, 103,104, 106, 107, 111, 112, 117, 120 ,121, 123, 124, 131, 133, 134, 136, 138, 171, 173, 188, 222, 241
    1856 (by-election) 135,173
    1857 132, 142, 145, 147, 150, 159, 167, 171, 273
    1859 133, 135, 144, 149, 150, 152, 171, 194, 224
    1865 144, 154, 157, 169, 170, 172, 185, 195, 223, 230
    1868 13,14, 169, 181, 183, 186, 194, 211, 219, 221, 223
    1874 181, 222, 224, 229, 233, 235, 240,241
    1880 233, 240, 245, 250, 253, 254, 256,258
    1881 (2 by-elections) 245, 247, 248
    1882 (by-election) 256
    1885 252, 253, 259, 260, 262, 266, 269, 271
    1886 (by-election) 262, 263
Elcho, Lord 177, 230
Ellice, Edward 176
Endowed Hospitals (Scotland) Act 207

Endowment schemes 244, 246, 249-253 , 256
Entail 246
Episcopalian Church 92, 105, 121, 125, 187
Ewart, William 62
Ewing, Archibald Orr 192
Exchange Bank of Scotland 84-87, 109, 127, 133
Eyre, Governor 175

Falkner's store, Manchester 163
Farmers' Alliance 238
Fawcett, Henry 167, 176, 181
Ferrier, James 122, 123
Fergusson, Sir James 177
Fettes College 253
Fettes, Sir William 253
Finlay, Robert 260-262
Fishery Board 198
Forrest, Sir James 31, 58-61, 66, 70, 92
Forster, WE 199, 203, 204
Free Church of Scotland 315
Freehold movement 146,147, 169
Fry, Elizabeth 98, 99
Fyfe, Andrew 153, 154, 172, 187, 195

George Watson's Trust 47, 207
Gibson-Craig, Sir James 26, 54, 58-63
Gibson-Craig, Sir William 52, 61-65, 74-80, 84, 89-93, 102, 104, 108, 135
Gladstone, William Ewart 114, 119, 149, 157, 167, 177-183, 191, 192, 197-204, 209, 211, 216, 221-223, 226, 227, 229, 230, 232, 233, 238-243, 245, 247, 248, 252, 255, 257-260 ,262-265, 267, 271, 274
Glasgow 7, 10, 13, 18, 20, 41, 50, 53,55, 57, 69,70, 72,74, 76, 85, 87, 92, 96, 105, 117,118, 126, 143, 144, 146, 148, 156,157, 160, 167, 172, 175, 179, 181, 186-189, 203, 210, 220, 223, 227, 233, 238, 242, 243, 252, 257, 259, 262, 265
Glasgow Herald 257
Glenbervie 186
Glencarron 238
Gordon, Edward 186, 205, 224, 227
Gordon, General 257
Gorrie, John 7, 153-156, 170, 185, 209
Graham, Sir James 33, 63, 74,
Graham, Robert Cunninghame 263
Grainger, Thomas 51, 103
Grant, Sir Alexander 208, 212, 214,
Grant, Andrew 236, 237
Granton 27, 30, 34, 86
Gray, John 63, 79
Greenock 10, 20, 95, 105, 146, 186
Grey, Earl 21, 33
Grosvenor, Lord Richard 243, 258

Haddington 10, 16, 181, 273

Hamilton, Sir William 51, 121-123
Harcourt, William 244-248, 250, 251, 264
Harrison, George 235, 236, 240, 261, 262
Harrogate 184, 185, 187, 188, 190
Hartington, Lord 233, 247, 258
Heiton, John 133
Hepburne-Scott, Walter (Master of Polwarth) 263
Herald 130, 142, 174, 194
Heriot, George 15, 48, 250
Heriot's Hospital 32, 113, 115, 142, 155, 168, 207, 208, 249
Heriot's Trust 15, 47, 249
Heriot-Watt College 15, 250
Hope, George 71, 201, 230
Hope, Lord 140
Horner, Leonard 11, 14
Huddersfield 145,146
Hudson, George 85-88
Hughes, Thomas 176
Hume, Joseph 61, 62
Hypothec 244

Independent committee (anti-Whig) 104-107, 109, 135, 172, 193, 221, 235
Inglis, John 123
Inspector of schools 44, 48
Inverness 238, 260, 262, 273
Inverness burghs (constituency) 260-262
Inverness-shire (constituency) 237
Ireland 30, 61, 76, 78, 80, 82, 88, 116, 127, 183, 189, 191,192, 197,198, 203, 219, 226, 247, 257, 263
Irish Church 179, 189, 198, 211, 258
Irish Coercion Bill 224
Irish Home Rule Bill 262, 263
Irish University Bill 219
Ivory, James 55, 57

Jamaica 9, 81, 96, 175
James Gillespie's Trust 47
Jameson, Robert 115
Jedburgh 158, 160, 165, 166, 271
Jeffrey, Francis (Lord) 11, 20, 21, 23, 24, 26
Jenkin, Fleeming 208
Jex-Blake, Sophia 212, 213
John Brown and Co 271
Johnston, Sir William 59, 104, 106-109, 135, 138, 139

Kelso 41, 45, 71, 114, 166, 183, 227
Kennington and Jenner 214
Kilmarnock 105, 237, 238, 259
Kinnaird, Lord 118
Kinross 53, 233, 243, 245

Labouchere, Henry 24, 27, 29, 33, 46
Laing, Samuel 147

Lancashire and Yorkshire Railway Company 88
Lausanne 217
Law of Scotland relating to Wills 186
Law, William 193
Lawson, Sir William 240
Learmonth, Sir John 26
Leatham, Edward 176
Leatham, Elizabeth 98
Leatham, William 176
Lee, John 44, 45
Leeds Mercury 95, 144
Leith 11,12, 20, 25, 27, 29, 30, 32, 36, 45, 50, 72, 83, 85, 86, 108, 114, 149, 150, 155, 192, 216, 236, 238,
  by-election, 236, 237
  docks 12, 26, 29, 32, 34, 36, 50
Lewis, David 172, 193, 208, 216, 221
Lewis, Sir George 153
Liberal Aggregate Committee 55, 57, 62, 104, 135, 171, 172, 220, 222, 223, 235
Liberal Central Association 240
Liberal Unionisn 266, 274
Lipton, Sir Thomas 266
Literary Institute 208
Livingston, Josiah 172
Livingstone, David 224
London School of Medicine for Women 213
Lothian, Marquess of 264
Lowe, Robert 178
Lucas, Margaret 255, 257
Lucy, Henry 241
Lunacy Board 197

Macaulay, Thomas Babington (Lord) 53-56, 62-67,74-81, 83, 84, 88-93, 105, 107-112, 134, 135, 174, 178, 274
Macdonald, Alexander 254
Macdonald, John (Lord Kingsburgh) 222, 223, 242
Macdonald, Roderick 260
MacDouall, Charles 121, 122
MacDougall, PC 122, 123
MacFie, Robert 216
Mackenzie, Forbes 117, 136, 169
Mackie, John Beveridge 114, 117, 158, 269, 270, 273
Madeira 81, 84, 96, 117, 132, 134, 161, 164,165, 200
Maginn, William 120
Maitland, Edward 77
Maitland, John 84
Manchester 7, 13, 54, 69, 73, 81,82, 84, 87, 88, 116, 129, 130, 146, 163, 164, 179, 200, 210, 223, 229, 230, 257, 261
Mann, Horace 94

Index

Manning, Cardinal 213, 267
Manuel rail accident 222
Married women's property 211
Marshall, Andrew 18
Marwick, Sir James 113, 142
Masson, David 213
Maule, Fox (Lord Panmure, Earl of
 Dalhousie) 7, 32, 40-43, 46, 58-63, 73, 75, 91
Mauritius 185, 209
Maynooth 88, 89, 91, 105, 108
McCrie, William 91, 172, 180, 187, 218
McGilchrist, James 63, 130
McLagan, Peter 246
McLaren, Agnes 45, 82, 100, 132, 155, 156, 159, 160, 175, 181, 183, 190, 191, 200, 201, 211-213, 256, 267, 272
McLaren, Anne 16, 17, 267
McLaren, Catherine (Oliver) 45, 82, 100, 132, 158-166, 189, 190, 191, 200, 201, 270, 273, 275
McLaren, Charles (1st Lord
 Aberconway) 99, 166, 184, 196, 222, 237, 242, 245, 254, 255, 262, 266, 267, 271, 275
McLaren, Duncan (sen)
 birth and boyhood 9, 10
 apprenticeship 10
 opens own draper's 13
 self-education 14
 burgess 15
 marries Grant Aitken 16
 her death and Anne's 16
 active Dissenter 18
 joins reformed town council 22
 opposes annuity tax 23ff
 city treasurer 29
 negotiates city-debt solution 31-37
 Committee of Dissenters 38
 foundation of Heriot schools 47, 48
 marries Christina Renton 44
 at Victoria's coronation 45, 46
 leaves council 37, 46
 writes for *Scotsman* 50
 supports farmers and traders 52
 children's health and Christina's death 47
 clashes with city Whigs 56
 disagreements with Macaulay 63-67, 74ff
 convenes conference of ministers 71
 leads anti-corn law London march 68
 valued by Bright and Cobden 72
 takes son John to Madeira 81
 leads attack on water company 83
 founds Exchange Bank 84
 railway investment 85-88
 Dissenter-Free Church alliance 88
 Macaulay's defeat 90, 91
 role in UP Church 95, 96
 marries Priscilla Bright 95-99
 Priscilla's health 99, 100

supports national education 94, 124
Lord Provost 103
Dissenter-Free Church split 103-106
fails to become MP 104-111
move to Newington House 131
Oliver becomes business partner 133
tackles public drunkenness 116
assiduous Lord Provost 112, 119
Trinity College Church row 115
access to buildings and parks 115
host to Harriet Beecher Stowe 118
appointment of professors 120-124
support for Scottish rights 126
Edinburgh Peace Congress 129-131
against Black in by-election 135
wins *Scotsman* libel case 141
setbacks to reform 146
launches freehold movement 147
encourages revived Bright 147
Royal Commission on roads 151
attacks Moncreiff on annuity Bill 152
return to town council 155
chair of Chamber of Commerce 157
supports Cobden on US civil war 157
dismay at Catherine's marriage 159-160
Oliver partnership dissolved 164
role in Social Science Congress 167
suburban property developer 168
supports housing improvements 169
death of Cobden 170
election to Parliament 173
agitation for Reform Bill 174
Queen's Park demonstration 178
Scottish Reform Bill 181
ill after Commons exhaustion 184
returned unopposed 189
Bills to end annuity tax 191
Row with James Robie 194
Church rates Bill 199
Commons disregard of Scottish
 affairs 198
death of Catherine 201
supports education Bills 203
role of religious instruction 205
boycotts Colebrooke commission 208
attacks Sir Alexander Grant 208
career advice to son John 209
support for women's rights 211
opposes Agnes's medical hopes 213
new Royal Infirmary 214
St Mary's Loch water project 215
defending the Forth 216
continental family trip 217
silver wedding 217
relations with trade unions 218
Queen's Park demonstration 218
new MP colleague 222

317

disestablishment campaign   225
road tolls abolished   228
sceptical on Liberal unity   234
Miidlothian campaigns   238
against Afghan war   239
  his largest majority   242
little help for John   243
reluctant retirement   245
campaigns for Heriot schools   249
disenchantment with Gladstone   257
backs disestablishment Liberals   260
last advice on government of Scotland   264
opposes Irish home rule   265
resigns presidency of Edinburgh South Liberals   265
death and funeral   267
monument in stone   269
a commissioned biography   269
McLaren, Duncan (jun)   45, 82, 134, 150, 158-164, 166, 169, 170, 175, 217, 256, 271
McLaren, Euphemia   9, 47
McLaren, Francis   271
McLaren, Grant (Millar)   17, 47, 82, 97, 100, 132, 159, 171, 190, 200, 256, 266, 270
McLaren, Helen (Rabagliati)   7, 98, 99, 165, 166, 212. 217, 230, 242, 254, 272
McLaren, Henry (2nd Lord Aberconway)   271
McLaren, Hernie   210, 213, 255, 256
McLaren, Janet   9, 47
McLaren, John (Lord)   16
  boyhood illnesses   47
  stays in Madeira and Jamaica   81, 82
  relations with Priscilla   97
  handwriting   100
  wants quadrilles   132
  career as advocate   142
  works on reform   149
  rupture with father   161, 162
  friendship with Oliver   161
  Social Science Congress organiser   318
  canvasses for father   172
  visits Algiers for health   185
  father's political aide   186
  fears for progress at Bar   186
  publishes legal volumes   186
  friends with Tory Nicolson   186
  attends Episcopal churches   186
  marries Ottilie Schwabe   189
  housekeeping advice from father   190
  seeks legal position   224
  Bright's advice   233, 234
  support for Schwabes   210
  son Hernie's health   213, 255
  role in candidate selections   233
  legal adviser on Tory Bills   225, 234

  political ambitions   225, 233, 234, 237
  promotes United Liberals   234
  father's disagreement   234
  Leith candidacy   236
  Midlothian campaigns   238
  chosen for Wigtown   238
  Gladstone's Lord Advocate   242
  defeated in by-election   242
  search for seat   243
  tensions with colleagues   244, 245
  opposes father on Heriot's   244
  MP for Edinburgh   245, 246
  Scottish MPs' frustration   246, 247
  Rosebery's role   247
  offered judgeship   247
  honorary LLD   255
  death of Hernie   255
  still consulted politically   258
  invitation to Gladstone   258
  praised as judge   270
  underwrites father's biography   270
  support for Liberal Unionism   270
  astronomer   270
  daughter marries Oliver's son   270
  death   270
McLaren, Katharine (Oliver)   270
McLaren, Martin   271
McLaren, Priscilla (Bright)   72, 73, 97-100, 102, 111-115, 129, 131-134, 145-151, 155, 156, 158-166, 168, 170, 171, 175, 180, 183, 184, 186, 187, 191, 194, 199, 200, 210-212, 216, 217, 224, 230, 236, 238, 245, 253-255, 257, 260-262, 265-267, 269-272, 275
McLaren Road   168
McLaren, Walter   99, 166, 217, 219, 224, 248, 255, 257, 260-263, 271
Melbourne, Lord   21, 42, 56, 64,
Melgund, Lord   95, 105, 108, 124, 135
Melville, Sir James   114
Melville, Lord   22, 34, 52
Miall, Edward   226, 227
Midlothian   21, 52, 56, 61, 72, 90, 117, 229, 232, 233, 238, 240, 241, 244, 248, 258, 259, 274
  elections   21, 52, 56, 61, 232, 233, 238, 240, 241, 244, 248, 258, 259, 274
Mill, John Stuart   174-176, 181, 187, 210-212
Millar, John   172, 190, 191, 256
Miller, Hugh   126, 144
Miller, John   172-175, 187-189, 191, 199, 207, 216. 219-223, 241
Molesworth, Sir James   114
Moncreiff, Sir Henry   127
Moncreiff, James (Lord)   7, 77, 78, 80, 108, 112, 124-127, 134, 140, 141, 147, 149-156, 171, 173, 174, 178, 179, 182-189, 191-194, 199, 202-204, 234, 235, 244, 249, 250, 251
Montpelier   213
Morning Chronicle   50

Index

Morning Star 144, 170
Muller, Eva (McLaren) 254, 272
Mundella, Anthony 251
Munro-Ferguson of Novar, Ronald 260
Muntz, George 147
Murray, John 33, 34
Musselburgh 236

Napier, Sir Charles 130, 131
Napier, McVey 65
National Association for the Vindication of Scottish Rights 126, 128, 197, 265
National Education Association of Scotland 95
National Liberal Federation of Scotland 262
National Society for Women's Suffrage 210
Neaves, Lord 90
Newcastle Daily Leader 269
New Edinburgh Anti-Slavery Association 211
Newington Church 267
Newington House 131, 134, 147,148, 157, 159, 162, 164,165, 168, 189, 191, 201, 213, 256, 257, 261, 267, 269, 270, 272 ,273
Nicolson, Badenoch 186, 224, 225
Nine Hour Factory Association 219
Nonconformists 54
Non-Intrusionists 58, 60, 63, 65, 67, 144
Norrie, William 154, 195
North British Advertiser 145
North Eastern Railway Company 88

Oban 144, 183, 184
Oliphant, Laurence 176
Oliver, Frederick Scott 270, 271
Oliver, John 81, 133, 134, 138, 158-166, 170, 190, 191, 200, 201, 267, 270, 271, 273
Oswald, James 73
Paisley 10, 20, 53,54, 85, 175
Palmerston, Lord 113, 128, 136, 145, 146, 149, 150, 152, 170, 173, 174, 257
Parks 114, 119, 178, 183, 218, 274
Parliamentary Reform Committee 149
Parochial Schools Bill 196, 203
Paterson, William 220, 221
Patronage Bill 225, 227, 228
Peace Society and conferences 128-131, 143, 144, 146,147, 175, 216

Peddie, Dick 237, 239
Peddie, James (sen) 18, 19
Peddie, James (jun) 18, 38, 39
Peebles 182, 237, 238,
Peel, Sir Robert 21, 33, 38, 42, 60, 63, 68, 77, 82, 85, 88-92, 112, 119, 150, 179, 223

Peel Terrace 168
Permissive Bill 236, 240, 241
Playfair, Lyon 187, 207, 212, 251
Pochin, Henry 254, 271
Pochin, Laura (McLaren) 237, 254 257, 271
Portobello 17, 47, 114, 236
Potter, TB 180
Poulton, Abraham 70
Prigging 15, 53
Princes Street Gardens 115, 116, 267
Prisons 44, 66, 150, 183
Pritchard, Dr 173

Quakers 73, 79, 92, 97-100, 117, 129, 131, 200, 211, 216, 254
Queen's Crescent 168
Queen's Park 114, 178, 218

Rabagliati, Andrea 7, 254, 267, 272
Rae, Sir William 26, 31, 46
Railways 8, 40, 45, 53, 84-88, 103, 116, 133, 143, 156, 168, 172, 183, 222, 229
Rainy, Robert 267
Raleigh, Thomas 261
Reform League 177, 179
Reform Acts 20-22, 66, 74, 104, 106, 146-150, 155-157, 169, 170, 172-181, 186, 188, 191, 210, 218, 257, 259, 260, 262, 273
Reid, George 272
Reid, James 232-234, 237, 240, 243
Relief Church 71, 92, 95
Religious instruction 40, 93, 95, 103, 124, 125, 204, 205
Renton (Dunbartonshire) 9, 10
Renton, Agnes (sen) 44, 73
Renton, Agnes (jun) 96
Renton, Christina (McLaren) 44-47, 96, 98, 257, 267
Renton, Henry 41, 47, 57, 71, 165, 166, 183, 200, 227
Renton, James Hall 256-258
Renton, William 99
Retailing 10, 13, 15, 271
Richards, Henry 217
Richmond and Gordon, Duke of 264
Ritchie, John 139, 140, 143
Roads and Bridges Bill 229
Road tolls 151, 228, 229
Robie, James 194-196
Robson, John 96, 160, 227
Robson, William 172
Rochdale 72, 73, 96, 98, 129, 149, 162, 174
Roman Catholic Church 39, 71, 78, 88, 92, 106, 125, 173, 200, 205, 231, 267, 272
Rose, Hugh 187, 218
Rosebery, Earl of 238, 242, 247, 248, 252, 264
Rosehall Church 267

319

Ross-shire by-election 260
Royal Commission on tolls 151
Royal Commission on worship 40, 41
Royal Infirmary (Edinburgh) 212-215
Royal Scottish Academy 214
Russel, Alexander 80, 138, 139, 142, 215, 223, 231, 252, 273
Russell, Lord John 40, 54, 66, 78, 79, 82, 89, 92, 93, 101, 104, 106, 135, 149, 150, 153-155, 170, 174, 202
Russell, Thomas 24, 38, 153
Rutherfurd, Andrew 30-33, 41, 42, 55, 57, 91, 104

Salisbury, Lord 259, 262, 264
School of Arts 14
Schwabe, Ottilie (McLaren) 186, 187, 189, 190, 210, 227, 235, 236, 243, 248
Scotsman, The 8, 14, 23, 24, 28, 33, 35, 38, 50, 51, 37-60, 70-72, 77-80, 82, 84, 85, 95, 103, 106-109, 111, 112, 118, 125, 135-144, 149, 150, 154-157, 171-178, 183, 189, 194, 208, 212, 214-218, 220, 222, 223, 235, 236, 240, 244, 246, 250, 256-259, 267, 268, 274
Scottish Liberal Association 262
Scottish Local Government Board Bill 264
Scottish Permissive Bill Association 241
Scottish Reformation Society 107
Secession (Church) 10, 17, 18, 39, 45, 69, 71, 92, 95
Secretary for Scotland 127, 198, 264, 275
Selkirk 181, 182, 237
Shaw-Lefevre, John 101, 116
Sheardale 172, 190, 256
Shearman, JB 70
Smiles, Samuel 10, 273
Smith, Sir Culling Eardley 61, 88-90, 104
Smith, John Benjamin 87-90, 94, 99, 102, 104, 106, 129, 135, 151
Smith, Madeleine 145
Smith, William 'Dictionary' 122
Social Science Congress 167
Society of Catholic Medical Missionaries 272
Spalding 271
Spittal, Sir James 14, 30, 32, 69
Stafford 242, 253, 254, 261
St Andrews University 18, 44, 95, 122, 123, 207, 250
Stair, Earl of 238
Stanley, Lord 188, 189
Stewart, Mark 242
St Giles' Cathedral 13, 41, 44, 267
St Mary's Loch 215, 216
Stirling 87, 94, 102, 128, 150, 172, 176, 228
Stott, JH 101
Stowe, Harriet Beecher 118

Stratheden, Lady 45
Struthers, Elizabeth 256
Sturge, Joseph 131, 147, 148
Sunday licensing 117, 118
Sunday trains 87, 90
Sutherland, Duke of 119

Tait's Edinburgh Magazine 86
Tait, William 23, 26, 55, 57, 86
Tamworth 147, 148
Taylour, Jane 212
Teinds 42, 102, 246
Temperance 45, 58, 117, 136, 202, 203, 228, 240, 254, 257
Terrot, Bishop 114
The Castes of Edinburgh 133
Thompson, Harry 87, 88
Thomson, Sir William (Lord Kelvin) 266
Times, The 51, 92, 127, 130, 131, 141, 142, 145, 211
Towers, John 134, 158, 162-165, 170
Traynor, John 241
Trinity College Church 115, 116, 183

United Free Church 271
United Presbyterian Church 18, 95, 143, 144, 193, 205, 206, 225-227, 231, 258-260, 267, 271

Ventnor 160, 195
Ventnor Terrace 168
Villiers, Charles 68, 73, 75, 76, 78
Vincent, John 273

Waddy, Samuel 256, 257
Wallace Monument 128
Waverley Park 168
Weekly Herald 174, 194
Weekly Journal 33,
Weir, William 70
West and South of Scotland Liberal Association 233
West End Liberal Association 234
Wigham, Eliza 211
Wigham, John 73, 75, 78, 79
Wigtown Burghs 223, 238, 242
Wigtown Free Press 199
Wilson, John (Christopher North) 120, 122
Witness, The 144, 194
Women's rights 8, 181, 210-213, 254-257, 270, 272
Women's Liberal Federation 272

York and North Midland Railway Company 85
York, Newcastle and Berwick Railway Company 85-87
Young, George 140, 141, 192, 193, 195, 197, 199, 204-206, 223